Divine Word and Prophetic Word in Early Islam

Religion and Society 7

MOUTON · THE HAGUE · PARIS

Divine Word and Prophetic Word in Early Islam

A Reconsideration of the Sources, with Special Reference to the Divine Saying or Ḥadîth Qudsî

WILLIAM A. GRAHAM
Harvard University

MOUTON · THE HAGUE · PARIS

ISBN: 90 279 7612 0

Printed in the Netherlands

To W. and W.

" حــبّ الهرّة من الايمان"

Preface

The present work was presented originally as a doctoral thesis at Harvard University in August, 1973. Since that time, the manuscript has undergone no major revision in substance, although numerous lesser alterations, additions, and corrections have been made.

The study grew out of my original interest in the ways in which, after the death of the Prophet, the Islamic community was able to develop new mechanisms of authoritative guidance for its collective life. In the attempt to examine specifically the early Muslim concepts of revelatory and prophetic authority, I was drawn in particular to the seemingly anomalous genre of Ḥadîth that is termed *qudsî*, "holy" or "divine": *viz.*, any report from Muḥammad in which he quotes direct words of God that are not found in the Qur'ân. While modern scholars had generally dismissed these "divine sayings" as late, "ṣûfî" forgeries, I soon discovered that a considerable number of these reports were to be found in the earliest available Ḥadîth collections. The presence of such first-person words of God among the early prophetic traditions caused me to question whether one could justifiably "read back" into the first-century Muslim worldview the later dogmatic distinctions between Qur'ân and Ḥadîth, revelation and inspiration, divine word and prophetic word.

Investigation of this question led to considerable evidence, in addition to that of the *ḥadîth qudsî*, or Divine Saying, which pointed to an essentially unitive understanding of divine and prophetic authority in the early Muslim community, an understanding that differed significantly from the interpretation that Sunnî Muslim scholarship was to develop by at least the third century of Islam. Thus I found myself involved in a double study: first, of the diverse materials that seemed to call for a general reappraisal of early Muslim notions of revelation and prophecy; and second, of the Divine Saying as a neglected genre of early material that challenges the assumption that there was from the beginning of Islam an absolute distinction between divine word and prophetic word.

These two separate but interrelated projects are represented in the present study by Parts I and II, respectively. Part III provides the technical and source material on which the investigation of the Divine Saying in Part II is based: the texts, translations, and sources of Divine Sayings drawn from the classical and earlier collections of Ḥadîth. Each part of the book involved exploration in the largely unsifted material of the Ḥadîth; if no more, perhaps this limited endeavor will call forth further efforts to mine the riches of this literature. Beyond this, it may, on the one hand, raise useful questions about our understanding of the early Muslim community, and, on the other, serve to rehabilitate the Divine Saying as an original part of the larger corpus of the Ḥadîth.

All works cited in the book can be found in the Bibliography, with the exception of a few sources that are mentioned only once and are described in full where they occur. All Qur'ân references are keyed to the numbering of the standard Egyptian text. Citation of the classical Ḥadîth collections is according to the chapter (*kitâb*) divisions and reference system of the *Concordance* and *Handbook* of Wensinck. Note, however, that the numbers rather than the names of the chapters are used throughout for brevity, except in the citation of introductory chapters (*muqaddimah*s) and chapters of Qur'ân interpretation (*tafsîr*s): e.g., Ibn Mâjah 37:33:4 [i.e., *kitâb* 37, *bâb* 33, ḥadîth 4], but Dârimî, *Muqaddimah*, 11:2 [i.e., *bâb* 11, ḥadîth 2], and Bukhârî, *Tafsîr*, S. 19:1 [i.e., the *bâb* that treats Sûrah 19, verse 1].

I welcome this opportunity to express my gratitude to those upon whom I have relied at one or more points in the preparation of this book: the many people here in Cambridge, in London, in Tübingen, and elsewhere who gave me advice, criticism, encouragement, and various kinds of material assistance as the original manuscript took shape between the autumn of 1971 and the summer of 1973. Among these I would mention in particular Mahmoud Ayoub, Annemarie Schimmel, John B. Carman, M. Tahir Mallick, Abdul Haqq Ansari, Maria Cedargren, Laila Abdel-Malek, and my father, W. Albert Graham.

Special thanks go to my wife, Margaret B. W. Graham, who often interrupted her own research to offer cogent criticism of successive drafts; to Rudi Paret, who gave me initial encouragement in 1972 and later provided invaluable detailed advice on the correction and improvement of the thesis text; and to Jacques Waardenburg, without whose persistence the thesis would never have become a book. For support in the publication itself I have both the Center for the Study of World Religions and the Center for Middle Eastern Studies at Harvard to thank.

Finally, I am particularly in the debt of three persons who gave me my primary guidance in the original study: Muhsin Mahdi, who encouraged me to venture into a neglected area of study and offered me sound advice along the way; Josef van Ess, whose kind invitation brought me to Tübingen in 1972 and whose generous and illuminating help greatly enriched the original project; and Wilfred Cantwell Smith, whose painstaking criticism and wise counsel greatly aided me in this endeavor, and whose long tutelage in the history of religion remains an inspiration.

The responsibility for this work and any inaccuracies that it may contain is, of course, entirely my own.

Cambridge, Mass.
January, 1975

WILLIAM A. GRAHAM

Contents

Transliteration

The transliteration of Arabic into English in the present work follows in general the method of the U.S. Library of Congress as outlined in the Cataloging Service Bulletin 49 (November, 1958), with the following important exceptions:

1. Circumflex is used instead of the macron for long vowels: e.g., û (not ū).
2. The *lam* of the definite article *al-* is assimilated to a following "sun letter": e.g., *ash-shams* (not *al-shams*).
3. The *a* of the definite article is dropped after an inseparable conjuction or preposition: e.g., *wa-l-insân, bi-l-ʿamal* (not *wa-al-insân, bi-al-ʿamal*).
4. The hyphen after inseparable prepositions, conjunctions, and other prefixes is always retained: e.g., *li-lladhî, bi-llâh* (not *lilladhî, billâh*).
5. *Alif maqṣûrah* is denoted by *á*: e.g., *ʿalá* (not *ʿalâ*).
6. Common Arabic names formed by a noun in construct to another are written as one word: e.g., ʿAbdallâh, Shamsaddîn, ʿAbdalmalik (exceptions are excessively long or less common construct names: e.g., Jamâl al-Millah wa-d-Dîn, Tâj al-ʿÂrifîn).
7. *Ibn* is transliterated uniformly as *b.*, except where the name begins with *Ibn*, or where Ibn so-and-so is the name commonly used to identify the person: e.g., Ṣâliḥ b. Muḥammad b. Nûḥ, but Ibn Ḥajar, Muḥyîddîn Ibn al-ʿArabî.

Abbreviations

In Part III, the Appendices, and the Bibliography, the most common Arabic proper names have been abbreviated as follows: ʿAbdallâh as *ʿAl.*, ʿAbdalʿazîz as *ʿAz.*, ʿAbdarraḥmân as *ʿAr.*, Ibrâhîm as *Ibr.*, and Muḥammad as *Muḥ.*

The following works have been cited throughout the book with the abbreviations indicated in the left-hand column below. Complete bibliographical information for each is available in the Bibliography.

Abû Dâwûd	Abû Dâwûd as-Sijistânî, *as-Sunan*
Abû al-Yamân	Abû al-Yamân al-Ḥakam b. Nâfiʿ, *Aḥâdîth*
ʿAlî al-Qârî	ʿAlî b. Sulṭân Muḥammad al-Qârî al-Harawî, *al-Aḥâdîth al-qudsîyah al-arbaʿînîyah*
Bell's Introduction	[Bell, Richard], *Bell's Introduction to the Qur'ân*, revised by W. Montgomery Watt
Blachère	Blachère, Régis, *Introduction au Coran*
Bukhârî	al-Bukhârî, *al-Jâmiʿ aṣ-ṣaḥîḥ*, edited by Krehl and Juynboll
Concordance	Wensinck, Arendt Jan, *et al.*, *Concordance et indices de la tradition musulmane*
Dârimî	ad-Dârimî, *as-Sunan*
EI	*The Encyclopaedia of Islam* (1913–1938)
*EI*²	*The Encyclopaedia of Islam New Edition* (1954–)
GAL	Brockelmann, Carl, *Geschichte der arabischen Litteratur* (2nd, revised edition)
GAL(S)	Brockelmann, Carl, *Geschichte der arabischen Litteratur: Supplement*
GAS	Sezgin, Fuat, *Geschichte des arabischen Schrifttums*, vol. I
Ghazzâlî	al-Ghazzâlî, *Iḥyâ' ʿulûm ad-dîn*
Hammâm b. Munabbih	Hammâm b. Munabbih, *Ṣaḥîfah*

Ibn Isḥâq	Ibn Isḥâq, *Sîrat rasûl Allâh*
Ibn Mâjah	Ibn Mâjah, *as-Sunan*
Ibn Sa'd	Ibn Sa'd, *Kitâb aṭ-ṭabaqât al-kabîr*, edited by Eduard Sachau *et al.*
Ismâ'îl Pâshâ	Ismâ'îl Pâshâ al-Baghdâdî, *Îḍaḥ al-maknûn fî adh-dhayl 'alá kashf aẓ-ẓunûn*
Ibrâhîm b. Ṭahmân	Ibrâhîm b. Ṭahmân, *al-Juz' al-awwal wa-th-thânî min mashyakhah Ibrâhîm b. Ṭahmân*
JA	*Journal Asiatique*
JASB	*Journal of the Asiatic Society of Bengal*
Jawâhir	al-Ḥurr al-'Âmilî, *al-Jawâhir as-sanîyah*
JRAS	*Journal of the Royal Asiatic Society*
Lisân al-'arab	Ibn Manẓûr, *Lisân al-'arab*
Kashf aẓ-ẓunûn	Ḥâjjî Khalîfah (Kâtib Čelebî), *Kashf aẓ-ẓunûn*, edited by Yaltkaya and Bilge
al-Mabânî	*Muqaddimat kitâb al-mabânî*, edited by Jeffery
al-Madanî	al-Madanî, *al-Itḥâfât as-sanîyah fî al-aḥâdîth al-qudsîyah* (1358/1939 edition)
Mu'jam	'Abdalbâqî, Muḥammad Fu'âd, *al-Mu'jam al-mufahras li-alfâẓ al-Qur'ân al-karîm*
Muslim	Muslim b. al-Ḥajjâj, *aṣ-Ṣaḥîḥ*, edited by Muḥammad Fu'âd 'Abdalbâqî
Musnad	Ibn Ḥanbal, *al-Musnad* (Cairo, 1313/1895)
Musnad (Shâkir)	Ibn Ḥanbal, *al-Musnad*, edited by Aḥmad Muḥammad Shâkir (1949–)
Muwaṭṭa'	Mâlik b. Anas, *al-Muwaṭṭa'*
MW	*The Muslim World*
Nasâ'î	an-Nasâ'î, *as-Sunan al-mujtabá*
Nöldeke-Schwally	Nöldeke, Theodor, *Geschichte des Qorâns* (2nd edition, vols. I, II, revised by Schwally
Nöldeke-Schwally (Bergsträsser)	Nöldeke, Theodor, *Geschichte des Qorâns* (2nd edition, vol. III, revised by Bergsträsser and Pretzl
RAAD	*Révue de l'Académie Arabe de Damas* (*Majallat majma' al-lughah al-'arabîyah bi-Dimashq*)
SEI	*Shorter Encyclopaedia of Islam*
Suhayl b. Abî Ṣâliḥ	Suhayl b. Abî Ṣâliḥ, *Nuskhah*

Tahdhîb	Ibn Ḥajar al-ʿAsqalânî, *Tahdhîb at-tahdhîb*
Tirmidhî	at-Tirmidhî, Muḥammad b. ʿÎsâ, *aṣ-Ṣaḥîḥ*
WZKM	*Wiener Zeitschrift für die Kunde des Morgenlandes*
ZDMG	*Zeitschrift der Deutschen Morgenländischen Gesellschaft*

Introduction

While much thorough and competent work on pristine Islam has been carried out in areas such as Qur'ânic studies and socio-political history, our understanding of early Muslim religious and intellectual life as a whole is still largely dependent upon reasonable hypotheses derived by "back-interpretation" from data belonging to the period of the crystallization of Muslim religious sciences, or *'ulûm shar'îyah*, in the second and third centuries A.H. Outside of purely Qur'ânic studies, any attempt to reach back into the intellectual world of the first generations of Muslims faces the considerable task of distinguishing the earliest layers of traditional materials from later interpolations.[1] Current scholarship is, however, revising backwards into the first century and a half of Islam the *terminus ad quem* for the entry into circulation of the majority of the Ḥadîth, or Tradition literature. It is increasingly being recognized that, with the exception of specifically legal material, most of the "classical" Ḥadîth, including the "fabricated" or spurious traditions (*al-mawḍû'ât*), can be dated from at least as early as the middle of the second/eighth century rather than the third/ninth century, when the major collections of Ḥadîth were compiled.[2]

Yet even with the vital and important new work being done in uncovering the early literary history of Islam, the emphasis and orientation of Western scholarship continues to center upon the "authenticity" of early materials and the related question of their "origin". In the case of the Ḥadîth, for example, the principal concerns have been the reliability of Ḥadîth as actual words of Muḥammad and his Companions[3] and, as a corollary of the predominantly negative assessment of this reliability, the identification of pre-Islamic and extra-Islamic sources for the content of these reports. Such concerns are not, however, the only nor necessarily the most important ones for scholarly and indeed historical investigation. Certainly there is also a need for an increased collateral concern among scholars with the early Muslim community itself and with the materials that *it considered* to be "authentic", the origin of which *it assumed* to lie, if not specifically with

Muḥammad, certainly ultimately with God, whatever their mode of transmission to the Community.

The most crucial kind of "authenticity" of a scripture or anything else of religious significance is, in the final analysis, its absolute authenticity in the understanding and faith of a particular individual or a particular group in a particular age. What a person or a community recognizes as true, has faith in as true, is as legitimate an object of scholarly concern as the equally elusive genesis or "original source" of an idea, an image, a myth, or even a text; and certainly it is more important than the latter in seeking to understand the person or group involved. This is not to say that it is not possible for the Islamics scholar to pursue among the heterogeneous materials of the Ḥadîth the religious legends, myths, and motifs that are mirrored in the common tradition of the ancient Near East.[4] No religious tradition arises in a cultural, religious, or linguistic vacuum, just as the Qur'ân could not have come in just any language, but had to be, for the peoples to whom it was first addressed, "an Arabic Qur'ân" (S. 12:2). The Qur'ân's own presentation of the pre-Islamic history of God's revelatory activity demonstrates how thoroughly the sending of Muḥammad and the revelations to him are felt as rooted in an earlier *Heilsgeschichte*, the knowledge of which is essential to the Muslim. Nevertheless, the scholarly concern with the precise "origins" and "authenticity" of materials with a pre-Islamic background such as those found in the Ḥadîth is only one type of concern. Of potentially greater significance for the historian who is trying to understand early Islam is the more subtle question of the meaning and function of such materials in the individual and collective life of the early Muslims.

The present study attempts first to reassess the early Muslims' understanding of their basic sources of authority and guidance, what they recognized as "authentic" guides for ordering their lives, shaping their dreams, and informing their faith. Its primary concern is with their perception of distinctions between Qur'ân and Ḥadîth, direct revelation and indirect inspiration, divine word and prophetic word. The study then focuses specifically upon some neglected materials that are included in the Ḥadîth literature but are explicitly quoted as words of God rather than words of Muḥammad, and which have come to be known generally under the rubric *ḥadîth qudsî* (plural: *aḥâdîth qudsîyah*), or Divine Saying.[5]

The Divine Saying represents a body of material that appears to have been seen originally as being closer to the Qur'ânic revelations than to the prophetic pronouncements of Muḥammad that form the core of the Ḥadîth (and to which the Divine Saying is now considered to belong). As such, it raises fundamental questions about the accuracy of the assumption that Qur'ân and Ḥadîth were perceived in the first century or so of Islam in the same way that they are perceived in more modern Muslim scholarship and especially in Western Islamics scholarship. If these Sayings are documents of early Islam, their very existence at least suggests that the early Muslim understanding of divine word and prophetic word was a primarily unitive one. This unitive understanding gradually faded in the face of an increasingly rigid bifurcation of the verbal inheritances of the Prophet's mission into the two "closed" corpora of Qur'ân and Ḥadîth. These Sayings are explicitly divine word, but they are equally explicitly reported by the Prophet in *his* words. Thus they may represent materials that reflect the point at which divine revelatory authority and human prophetic authority most clearly coalesced in the eyes of early Muslims. They are at once divine word and prophetic word, and as such they force us to rethink our interpretation of early Islamic concepts of revelation and prophet.

Notes to "Introduction"

1. Cf. the statement of Josef van Ess concerning the Ḥadîth: "Viele schriftliche Aufzeichnungen gehen den kanonischen Sammlungen voraus: ihre Autoren sind in den Isnaden verzeichnet. Allerdings reichen die uns erhaltenen Quellen nur selten über die Schwelle des 1. Jh's in die Frühzeit hinab, und da dies jener kritische Zeitpunkt ist, indem das Ḥadīṯ als theologisches bzw. juristisches Argument und als 'Machtmittel' Bedeutung gewann und damit auch Fälschungen oder wohlmeinenden Korrekturen gegenüber besonders anfällig wurde, ist für die Genese einer einzelnen Ueberlieferung häufig doch nicht viel gewonnen; durch frühe Schriftlichtkeit wird nicht unbedingt Echtheit verbürgt" ("Zwischen Ḥadīṯ und Theologie", p. 1).
2. See A. J. Wensinck, *The Muslim Creed* (Cambridge: The University Press, 1932), p. 59, and Rudi Paret, "Die Lücke in der Ueberlieferung über den Urislam" (1954). The Paret article lays out in clear fashion the reasons for the lesser reliability of strictly legal ḥadîths as opposed to the greater mass of non-legal Ḥadîth material. Of recent works on the reliability of the early preservation and trans-

mission of Ḥadîth, the most significant are the impressive, if occasionally overly sanguine, studies of Nabia Abbott (*Studies in Arabic Literary Papyri* [1957–67], esp. I, 1–31; II, 1–83) and Fuat Sezgin (notably his Turkish study of Bukhârî [Istanbul, 1956] and vol. I [1967] of his *Geschichte des arabischen Schrifttums*, esp. pp. 53–84). Soon to be added to these, and potentially of more importance for the problem of using the Ḥadîth for reconstruction of early Islamic intellectual history, will be the forthcoming book of Josef van Ess, *Zwischen Ḥadiṯ und Theologie* (1975? This study is to be an elaboration of some of the concerns evidenced in a paper of the same title given in Cambridge, Massachusetts, in April, 1971, which I have been able to use). Of previous works, also important are the contributions by M. Hamidullah in his edition of and commentary on the *Ṣaḥîfah* of Hammâm b. Munabbih (1953) and by M. M. Azmi in his *Studies in Early Hadîth Literature* (1968). Cf. also the work of M. Z. Ṣiddîqî, especially his *Ḥadîth Literature* (1969). The substantial core of early material in the Ḥadîth was early recognized by Aloys Sprenger (notably in his article, "On the Origin and Progress of Writing Down Historical Facts among the Musalmans" (1856). Goldziher, the father of the critical study of the Ḥadîth as a source for the study of Islamic history of the second and third centuries A. H., himself recognized also the existence of a "Grundstock" of reports in the Ḥadîth that originated with the Prophet and his contemporaries (*M. Studien*, II, 4–5). Much later, when enthusiasm for historical reconstructions based upon Goldziher's analysis of the layers of late forgeries in the Ḥadîth led many Western scholars to adopt a hypercritical attitude towards the reliability of the entire corpus of Ḥadîth, Johann Fück (esp. in his article, "Die Rolle des Tradionalismus im Islam" [1939]) and, still later, James Robson (in various articles, esp. "The Isnad in Muslim Tradition" [1953]) both emphasized the genuine elements and basic reliability of the Ḥadîth as a repository not only of late forgeries but also of early Islamic traditional materials.

3. "Companion" and "Follower" are used throughout as technical terms equivalent to the Arabic *ṣaḥâbî* and *tâbiʿî*, respectively. The former denotes generally a person who knew the Prophet and the latter a member of the first succeeding generation after that of the Prophet and Companions.
4. The use of the terms *legend* and *myth* here is fraught with difficulties primarily because of the unfortunate connotations that have accrued in Western usage to both and have given them the negative implication of *untrue* traditional accounts. This problem is compounded by the fact that for most Muslims the words are particularly foreign and even repugnant usages in the Islamic context. If, however, they are understood in their proper sense as traditional narratives that express religious truths inaccessible to rationalist or literalist modes of

expression, both words can be used to describe many of the kinds of material from the Ḥadîth that are relevant to the concerns of the present investigation. The Qur'ân itself – or, in Muslim terms, God Himself in the Qur'ân – uses "legends" about previous peoples to admonish the hearers of the Qur'ân with clear "signs" (*âyât*). In the life of faith, these are authentic and true accounts of the ways of God with man. It is in this sense of true stories that the two terms are used in the present study, where a somewhat arbitrary distinction between them has been adopted: *legend* is used to refer to accounts of previous events involving people on earth, while *myth* is used to refer to accounts of past, present, or future extraterrestrial events, generally involving God and the angels or Devil, or the events on the Day of Resurrection.

5. Note that *Divine Saying*, as a technical term, is capitalized throughout this study, while *divine word* and similar formulations are not. See also below, p. 47, n. 108.

PART ONE

Revelation in Early Islam

1

The Early Muslim Understanding of the Prophetic-Revelatory Event

A. The Unity of the Prophetic-Revelatory Event as the Basis of Muslim Traditionalism

"In the time of the Apostle of God, people were judged by revelation. Then revelation was cut off, and now we judge you by those works of yours that are apparent to us ...."[1] While Muḥammad still lived and prophecy and revelation in Islam continued, an order of existence prevailed that was unattainable in subsequent times. Human affairs stood under the special "judgment" of the prophetic-revelatory event, which illumined not just appearances, but realities in human life. For most Muslims, the "cutting off" of revelation at the Prophet's death marks not only the end of one historical order and the beginning of another, but also the transition from one order of being to another.[2] Once past, "the time of the Apostle of God" became – most vividly for those who had participated in it and the early Muslims after them, but in a real sense for all Muslims – a wholly different mode of time: a time made holy by divine activity, "a time out of time", what Mircea Eliade has called "sacred time".[3] All succeeding generations would look back upon the time of the Prophet as the paradigmatic age, the era hallowed by the divinely ordained mission of Muḥammad and the divine revelation communicated through him. No other age could attain its perfection, no ensuing accomplishments equal its glories.

The hallmarks of this age are divine revelation and prophetic[4] activity. In religious terms, the *laylat al-qadr*, the "night of power" in which the Qur'ân symbolically "came down", is indeed "better than a thousand months" (S. 97:3) – or a thousand years. Similarly, the Prophet is "the best of men", and every Muslim who experienced his loss could join the Companion, Ḥassân b. Thâbit, in his lament: "I was in a flowing stream [while Muḥammad lived], and [now removed] from it, I have become one thirsty, alone."[5] Prophecy and revelation had dried up like an evanescent desert stream; historical time had replaced sacred time.

This elevation of the time of prophet and revelation out of the realm of "ordinary" time is the recognition of the "breaking" of historical time from outside of history, the irruption of the infinite into the finite. Thus it could be said that "revealing" (*waḥy*) was "cut off", for here *waḥy* is not meant as a synonym for "book" or "scripture"; rather, it is to be understood as an activity coextensive with the life of the bearer of revelation, the Prophet. It is only comparatively late that the verbal noun *waḥy* becomes a concrete noun that refers primarily to a text rather than a happening. In the early period, "as against the lifeless and abstract character of the written word in isolation, revelation is seen to be an activity of God directed towards human beings and expecting a response from them. Thus it is imbedded in the texture of life."[6] This divine activity was the prophetic-revelatory event in which Muḥammad as God's messenger mediated God's word explicitly in divine "recitations", or *qur'âns*, and implicitly in his own words and actions to his people. Their response was *islâm*, "submission" to the will of God as revealed by prophet and revelation, the two conjunct elements of the divine activity in the Muslim view. They were and are distinct from each other, yet they were and are inseparably intertwined. It was no more possible for later generations of Muslims to understand and to live by the Qur'ân without the Ḥadîth ("tradition", "report", "story"; in general, the accounts of the words and deeds of the Prophet) than it was for Muḥammad's Companions to receive *qur'âns* without the person of the Prophet to bring them, to interpret them, and to use them in directing the new society of the *Ummah*, or Muslim community. Revelation and prophetic mission are together the essence of the transhistorical, sacred event that stands at the beginning of Islamic history.

Psychologically and religiously, the Islamic era dates from the "cutting off" of revelation at the death of the Prophet. If the Hijrah from Mecca to Medina marks the birth of the Muslim community, it is Muḥammad's passing that signals its coming of age. Bereft of the guidance of its charismatic prophet-founder and the "revealing", the ongoing revelation, which he brought, the *Ummah* was now on its own. This is the moment in the history of a nascent religious tradition when, as Max Weber puts it, the charisma of the founder (and, in Islam, of his revealed message) undergoes a "routinization" (*Veralltäglichung*) in which it is "rationalized" (*rationalisiert*) into new patterns of authority within the charismatic community.[7] The transition is, in other words, from an active divine guidance that is still unfolding in the time of the prophet-founder to a "completed" or "closed" divine guidance mediated by structures and mechanisms developed by the community. In Weber's words, after the death of the founder, "die charismatische Gemeinde fortbesteht (oder: *nun* erst *ent*steht)."[8] In the case of Islam, the *Ummah* had now in a sense to reconstitute itself as a post-prophetic, post-revelatory community and to begin to work out its own destiny in the light of its understanding of the prophetic-revelatory event that had brought it into being.

In general terms, Islamic history is the history of Muslim interpretation and implementation of the divine will that it saw communicated in the prophetic-revelatory event. In concrete terms, it is the history of the development of the legal, social, political, and other religious institutions that enabled the *Ummah* to continue in at first rapidly changing circumstances as a community guided by a theocentric ideal. The early stages of this development are clearly seen in the process by which the initially unitary, undifferentiated *ʿilm* ("knowledge", especially knowledge of essential facts; ultimately knowledge of God's will) of the early community gradually crystallized into the distinctive *ʿulûm* (plur. of *ʿilm*), or "sciences", of later Islam.[9] This process, in all the emerging spheres of intellectual life during the first century of Islam, was naturally built upon the two primary sources of *ʿilm* available to the Community: the verbal revelations brought by Muḥammad and his divinely-inspired words and example. The former were soon given formal shape in the official text of the Qurʾân; the latter were much more slowly verbalized and then codified in the form of ḥadîths and later formally identified as *sunnat an-nabî*, "the way (*sunnah*) of the Prophet".

It is in this natural reliance upon the historical inheritances from the prophetic-revelatory event that the origin and meaning of Muslim traditionalism is to be sought. If a sacred event is an historical as well as a mythical reality,[10] it serves all the more powerfully as the source of guidance and authority for the *Leben im Heil* that every religious community seeks. Traditionalism here means continuing contact in historical, "profane" time with transhistorical, sacred reality that transforms everyday, "profane" reality. Abandoned in a sense to history, Islam looked back – and continues to do so – to a time that is essentially beyond history. When "revealing" ended and prophecy ceased, the revelations and prophetic guidance already given became the only fixed standards upon which life could be patterned.

Yet the *Ummah* could be and indeed had to be the arbiter of the crystallization, preservation, and application of these standards. Thus the element in the developing traditionalism that offered a measure of adaptability and flexibility in applying the norms of prophetic and revelatory guidance to new situations was the agreement or consensus (*ijmâʿ*) of the Community. Naturally enough, the living *sunnah* ("way", "practice") of the charismatic *Ummah* (and the Medinan community in particular), which was rooted in the *sunnah* of the Prophet, became the active, practical standard of authoritative faith and practice.

It would, however, be a mistake to see this living *sunnah* of the community of the Companions and early Followers as ever having been consciously set up as a standard different from what was understood to be the *sunnah* of the Prophet. What the post-prophetic community practiced was perceived as but the continuation of what the community in Muḥammad's time had practiced. The relatively recent scholarly theory that the stress on the *sunnat an-nabî* developed only after A.H. 150 in legal circles as an *ex post facto* confirmation of the living *sunnah* of the community,[11] must be modified in light of the most recent investigations into the early history of the development of the Ḥadîth.[12] This theory rests not only upon a rather selective reading of the early legal sources, but also upon a misperception of the basis of Muslim traditionalism, which is the conviction of the sacred nature of the prophetic-revelatory event. Whatever the number of late ḥadîths ascribed to the Prophet, or however late the formal development of *sunnat an-nabî* as a conscious legal principle, the community always and ever understood its authoritative source of *ʿilm* and guidance to lie in the Revelation and the practice of its bearer. The later fabrication of ḥadîths is not a sign of the late appearance of emphasis on the *sunnat an-nabî*.

The explicit divine "recitations" and the divinely guided words and actions of the Prophet were from the beginning the only natural recourse for ultimate authority in making any judgment that could claim to be based upon true *ʿilm*. One senses that the traditional accounts of the special aura that surrounded the recitation of the revelations and the telling of stories about the Apostle of God mirror the pietism of the earliest days of Islam, whatever the actual date of origin of the reports themselves. There is a touching naïveté to the story of how one of the Companions had a horse that tried to bolt away one night from his courtyard when this Companion began to recite the divine word. He went out to see what had happened to the animal, but found nothing that could have frightened it. When he told this to Muḥammad the next morning, the latter explained the incident by saying: "That was the *sakînah*[13] that descended with the recitation."[14] Compare this with the story of ʿAmr b. Maymûn about the Companions' reverence for the sayings of Muḥammad:

> I kept frequent company with ʿAbdallâh b. Masʿûd for a year, during which time I never heard him report an ḥadîth from the Apostle of God nor say, "the Apostle of God said", save for one day when he reported an ḥadîth. [As] there came to his tongue, "the Apostle of God said", fear came over him so that I saw the sweat stream from his brow. Thereupon he said, "May it please God, either somewhat more than that, or about that, or somewhat less than that [was what Muḥammad said]."[15]

Such accounts underscore the special qualities ascribed to both the divine word and the word of the Prophet in early Islam. They point up the fact that, as religious phenomena, both are sacred word, "the word of life", the word of power, the saving word.[16] As such, they possessed from the beginning, from the time of the Prophet, a divine authority. Long before ash-Shâfiʿî's (d. 204/820) codification of Muslim thinking about the relationship of Qur'ân, *sunnat an-nabî*, communal consensus (*ijmâʿ*), and individual reasoning (*qiyâs*) into a formal theory of *uṣûl*, or "sources" (literally: "roots"), of authority,[17] the former two of these "sources" had established themselves as the primary loci of definitive guidance in Muslim life.[18] What is less clear, however, is that the formal and especially the theological distinctions between the Qur'ân and the Ḥadîth (which is considered to be the guide to the *sunnat an-nabî*) began by being perceived and understood in the way that later Muslim theory defined them.

B. The Unity of Prophetic Word and Divine Word as Channels of Authority

The Islamic distinction between the word of God preserved in the Qur'ân and the word (and example) of Muḥammad preserved in the Ḥadîth has an important theological basis. The distinction represents an attempt to preserve the absoluteness and uniqueness, the "partnerlessness", of God by careful separation of His word from the limited, human words of His apostles and prophets. The Qur'ân as divine word is immutable and absolute; in due course, Muslim theology even insisted that it was uncreated, existing eternally as the divine attribute of speech (*kalâm Allâh*). The Ḥadîth as vehicle of the prophetic *sunnah* is mutable and historically contingent; thus the Islamic "science of Tradition" (*'ilm al-ḥadîth*) maintained that an ḥadîth from Muḥammad is divinely inspired in its meaning, but not verbally revealed (and hence not "fixed" as to wording) like the Qur'ân. Such dogmatic distinctions belie, however, both the later effective importance of Qur'ân and Ḥadîth in Muslim piety and also, as will be seen, the early understanding of the division between the two insofar as it can be accurately reconstructed.

Whatever the sophisticated theological distinctions between the divine *kalâm* and the prophetic Ḥadîth, psychologically the person of the Prophet and the importance of the pattern of his life (*sîrah*) have always occupied a central place in Muslim faith[19] – a place derived from the implicit recognition that the divine hand was at work in the person and sending of Muḥammad, to the extent that his historical and eschatological rôle in God's *Heilsgeschichte* also takes on aspects of eternity. The theologians themselves recognized the very special human status of Muḥammad and previous prophets in their doctrine of *'iṣmah*, or "protection" of the prophets from error. Similarly, the legists' reliance upon the *sunnat an-nabî* as reconstructed from the Ḥadîth reached a point where "the *sunnah* is judge over the Qur'ân, and not the Qur'ân over the *sunnah*".[20] As a further example, one need only mention the spiritual rôle assigned the Prophet in mystical and popular piety, where he takes on the aspect of the perfect man, the soul's guide, the intercessor on the Last Day, and even the divine Light. The great Swedish Islamicist, Tor Andrae, has devoted an entire book to a sweeping analysis of the varied ways in which Islam gradually elevated its Prophet into an almost superhuman figure whose example stands beside the Qur'ân as an authoritative guide to God's will.[21]

The present study is an attempt to discern some of the ideas and attitudes of the earliest period of Islam about revelation and prophet.[22] What were the early – one might say, the "pre-theological" – Muslim concepts of divine word and prophetic word and the relation between them? There is evidence that in the formative decades of Islam, for those for whom the Qur'ân and Ḥadîth were still primarily oral rather than written facts,[23] the distinctions between revelation and prophetic inspiration were, even though present in some degree, less absolute, and certainly less important than the overwhelming awareness of one's being close to what has here been termed "the prophetic-revelatory event". In the early sources, there are glimpses of a more unitary understanding of its own origins by the early *Ummah*, and a broader interpretation of revelation than was later the case. It appears that for the Companions and the early Followers of the Prophet, the divine activity manifested in the mission of Muḥammad was a unitary reality in which the divine word, the prophetic guidance, and even the example and witness of all who participated in the sacred history of the Prophet's time, were all perceived as complementary, integral aspects of a single phenomenon.

It is, on the one hand, indisputable that from the time of Muḥammad himself there existed a clear sense of theological dangers in any quasi-divinization of the Prophet or confusion of his judgments with those of God. The Qur'ân calls upon Muḥammad to say: "I am only a man like you, one to whom it has been revealed that your God is one God ...."[24] There are several similar statements in the Ḥadîth by the Prophet himself that show him at pains to stress his own fallibility and relative insignificance *vis-à-vis* the perfection and majesty of the Qur'ân. Most of these involve stories in which Muḥammad stresses that he has been given no special, superhuman knowledge, usually by echoing the Qur'ânic word, "I am only a man".[25] One of the early revelations shows clearly that it was God's grace, not Muḥammad's inherent merit, that led to success: "Did He not find you erring and guide you?" (93:7) Both the message of the Qur'ân and the preaching of the Prophet carry an unmistakable emphasis upon the unimportance of the messenger relative to the divine message itself.[26]

This emphasis was clearly aimed at the preservation of the ultimacy of God from any idolatrous "association" of His earthly representative with Him. That the early *Ummah* had some sense of this is most vividly illustrated in the story of the events immediately after the Prophet's death. The faithful but precipitate 'Umar tried at once to reassure the people (and himself) by claiming that Muḥammad was not really dead, but only "gone away like Moses".[27] Abû Bakr, however, interrupted his speech and addressed the

Muslims: "As for those of you who used to serve and worship[28] Muḥammad, verily Muhammad is dead! And as for those of you who used to serve and worship God, verily God is alive and never dies!"[29] Then he proved his point by quoting a Qur'ânic *âyah*: "Muḥammad is but a messenger; messengers before him have passed away. If he should die or be killed, will you then take to your heels ...?" (3:144) At this, the people recognized the truth of his words, and, the reports say, it was as if they had not known that God had revealed these words before they heard them from Abû Bakr.[30] In their response to them, the Muslims showed that they were prepared to face the future without their beloved Prophet, firm in their faith in the God that his mission had served.

On the other hand, whatever the faithfulness of the early Community to the ideal of a "pure" monotheism unsullied by misguided elevation of Muḥammad to a divine or semi-divine plane, it must have been extremely difficult for those close to the Prophet to keep the authority of the divine judgments communicated as *qur'âns* distinct from the authority of his own judgments as God's Apostle. The Qur'ân itself – not to mention the Ḥadîth literature – uses the formula "God and His Apostle" as though their authority for men were indivisible. Muḥammad was sent, after all, "as a mercy to all beings" (*raḥmatan li-l-ʿâlamîn*: S. 21:107). The faithful are admonished: "your comrade [i.e., Muḥammad] is not astray, nor does he err. Neither does he speak from caprice" (53:2–3); or: "Obey God and His Apostle" (8:20); or: "Verily, in the Apostle of God you have a good example" (3:21). If the Muslims accepted his "mission" (*risâlah*), how could they help but ascribe to him the magical and spiritual qualities, the *barakah*, of the saint or holy man? Even in the face of the Arab tradition of the leader as *primus inter pares*, the chosen bearer of revelation was still a man set apart by his intimacy with the divine word. As God's prophetic voice, Muḥammad's own personal, human words and deeds necessarily carried no small measure of divine authority for those around him.[31]

The apparently contradictory evidence as to the relative importance of the Prophet's word and example *vis-à-vis* the divine word in the time of Muḥammad and the early days of Islam must be squarely confronted. Andrae has tried to explain the apparently contradictory Qur'ânic materials by using the Qur'ân to investigate the prophetic self-consciousness of Muḥammad himself.[32] He postulates a gradual change in Muḥammad's own consciousness of his rôle as his historical mission progresses. Thus he theorizes about an initial unity of prophetic consciousness and divine revelation (seen especially in the early Meccan Sûrahs), which gradually dissolves (in the Medinan revelations) as the idea of a concrete "Book" grows more prominent, and as Muḥammad's evaluation of his own rôle recedes before the massive fact of God's holy scripture. According to this interpretation, Muḥammad's awareness of "his personal importance as God's Apostle" was, at the outset of his mission, "equally as free and 'regal' [*königlich*]" as that of the greatest Hebrew prophets,[33] but changed later on as his relation to the revelations became more and more stylized and objectivized and his "theory" of the recurring revelation of scriptures taken from God's divine Book (the *Umm al-kitâb*) developed.[34]

Whatever accuracy there may be in Andrae's interesting hypothesis about the personal psychology of Muḥammad, the apparently conflicting ideas about the relative authority of the prophetic life (*sîrah*) as model and the divine *kalâm* as commandment were all preserved and known in the early *Ummah*. The simplest explanation appears in this case to be the best: that all these ideas were accepted and integrated into the Community's understanding of its origins. In the minds of Muḥammad's Companions and early Followers, and very likely in the Prophet's own mind, the emphasis upon his humanity and the consequent limitations of his words and deeds did not contradict the sense of his unique rank as the final Prophet and Apostle of God and of the consequent divine authority of his words. For the life of faith, both perceptions were true. Just as the time of the Prophet and Revelation was at once an historical reality and a mythical paradigm, a moment in history and beyond history, so the humanity and fallibility of the Prophet coexisted with the trans-human significance of his mission and function in the eyes of the Community. Empirically, Muḥammad was certainly "only a man"; yet, at the same time, he was God's intimate, His Prophet, and the leader and lawgiver of the new community.[35] Theologically, the Prophet's words were on a plane inferior to that of the divine revelations; psychologically and religiously, Muḥammad's rôle as the instrument of the divine word imbued his own words and actions with the force of divine authority.

Such a complexity in the early understanding of divine word and prophetic word can be seen specifically when one attempts to reconstruct the early Muslim attitudes toward Qur'ân and Ḥadîth. There are, on the one hand, numerous indications that the first one or two generations of Muslims had a much less fixed notion of the boundaries of the Qur'ânic corpus itself than did those who came later. At least until the ʿUthmânic redactors some two decades after Muḥammad's death brought the separate *qur'âns* that had been revealed to the Prophet "between two covers" (*bayn ad-daffatayn*), and perhaps for some time thereafter, the intimate involvement of the Prophet with the revelatory process that produced the *qur'âns* appears to have been a natural and unproblematic assumption for the Community. The contemporaries of the Prophet and even their immediate successors were close enough to the active, ever-unfolding, often *ad hoc* Qur'ânic revelations to have recognized that the *qur'âns* were in a sense prophetic word as well as divine word. Nor did that recognition lessen the force of the *qur'âns* for them as revelation.

On the other hand, the boundaries of the non-Qur'ânic, prophetic words of Muḥammad were apparently far less clearly defined than those of the *qur'âns*. The formal notion of the Ḥadîth as the corpus of prophetic word and deed, and even the standardized form for an individual ḥadîth report, developed only gradually in the course of about the first one-hundred or one-hundred-and-fifty years of Islam.[36] In the evolved, technical sense of the word, *ḥadîth* refers to any report or narrative (and collectively to all such reports), the "text" of which is ascribed either to the Prophet himself or to one of the Companions, and which is attested to by a chain (or chains) of supporting authorities or transmitters (the *isnâd*). The *isnâd* ("support") begins with the last person reporting the tradition and extends backwards from transmitter to transmitter, ending properly only with Muḥammad himself, or sometimes a Companion. This description, however, is a normative pattern rather than an exact representation of the contents of every report that may be given the name *ḥadîth*, even within the "standard", or "classical", collections of Ḥadîth.

When one examines the Ḥadîth literature, it becomes rapidly apparent that even within the framework of the Prophetic Tradition, or *ḥadîth nabawî*, which reports specifically the words or actions of Muḥammad, a wide variety of other "authorities" may be quoted by the Prophet himself. These may take the form of words of previous prophets, earlier scriptures or "Books", or angels or devils as well. Muḥammad is even on occasion quoted as having transmitted direct, non-Qur'ânic words of God Himself that he had received or recognized as authentic revelations. Thus it can be argued that the boundaries of divine word and prophetic word were apparently much more loosely defined in the thinking of the first century or so of Islam than was possible, at least among the religious scholars, in later times.

For an understanding of the early Muslim attitudes toward revelation and the prophetic-revelatory event, the unity of divine word and prophetic word is ultimately more significant than are the undeniable distinctions between the two. If too mechanical a line is drawn between verbatim Qur'ânic revelation communicated through Muḥammad and implicit, non-Qur'ânic revelation and inspiration granted him as a function of his prophethood, the early Community's essentially unitive understanding of God's activity in the sending of His Apostle is distorted. The "pre-theological" Muslim understanding of revelation was focussed not solely upon a scriptural revelation, but upon a revelatory event in which a scriptural revelation was the principal, but not the only aspect of God's revelatory activity. In the next chapter, specific evidence from traditional sources for the existence of such an "open" understanding of revelation in the early period will be examined.

Notes to Chapter 1: "The Early Muslim Understanding of the Prophetic-Revelatory Event"

1. Ascribed to ʿUmar b. al-Khaṭṭâb, second Caliph, or "Successor", of the Prophet: *inna unâsan kânû yu'khadhûna bi-l-waḥy fî ʿahd rasûl Allâh wa-inna-l-waḥy qad inqaṭaʿa wa-innamâ na'khudhukum al-ân bi-mâ ẓahara la-nâ min aʿmâlikum* (Bukhârî 52:5).
2. This interpretation of the perceived discontinuity between the time of the Prophet and the Revelation and that of subsequent history must be qualified somewhat for Shîʿî Muslims. They would understand God's active revelation as having continued, albeit in different form, after Muḥammad in ʿAlî and the succeeding divinely guided Imâms.
3. *The Sacred and the Profane*, ch. 2. Eliade uses the term primarily with reference to "a primordial mythical time made present", which is "indefinitely recoverable, indefinitely repeatable" through its reactualization in religious ritual (pp. 68–69; cf. pp. 81, 104–107). Eliade does, however, note that the Judeo-Christian – especially the Christian – case is unique in that in it an historical (rather than a mythical, "original") time is sanctified, and the cyclical, cosmic concept of time "is left behind" (pp. 72, 110–113). He does not, however,

mention the Islamic case, in which there is also an historical event that is sanctified by the personal intervention of God. The sending of Muḥammad, like the life of Christ or the Sinai event, is a sacred time in some ways discontinuous with the rest of historical time; and it, like them, is an "original" time insofar as it is a new beginning. The Islamic case also points to two facets of the notion of sacred time to which Eliade's approach does not sufficiently do justice: the fact that *historical* sacred time is *also mythical,* in that myth deals with eternal truths; and the fact that an historical sacred time sanctifies to a certain degree subsequent historical time for the community that has its origins in that sacred time. In this sense, there is no "profane" time after the sacred historical event has occurred, for the sacred event gives meaning to all subsequent events: "The striking revelations of divine activity affect our conception of the world we see. Everything is then seen and understood in the light of those revelations" (W.B. Kristensen, *The Meaning of Religion,* p. 379).

4. The term *prophetic* (also *prophet*, *prophecy*, etc.) is used throughout this study in its strictly Islamic sense: of or pertaining to Muḥammad and/or the other persons referred to in the Qur'ân as prophets. The term *prophet* (*nabî*) in this usage is roughly the equivalent of *apostle* or *messenger* (*rasûl, mursal*), even though technically there may be some functional differences between them in Qur'ânic and later Islamic usage. For a fuller treatment of the subject, see: A.J. Wensinck, "Muḥammad und die Propheten"; W.A. Bijlefeld, "A Prophet and More than a Prophet?"; J. Jomier, "La notion de prophète dans l'Islam".
5. Ibn Isḥâq, 1026 / Guillaume, *Life*, 690 [N.b.: All references to Ibn Isḥâq are followed by references to the English translation by Guillaume. The responsibility for all translations in this study is, however, my own].
6. Watt, *Islamic Revelation in the Modern World*, p. 6.
7. *Wirtschaft und Gesellschaft*, pp. 178–188, esp. p. 182; cf. pp. 317–367, *passim.*
8. *Ibid.*, p. 182.
9. "The *ʿilm* of the earliest period was integral but composite. It drew on the Qur'ân, *ḥadîth* and *sunnah*, and law and custom without any clear differentiation between *ʿilm al-Qur'ân* and *ʿilm al-ḥadîth* and *ʿilm al-fiqh*, each of which was later to develop into various branches" (Abbott, *Papyri*, II, 14).
10. Cf. n. 3, above (near the end). With the passing of time, every event of religious significance gradually takes on a mythical aspect. This does not mean that the "mythologization" of an historical event represents a distortion of reality. On the contrary, "myth-making" or "mythologizing" is the process by which an historical reality is recognized as having ultimate, transhistorical meaning (see also above, Introduction, n. 4). The myth founded upon an historical reality is recognized as having ultimate, transhistorical meaning. The myth

founded upon an historical reality can be threatened by its tie with history (when historicism prevails), whereas a so-called "cosmic" myth without palpable historical nexus (and therefore inaccessible to the methods of historicism) cannot; but the "historical" myth carries for the man of faith the double force of history *and* myth, of temporal *and* eternal reality.

11. Joseph Schacht, *Origins of Muhammadan Jurisprudence*, pp. 1–5, 40–80, 133–137, 176–179.
12. Primarily those of Abbott and Sezgin; secondarily those of Azmi and Hamidullah (see above, Introduction, n. 2). For specific discussion of the reliability of the Ḥadîth and the early emphasis on the Prophet's words and deeds, see Abbott, *Papyri*, II, 6–7, 11, 22–23, 78–79; Fück, "Rolle des Traditionalismus", p. 19; G. von Grünebaum, "Von Muḥammads Wirkung und Originalität", 29–30; and Goldziher, *M. Studien*, II, 4–5.
13. *Sakînah* is a Qur'ânic term (S. 2:249; 9:26, 40; 48:4, 18, 26). The basic Arabic sense of the word is "tranquillity", but the Qur'ân uses it primarily in an expanded sense as "some kind of aid sent down to believers from Heaven" (Jeffery, *Foreign Vocabulary*, p. 174). It would appear that some of the richness of the Hebrew *shekinah* has attached itself (probably through the medium of the Syriac: *ibid., op.cit.*) to the basic Arabic word, so that it conveys the sense of the active presence or manifestation of the presence of God (cf. George A. F. Knight, "The *Shekhinah* in Jewish and Christian Thinking", p. 1). On the subject, see also: Goldziher, *Abhandlungen*, I, 177–204; Paret, *Kommentar*, p. 52 (to S. 2:248), and references there; M. Grünbaum, "Beiträge zur vergleichenden Mythologie aus der Hagada", p. 109.
14. *Tilka as-sakînah tanazzalat bi-l-qur'ân* (Bukhârî, *Tafsîr* S. 48, no. 2). I understand *qur'ân* in this context to mean not "the Book" as a whole, but the specific "recitation" (i.e., the act of reciting the particular *âyah* or Sûrah) that the man was engaged in on the occasion in question.
15. Ibn Saʿd, III, i, 110. This and similar accounts are noted by Ignaz Goldziher, "Kämpfe um die Stellung des Ḥadîṯ im Islam", p. 860.
16. Cf. van der Leeuw, *Religion in Essence and Manifestation*, II, 403–407, 418–421; cf. II, 435–446.
17. Through his *Risâlah*. Note that the *uṣûl* are actually *media* rather than *sources* of authority, since ultimately God alone is the Source of authority. It is only within the temporal sphere that the *uṣûl* serve the Community as the immediate "sources" for man's knowledge of God's authority, i.e., for man's "understanding" (*fiqh*) of the divine "ordinances" (*sharâ'iʿ*). Beyond the contingent, temporal sphere, only God is the true "Source" of authority for the Muslim. See W. C. Smith, "Law and Ijtihad in Islam", pp. 111–112.

18. The Qur'ân and *sunnah* are in fact called "the two sources" (*al-aṣlân*) by Shâfi'î himself. In his theory of the *uṣûl*, all other *uṣûl* are secondary to these two, even *ijmâ'* and *qiyâs*, which are seen as authoritative only where a decision cannot be reached through the *aṣlân* (Schacht, *Origins*, p. 135).
19. Cf. the discussion of *sunnat an-nabî* in Section A of the present chapter. Note that while the literary genre of the *sîrah*, or "life" of the Prophet, was not used as a source for the prophetic *sunnah* in legal matters, the life of Muḥammad depicted in the kind of accounts found in Ibn Isḥâq/Ibn Hishâm, Ibn Sa'd, or the Ḥadîth has served all subsequent generations of Muslims as a pattern for their own lives. On this aspect of Muslim "traditionalism", see the important study of J. Fück: "Die Rolle des Traditionalismus im Islam".
20. *As-sunnah qâḍiyah 'alá al-qur'ân wa-laysa al-qur'ân bi-qâḍin 'alá as-sunnah* (Dârimî, *Muqaddimah*, 49).
21. *Die Person Muhammeds in Lehre und Glauben seiner Gemeinde* (1918).
22. By "earliest period" here is meant roughly the first century or century and a half after the time of the Prophet. It is recognized that one cannot place absolute reliance upon the ḥadîth materials as documents of this "earliest period", but, as noted in the Introduction above, these materials do contain much that dates at least from the middle of the second century. Thus they can provide valuable insights into the early community and its thinking even where they do not represent the actual words of Muḥammad.
23. This is not to deny that much of the Qur'ân and many ḥadîths were from the beginning written down as well as memorized (cf. Abbott, *Papyri*, II; *GAS*, pp. 53–84; also Widengren, *Hebrew Prophets*, chs. I, II). However, as the present chapter and especially Chapter 2 attempt to show, neither was thought of at the outset (in the case of the Qur'ân, up to the time of the 'Uthmânic Qur'ân redaction; in that of the Ḥadîth, up to at least the end of the first century) as a fixed book or books in the same way in which they were later understood.
24. *Qul innamâ anâ basharun mithlukum yûḥá ilayya innamâ ilâhukum ilâhun wâḥidun* (41:6; also at 18:110; cf. 17:93). For a full discussion of the humanity of Muḥammad and earlier prophets in the view of the Qur'ân, see Pautz, *Muhammeds Lehre von der Offenbarung*, pp. 234–235; cf. Nöldeke-Schwally, II, 82–83.
25. *Innamâ anâ basharun* (Bukhâri 8:31:3; 90:10; 93:20:1; 93:29:1; 93:31; Muslim 45:88–95; *Muwaṭṭa'* 36:1; further references at *Concordance*, I, 183a, "bashar"). Robson, "The Material of Tradition", p. 179, gives other salient examples and references. Cf. also Muḥammad's statement that he has to "ask God for forgiveness more than seventy times a day" (*Musnad*, II, 282).

26. For the Muslim, "to say 'and Muḥammad is the apostle of God' is to commit oneself to a belief, not about the person of Muḥammad, but about the validity of what he brought. The personality of Muḥammad is *essentially* [italics mine] irrelevant. To declare that he is a prophet is to accept the Qur'ân as binding (and therefore the community that lives according to it as embodying on earth what is of divine prescription)" (Smith, *Islam in Modern History*, p. 19. n. 18).
27. The reference to Moses is found only in the account given by Ibn Isḥâq, pp. 1012–1013 / Guillaume, *Life*, 682–683. The idea is apparently that Muḥammad would return to his people shortly – but in the flesh and not as a Messiah (cf. Andrae, *Person Muhammeds*, pp. 22–23).
28. The verb here is *yaʿbudu*, from ʿ-B-D, "to worship", "to serve". As such it is used in the religious sense only with God as its object. In the present context, where the point is that only God is deserving of *ʿibâdah*, not Muḥammad or any other man, the sense of the word is best preserved by translating it with both "worship" and "serve", since these are the dual aspects of the proper relationship of man to God. In the Muslim view, man *belongs* to God: "*ʿAbd*, literally 'slave', is best rendered theologically by our 'creature'" (D.B. Macdonald, "ʿĪsā", *SEI*, p. 173a). Cf. the censorious Muslim reference to the fact that the Christians "serve and worship" (*taʿbudu*) Jesus (*Musnad*, I, 318).
29. *Ammâ baʿdu fa-man kâna minkum yaʿbudu Muḥammadan fa-inna Muḥammadan qad mâta wa-man kâna yaʿbudu Allâha fa-inna Allâha ḥayyun lâ yamûtu* (Bukhârî 23:3:1).
30. Basically the same story is told in several places in addition to those in Ibn Isḥâq and Bukhârî cited in nn. 27 and 29 above: Bukhârî 62:5:12; 64:83:19; Ibn Mâjah 6:65:1; *Musnad*, VI, 220; Ibn Saʿd, II, ii, 53–57 (various reports).
31. The tendency to idolize Muḥammad's person may of course be quite different from regarding his words and acts as divinely inspired. The fact remains, however, that the divine authority of his rôle as God's Apostle was a major factor in the tendency to divinize his person. It is Muḥammad the bearer of revelation and messenger of God to his people who becomes the paradigm for Muslim life.
32. *Person Muhammeds*, pp. 7–24.
33. *Ibid.*, p. 10.
34. *Ibid.*, pp. 12–14. Andrae goes on, however, to demonstrate that despite the growing sense of the importance of the Revelation in Muḥammad's consciousness, he still claimed for himself substantial privileges as the chosen bearer of revelation to his community (pp. 14–24). Still, as Andrae points out, one cannot in any way charge his Companions with idolatrous veneration of his person (pp. 24–25).

35. Cf. Widengren's statement with respect to the pre-Islamic notion of the identification of the *nâmûs* [νόμος], or "law", with the *rasûl*: "It would on the whole seem to have been a common idea that the religious Law, as an expression of true revelation, is attached to the person of the Apostle – in a way incarnate in him. The Apostle is not only the guarantee of the truth of the religious scripture that he brings; he is somehow also in his person the outward, living expression of that religious Law. His own person is equally important as [*sic*] the revealed book that he brings" (*Muḥammad the Apostle*, p. 101).
36. This holds true without reference to the question of the "authenticity" of the Ḥadîth as actual words of the Prophet (see Introduction). The *formal* criteria of the *isnâd*, for example, could not have developed until several generations of Muslims had transmitted reports from the Prophet and the need arose for a standard form as a guarantee against the forgeries that were clearly developing apace from at least the time of the first civil war during ʿAlî's Caliphate (35/656–40/661). Cf. Robson, "Isnâd in Muslim Tradition", and Horovitz, "Alter und Ursprung des Isnād".

2

Concepts of Revelation in Early Islam

The precise nature of any spiritual experience is necessarily "closed" to non-participants; the encounter with "the wholly Other"[1] does not present itself except symptomatically, i.e., in its accompanying phenomena, or *Begleiterscheinungen.* Thus the prophetic experience of Muḥammad, the revelatory process that produced the *qur'âns* that he transmitted and that sustained him in the tasks that he felt were his to do, was and is fundamentally unobservable except in its fruits: for Muslims, in the Qur'ân and the prophetic example; for others, in the response that it has elicited and continues to elicit from Muslims. While the phenomenologist or the historian of religion is not able to penetrate the mystery of Muḥammad's spiritual experience itself, he or she can legitimately seek to discern the Muslim's understanding of that experience. It is possible to try to reconstruct from the classical sources certain aspects of the attitudes in the early *Ummah* towards the revelatory process and its concrete products. Of these products, the verbatim revelations that became the Qur'ân are the most important (but not the only) ones that have to be considered.

A. The Early Muslim Understanding of Qur'ânic Revelation

The early Community was apparently able to view the Qur'ân both as the word of God and as the word of Muḥammad, insofar as God's words came to the Prophet as an integral part of his prophetic experience. While the dogmatic distinction of later Islam between the fundamental nature of the divine word and that of the human words that issued from the same prophetic lips preserves the "immaculateness" of the Qur'ânic revelations, it does so in a somewhat artificial and literalistic way. One modern Muslim Islamicist has pointed out that in fact no *qur'ân* could have been wholly exterior to Muḥammad:

> When ... during the second and third centuries of Islam, acute differences of opinion ... arose among the Muslims about the nature ofRevelation, the emerging Muslim 'orthodoxy' ... emphasized the *externality* of the Prophet's Revelation in order to safeguard its 'otherness', objectivity and verbal character. The Qur'ân itself certainly maintained the 'otherness', the 'objectivity' and the verbal character of the Revelation, but had equally rejected its externality *vis-à-vis* the Prophet.[2]

As proof-texts, he cites the "bringing down" of the Revelation upon Muḥammad's heart mentioned in Sûrahs 2:97 and 26:193–194, then he goes on to criticize the inability of "orthodoxy" "to say both that the Qur'ân is entirely the Word of God and, in an ordinary sense, also entirely the word of Muḥammad," while "the Qur'ân obviously holds both, for if it insists that it [the Revelation] has come to the "heart" of the Prophet, how can it be external to him?"[3]

There are several indications that the relationship of the Prophet to the specifically Qur'ânic revelations was early understood in much more complex ways than was generally recognized later on. The traditional Muslim theory has tended to be that Muḥammad received all the *qur'âns* orally from Gabriel as explicit verbal revelation given when the latter appeared to him, either in a trance, or "waking vision",[4] or in a dream-vision.[5] In both kinds of revelatory experiences, the stress has been upon the didactic, "external" nature of Gabriel's "teaching" of specific "texts" to the Prophet, for theological reasons such as those cited by Fazlur Rahman in the passage above. The traditional accounts, however, contain also hints of a less rigid understanding of the modes of revelation. Note the following tradition:

> The Apostle of God used to say, "Revelation used to come to me in two ways. [Sometimes] Gabriel would bring it to me and tell it to me as one man speaking to another, and that would [afterwards] be lost to me. And [sometimes] it would come to me as with the sound of a bell, so that my heart would become confused, [but] that would not be lost to me."[6]

According to this version, the revelations "kept" by Muḥammad were apparently precisely those that were *not* overtly discursive or visionary in nature, but less clearly defined experiences of "the heart".[7]

Modern scholarship, taking up traditional Muslim concern with the "modes", or *kayfîyât*, of revelation to Muḥammad,[8] has called attention to the fact that the evidence of Qur'ân and Ḥadîth suggests that it was understood in early Islam that the *qur'âns* came to the Prophet in various ways.[9] Andrae has tried to show that many of the revelations came as "auditory" rather than visionary experiences.[10] Along the same lines, Richard Bell has attempted to demonstrate that the verb *awḥá* in the Qur'ân is better understood as "to suggest" rather than simply as "to reveal" in a general sense. In other words, the true Qur'ânic sense of the word is that of "prompting" or "inspiring" an idea in the mind of the Prophet rather than handing down a set "text". Thus he concludes that the revelatory process should be understood as one of divine inspiration out of which Muḥammad produced the actual *qur'âns*.[11] Building upon Bell's work, Montgomery Watt postulates three basic "modes" of God's communication which he finds in Sûrah 42:51: through *waḥy*, understood as "suggestion"; "from behind a veil", without a mediator; and by a messenger. He finds evidence of all three types in the Qur'ân, as well as the Ḥadîth.[12]

While none of the aforementioned interpretive efforts is capable in the final analysis of penetrating to the mystery of the revelatory experience itself, all do reveal the variety of materials in the sources that suggest that the Prophet's revelatory experience was at the outset understood in a complex fashion. One particular aspect of this complexity is the traditional evidence that Muḥammad received Qur'ânic revelation directly from God as well as through the medium of Gabriel.[13] In his study of prophecy and revelation in the Near East, Geo Widengren has suggested that in the traditional (including the Qur'ânic) accounts of the revelatory experience of Muḥammad, two basic patterns common to the Near East generally have merged. One of these is the notion of a heavenly Book that is brought to a prophet as a single unit, as a "scripture", by a heavenly messenger (who is a kind of spiritual alter-ego); the other is the concept of a heavenly journey or ascension of a prophet (often guided by a heavenly messenger) into the divine presence, where he receives directly from God Himself both revelation for his people and esoteric knowledge meant only for him.[14] While the present concern is not to trace older Near Eastern patterns of revelatory experience in the prophetic career of Muḥammad, or in subsequent Muslim interpretation of that career, these dual aspects of the latter's experience are evident in Qur'ân and Ḥadîth, and they point to at least an implicit Muslim awareness of considerable variety in the spiritual life of the Prophet.

This is most evident in the traditions about the famous *miʿrâj*, or "ascent [to Heaven]", which is mentioned in Sûrahs 81:19–25 and 53:1–12, 13–18.[15] This was apparently a visionary experience,[16] and it is linked traditionally with the *isrâʾ*, or "night journey", referred to in Sûrah 17:1,[17] and even on occasion with the story of the cleansing of Muḥammad's heart by the angels.[18] The idea of this journey, in which the Prophet is said to have met God face face and even to have received revelation from Him,[19] exists alongside the traditional tendency to view Gabriel as the sole medium of revelation to Muḥammad.[20] Later tradition, moreover, could even maintain that Muḥammad received some parts of the Qurʾân itself directly from God on the *miʿrâj*, specifically the somewhat problematic prayers that appear in the *Fâtiḥah* (the opening Sûrah of the Qurʾân) and in the *khawâtim al-Baqarah*, or "seals" (i.e., the closing verses, or *âyah*s, 284–286) of Sûrah 2, *al-Baqarah*.[21] One version, albeit a late one, says that God taught Muḥammad the entire Qurʾân on the *miʿrâj*, and thereafter Gabriel had only to "remind" him of a particular part when it was to be revealed to the community.[22] Muslim tradition has also associated the *miʿrâj* with various *non-Qurʾânic* revelations from God to the Prophet, such as the prescription of the five daily *ṣalât*s and the communication of the Divine Sayings that are considered in the present work.[23] The question of the nature of the heavenly journey – i.e., whether it was corporeal or visionary – became a major issue in later theological discussion, principally with regard to the "seeing of God" (*ruʾyat Allâh*) by Muḥammad on the *miʿrâj*.[24]

While it is evident that the mythological development of the *miʿrâj* was a late phenomenon,[25] the heavenly-journey motif goes back to the Qurʾân itself. The general concept of Muḥammad's special communication with Heaven in addition to the revelatory encounters with Gabriel is very old, however rudimentary it may have been in the beginning relative to later embellishments. There was apparently criticism of the Prophet about the *miʿrâj* from scoffers when he first told of it, and, as Widengren has pointed out, such a journey must have been seen – even if unconsciously – as a natural or even necessary sign of a *rasûl Allâh*.[26] Such a face-to-face encounter with the Divine was necessarily tied up with the revelation of the divine word, however strong the emphasis upon the mediation of a messenger in the revelatory process.

In addition to the question of how the revelation of the *qur'âns* was understood to have been effected, there remains the major issue of the early *Ummah*'s understanding of the nature and scope of the Revelation as a holy scripture. So long as the Prophet was alive, the "Revealing" was, as has been suggested, an active, ongoing reality. It was only after the death of Muḥammad that the Qur'ân received two covers and a fixed content.[27] How could it have been otherwise, since it existed as an open-ended series of *qur'âns* until "closed" by the Prophet's passing? There is ample evidence that the idea of a completely fixed divine Book left behind by the Apostle of God is again a dogmatic development of later Muslim scholarship.[28] The early Community seems to have been more capable than that of a later day of recognizing that the divine word remained divine, whatever minor formal vagaries it might undergo in the all too human hands of the faithful (including the Prophet himself). Although many if not all of the Sûrahs were already written down and a formal collection of the revelations was probably being prepared before Muḥammad died,[29] it is clear that the finalization of a single, authoritative 'text' of the revelations took place – and could take place – only later on.[30] This in no wise contradicts the clear Qur'ânic evidence that the many separate *qur'âns* brought by the Prophet were intended and understood to be parts of a single Qur'ân which would be "the Book", *al-kitâb*, but it does remind us that there was a human history of the *text* of the Qur'ân.

This latter fact is emphasized here not to demean in any way the Qur'ân as scripture, but to underscore the fact that for the earliest Muslims the divine word was a less fixed, more active reality than later literalist tendencies would indicate. Such a phenomenon is hardly unique in the history of revealed religion: dogmatic literalism with respect to the revealed word is usually a product of a crystallized religious structure, not a phenomenon encountered when a young community still feels itself close to active revelation and prophetic activity.

This is further borne out in the Islamic case by the evidence that the early Muslims were able to recognize and accept Muḥammad's own *active*, *intimate*, *human* involvement in the revelatory process. Otherwise, how can one explain the preservation of a tradition such as that concerning the final words of Sûrah 23:14 ("So blessed be God, the Best of Creators!")? These words are said to have been the awed exclamation of one of Muḥammad's scribes at the beauty of the opening portion of Sûrah 23, which the Prophet was dictating to him. When this scribe uttered these words, Muḥammad told him that they were exactly what belonged at that place, and so they were included.[31] There is also evidence that Muḥammad's rôle as bearer of God's word involved some apparent redaction in putting the revealed material together. Once he is said to have removed a passage just dictated; on another occasion he was inspired to add to a previous revelation words that were revealed later on.[32]

The Qur'ân itself indicates that God willed certain passages to be forgotten or abrogated by the revelation of other verses (2:106; 87:6–7; 13:39). If, however, God "exchanges" one *âyah* for another, this does not mean that Muḥammad has made it up (16:101). God also "abrogates what Satan interjects" into the reciting (22:52). This question of *an-nâsikh wa-l-mansûkh* ("the abrogating and the abrogated"), which has been taken up at length by Muslim scholarship, is especially interesting as a further index of the fluid state of the Qur'ânic word during the time of "the Revealing".[33] Muslim tradition has even preserved a substantial number of "abrogated verses" that are said to have been at one time a part of the Qur'ân.[34] If the early Muslims were able to integrate – whether consciously or unconsciously – in their understanding of revelation both Muḥammad's active rôle with respect to the formal structure of the divine word and the possibility that some early revelations would be supplanted, abrogated, or deleted at a later date, then this understanding of revelation was surely a much less rigid one than the later, reified notion.

When one comes to the history of the Qur'ânic text itself,[35] it is also apparent that the early *Ummah* was well aware that many variant readings and arrangements of the revelations had been preserved after the Prophet's death, and also that human error, forgetfulness, and chance had threatened the careful and exact preservation of the texts of the revelations from the beginning.[36] Yet this awareness apparently did not compromise the holy, revealed nature of the Book in the Community's eyes. Goldziher exaggerates grossly when he says that there is no other canonical or revealed religious scripture whose text exhibits as much variation and uncertainty as that of the Qur'ân,[37] but he is surely correct when he observes that in the early years after Muḥammad's death there reigned apparently a casual, at times even individualistic, sense of freedom concerning the actual constitution of the Qur'ân text, almost as if people were not overly concerned about whether or not the text was transmitted in its absolutely earliest form.[38]

It is well known that the text of the Qur'ân was finally officially established some twelve to twenty years after Muḥammad's death, under the Caliph ʿUthmân (23/644–35/656),[39] apparently precisely because of the development of regional recensions of the holy Book that were at variance as to particular readings, overall Sûrah-arrangement, and even on occasion the number of Sûrahs included in the text.[40] The existence of these early recensions or codices (*maṣâḥif*, plural of *muṣḥaf*) in addition to the Medinan one that served as the model for the ʿUthmânic text is amply confirmed by later works.[41] While most differences between these codices and the standard text are minor,[42] there is one difference between the highly regarded codex of Ibn Masʿûd (d. 33/652–653) and the ʿUthmânic text that is significant here.

Ibn Masʿûd's version reportedly did not include the *Fâtiḥah* (Sûrah 1) or the *Muʿawwidhatân*, the two "prayers for refuge" that make up Sûrahs 113 and 114.[43] These three Sûrahs, like the earlier-mentioned prayer in the *khawâtim al-Baqarah*,[44] are problematic in that they take the form of first-person plural prayers addressed to God and give no specific indication (such as the imperative, "Say!" [*Qul*], placed before many Qur'ânic passages meant to be recited by Muḥammad or the Muslims) that God is speaking. Muslim tradition has recognized the unusual status of these three Sûrahs, which "frame" the rest of the Qur'ân almost as invocation and (double) benedictory talisman against the powers of evil.[45] It may be speculated that they are examples of materials from the Prophet that were considered by some of the Companions to belong to the Qur'ânic revelations and by others to belong to some other form of revelation or to be prayer formulas especially favored by the Prophet. This question deserves some serious study as a possible indication of a lack of fixed boundaries between divine and prophetic word in at least some cases in the early *Ummah*.

The widely recognized reading variants, or *qirâ'ât*, for certain words and phrases in the Qur'ân have been explained in Islam through a statement ascribed to the Prophet in the Ḥadîth: "the Qur'ân was revealed *ʿalá sabʿat aḥruf*",[46] that is, in seven different ways or, as it is usually interpreted, in seven different forms of recitation.[47] This is said to have been Muḥammad's answer in a dispute over wording differences in Sûrah 25 between two of his Companions.[48] By this, he apparently meant that "all [of the readings] are correct", a statement that he is said to have made on another occasion, when his scribe corrected a phrase that he had just dictated.[49] Goldziher has shown how the tradition of the seven different modes of recitation allowed the early variants to be used in the interpretation of the Qur'ân.[50]

These variants have been attributed by Muslim Qur'ân scholarship to scribal errors,[51] but another explanation would be that Muḥammad recited the same Qur'ân in varying fashion at various times.[52] Such a "freedom" on the part of Muḥammad and of the early Muslims in the treatment of the details of the revelation would not have to represent a lack of faith or seriousness of faith, but rather could indicate confidence born of firmness and freshness of faith, concern for content and relatively less concern with literal form. Certainly with respect to the arrangement of *âyah*s within a Sûrah, this seems particularly likely. One reason that Muḥammad himself had scribes write down the revelations from very early on in his mission was presumably to "fix" in a particular form or sequence revelations received at different times, to make clear what revelations had been abrogated, or possibly, as will be seen, to distinguish *qur'ân*s from other types of divine-prophetic guidance. Such facts would not in any case have disturbed contemporaries' sense of the authority of the divine word, however repugnant such suggestions might be to Muslims of later centuries. The early community was aware that its divine word was preserved by human hearts, recited on human tongues, and written in human books.

B. The Early Muslim Understanding of "Extra-Qur'ânic" Revelation

It has been suggested that in many respects the authority of the Prophet was and is inseparable from that of the Qur'ân, and that Muḥammad's intimate, personal involvement in the revelatory process was understood in the early Muslim generations as a natural corollary of his office. The "unity" and "freedom" in the early Muslim understanding of revelation becomes still clearer when one turns to the specific question of non-Qur'ânic channels of divine authority. The clear locus of such modes of revelation, like that of the *qur'ân*s themselves, was the person and activity of the Prophet. One modern scholar has remarked that, on the basis of his study of the Ḥadîth literature, it appears, that revelation could come to the Prophet in different ways, and that what came to him, while all of divine origin, was treated on different levels. The Qur'ân was the highest level, but it would seem that Muḥammad could receive a type of inspiration not so high.[53]

Certainly the Qur'ân could never have stood alone as the sole bulwark of faith, even though it is the *muʿjizah*, the clear "miracle", which confirms the divine authority of Muḥammad's mission. In Islamic terms, this is not so because of any limitations of the Qur'ân, but because of man's limitations. The Qur'ân, "being the Word of God, is too sublime to interpret and decipher without the aid of the Prophet."[54] The later working-out of a legal theory of the relative authority of prophetic Ḥadîth and divine Book, as described in Chapter 1, tended to make the authority of the Ḥadîth co-ordinate with that of the Qur'ân. Building upon the Qur'ânic word, "Verily, in the Apostle of God you have a good example" (33:21), and fortified with ḥadîths such as "God ordained (*sharaʿa*) for your Prophet paths of right guidance (*sunan al-hudá*)",[55] this tendency could even reach the point of practically equating the prophetic word with the divine word: Anas b. Mâlik is quoted as saying, "Accept my reports, for I have received them from the Prophet, and he from the angel Gabriel, who got them from God."[56] Suyûṭî even reports a tradition that "Gabriel used to descend with the *sunnah* just as he descended with the Qur'ân."[57]

Goldziher long ago stressed the relatively late development of much of such glorification of the status of the *sunnat an-nabî*, and Schacht and others have since given this idea further emphasis. Goldziher himself, however, also recognized that in the very beginning the words of the Prophet had probably been treated almost as revelation in themselves. He notes that in those circles in which the Ḥadîth of the Prophet was cultivated after the latter's death, the religious importance of whatever was ascribed to Muḥammad was much greater than it came to be in later jurisprudence *per se*:

> The feeling was that God's revelations to Muḥammad were not exhausted with the Qur'ân. It was presumed that the holy Book included those revelations that God intended to be communicated to the masses, but not the sum of all those revelations with which God favored His chosen Prophet.[58]

It is these "extra-Qur'ânic" revelations and the testimony to them in the Ḥadîth that have now to be considered. They take many different forms and admit of only very loose classification, but as a whole they are a significant indication of the reassessment that is needed in the commonly accepted understanding of the distinction between prophetic and divine word in Islam.

There are numerous traditions that point simply to the fact that the Prophet knew of things that were closed to all mortals save the prophets. One of the common types of this kind of tradition is that involving predictions by Muḥammad either about future events that would befall his community after his death or about the events on the Day of Resurrection and the characteristics of the next world. Most of the former are *ex post facto* attempts to justify or to condemn a particular event or group by stressing Muḥammad's special knowledge (and approbation or disapprobation) of these later peoples or happenings.[59] Some of the eschatological "predictions" are also tendentious in nature, but their general thrust is true to the prophetic function of Muḥammad as it is depicted in the Qur'ân. They deal usually with the details of the final Judgment and/or the fate of various types of people (e.g., martyrs, sinners, "holy warriors", apostates, etc.).[60] They are often not unlike Qur'ânic promises and threats and are generally less actual "predictions" than apodictic reminders of divine requital of good and evil deeds. Thus Muḥammad can reassure his people that though they are the last to receive a prophet, they shall be "first on the Day of Resurrection",[61] or that the lowest of them in Paradise shall still have whatever he desires.[62] These are the words of a prophet.

Another major type of tradition about Muḥammad's special knowledge is that containing his interpretation, or *tafsîr*, of particular *qur'âns* for his followers. Such exegetical activity would have been a natural and necessary part of his rôle as bearer of revelation. While the exegetical ḥadîths burgeoned in later times, principally through pious forgery,[63] it is only logical that Muḥammad's explanations of certain Qur'ânic passages should have been the basis of the earliest *tafsîr*. A later age went considerably beyond this to invest such explanations with direct divine authority, and it is difficult to say whether this was only a later development. In an ḥadîth quoted by Ibn ʿAbdalbarr it is stated that whenever a revelation was sent down to Muḥammad, Gabriel was present with the appropriate *sunnah* that would explain (*tufassiru*) it.[64]

Muḥammad's special knowledge of the future and of the meaning of the divine word belongs primarily to the category identified by Muslim scholarship as *ilhâm*, personal "inspiration" (as opposed to *waḥy*, general "revelation").[65] There are, however, more explicit kinds of "extra-Qur'ânic" revelation. In one report, Muḥammad says, "Verily, I was given the Book, and with it something similar ...",[66] which is identified in a different version of the ḥadîth as *al-ḥikmah*, "wisdom", especially esoteric wisdom.[67] This is in accord with both Andrae's and Widengren's emphasis upon a tradition of secret or "concealed" knowledge given Muḥammad by virtue of his function as a *rasûl* and communicated directly to him by God (primarily on the occasion of his ascension).[68] In the eyes of the faithful, the Prophet held a favoured place in God's counsels; some held that he had even seen Him and been spoken to by Him.[69] Therefore it is no surprise to find Ṭabarî quoting him as saying: "And He [God] revealed to me secrets that I am not allowed to communicate."[70] As an initiate in the divine confidence, Muḥammad was granted "the knowledge of those who came before and those who come afterwards".[71] One tradition has him say, "By Him in whose hand is the soul of Muḥammad, if you knew that which I know, you would weep much and laugh little."[72] Even more explicit is the following:

> I have been given the keys to all things save five: with God is the knowledge of the Hour [of Judgment]; He sends down the rain; He knows what is in the wombs; no one knows what he shall get tomorrow; and no one knows in what land he will die. Verily, God is the All-Wise, the Omniscient.[73]

While many such statements of Muḥammad's "special knowledge" are undoubtedly late, often mystical, developments, the pattern of the *rasûl*'s esoteric knowledge is an ancient, pre-Islamic one, and would have been naturally appropriated in the early interpretation of Muḥammad's prophethood.[74]

What Montgomery Watt remarks about the early period of revelation to the Prophet can be said of his entire mission: "There may also have been revelations of a more private character which Muḥammad did not consider to form part of the Qur'ân."[75] While tradition has it that the last revelation was given to the Prophet on the "Farewell Pilgrimage" some three months before his death,[76] there is a well-attested ḥadîth that states that the flow of revelation not only did not cease until the moment of death, but even increased: "God continued revealing to the Apostle of God before his death up to the time that he died, and most of the Revelation [came] on the day in which the Apostle of God died."[77] This is perhaps to be linked with the reports that Gabriel appeared to the Prophet on each of the three days before he died.[78]

Certainly the Ḥadîth literature gives ample testimony of a strong notion that Gabriel not only brought God's *âyah*s to the Prophet, but came with other specific messages for him. These messages can only be seen as a type of "extra-Qur'ânic" revelation, in that they were apparently thought to have been communicated in the same fashion as the *qur'âns*,[79] that is, in visionary appearances of Gabriel to Muḥammad. One well-known example is the incident at the battle of Badr, when Muḥammad saw him (in a dream) come to aid the Muslims, "with the dust [of riding] on his teeth".[80] In other traditions, the Prophet relates specific words that the angel spoke to him.[81] One such ḥadîth is reported by Bukhârî on the authority of 'Â'ishah: "The Prophet said: 'Gabriel called me and said, "God has heard the words of your people and what they reply to you".'"[82] Also, as will be seen below, some explicit, non-Qur'ânic Divine Sayings are related from God by the Prophet on the authority of Gabriel. In addition, if Gabriel was from the beginning identified by Muslims with the "spirit of holiness" (*rûḥ al-qudus*) mentioned in the Qur'ân (2:87, 253; 5:110; 116:102), there is the further implication that the "spirit" may have been thought to give the Prophet guidance of a more general sort in addition to that in the *qur'âns*.[83]

The picture of divine communication with Muḥammad in the Ḥadîth shows him to have relied on revelation for guidance in almost all situations. When he was asked a question, "he did not answer until revelation came to him from Heaven."[84] There are numerous examples of ḥadîths about revelations to Muḥammad that enabled him to avoid danger, exercise wise judgment, give guidance, and answer questions.[85] There may even be a reference to such non-Qur'ânic divine communications in one Companion's story of how those around the Prophet were afraid to behave frivolously in his presence "for fear that something would be revealed concerning us."[86] Nöldeke goes so far as to say of such non-Qur'ânic *ad hoc* revelation that it appears to be one of the most reliable kinds of Ḥadîth material precisely because no specific texts have been preserved. He argues that even if such episodes were to be regarded as fables, one would still have in these reports a generally valid picture of the Prophet's state of mind, for the common characteristic of a prophet is to be in almost constant touch with the Divine and to receive guidance not only in important affairs but even in the tiniest everyday matters.[87]

This notion of reliance upon a Prophet whom God has closely guided in all his activity is further demonstrated in the many ḥadîths that deal with Muḥammad's dreams and his interpretation of his own and others' dreams.[88] One well-known tradition asserts that "the dreams of the prophets are *waḥy*",[89] and certainly Muḥammad's dreams were closely associated with the Revelation. Before the Qur'ânic revelations began, it was through dreams that he received his call to be a prophet: "The first sign of prophethood given the Apostle of God was authentic dreams (*ar-ru'á aṣ-ṣâdiqah*)".[90] According to tradition, Muḥammad received dreams that guided him in his decision-making;[91] other dreams revealed future events in the *Ummah*;[92] and still others served him as symbolic paradigms for the instruction of his followers.[93] One dream even confirmed the Prophet's special status: in it he saw himself given "the keys of the treasures of the earth".[94] The special revelatory value of dreams in the eyes of Muslim tradition is further demonstrated by the statement of the Prophet on the day of his death that the only thing left of prophecy is the sound dream (*ar-ru'yâ aṣ-ṣâliḥah*).[95] Similar to this are his words, "The dream of the man of faith is one forty-sixth of prophecy".[96]

Such traditions point, moreover, to a wholly different aspect of "extra-Qur'ânic" revelation in early Islam that deserves at least cursory mention: revelation granted to others besides the Prophet. Muḥammad is quoted as calling upon God to aid Ḥassân b. Thâbit, the poet, with the "spirit of holiness".[97] Even more explicit are his statements about ʿUmar: "God has placed truth upon ʿUmar's tongue and in his heart",[98] and "In the past there were among the peoples those who were spoken to (*al-muḥaddathûn*). Verily, if there were one of them among this people, it would be ʿUmar b. al-Khaṭṭâb."[99] As the great Muslim historian Ibn Khaldûn points out, such traditions point to special inspiration granted some of those around the Prophet and similarly thought to have been given the Shîʿî Imâms and certain of the saints.[100] Accounts of some schismatic groups in later Muslim heresiography indicate that the idea was also encountered that "the Apostles (*ar-rusul*) never cease, and the apostolic mission (*ar-risâlah*) never ceases",[101] or that "revelation (*al-waḥy*) never ceases".[102] The whole question of *continuing* revelation or infallible guidance after the death of Muḥammad lies at the heart of the Shî'î-Sunnî split in Islam.[103] A systematic study of the roots and development of the various forms of this notion and their relation to early Muslim ideas of inspiration of and revelation to Muḥammad and others is needed. The explicit and implicit consequences of early ideas of "extra-Qur'ânic" and "post-Qur'ânic" revelation were important for many of the theological issues that later assumed great importance in Islam.

Also relevant to the question of "extra-Qur'ânic" revelation is the Qur'ânic and prophetic concept of the past history of revelation. The idea of God's previous revelations to other peoples contains an inherent potential for recognition (on the part of Muslims) of, for example, some parts of Jewish and Christian scriptures as genuine remains of these former revelations. The many quotations or paraphrases of such materials in ḥadîths[104] and even the later Muslim efforts to find portents of Muḥammad in earlier scriptures[105] imply some recognition of the revealed nature of at least parts of these books. Revelation in the traditional Muslim view could be "pre-Qur'ânic" as well as Qur'ânic and "extra-Qur'ânic".[106] Previous studies have traced Muslim "borrowings"; serious attention needs now to be given to *conscious* Muslim use of materials from other traditions such as is seen in the "Israelite stories" (*al-isrâ'îlîyât*).[107]

All of the preceding evidence of an early Muslim notion of revelation outside of or in addition to the *qur'âns per se* is more or less indirect in nature. In the general category of Ḥadîth, however, there are a number of traditional reports in which direct words of God that are not found in the Qur'ân are quoted. This kind of divine word has come to be known in Islam primarily as *ḥadîth qudsî* (plur., *aḥâdîth qudsîyah*), sometimes also as *ḥadîth ilâhî* or *ḥadîth rabbânî*. These three terms, each of which is perhaps best rendered in English as Divine Saying,[108] are used generally by Muslim and by Islamics scholars as synonymous catchwords for a variety of statements traditionally ascribed to God, but which do not occur in the Qur'ân. Most of these Sayings involve simply a direct-discourse statement of God that is quoted on the authority of Muḥammad or, in other words, one that is set in the framework of a Prophetic Tradition (*ḥadîth nabawî*). Many of them take the form of some of the kinds of "extra-Qur'ânic" revelation already discussed above, such as divine words to a previous prophet or to Gabriel. Some are even found, principally outside the formal Ḥadîth literature, with no *isnâd* at all or with one that goes back to someone other than the Prophet.

Oddly enough, despite the implications that the very existence of such a kind of material has for an understanding of early Muslim concepts of revelation and religious authority, virtually no exensive consideration has been given to the Divine Saying either among Muslim or Western scholars. There is, to begin with, considerable unclarity among Muslims as to the formal characteristics of the Divine Saying and the precise dimensions of the genre as a whole,[109] and even the use of the term *ḥadîth qudsî* appears to be a comparatively late development in Islam. Western scholarship, for its part, has given no really serious attention to this phenomenon, and what emphasis it has received in the West has tended to be extremely superficial.

While the Divine Saying appears to have played no significant rôle as a special source of revealed authority in Muslim legal and theological discussions, it has had special significance in the spheres of popular and mystical piety. This does not, however, justify the attitude adopted by many Western scholars that the Divine Saying is a late, primarily third-century product of Ṣûfî piety and mystical experimentation. On the contrary, the very earliest collections of Ḥadîth as well as the major, "classical" collections contain Divine Sayings. These latter examples therefore represent the clearest early examples of explicit, non-Qur'ânic revelations available. Their existence tends to confirm the generally unitive nature of the early Muslim understanding of divine revelation and prophetic inspiration, for they lie somewhere between the divine word of the *qur'ân*s and the prophetic word of the Ḥadîth as a whole. As such, they deserve special considerations as a unique, if diverse body of Muslim religious tradition that has heretofore been largely neglected. It is to these Sayings that the remainder of the present study is devoted.

NOTES TO CHAPTER 2: "CONCEPTS OF REVELATION IN EARLY ISLAM"

1. On "the wholly Other" (*das ganz Andere*), see Rudolf Otto, *Das Heilige*, esp. pp. 31 ff. Concerning the "closed" nature of experience itself, cf. the statement of Gerardus van der Leeuw: "Phenomenology is the systematic discussion of what appears. Religion, however, is an ultimate experience that evades our observation, a revelation which in its very essence is, and remains, concealed" (*Religion in Essence and Manifestation*, II, 683).
2. Fazlur Rahman, *Islam*, p. 31.
3. *Ibid., loc. cit.*
4. There are numerous accounts attributed to Companions of the Prophet that tell how a revelatory "trance" could come upon Muḥammad suddenly, even in the midst of a group of people. Cf. Bukhârî 1:2; 1:3 [towards the end]; 1:4; 25:17; 26:10:1; 52:15 [towards the end]; 59:6:1; Ibn Saʿd, I, i, 131–132. See also Robson, "The Material of Tradition", p. 178.
5. For accounts of revelation to Muḥammad "in sleep" (*fî-n-nawm*), see Bkh. 1:2; 1:3; 1:5; Ibn Saʿd, I, i, 131. On Muḥammad's revelatory experience in general, see Andrae, *Mohammed*, pp. 38–42; Watt, *Muhammad in Mecca*, pp. 46–58.
6. Ibn Saʿd, I, i, 131. A different version is given by Bukhârî (1:2), in which both types of revelation are similarly described, but there is no indication that in one kind or the other Muḥammad failed to retain what had been revealed, as appears to be the case here. It does say that the "bell" experience was "the more/most severe" (*ashaddu*) kind of revelation for him. Cf. Watt's translation of this version of Bukhârî in *Mecca*, p. 55.
7. Even those accounts of the explicit "teaching" of *qur'âns* to Muḥammad by Gabriel (various accounts in Suyûṭî, *Itqân*, pp. 100–101; cf. Tahânawî, *Kashshâf*, II, 1164) do not preclude entirely the Prophet's "internal" involvement in the revelatory process. Note that in one such account, in which Muḥammad says that Gabriel recited the first revelation (S. 96:1–5) to him so that he was able to memorize it, he closes by saying: "I awoke from my sleep, and it was as though these words were written on my heart" (from Ṭabarî, *Ta'rîkh*, as quoted in Jeffery, ed., *Islam*, p. 19). Cf. also S. 53:1–12.
8. See Watt, *Mecca*, pp. 54–58; Suyûṭî, *Itqân*, pp. 91–93.
9. Note the important summary of these "various ways" in Nöldeke-Schwally, I, 20–24, and ff., drawn largely from Suyûṭî, *Itqân*, pp. 102–103, which see. Many of the "modes" listed seem, however, to refer to non-Qur'ânic revelation, which will be considered in Section B of the present chapter.
10. *Mohammed*, pp. 39–42.

11. "Muḥammad's Visions"; cf. *Bell's Introduction*, pp. 18–25.
12. *Mecca*, pp. 52–58; cf. Watt, *Islamic Revelation*, ch. I.
13. Cf. Robson, "Material", pp. 177–178.
14. *Muḥammad the Apostle*, chs. IV, V (esp. pp. 97–98), VI (esp. pp. 142ff.).
15. On the subject, see J. Horovitz's article, "Miʿrādj", *SEI*, s.v., and the literature cited there. In addition, see the important treatment of the subject by Widengren, *Muḥammad the Apostle*, chs. IV–VI, esp. ch. V, "Muḥammad's Miʿrâj"; cf. Widengren, *Hebrew Prophets*, p. 106, and Andrae, *Person Muhammeds*, pp. 68–85.
16. Cf. S. 17:60, where the *ruʾyâ* sent by God is often interpreted as a reference to the *miʿrâj* experience. Cf. Ṭabarî, *Tafsîr*, XV, 13: *wa-ṣâra al-amr ʿindahu ka-baʿḍ aḥlâm an-nâʾimîn*, "It was for him like some of the dreams of sleepers" ["ein traum, wie ihn die träumenden schauen" [*sic*], as Andrae translates it (*Person Muhammeds*, p. 73)]. Bukhârî, *Tafsîr* S. 17:60, no. 9, has "a vision of the eye" (*ruʾyâ ʿaynin*) that the Apostle saw". But see Paret, *Kommentar*, pp. 302–303, for references to other traditional interpretations.
17. See B. Schrieke, "Isrāʾ", *SEI*, s. v., and "Die Himmelsreise Muhammeds", for comprehensive treatments of the ascension and the night journey. See also Nöldeke-Schwally, I, 134–136; II, 85–88.
18. In various places: e.g., Bukhârî 8:1:1; Muslim 1:263; further references at *Concordance*, III, 267a. Cf. article by J. Horovitz on the *miʿrâj* cited in n. 15 above and the same author's "Muhammed's Himmelfahrt"; also Andrae, *Person Muhammeds*, pp. 85, 52–55, and Robson, "Material", pp. 178–179.
19. Muslim even cites an ḥadîth concerning the "*isrâʾ* to heaven" in which Muḥammad says: "And so God revealed to me what He revealed" (*fa-awḥá Allâh ilayya mâ awḥá*) (1:259, near the end; cf. *Musnad*, III, 148–149).
20. Cf. Tahânawî, *Kashshâf*, II, 1162 (middle of the page).
21. Muslim 1:279; 6:253; further references in *Concordance*, II, 10b. Cf. Suyûṭî, *Laʾâlî*, p. 39 (line 7 from the bottom), and translations of same in Widengren, *Muḥammad the Apostle*, pp. 105–106, and Jeffery, ed., *Islam*, p. 45. These passages are problematic because of their external form (see below, p. 29). On S. 2:284–286 specifically, see Widengren, *ibid.*, *loc. cit.*, and Nöldeke-Schwally, I, 185.
22. Quoted from az-Zurqânî by Widengren, *Muḥammad the Apostle*, p. 108; also by Andrae, *Person Muhammeds*, p. 69.
23. The story of the remission on the *miʿrâj* of the original divine command of fifty formal Prayers per day and the final command of five is found at Bukhârî 8:1:1. Concerning the communication of the Divine Sayings on the *miʿrâj*, see Tahânawî, *Kashshâf*, II, 280.

24. Surveys of the varied Muslim treatment of the question are found in Stieglecker, *Glaubenslehren*, pp. 361–371, and Andrae, *Person Muhammeds*, pp. 71–85.
25. Andrae, *ibid.*, pp. 68, n. 1, and 82–88.
26. Widengren, *Muḥammad the Apostle*, chs. IV, V.
27. Nöldeke-Schwally, I, 44–45; Blachère, pp. 18–27.
28. Jeffery, *Materials*, pp. 4–5. Cf. Suyûṭî, *Itqân*, 146, and the traditions that tell how Gabriel used to come once a year to recite the whole Qur'ân with the Prophet (and twice in the year that he died): Ibn Sa'd, II, ii, 3–4.
29. There were, in fact, several "scribes of the revelation" (*kuttâb al-waḥy*) in the Prophet's time: see Nöldeke-Schwally, I, 45–46; Widengren, *Hebrew Prophets*, pp. 45–47; Blachère, pp. 12–13.
30. Jeffery, *Materials*, pp. 5–8; Nöldeke-Schwally, II, 1–121, esp. 1–11, 47–62.
31. Nöldeke-Schwally, I, 46–47 (with references to the *Tafsîr* literature). For references to numerous examples from Bukhârî of revelation "als Folge von Beeinflussung durch Ideen Anderer", see O. Rescher, *Sachindex*, s. v. "Offenbarung".
32. Nöldeke-Schwally, I, 46–48; II, 1–5. See also Widengren, *Hebrew Prophets*, pp. 49–51; *Bell's Introduction*, p. 107 (cf. p. 113).
33. On abrogation, see Blachère, pp. 241–242; Jeffery, ed., *Islam*, pp. 66–68; Franz Buhl, "Ḳur'ān", *SEI*, p. 251b.
34. This group of "original parts of the Qur'ân" is treated in some detail by Nöldeke-Schwally (I, 234–255), drawing upon the work by Hibatallâh, *an-Nâsikh wa-l-mansûkh fî-l-Qur'ân.* On Hibatallâh (d. 410/1019), see *GAS*, p. 47.
35. Cf. Blachère, pp. 27–135; Nöldeke-Schwally, II, 1–121; Nöldeke-Schwally (Bergsträsser), III, 1–115.
36. Numerous instances are given in ch. IV of *al-Mabânî*, pp. 78–116, *passim.* One tradition even tells of how a small scroll was neglected while the Companions were "busy with the Prophet's death" and consequently was eaten by a household goat (*dâjin*) (*ibid.*, pp. 87–88).
37. *Richtungen*, p. 2.
38. *Ibid.*, p. 33.
39. For a reconstruction of the process, see Nöldeke-Schwally, II, 47–119, and Blachère, pp. 52–62.
40. Nöldeke-Schwally, II, 8–50; Blachère, pp. 35–45; Jeffery, *Materials*, pp. 8–9; Goldziher, *Richtungen*, pp. 2–31.
41. E.g., the three fourth/tenth-century books on the subject of the early codices, each of which bears the title, *Kitâb al-maṣâḥif* (Jeffery, *Materials*, pp. 9–18).

Note that Jeffery's *Materials* contains the text of one of these three works, that of Abû Dâwûd as-Sijistânî.

42. Cf. Goldziher's numerous examples in *Richtungen*, pp. 1–54.
43. Nöldeke-Schwally, II, 39–42.
44. Cf. above, p. 28.
45. Suyûṭî, *Itqân*, 186–187; further references at Nöldeke-Schwally, II, 41, n. 1. Cf. the ḥadîth concerning these verses (and, in addition, the *âyat al-kursî*) in al-Madanî, p. 92 (no. 495).
46. Bukhârî 44:4:3; Muslim 6:264, 270, 272, 274; further references at *Concordance*, I, 448a.
47. Goldziher, *Richtungen*, pp. 37–39; Blachère, pp. 116–131.
48. Nöldeke-Schwally, I, 48.
49. Goldziher, *Richtungen*, p. 35.
50. *Ibid.*, pp. 40–51. Note the statement quoted on p. 50 from Ibn al-Munayyir that "all seven modes of recitation (*aḥruf*) were communicated to Muḥammad through the angel Gabriel".
51. *Ibid.*, 31–32; cf. *al-Mabânî*, ch. IV, *passim.*
52. Widengren, *Hebrew Prophets*, p. 48, stresses the view "that on various occasions Muḥammad would recite the same Sûrah in a different wording, and that this variation was from the outset preserved in the different readings in which the Sûrah circulated, both in oral and written transmission." It is not clear here how precisely Widengren uses the word *Sûrah*, but in context it appears to be used very loosely. Judging from the variant *maṣâḥif* readings, it would seem that such reading variations were most common for specific *âyahs* or short segments of longer Sûrahs.
53. Robson, "Material", p. 178.
54. Nasr, *Ideals and Realities*, p. 82.
55. Muslim 5:257. Goldziher quotes the same tradition from Abû Dâwûd in *M. Studien*, II, 20.
56. Goldziher, *ibid.*, *loc. cit.*, from the *Sunan* of Tirmidhî.
57. Suyûṭî, *Itqân*, p. 102; Dârimî, *Muqaddimah*, 48.
58. Goldziher, "Kämpfe", p. 863 (my translation).
59. Numerous examples in Goldziher, *M. Studien*, II, 33–125, *passim*; also Robson, "Material", pp. 267ff. For specific examples from as early as the end of the first century A.H., see Hammâm b. Munabbih, nos. 29, 125, 128.
60. A prominent example of a particularly long tradition about the fate of various people at the Last Judgment is found at Muslim 1:302.
61. Bukhârî 97:35:6; Hammâm b. Munabbih, no. 1.
62. Muslim 1:301.

63. See Nöldeke-Schwally, II, 162–163; Goldziher, *Richtungen*, 64.
64. Ibn ʿAbdalbarr, *Jâmiʿ*, II, 191. Note the many other traditions in the same section that contain similar material about the *sunnah* and the Book and the distinction between the two. Note also the "reified" use of the term *sunnah* in the ḥadîth in question. It is used here in the sense of *specific* "ḥadîths" rather than the older sense of "way" or "path" (which can be derived from an ḥadîth, but is not strictly the same as an ḥadîth!). This leads one to suspect that the tradition is a product of a relatively late period.
65. The particular ḥadîth about Gabriel's having brought the *sunnah* to explain the Qur'ân would not, however, belong to the category of *ilhâm* in the terms of Muslim religious science, where the latter concept is treated as a wholly internal kind of "suggestion" that takes place "in the heart" entirely, without any visionary experience of a divine messenger. On the distinction between *ilhâm* and *waḥy*, see: Jurjânî, *Taʿrifât*, p. 35; Tahânawî, *Kashshâf*, II, 1308; cf. D.B. Macdonald, "Ilhām", *EI*², s.v., and "The Doctrine of Revelation in Islam", esp. pp. 116–117; also Massignon, *Essai*, pp. 42, 224, 260 (note that Massignon translates *ilhâm* as "inspiration privée", *waḥy* as "révélation angélique").
66. *Innî ûtîtu al-kitâb wa-mithlahu maʿahu* (Abû Dâwûd 39:9).
67. *Al-Mabânî*, p. 81; cf. Paret, *Kommentar*, p. 68 (on S. 3:48), and Widengren, *Muḥammad the Apostle*, pp. 129–131, concerning *ḥikmah*.
68. See above, Section A, pp. 28–29.
69. Cf. Section A, above; see also Robson, "Material", p. 177; Andrae, *Person Muhammeds*, pp. 68ff.; Widengren, *Muḥammad the Apostle*, pp. 102–114, 214–216.
70. *Tafsîr*, XXVII, 26; also translated by Andrae, *Person Muhammeds*, p. 70. In an earlier portion of the same ḥadîth in Ṭabarî, it was revealed to Muḥammad "what was in Heaven and what was on earth". *Musnad*, IV, 66, has this latter account without the former mention of "secrets": *ḥattá tajallá lî mâ fî as-samawât wa-mâ fî al-arḍ*, "... until it was made manifest/revealed to me what was in Heaven and what was on earth" (cf. Goldziher's translation of this passage in *Vorlesungen*, p. 124).
71. From al-Qastallânî's *Mawâhib*, as quoted by Andrae, *Person Muhammeds*, p. 70, and Widengren, *Muḥammad the Apostle*, p. 108.
72. Hammâm b. Munabbih, no. 14; quoted by Sarrâj, *al-Lumaʿ* pp. 377–378.
73. *Musnad*, II, 85–86.
74. Widengren, *Muḥammad the Apostle*, p. 106. Cf. Widengren's companion study, *The Ascension of the Apostle and the Heavenly Book*, for detailed analyses of earlier ascension accounts in the ancient Near East.

75. *Mecca*, p. 49.
76. Muslim 54:3–5; Bukhârî 2:33:2. The *âyah* that is cited is that of S. 5:3: "Today I have consummated your religious observance (*dîn*) for you, I have completed My blessing upon you, and I have confirmed *islâm* as your religious duty (*dîn*)." Modern scholarly opinion differs on the placement of this *âyah* in the last year of Muḥammad's life: cf. Paret, *Kommentar*, p. 114, and further references there.
77. *Inna Allâh tâbaʿa al-waḥy ʿalá Rasûl Allâh qabla wafâtihi ḥattá tuwuffiya wa-aktharu mâ kâna al-waḥy yawm tuwuffiya rasûl Allâh* (Muslim 54:2; cf. Bukhârî 66:1; *Musnad*, II, 236). The same tradition is quoted from Ibn Saʿd, II, ii, 2, by Goldziher, "Kämpfe", p. 863, n. 3 (where the vol. number is incorrectly given as "III"). Concerning the transitive use of *tâbaʿa*, see the editor's note to Ibn Saʿd, II, ii, 2, on p. 3 of the "Anmerkungen" to vol. II, ii.
78. Ibn Saʿd, II, ii, 48–49.
79. Cf. the tradition quoted above, p. 33, to the effect that Gabriel brought "the *sunnah* just as" he did the Qur'ân.
80. Ibn Isḥâq, p. 444/Guillaume, p. 300.
81. E.g., Bukhârî 59:7:4; 1:37:1; Muslim 1:57; *Musnad*, II, 231 (two different accounts); Ibn Saʿd, I, i, 113. All of these ḥadîths report words of Gabriel to the Prophet about various matters.
82. Bukhârî 97:9:4.
83. Concerning the Muslim concept of the *rûḥ al-qudus*, see Ahrens, *Muhammed*, pp. 133–134; E. E. Calverley, "Nafs", *SEI*, s. v.; O'Shaughnessy, *Meaning of Spirit*, pp. 42–51; Bell, "Muhammed's Visions", p. 148 and *passim*; D. B. Macdonald, "ʿĪsā", *SEI*, s. v.
84. Ibn Bashkuwâl, *as-Sîlah fî ta'rîkh a'immat al-Andalus* (ed. Francisco Codera, 2 vols. in 1, *Bibliotheca Arabico-Hispana*, vols. I, II [Maitriti, 1883]), I, 314: ... *fa-lâ yujîbu ḥattá ya'tîhi al-waḥy min as-samâ'*. This passage is quoted by Goldziher, "Kämpfe", p. 864.
85. Examples drawn from al-Wâqidî can be found in Nöldeke-Schwally, I, 259.
86. Bukhârî 67:80:2: *haybata ann yunzala* [*yanazzala*] *fînâ shay'*.
87. Nöldeke-Schwally, I, 259.
88. See Book 91, "Ta'bîr ar-ru'á", of Bukhârî's *Ṣaḥîḥ*, for examples. On dreams and dream-interpretation generally in Islam, see T. Fahd, "Les songes et leur interprétation selon l'Islam"; N. Bland, "On the Muhammedan Science of *Ta'bîr*, or Interpretation of Dreams"; N. Vaschide and H. Pieron, "La rêve prophétique dans la croyance et la philosophie des Arabes". Specifically on the dreams of the Prophet, see Hamidullah, *Prophète*, II, 683–684.
89. Bukhârî 4:5; 10:161:3.

90. Ibn Isḥâq, 151 / Guillaume, *Life*, 105.
91. al-Wâqidî, *K. al-Maghâzî*, I, 208–209 (= Wellhausen, *Muhammed in Medina*, pp. 104–105).
92. E.g., Bukhârî 62:5:9; 62:6:4.
93. E.g. Bukhârî 62:6:2, 3; 91:18. For other references to various types of dreams of Muḥammad, see *Concordance*, II, 205–206 ("ru'yâ").
94. Bukhârî 96:1; also 91:11; cf. Hammâm b. Munabbih, no. 134; apparently in contradiction of S. 6:50: *qul lâ aqûlu lakum ʿindî khazâ'in Allâh wa-lâ aʿlamu al-ghayb*, "Say, 'I do not say to you that I possess the treasures of God, and I do not know the Hidden ...'" (also at S. 11:31). Cf. Widengren, *Muḥammad the Apostle*, pp. 169–170, on the "treasures" granted the Apostle.
95. Bukhârî 91:5; cf. Muslim 4:207, 208; *Muwaṭṭa'* 52:2, 3.
96. Bukhârî 91:4:2–4; *Musnad*, II, 233, 269; Hammâm b. Munabbih, no. 48.
97. Bukhârî 8:68; 59:6; 78:91; many further references at *Concordance* I, 139a ("ayyada"), and V, 320a ("qudus"). Cf. Tirmidhî 41:70:1; al-Ḥâkim an-Naysâbûrî, *al-Mustadrak*, III, 287 (incorrectly cited in Abbott, *Papyri*, II, 7, n. 25, as vol. "II"). In these latter two versions of the ḥadîth, it is not said that Muḥammad *asked* God to aid Ḥassân, but that "God aids Ḥassân" with the *ruḥ al-qudus*. Cf. above, n. 83, for literature on the *rûḥ al-qudus*. For another ḥadîth that mentions the *rûḥ al-qudus* as an aid to ordinary men, see Muslim 44:157.
98. Tirmidhî 46:17:2; Ibn Saʿd, II, ii, 99. Cf. Ibn Saʿd, II, ii, 100, where it is said that ʿUmar possessed nine-tenths of all knowledge.
99. Bukhârî 60:54; Muslim 44:23; other references at *Concordance*, I, 434a. As is noted by Bukhârî after the version cited above and in *Lisân al-ʿarab*, II, 439, the term *muḥaddath* [not *muḥaddith*, as read by Houdas and Marçais, *Les traditions islamiques*, II, 529!] means "inspired" (*mulham*). This is a term applied in "Twelver" Shîʿî sources to all the Imâms, according to traditions cited by al-Kulînî, *Kâfî*, I, 531, 534 (in two places).
100. *Muqaddimah* (Rosenthal), II, 203; cf. I, 223. See also n. 99 above.
101. Ash-Shahrastânî, *al-Milal wa-n-nihal*, p. 136. The statement refers to the views of the party of the Mansûrîyah. Al-Ashʿarî makes a similar statement in his *Maqâlât*, p. 9.
102. Quoted by Widengren, *Muḥammad the Apostle*, p. 46, from al-Maqdisî, concerning the views of the Khurramîyah. Al-Ashʿarî says of this group [the "Khurramdînîyah" according to his classification] that they claim that the prophets come in an unbroken succession after Muḥammad, and that their line does not cease (*Maqâlât*, p. 438).
103. Cf. W. M. Watt, "Early Discussions about the Qur'ân", pp. 34–35. Watt notes

the view ascribed to some of the Rawâfiḍ, that even the Qur'ân can be abrogated by the Imâms (ref. to Ashʿarî, *Maqâlât*, p. 611) (*ibid.*, p. 35, n. 33). Cf. Ashʿarî's comment in another place that some groups of the Rawâfiḍ claim that the Imâms can abrogate the divine ordinances, or *sharâʾiʿ* (*Maqâlât*, p. 438).

104. Cf. Tor Andrae's statement concerning "Schriftworte" that are "quoted" from other scriptures in the Muslim sources: "Die Worte 'Gott sagt in der Tora' oder 'ich habe in einem Buch der Schriftbesitzer gelesen' wurden zu einer Formel, mit der man ohne Bedenken einfach Worte anführt, die man besonders erbaulich fand oder von deren Wahrheit man felsenfest überzeugt war" (*Islamische Mystiker*, pp. 31–32). Cf. Goldziher, "Neutestamentliche Elemente in der Traditionslitteratur des Islam", and *M. Studien*, II, 382–400; Bell, *Origin*, pp. 191–199.
105. Cf. Stieglecker, *Glaubenslehren*, pp. 537–567; Watt, "The Early Development of the Muslim Attitude to the Bible", pp. 57–59.
106. Bell, *Origin*, pp. 100–101; cf. Wielandt, *Offenbarung und Geschichte*, p. 31. Nor is the idea foreign to the Qur'ân itself, as Rudi Paret has reminded me in a letter of 27 December, 1973: the concept of the *ṣuḥuf al-ûlá* (S. 20:133; 87:18f.; 53:36f.) is ample indication of this.
107. Many of these traditions, quoted generally on the authority of converted Jews such as Wahb b. Munabbih, are found in Ibn Hishâm's *at-Tîjân li-maʿrifat mulûk az-zamân fî akhbâr Qaḥṭân*. Kaʿb al-Aḥbâr was another converted Jew who was a well-known transmitter of such accounts: see Wolfensohn, "Kaʿb al-Aḥbâr", esp. ch. III. Specifically on the *isrâʾîlîyat*, see: G. H. A. Juynboll, *Authenticity*, pp. 121–138, and "Aḥmad Muḥammad Shâkir ... Ibn Ḥanbal's Musnad", p. 239; Goldziher, "Mélanges judeo-arabes: Isra'iliyyat"; Naʿnâʿah, *al-Isrâʾîlîyât*. Further references are given in Husām al-Alousī, *Problem of Creation*, p. 157.
108. "Holy" or "sacred" would be other equivalents for *qudsî*, but "divine" expresses more clearly the Muslim understanding of this type of ḥadîth as a particular kind of revelation from God (hence the synonymous terms, *ilâhî* and *rabbânî*, "divine"). The word *ḥadîth* itself is impossible to render in English by one word that is satisfactory for all senses of the original. "Tradition" is the usual translation, but this does not convey the inherent sense of *something spoken* or *narrated* (especially in the sense of *something new that is reported*; cf. the German *Nachrichten*, or, less satisfactory, the English "news") that the Arabic root does. Nor does it convey, except where specifically so defined, the technical sense of *ḥadîth* as a report from or about the Prophet that is accompanied by a chain of transmitting authorities for the

accuracy of the report. Since, however, "tradition" has been used by convention as an English equivalent for *ḥadîth* in the technical sense, this usage has been followed throughout the present work, with the one exception of the present rendering of *ḥadîth qudsî* (and a few glosses of it as "word" or "report", where the intended meaning is clear). In the present case, it seems preferable to emphasize by the use of "saying" the specific words of God quoted in the text of the so-called *ḥadîth qudsî* rather than the entire ḥadîth (which includes the chain of authorities and any frame-story there might be for the divine word proper). This emphasis has firm precedent in Arabic usage, where *ḥadîth qudsî* most often refers only to that part of the full tradition wherein the specific divine word is quoted even though it would also be used by extension for the whole ḥadîth, including transmitters and additional textual material. It is also supported in Western scholarship by the similar usage of the great German orientalist, Hellmut Ritter, who translates *ḥadîth qudsî* with *Gottesspruch* (*Meer der Seele*, p. 28, n. 1, and *passim*). The use of the English term also serves to emphasize what will be demonstrated in Chapter 3: that the Arabic technical term is itself a relatively late development.

109. It is interesting to note the varying estimates of the number of so-called *aḥâdîth qudsîyah* among Muslims. Tahânawî, for example, says that they number about 100 (II, 280), while Seyyed Hossein Nasr says that there are only about forty (*Ideals and Realities*, p. 83)! In Part III of the present study, ninety separate Sayings or "families" of Sayings of this type have been collected from the "standard" and earlier Ḥadîth works. Many others can be found in the major Ṣûfî compendia (see Chapter 3, C) and in the later collections of Divine Sayings (see Chapter 3, C, and Appendix A), where, for example, one writer (al-Madanî has collected 858 such Sayings in one volume, albeit with numerous repetitions and variants of the same tradition).

PART TWO

The Divine Saying

3

The Divine Saying as Problem

If the Divine Saying, or so-called *ḥadîth qudsî*, is to be investigated in the light of the question of early Muslim understanding of revelation and prophetic inspiration, primary attention must be focused upon those non-Qur'ânic Divine Sayings that were preserved in the form of ḥadîth reports early in the history of Islam. It is not, however, possible to deal only with the earliest Divine Sayings and to ignore the subsequent history of this genre of material. The nature and extent of the early Divine Saying can only be assessed after the later developments in its use and interpretation have been properly understood. Furthermore, because modern Islamics scholarship has fastened upon only certain limited aspects of the Divine Saying as a phenomenon in Muslim life, it is necessary to understand how the presently held scholarly conceptions and misconceptions have been developed.

The present chapter presents, therefore, a survey of, first, the rather limited Western scholarly treatment of the Divine Saying, then the longer history of Muslim discussion and theory concerning this unique body of literature, and finally the various kinds of Islamic sources in which the Divine Saying is found. Such considerations are prerequisites for the re-assessment of the Divine Saying as an authentic document of early Islam that the present study proposes.

A. The Divine Saying in Western Scholarship

Islamics scholarship in the West has devoted relatively little attention to the phenomenon of the Divine Saying. Apparently the first reference to *ḥadîth qudsî* in a published source is that of Joseph von Hammer-Purgstall in an article in 1851 on Rûmî, where it is defined as "holy or heavenly tradition, such words of tradition in which ... God Himself speaks and which were revealed to the Prophet either through Gabriel or in a dream".[1] Only a few years later, in the second volume (1865) of his monumental *Arabic-English*

Lexicon, E. W. Lane cites two brief and generally similar definitions of *ḥadîth qudsî* taken from Muslim lexicographers,[2] but as late and comprehensive a work as the first edition of the *Encyclopaedia of Islam* (1913–1938) has no separate article on the subject, and its "Ḥadīth" article has only a minimal reference to it.[3] Oddly enough, even the greatest of Western Islamicists, Ignaz Goldziher, makes no mention of Divine Sayings in his study of the Ḥadîth literature in Volume II of his *Muhammedanische Studien* (1889), although he does refer to them in the course of a later article (1907).[4] The only consequential scholarly consideration of the subject prior to the First World War is that by Nöldeke and Schwally in the second edition (1909) of Nöldeke's *Geschichte des Qorâns*,[5] where it is treated as one sub-category of "those revelations of Muḥammad not contained in the Qur'ân".[6] Here several examples are given, along with references to their occurrence in the classical sources, and the Divine Saying is recognized as "extra-Qur'ânic revelation" (*ausserqorânische Offenbarung*), along with such materials as "omitted" portions of the Qur'ân and non-Qur'ânic *ad hoc* revelations to the Prophet (see above, Chapter 2, B).

It was, however, only in 1922 that an entire article was devoted to the Divine Saying by a non-Muslim scholar, Samuel Zwemer.[7] While this study is elementary and ultimately unsatisfactory, it has remained the standard reference source for later scholars to the present time. In the article, Zwemer deals primarily with three late collections of Divine Sayings: those of Ibn al-ʿArabî (d. 638/1240), Muḥammad al-Madanî (d. 881/1476), and Muḥammad al-Munâwî (d. 1031/1621).[8] Although he does recognize that some of these "direct revelations of God to former Prophets and also to Mohammed himself" are also found in the "canonical" collections of Ḥadîth (p. 264), Zwemer does not devote any attention to specific instances of early citation. Thus it is not surprising when he concludes that a characteristic of the Divine Saying is a weak chain of transmitters, or *isnâd*, for none of the three collections that he uses gives full *isnâd*s throughout. Zwemer is inclined to see such ḥadîths in general as illustrating the "looseness of the whole fabric of tradition", and he in effect dismisses them as a "system of pious frauds" that have been fostered by "deception" in the cause of Islam (pp. 270–271). He is particularly interested in the "sources" of these ḥadîths and focuses upon the examples that he can find in the three collections that appear to him to be "Old and New Testament fragments", "stray verses from other Apocryphal writers", and "*abrogated* verses of the Koran" (p. 269). It is only at the end of his article that Zwemer really begins to wrestle with the Divine Saying on its own terms and ends by pointing to several questions that are raised by the mere existence of these ḥadîths, notably their relation to the Qur'ân, to previous revelations to other prophets, and to the remainder of the Ḥadîth literature (p. 275). In sum, the principal value of his study is as a point of departure rather than a significant advance in knowledge about the Divine Saying.

More recently, Louis Massignon has devoted some attention to the subject with respect to the rôle of these Sayings in mystical usage. In this context, he classifies them primarily as one kind of *shaṭḥ* (plur., *shaṭḥîyât*), "ecstatic saying" or "divinely inspired utterance", a phenomenon well known among the Ṣûfîs.[9] He states rather disingenuously at one point that "the *ḥadîth qudsî* was, in the beginning, the indirect way of placing in circulation 'theopathic phrases', by tracing them back to scriptures in which God speaks in the first person".[10] He calls the *ḥadîth qudsî* an "aberrant branch of tradition",[11] and links it with the kind of ḥadîth called *mursal*, or, as he translates it, "lax" (*relâché*).[12]

The *ḥadîth mursal* is an ḥadîth in which one or more links *at the end* of the chain of transmitters are missing,[13] and Massignon is specifically concerned with those traditions that were falsely, but with the pious intent of religious edification, attributed by later Muslims to Muḥammad and other prophets through an apocopated, or *mursal* chain of transmitters. Such ḥadîths, he argues, were commonly received in either ecstatic or dream-encounters with a prophet after his death and were regarded by their perpetrators as wholly authentic communications from the divine realm. Similarly, he sees the Divine Saying, or *ḥadîth qudsî*, as the form in which divine words were placed in circulation by pious Ṣûfîs. Given at first as *mursal* traditions from Muḥammad, John the Baptist, Moses, or some other prophet, these ḥadîths finally (as in the *riwâyât* of al-Ḥallâj) became ecstatic divine words supported by an *ilhâmî* ("ecstatic", "inspired") *isnâd* rather than an historical line of transmission.[14]

Massignon's entire emphasis is thus upon the mystics' use of the Divine Saying, which he apparently sees as a phenomenon that develops relatively late. While he calls the *ḥadîth qudsî* and *ḥadîth mursal* phenomena of "primitive Islam", he speaks of them as types of ḥadîth that grew up principally in the third/ninth century among the mystics as means of giving expression to ecstatic experience.[15] This position is also taken over by Louis Gardet and G.-C. Anawati in their *Mystique musulmane,*[16] where the Divine Saying is even defined as an ḥadîth "en lequel Dieu, durant une expérience mystique, parle à la première personne".[17] Neither Massignon nor Gardet and Anawati are interested in exploring the possibility that this kind of Saying was in circulation from very early on in Islamic history and was not in every instance the product of ecstatic experience.

The other side of the more recent treatment of the Divine Saying is seen in the work of James Robson, who as an Ḥadîth specialist approaches the phenomenon in a wholly different context from that of mystical experience, namely that of the Ḥadîth as a genre of Islamic literature. In a brief and rather insufficient article on the Divine Saying in the new edition (fascicles from 1954) of the *Encyclopaedia of Islam,*[18] and in the course of a more satisfactory treatment in a 1951 article,[19] Robson considers the Divine Saying primarily as a traditional category of the Ḥadîth, distinguished from other ḥadîths by its form and content, not by its alleged sources, purposes, or "authenticity" relative to other ḥadîths. He notes the important question that this kind of material raises: whether, and if so, in what way, one may speak of different levels of revelation in Islam. He also stresses that a remarkable number of these Sayings are found in the "canonical" collections of Tradition.[20] Nonetheless, he, like Zwemer, concentrates on the Biblical "borrowings" in the later Divine Sayings, especially those in al-Madanî's collection, rather than upon the Divine Saying as a phenomenon in and of itself. In the final analysis, he is not prepared to treat these traditions as documents of any great antiquity or as essentially more than examples of later Muslim utilization of non-Muslim materials.

Finally, there remains one very brief but significant mention of the Divine Saying by a contemporary scholar that is relevant here. Nabia Abbott, in her important study of Arabic papyri, raises at one point the question of the possible rôle of the Divine Saying and other types of non-Qur'ânic revelation in the early history of Islam. In particular, she speculates as to whether or not "ʿUmar's fear of competition" of the Ḥadîth with the Qur'ân[21] might not have been exacerbated by precisely such "extra-Qur'ânic" revelations as those that take the form of the so-called *ḥadîth qudsî.*[22] While this remains an open and tentative possibility, the importance of her interest in the Divine

Sayings as first- or second-century documents rather than third-, fourth-, fifth-, or sixth-century documents cannot be over-emphasized.

If there is the possibility that these Sayings were important in the early period, or even if it can be shown that they are part of the earliest stratum of the Ḥadîth literature, they pose interesting questions about the early Muslim understanding of revelation and about aspects of their history as a specific genre of religious tradition in Islam that Western scholars have heretofore largely ignored.

B. The Divine Saying in Muslim Scholarship

It will be seen in Chapter 4 that the Divine Saying can be traced in Islamic usage back to the earliest Ḥadîth documents presently available. Muslim scholarly interest in the definition and explanation of this singular form of tradition appears, however, to have come only relatively late, and then with relatively little emphasis placed upon it.

The earliest discussion of the kind of traditional report later described as *ḥadîth qudsî*, *ḥadîth ilâhî*, or *ḥadîth rabbânî*, which the present investigation has uncovered is *not* in a work on the "sciences of Tradition" (*ʿulûm al-ḥadîth*), as might be expected, but rather in an anonymous introduction to the Qur'ânic sciences (*ʿulûm al-Qur'ân*), *Muqaddimat kitâb al-mabânî fî naẓm al-maʿânî*, which was written ca. 425/1033.[23] This particular treatment of the Divine Saying is part of a longer discussion of various revelations given Muḥammad "as [apostolic?] communication, not as a *qur'ân* recited or written".[24] It states that one such kind of revelation is

> that which was related from the Prophet as what he said as a statement from his Lord. [Such as:] he said, "Every action of the son of Adam belongs to him except fasting. It belongs to Me, and I reward it",[25] and his statement, "I fulfill My servant's expectation of Me, let him think what he will of Me".[26] There are many similar reports. It is known, and known with certainty, that he [Muḥammad] only knew and related [this kind of saying] by revelation and "apostolic" communication (*bi-waḥy wa-risâlah*) from God. Therefore, whoever claims that these words are from God and are His "revealing" (*waḥy*) and His "sending down" (*tanzîl*), he has spoken

> the truth, for it [this kind of saying] is a prescript (*ḥukm*) that He ordained and revealed and sent down. It is not permissible that any of it be recited in the Prayer (*ṣalât*), for it was not sent down in the same arrangement (*naẓm*) in which the rest of the Qur'ân (*sâ'ir al-Qur'ân* [!]) was sent down – which [book] has been given us to recite, which is written in the codices (*maṣâḥif*), and the transmission of which has come to us as generally accepted from one generation to the next.[27]

Here one sees already a concern to distinguish such Divine Sayings as to their internal arrangement or form (*naẓm*) and their ritual use (in the Prayer[28]) from verses of the Qur'ân, which are specifically designed to be recited. The Sayings are referred to simply as "reports" (*akhbâr*), and, moreover, no mention is made of their relation to Prophetic Traditions. The final sentence about the well-attested status of the text of the Qur'ân (i.e., that it is not an "isolated" report, but one attested by many different transmitters in each generation of Muslims) implies perhaps that the texts of the Divine Sayings are not so well established; however, the major question as to whether such Sayings are to be considered revelation is answered in the affirmative. What is most striking here is the use of the phrase, "the rest of the Qur'ân" (*sâ'ir al-Qur'ân*), which places the Divine Saying in the category of Qur'ân. The distinctions between the two are clearly drawn, but this rather surprising usage indicates that the Divine Saying was seen at this time as fundamentally closer to the Qur'ân than to ordinary ḥadîth reports: it is seen as a kind of divine word. The puzzling fact is that the author apparently knew no specific name for this kind of revelatory word. The absence of a technical designation such as *ḥadîth qudsî* suggests that at this time it had not yet become necessary to give such materials a formal classification. The Divine Saying had not yet become a particularly problematic genre of material for Muslim scholarship.

The apparent want of any formal term for the Divine Saying as a particular type of report until relatively late is further borne out by the absence of any such designation in the oldest manuals of the "sciences of Tradition"or the early Arabic lexicons.[29] Nor does the early *fiqh* handbook of Abû al-Ḥusayn al-Baṣrî (d. 436/1044) offer any discussion of the Divine Saying. Thus, if the witness of the *Mabânî* and such materials as these can be accepted as representative, early medieval Muslim scholarship was not concerned about precise, technical discrimination of the Divine Saying from among other types of Ḥadîth. The only crucial distinction was between it and the Qur'ân proper, for it was the Qur'ân that it most closely approximated.

The earliest evidence of a specific name for the Divine Saying in Muslim usage comes from the sixth/twelfth century, in the title of a work by one Abû al-Qâsim Ẓâhir b. Ṭâhir b. Muḥammad ash-Shaḥḥâmî an-Naysâbûrî (d. 533/1138): *Kitâb al-aḥâdîth al-ilâhîyah.*[30] This of course may or may not represent the usage of the original author, since titles of many Arabic works stem from the hands of manuscript copyists or the author's pupils and do not come from the writer himself. One is on firmer ground, however, at the end of the sixth century, with the collection of Divine Sayings compiled in the year 599/1201–2 by Ibn al-ʿArabî, for he uses the term *ḥadîth ilâhî* in his prefatory remarks to one of the sections of his collection.[31] While he unfortunately does not discuss the Divine Sayings that he has collected either as a genre type or as particular category of ḥadîth, his use of the term *ilâhî* suggests that this term, rather than the later more common *qudsî*, may be the oldest name given to the Divine Saying.

The first use of the term *qudsî* for the Divine Saying that these investigations have uncovered is apparently at least a century later than Ibn al-ʿArabî. It occurs in a discussion of the Divine Saying that is often quoted by later Muslim scholars, who ascribe it to one aṭ-Ṭayyibî, presumably Abû ʿAbdallâh al-Ḥusayn aṭ-Ṭayyibî (d. 743/1342).[32] He is quoted as saying that

> the Qur'ân is the expression (*lafẓ*) sent down to the Prophet through Gabriel, and the divine [saying] (*wa-l-qudsî*) is reports of God (*akhbâr Allâh*), the meaning of which [comes] through inspiration (*ilhâm*) or dream (*manâm*), and which the Prophet reported to his people in his own wording (*bi ʿibârat nafsihi*). And the rest of the ḥadîths (*sâ'ir al-aḥâdîth*) are not ascribed to God nor related from Him.[33]

Although the Divine Saying is here called only *al-qudsî*, not *al-ḥadîth al-qudsî*, it is clear that, in contrast to the discussion quoted earlier from the *Mabânî*, the Divine Saying is reckoned as a part of the Ḥadîth; compare the use here of *sâ'ir al-aḥâdîth* with the *Mabânî*'s *sâ'ir al-Qur'ân*. Nonetheless, the primary concern in this discussion is still to distinguish the Divine Saying from the Qur'ân, not from the Ḥadîth, although the last sentence does go on to this as well. The Qur'ân is identified with revelation sent through Gabriel, the Divine Saying with revelation received in an apparently "internal" fashion, perhaps "in the heart", as later Muslim writers were to describe it. For the first time the scholastic distinction is made between divine word that is revealed in both "expression" and "meaning" (i.e., the Qur'ân) and that which is revealed in its meaning only, its expression being the human creation of Muḥammad. By the time of aṭ-Ṭayyibî, formal distinctions between Qur'ân and Divine Saying are not sufficient: one must distinguish the two as two different types of revelation, one the verbatim divine word, the other the divinely inspired prophetic word.

The same type of theological concern with the unique status of Qur'ânic word is seen in more sophisticated form in a slightly later discussion of the Divine Saying by the great Muslim philosopher and historian, Ibn Khaldûn (d. 808/1406). In the *Muqaddimah* to his universal history,[34] he speaks of the Divine Saying (without giving it a name) as follows:

> ... the Qur'ân is alone among the divine books, for it was received by our Prophet as a recitation (*matlûwan*) just as it is, in its [present] words and phrases, in contradistinction to the Torah, the Gospel, and other heavenly books. The prophets received them in the state of revelation according to their sense (*fî ḥâl al-waḥy maʿânî*), and they expressed them, after their return to the normal human state, in their own normal words. Therefore those books do not have "miraculous inimitability"(*iʿjâz*), for *iʿjâz* is peculiar to the Qur'ân. They [the other prophets] received their books in the same way that our Prophet received the concepts (*maʿânî*) that he traced back to God, as are found in many ḥadîth reports (*allati yusnidu ilá Allâh kamâ yaqaʿu fî kathîr min riwâyat al-aḥâdîth*).[35]

Here Ibn Khaldûn attempts to integrate the Divine Saying into a larger scheme of divine revelation down through the ages. It is *waḥy*, just as the "divine books" of other prophets are *waḥy*, but both it and earlier "divine books" were revealed by a kind of inner inspiration, conceptually rather than verbally, while the Qur'ân alone stands out as a verbatim "recitation" of the living God, which is accordingly inimitable, unique. This line of argument is one of the most sophisticated Muslim treatments of the Divine Saying, as well as being an interesting Muslim interpretation of revelation in a universal context. However, almost all subsequent discussions of the subject by Muslim scholars evidence much the same concerns: to distinguish the Divine Saying as revelation from the Qur'ân as revelation and to identify it as a sub-genre of the Ḥadîth.

A contemporary of Ibn Khaldûn who is usually quoted in later treatments of the Divine Saying is "al-Kirmânî", presumably Muḥammad Yûsuf al-Kirmânî, an Ḥadîth scholar who died in 786/1384.[36] He also stresses the distinction between the Divine Saying (which he calls specifically *ḥadîth qudsî*, the earliest such usage found in the present investigation) and the Qur'ân as consisting chiefly in the "miraculous inimitability" (*iʿjâz*) of the latter and its revelation through Gabriel, neither of which applies in the case of the Divine Saying. Al-Kirmânî also notes the alternate terms *ilâhî* and *rabbânî* for the Divine Saying, and he says that although the usual ḥadîths ascribed to Muḥammad alone and not to God are not entirely different from the *ḥadîth qudsî* (since all of the Prophet's words are authoritative), the latter is marked by "His [God's] purity of essence" (*tanzîh dhâtihi*) and "His glorious and perfect attributes" (*ṣifâtuhu al-jalâlîyah wa-l-kamâlîyah*).[37]

Chronologically, the next treatment of the subject that is commonly cited by later authors is that of al-Jurjânî (d. 816/1413),[38] who describes briefly the Divine Saying in his lexicon of technical terms, *at-Taʿrîfât* (s.v. "ḥadîth qudsî"). His definition, which is substantially the same as those of aṭ-Ṭayyibî and al-Kirmânî, emphasizes that the Qur'ân is superior to the Divine Saying because not only its meaning but also its expression was "sent down" (*munazzal*) (a position common among most Sunni scholars, but not always insisted upon by Muʿtazilî scholars).[39]

The earliest treatment of the Divine Saying of any extent appears to be that of Ibn Ḥajar al-Haythamî (d. 973/1565) in his *al-Fatḥ al-mubîn*, a commentary on an-Nawawî's *Arbaʿûn*.[40] He begins by distinguishing the Qur'ân as "recited revelation" (*waḥy matlû*) from the *ḥadîth qudsî* as "revelation reported from Muḥammad from his Lord" (*al-waḥy al-marwî ʿanhu ṣallá Allâh ʿalayhi wa-sallam ʿan rabbihi*).[41] Then he divides "speech ascribed to God" (*al-kalâm al-muḍâf ilayhi taʿâlá*) into three parts, as follows:[42]

1. The Qur'ân. It is the noblest of the three, distinguished by its inimitability (*iʿjâz*); it is an eternal miracle (*muʿjizah bâqiyah ʿalá mamarr ad-duhûr*), preserved from all change and alteration; it may not be touched by the

unclean (*al-muḥdith*) nor recited by the ritually impure (*al-junub*)[43] nor related according to its sense alone; it is designated for use in the Prayer, is called a "recitation" (*qur'ân*), and each letter of it, when recited, is equivalent to ten good deeds (*ḥasanât*); selling it is forbidden according to Ibn Ḥanbal, and merely reprehensible (*makrûh*), according to Ibn Ḥajar; and its parts are called *sûrah*s and *âyah*s. Each of the preceding is a characteristic peculiar to the Qur'ân and not applicable to the following two kinds of "speech attributed to God".

2. The books of the Prophets *before* they were changed and altered [no further explanation of this category is given].
3. "The remainder of the *aḥâdîth qudsîyah*".[44] They are isolated reports (*mâ nuqila ilaynâ âḥâdan*)[45] from the Prophet with their *isnâd* from God; they are part of God's speech (*kalâm Allâh*)[46] and are ascribed to Him (*tuḍâfu ilayhi*); their composition is traced to Him, for He spoke them first, and they may be ascribed to the Prophet because he reported them from God, in contradistinction to the Qur'ân (*bi-khilâf al-Qur'ân*), which is not ascribed to anyone except God; with respect to the Qur'ân one says "God said", and with respect to these ḥadîths, one says "the Apostle of God said in that which he related from his Lord" (*qâla rasûl Allâh fîmâ yarwî ʿan rabbihi*). The *ḥadîth qudsî* differs from the rest of the *sunnah*, and the verse "He does not speak out of caprice" [S. 53:3] indicates that it is revelation, as do the Prophet's words, "I have been given the Book and with it something similar".[47] These ḥadîths are not limited to only one of the various modes of revelation (*kayfîyât al-waḥy*), but may come down by any one of them: in a dream-vision (*ru'yâ an-nawm*), as implantation in the heart (*al-ilqâ' fî rûʿ*), or on the tongue of an angel (*ʿalá lisân al-malak*). There are two ways to introduce an *ḥadîth qudsî*: that of the ancients (*as-salaf*), "the Apostle of God said in that which he related from his Lord" [see above], and also that which has "God said in that which the Apostle of God related from Him" (*qâla Allâh fîmâ rawâhu ʿanhu rasûl Allâh*), and both have the same meaning.

Here the primary emphasis is upon the Divine Saying as divine word. It is clearly placed in the context of direct revelation, and an attempt is made to work out the theological distinctions between it and other types of revelation.

The only identifying characteristic that is cited for it is, however, the formula with which it is introduced, which is a purely formalistic way of distinguishing it from a Qur'ânic text.[48]

Many of the same points are covered by 'Alî al-Qârî al-Harawî (d. 1014/1606) in the introduction to his collection of forty Divine Sayings.[49] He notes that the verbal expression of the Divine Saying was entrusted entirely to Muḥammad, the meaning only being revealed by God, "sometimes through Gabriel, sometimes through revelation (*waḥy*), inspiration (*ilhâm*), and dream (*manâm*)". The Qur'ân, on the other hand, was revealed only through "the trusted spirit of God" (*rûḥ Allâh al-amîn*), evidently referring to Gabriel, and it is bound by its exact expression on "the Preserved Tablet" (*al-lawḥ al-maḥfûẓ*) in heaven. Its transmission is absolutely verified by multiple transmission through every generation. He goes on to say that there are specific legal ways in which Divine Sayings are recognized by religious scholars to differ from the Qur'ân: the Prayer is not valid when they rather than Qur'ânic verses are recited; the ritually impure (*al-junub*) may touch and recite them, as may the menstruating (*al-ḥâ'iḍ*) and those who have given birth (*an-nafsâ'*),[50] again unlike the Qur'ân; the rejection of them does not make one a *kâfir* (a "denier of God", or "unbeliever"), as does the rejection of the Qur'ân; and they do not carry, as does the Qur'ân, any "miraculous inimitability" (*i'jâz*).[51]

The preceding represent the bulk of traditional Muslim scholarly interpretation of Divine Sayings, these being the authorities quoted by later writers such as Abû al-Baqâ' al-Kaffâwî (d. 1094/1683),[52] Muḥammad 'Alâ' b. 'Alî at-Tahânawî (fl. 1158/1745),[53] Muḥammad Râghib Pâshâ (d. 1176/1763),[54] Muḥammad Jamâladdîn al-Qâsimî (d. 1334/1914),[55] and two present-day Ḥadîth-scholars, Ṣubḥî aṣ-Ṣâliḥ[56] and Muhammad Tayyib Okiç.[57] In general, such later authorities do not add anything substantially new to the earlier expositions, but content themselves with a summary and/or quotation of the latter. Al-Qâsimî presents the most complete compilation of earlier views, while aṣ-Ṣâliḥ attempts to describe the Divine Saying without excessive reliance upon quotation of earlier sources. The latter describes such Sayings as exhortations (*mawâ'iẓ*) of Muḥammad to his Companions which he related from God. He goes so far as to say that they were *not* sent down as revelation (*laysat waḥyan munazzalan*), nor were they usual ḥadîths (*ḥadîth 'âdiy*), but rather sayings that Muḥammad set apart from the rest of his words by introducing them with a special expression (*ʿibârah*) that showed that they came from God. These ḥadîths were told, of course, in a style wholly different from that of the Qurʾân, but they still carry with them a touch of the atmosphere of the realm (*ʿâlam*) of the Holy (*al-qudus*) and the Unseen (*al-ghayb*).[58]

In other published discussions of the Divine Saying by modern Muslim religious scholars in Egypt, one finds also that the same traditional distinctions and definitions are given. Interestingly enough, however, in an article reporting a round-table discussion of Muslim religious scholars on the subject, one participant argues that *both* the meaning (*maʿná*) *and* the wording (*lafẓ*) of the Divine Saying were given to Muḥammad by God.[59] Most of his colleagues participating in the discussion stand by the traditional opinion that the expression (*taʿbîr*) of the Divine Saying is from the Prophet, not God, but one says that it is uncertain whether it is God's or Muḥammad's. He maintains that the real distinction between the Divine Saying and the Qurʾân is that the latter is "inimitable" (*muʿjiz*).[60] In both this and a second article, another interesting point is made: that the transmission of a Divine Saying, unlike that of the Qurʾân, involved the Prophet's own "personal effort and decision" (*ijtihâd*) in formulating the revealed word.[61] In yet a third modern Muslim periodical article, one finds only a repetition of the standard definitions by ʿAlî al-Qârî, at-Tahânawî, etc., which have been dealt with above.[62]

While most Muslim discussion of the Divine Saying, both in the past and especially in more recent times, has tended to concentrate on the formalistic definitions and on rather mechanical distinctions between it and the Qurʾân, there is one further treatment of the subject that approaches it in a somewhat different fashion.[63] As the only interpretation with a distinctly mystical, or Ṣûfî, orientation that has come to the attention of the present writer, it bears some consideration here. It is reported by al-Qâsimî, and is attributed to one Najm al-ʿĪrfân ʿAbdalʿazîz ad-Dabbâgh as reported in a work by a disciple of his, Ibn al-Mubârak as-Sijilmâsî (d. 1156/1713).[64] Ibn al-Mubârak's exposition takes the form of a dialogue with his Shaykh in which the relations among the Qurʾân, the Divine Saying (*ḥadîth qudsî*), and the Prophetic Tradition (*ḥadîth nabawî*) are discussed, and the Shaykh's interpretation is elicited.

The basis of ʿAbdalʿazîz's interpretation is the metaphor of "light" (*nûr*;

plur., *anwâr*), which represents both the content of revelation to the Prophet and the experience of revelation itself. Thus the Qur'ân, Divine Saying, and Prophetic Tradition, all of which issued from Muḥammad's lips, are "lights" of his (p. 66);[65] yet they were given to him in moments of divine communication that involved the activity of "the lights of the Divine Truth" (*anwâr al-Ḥaqq*) (p. 68).[66] Everything that the Prophet said is "a revelation revealed" (*waḥy yûḥá*) (p. 68) and came to him through "lights" that "moved upon" (*habba ʿalâ*) his soul (p. 67), each in a different fashion according to whether it involved the revelation of a *qur'ân*, that of a Divine Saying, or that of a regular ḥadîth of the Prophet. The three types of "light", or revelation, are distinguished from one another by their essential natures and the modes in which they were revealed to Muḥammad. Thus the distinctions among them are delineated primarily in ontological and psychological terms. Significantly, there is no mention of formal or ritual distinctions among the three.

The ontological distinctions that emerge from his explanations are as follows: the "light" of the Qur'ân is eternally pre-existent (*qadîm*) and belongs to the essence of the Divine Truth (*dhât al-Ḥaqq*); the "light" of the Divine Saying is not pre-eternal and belongs to the spirit of the Prophet (*rûḥ an-nabî*); the "light" of the Prophetic Tradition is not pre-eternal and belongs to the essence (here, the human person) of the Prophet (*dhât an-nabî*). The difference between the latter two, contingent "lights" is further clarified by the explanation that the "light" of the spirit of the Prophet, which is created from the "highest realm" (*al-mala' al-aʿlá*), is closely related to the Divine Truth, while the "light" of the person of the Prophet, which is created from dust (*turâb*), is closely related to created being (*al-khalq*) (p. 66). Neither of these two can, of course, approach the sublimity of being of the Qur'ân, which is set apart from them by its "miraculous inimitability", or *iʿjâz*, which is evident to anyone with intelligence. The speech of God has a wholly different quality from all other speech which clearly reveals it to be God's word when it is heard. How else could the contemporaries of Muḥammad have been persuaded to turn to Islam and abandon the religious orientation of their fathers? Everyone who lets the words of the Qur'ân flow over his heart knows by necessity that it is God's word, for its greatness is that of the divine lordship (*ar-rubûbîyah*), and it is through it that God and His attributes are known (p. 69).

As for the psychological distinctions that are to be seen in the Shaykh's presentation, these center around the question of why the Divine Saying, unlike the Qur'ân, is the speech (*kalâm*) of the Prophet rather than of God. He points out that all three types of revelation under consideration were accompanied by the "lights" of revelation and came to Muḥammad when he was in the state of "witnessing" (*mushâhadah*), which is a kind of abiding in the awareness of the divine presence and was a permanent characteristic of Muḥammad's prophetic consciousness. Yet each of the "lights" was experienced by the Prophet in a different manner. When it involved a *qur'ân*, he heard the word of God (*kalâm al-Ḥaqq*) along with the "lights", or an angel descended to him (p. 67). In these instances, what he spoke was not of his own choosing; he was as a man with a fever, the intensity of which causes him to lose consciousness and be unaware of what he says. This unconscious, ecstatic state is that in which the "lights" became so radiant that the Prophet's senses were wholly overwhelmed from outside himself (p. 68).

The "lights" of the Divine Saying, on the other hand, came without his actually hearing the word of God, and they came in such a fashion as to confuse his mind. Thus his conscious state was altered, but not abandoned, and through the bewildering experience of these "lights", "that which was concealed became manifest and was attributed to the Lord" in the form of a Divine Saying (p. 67). In such instances, his words were of his own choosing; he was as a man raging with fever but who does not lose consciousness. In this state the "lights" were *anwâr 'âriḍah*, or "temporary lights", and even though they shone powerfully, they did not overwhelm his senses completely, as did the "lights" of a *qur'ân* (p. 68).

As for the Prophetic Tradition, or normal utterance of the Prophet, it came with the "tranquil light" (*nûr sâkin*) in Muḥammad's own person (*dhât*), and this "light" was a permanent one that never left him. In this state, his words were of his own choosing; he was as a man with a normal temperature and correspondingly normal consciousness. The "lights" were then "constant lights" (*anwâr dâ'imah*), which were an inherent attribute of his noble being as God's Apostle and informed all of his words (p. 68).

In this fashion, the Shaykh presents a metaphorical picture of the three levels of experience that produced the utterances of the Prophet, whether *qur'ân*, Divine Saying, or Prophetic Tradition. These correspond, of course, to the different ontological qualities of the three kinds of revelation. Finally, in addition to these distinctions, he does present also some *effective* distinctions between the two lower levels of utterance, the "divine" and "prophetic" ḥadîths. The Divine Saying, being of "the sciences of the spirit" (*ʿulûm ar-rûḥ*), deals with God in three ways: by declaring His greatness, showing the extent of His dominion and His generosity, and revealing His mercy (p. 66) [which are, as will be seen below, indeed the major themes of the earliest examples of the Divine Saying]. On the other hand, the Prophetic Tradition speaks of that which will be of benefit to people by relating the permissible and the forbidden, and by urging to obedience through threat and promise (p. 67). Thus, in addition to ontological and psychological distinctions, the Divine Saying and the Prophetic Tradition are separated in this view by differences of purpose and content.

This particular Ṣûfî interpretation completes the consideration of Muslim descriptive and theoretical treatments of the Divine Saying. On the basis of the sources that have been used, two principal observations about the Muslim understanding of the Divine Saying over the centuries suggest themselves. First, it appears that the use of the specific term, *ḥadîth qudsî*, for such sayings is a comparatively late development, the earliest attested instances of it coming only in the middle of the eighth/fourteenth century. The earliest discussion of the Divine Saying, in the *Kitâb al-Mabânî* (ca. 425/1033), gives no name at all to this kind of tradition. In the earliest verifiable use of a specific name, in the year 599/1201–2, Ibn al-ʿArabî refers to it as *ḥadîth ilâhî*, not *ḥadîth qudsî*; yet even here, he seems to be more inclined to designate such sayings simply as "ḥadîths traced back to God". Prior to the eighth century of Islam, the only other mention of these Sayings by name – if it can be relied upon – is in the title of a collection of Divine Sayings, where they are also called *aḥâdîth ilâhîyah*, not *aḥâdîth qudsîyah*.[67]

Second, and more important, is the evidence that, parallel with the gradual growth of interest in identifying the Divine Saying by specific terminology there developed an increasing need to identify the Divine Saying with the Ḥadîth and more sharply to distinguish it from the Qurʾân. In all of the Muslim discussions of the Divine Saying, the prime concern is to show how it differs from the Qurʾân; it is, however, only in the later discussions that a specific effort is made to identify it as a sub-category of Ḥadîth and to show how it differs from the Prophetic Tradition, or *ḥadîth nabawî*, as well as from the Qurʾân. In the older discussions, the Divine Saying appears to have been seen simply as a special type of report, or *khabar*,[68] which reported something that God had said, but not in the form of a *qur'ân*. The formal identification of the Divine Saying as a kind of Ḥadîth in the technical sense of the human words of Muḥammad does not seem to have been necessary or desirable; the Divine Saying was an ḥadîth only in the most general sense of the word – in much the same way as the Qur'ân itself was said to be "the best ḥadîth".[69]

The crucial point was and is that the Divine Saying is a kind of divine word: specifically a word of the Lord spoken by His prophet Muḥammad, and hence a prophetic word in the fullest sense of the term. In the later as well as the earlier discussions of the Divine Saying, it is abundantly clear that this kind of Saying represents a type of material that is both God's and Muḥammad's. While the emphasis upon the gulf between the Divine Saying and the Qur'ân increased with time, and its closeness to the Prophetic Tradition was correspondingly emphasized, not even the most recent Muslim writers would deny that the Divine Saying occupies a special place between Qur'ân and Ḥadîth proper as both divine and prophetic utterance.

C. The Divine Saying in Muslim Piety

Theoretical, scholarly discussions of the Divine Saying can take one only so far. It is in its rôle as a religious text that the Divine Saying must ultimately be understood. In seeking the Divine Saying as it is found in Muslim usage, several principle sources suggest themselves: (1) specific collections of Divine Sayings, (2) collections of Shî'î Ḥadîth, (3) works dealing with pre-Islamic history and especially with previous prophets (e.g., the *qiṣaṣ al-anbiyâ'* literature), (4) Ṣûfî literature, and (5) the standard Sunnî Ḥadîth collections. For the purposes of an examination of the early Divine Saying as it was preserved in Sunnî tradition, the last-named collections (together with the earlier small collections that are available) are the basic sources and will therefore be given separate and more detailed consideration in Chapter 4 and Part III. Adequate treatment of the other four kinds of material would require separate studies of their own, but in order to place the present consideration of the earliest attested Divine Sayings in the perspective of the wider collection and use of the Divine Saying in Islam, it is important to survey very briefly here the other four groups of material listed above. Perhaps such a survey will also serve as an agenda for further study in the future.

Collections of Divine Sayings. These are apparently a rather late phenomenon in Islam. The oldest collection that the present writer has found dates only from the first third of the sixth/twelfth century.[70] One may, however, reasonably suppose that perhaps here as elsewhere the collecting of materials antedates the oldest extant manuscripts. Appendix A gives an annotated, chronological list of those Arabic collections of Divine Sayings that have been identified in the course of the present investigation. On the basis of the three printed Sunnî[71] collections examined (those of Ibn al-ʿArabî, Muḥammad al-Madanî, and ʿAlî al-Qârî), such works apparently draw primarily upon the "classical" and other later Ḥadîth compendia; e.g., Mâlik's *Muwaṭṭa'*, Ibn Ḥanbal's *Musnad*, and the standard "six books" of Ḥadîth, plus works of men like aṭ-Ṭabarânî (d. 360/971),[72] ad-Dâraquṭnî (d. 385/955),[73] al-Bayhaqî (d. 458/1066),[74] and others.

Because of the almost uniformly pietistic, sermonic, mystical, and eschatological content of the Divine Saying both early and late, such collections of Sayings appear to have been compiled less for pragmatic purposes of a legal or doctrinal nature than as acts of pious scholarship, much as one has been wont in Islam to make collections of forty "most beautiful" ḥadîths.[75] This is at least the case with the collection of Ibn al-ʿArabî, *Mishkât al-anwâr*, which was compiled, according to the author's own prefatory remarks to the work, in accordance with the Prophetic Tradition: "Whoever preserves for my community forty ḥadîths of the *sunnah*, I shall be intercessor for him on the Day of Resurrection."[76]

Shîʿî Ḥadîth Collections. One of the collections of Divine Sayings listed in Appendix A is that of al-Ḥurr al-ʿÂmilî (d. 1099/1688), a well-known Shîʿî Ḥadîth scholar. His collection points up the fact that the Divine Saying has also played a rôle in the Shîʿî tradition, for it contains a large number of ḥadîths with *isnâd*s that are traced to the Imâms as well as a number from the Prophet. These Sayings appear to be drawn from the major Shîʿî Ḥadîth collections, notably the *Kâfî* of al-Kulînî (d. 328/939).[77] While there are a number of Divine Sayings in the collection of al-ʿÂmilî that are also found in the same or a similar form among the Sayings collected in Part III, the majority of the Sayings in this collection are peculiar to Shî'î sources. It is interesting to note that the work is organized into separate chapters, each of which presents Divine Sayings that were given by God to a different prophet or Imâm. Thus there are Sayings quoted on the authority of Adam, Noah, Abraham, Jacob, Joseph, Shu'ayb, Moses, David, Daniel, Jesus, Muḥammad, 'Alî b. Abî Ṭâlib, and each of the next six Imâms after 'Alî. The presentation, in chapter XII of the collection,[78] of various versions of the so-called "Tablet of Fâṭimah" (*lawḥ Fâṭimah*) which was supposed to have been revealed in addition to the Qur'ân, is also of special interest, and would bear specific consideration as a unique kind of Divine Saying that could hardly be called an *ḥadîth*.[79]

Another source for some of the Sayings in al-'Âmilî's collection is the eighth Imâm of the "Twelver" Shî'ah, 'Alî ar-Riḍâ' (d. 203/818).[80] A short collection of ḥadîths ascribed to him has recently been published, and it contains some sixteen Divine Sayings among its other material.[81] None of these Sayings is, however, found among those Divine Sayings from Sunnî sources that are presented in Part III of this study.

The Divine Saying in Shî'î Islam, as the aforementioned sources indicate, is a unique phenomenon that deserves attention in and of itself. Such a study might well begin with the collection of al-'Âmilî and the Divine Sayings in the booklet of ar-Riḍâ'. A thorough search of the *Kâfî* would also yield a considerable number of Divine Sayings.[82] The central question of the Shî'î view of "extra-Qur'ânic" revelation, especially with respect to the revelatory nature of the speech of the Imâm, needs particular consideration.

Accounts of pre-Islamic peoples and prophets. Numerous Divine Sayings are found throughout Islamic literature in the extensive legendary stories of God's dealings with the communities and prophets before Muḥammad, especially those of Israel. These accounts often take a Midrash form in which words of angels and prophets, as well as those of God Himself are quoted.[83] The two names that are traditionally most often associated with this kind of material are those of Ka'b al-Aḥbâr (d. ca. 32/652)[84] and Wahb b. Munabbih (d. ca. 110/729),[85] both of whom were Jewish converts to Islam who were renowned for their learning and for their knowledge of Jewish lore in particular. Within the "classical" Ḥadîth literature itself, there are a considerable array of *Isrâ'îlîyât*, or "Israelite stories",[86] and other legendary accounts, many of which include Divine Sayings, which go back to these two men.

It is, however, in material other than the formal Ḥadîth that such reports are especially evident. For example, many of the Divine Sayings in Ibn al-ʿArabî's *Mishkât* that are not found in the "standard" or "classical" Ḥadîth collections are quoted from Kaʿb.[87] The most important sources in which these kinds of material are collected are, however, the pre-Islamic or universal "histories" of men like Ibn Hishâm[88] and al-Masʿûdî[89] and in the *Qiṣaṣ al-anbiyâ'* literature.[90] A substantial study could be made of the legends about God and the Divine Sayings that they include from these sources alone. There are, of course, other genres of Islamic writing that also contain these kinds of legend and myth, most notably the *Tafsîr* works and literature associated with or dealing with the Islamic preachers and storytellers (*quṣṣâṣ*).[91] In addition, many of the stories of the words of angels or of God to earlier prophets are quoted by the Ṣûfîs and must be reckoned with as the source of a number of the Divine Sayings that are found in mystical writings.

Ṣûfî literature. It is among the Ṣûfîs that the Divine Saying is given its most significant rôle in Muslim piety as a mode of direct divine communication outside of the Qur'ân. Seyyed Hossein Nasr, a modern Muslim interpreter of Islam to the West, has said regarding Divine Sayings and the Ṣûfîs: "Sufism is based on these sayings and many a sufi knows them by heart and lives in constant remembrance of their message."[92] As indicated in Section A of the present chapter, the Ṣûfî predilection for the Divine Saying has been the focus of greatest Western interest in the Divine Saying as a distinct phenomenon. This has tended, especially as a result of the influence of Massignon, to obscure other aspects of the Divine Saying in Islam. While the present study seeks in part to redress this imbalance in previous study by concentrating upon the early Divine Saying in the Ḥadîth, this is not to deny the fact that it is among the mystics of Islam that the Divine Saying has received fullest attention and greatest importance as "extra-Qur'ânic" revelation. On the contrary, the frequent incidence of Divine Sayings in the earliest Ḥadîth materials and the fact that they reflect those concerns that were later associated with *taṣawwuf*, or mystical piety,[93] is another argument for the deep roots of *taṣawwuf* in the earliest forms of Muslim piety.

The first important point about the Divine Saying in Ṣûfî literature is that it does not represent a special or different kind of Divine Saying from that found in other materials, including the "classical" Ḥadîth literature. Instead, the Divine Sayings that are quoted in Ṣûfî writings present a cross-section of those found in most other sources and share a considerable amount of common material with these. A great many of the Divine Sayings in Ṣûfî sources are, for example, well attested in the formal Ḥadîth. While the Ṣûfîs do not generally quote full *isnâd*s for such Sayings (their concern here as elsewhere being not the formal attestation but the witness of the truth of the words themselves), they do report the same "texts" (*matn*s) from the Prophet that are found in the major Ḥadîth collections. A random sample of Ṣûfî citations of many of the Divine Sayings found in the major collections is given in Part III of this study in the critical apparatus of the appropriate Sayings (under the heading, "Other References"). These citations give sufficient indication of Ṣûfî reliance upon "traditional" Divine Sayings from the prophetic Ḥadîth to rebut effectively the notion that the Divine Saying can be generally identified with ecstatic sayings that have been clothed by the mystics in the garb of *mursal* ḥadîths, as Massignon and others have implied.[94]

There are, of course, numerous instances in Ṣûfî writings of the kind of *mursal* Divine Sayings that Massignon has emphasized. The quotation of legends that report God's words to previous prophets is, as was indicated earlier, especially common. An example of such a report is given without *isnâd* by Abû Ṭâlib al-Makkî simply as "one of the reports (*akhbâr*) of David": "God revealed to him [David]: 'The most beloved of those who love is he who serves and worships Me not for something in return, but because of My right of Lordship'."[95] Such Sayings do tend to be reported in this manner directly from an earlier prophet or earlier "Book", which does make them technically *mursal* ḥadîths.[96] It would, however, be an error to see this as primarily an indication that the Ṣufîs invented Divine Sayings and then sought to give them traditional authority by ascribing them to an earlier prophet or scripture in the manner of an ḥadîth report. Rather, one must recognize that the Ṣûfîs were not overly concerned with the formal criteria, specifically the *isnâd*, of Ḥadîth scholarship, any more than were authors like al-Mas'ûdî or al-Kisâ'î, who made use of similar materials in their historical and biographical legends. The absence of the apparatus of the formal ḥadîth is not proof of the "inauthentic" nature of a Ṣûfî report any more than the presence of such an apparatus is proof of its "authenticity" in reductionist terms.

More important, and more uniquely "Ṣûfî", than words of God to other prophets are the Divine Sayings that are quoted not as words of God to Muḥammad but as words to particular Muslims, i.e., particular Ṣûfîs. These are, as Massignon has indicated, essentially a kind of "ecstatic saying" (*shaṭḥ*) that has been received directly by the individual from God. They are, in other words, statements revealed in the course of mystical experience of or communion with the Divine, fruits of the intimacy (*uns*) or nearness (*qurb*) of the mystic to God. In such cases, no *isnâd* is needed, for the mystic is reporting a direct, personal revelation from his Lord, as in the report ascribed to al-Junayd (d. 297/910): "Once I was sick and prayed to God to heal me. He said to me in my inmost self (*fa-qâla lî fî sirrî*), 'Do not come between Me and your [own] self (*nafs*)'."[97] The voice of the "inmost self" or the "heart" (*qalb*) becomes for the Ṣûfî the absolute assurance of the "authenticity" of a word from God; under such circumstances a human "support", or *isnâd*, is hardly necessary, for the mystic himself becomes the "mouthpiece" of God.[98] It is interesting to note how this kind of "support" eventually does take the form of a spiritual *isnâd*: in the quotation of a Divine Saying in Ibn Ḥajar's *Iṣâbah*, one finds "my heart related to me from/on the authority of my Lord ..." (*ḥaddathanî qalbî ʿan rabbî*),[99] where the sole "authority" for God's words is the direct experience of the heart rather than transmission from Muḥammad.

In the Divine Sayings that appear among the mystics as *shaṭḥîyât* (plur. of *shaṭḥ*), one is dealing with a different kind of "extra-Qurʾânic" revelation from that of the Prophetic Traditions in which Divine Sayings are quoted on Muḥammad's authority. The latter also occupy, however, a prominent place in the Ṣûfî tradition. Some of the favorite Divine Sayings of the mystics are in fact those attributed to God's communication with Muḥammad and generally recognized in Islam as non-Qurʾânic reports revealed to him. Such is the case with the central portion of Saying 49 in Part III, "My servant continues drawing nearer to Me ... until I become his ear with which he hears, his eye with which he sees ...", which is perhaps the most famous of all Divine Sayings among Muslims generally and the Ṣûfîs in particular.[100]

There are also Prophetic Traditions quoted by the Ṣûfîs that report divine words that are not found in the formal Ḥadîth sources. One example is the tradition cited by al-Kalâbâdhî (d. 385/995) from Abû al-Qâsim al-Baghdâdî from an unnamed Ṣûfî. It is introduced by the anonymous Ṣûfî with a phrase that is typical of those used in the formal Ḥadîth for Divine Sayings:[101] "In that which [Muḥammad] said, reporting from God (*fî qawlihi ʿalayhi as-salâm khabaran ʿan Allâh*): 'Whoever is so taken up with remembering Me that he neglects to petition Me, I grant him a nobler gift than that which I give to supplicants'."[102]

Some of the most famous Ṣûfî Divine Sayings are in fact ones that do not occur in the major Ḥadîth collections but have been circulated widely among the Sûfîs and are variously ascribed to Muḥammad, other prophets, or to individual Ṣûfîs themselves. A good example is that in which God says, "I was a hidden treasure (*kuntu kanzan makhfîyan*) and wanted to be known. Therefore I created the creatures, that they might know Me."[103] Another is the word of God that is variously described as referring to qualities like "sincere devotion" (*al-ikhlâs*)[104] and "knowledge of the inner meaning" (*ʿilm al-bâṭin*):[105] "It is a secret of My Secret (*huwa sirr min sirrî*); I placed it in the heart of My servant ...." Still another is the well-known Saying, "He who knows himself, knows his Lord" (*man ʿarafa nafsahu fa-qad ʿarafa rabbahu*).[106]

There are many others to be found in any Ṣûfî work, so firmly have they entrenched themselves in mystical piety – and in popular Muslim piety as a whole, for every Muslim knows at least one or two by heart. There have been, of course, strange uses made of the Divine Saying: witness the remarkable Saying that is on occasion popularly ascribed to the Lord: "The love of cats is a part of faith" (*ḥubb al-hirrah min al-îmân*).[107] This, however, is an extreme, and it does nothing to detract from the venerable heritage of the Divine Saying in Muslim spiritual life, which, as the remainder of this study will show, is as old and established as that of any other type of traditional report in Islam. Whatever assessment one may wish to make about the historical "origin" or "authenticity" of the Divine Saying as it has been cultivated among the Ṣûfîs and in the everyday, popular tradition of Islam, it cannot be denied that "the presence of these sayings indicate [*sic*] how deeply the roots of Islamic spirituality are sunk in the sources of the revelation itself".[108]

Notes to Chapter 3: "The Divine Saying as Problem"

1. "Heilige oder himmlische Ueberlieferung, solche Worte der Ueberlieferung, in denen ... Gott selbst spricht und welche dem Propheten entweder durch Gabriel oder im Traume geoffenbaret worden [sic]", "Bericht über ... den türkischen Commentar des Mesnewi Dschelaleddin Rumi's", *Sitzungsberichte der Kaiserlichen Akademie der Wissenschaften zu Wien* (Philos.-Hist. Classe), VII (1851), 637.
2. *Viz.*, Abû al-Baqâʾ and al-Jurjânî, both of whom are mentioned below in Section B of the present chapter. Lane's definition occurs s. v. "ḥadîth", II, 529b.
3. II, 190. The article is by Th. W. Juynboll.
4. "Kämpfe um die Stellung des Ḥadîṯ im Islam", pp. 863–864.
5. I, 256–259. In the original, one-volume edition of 1860, Nöldeke does devote considerable attention to "Offenbarungen, die in unserem Qorân fehlen, aber anderweitig erhalten sind" (pp. 174–188), but he mentions the *ḥadîth qudsî* only once, as a possible form taken by "original parts of the Qur'ân" that were left out of the final text (p. 174).
6. "Die im Qorân nicht erhaltenen Offenbarungen Muhammeds", I, 234–261.
7. "The So-called Hadith Qudsi" (also translated into German: see Bibliography).
8. See Appendix A for further particulars of these three collections. Zwemer discusses them in his article on pp. 265–267 and translates excerpts from them on pp. 272–274.
9. In his article, "S̲h̲ath", *SEI*, p. 533.
10. "Le *hadîth qudsî* a été, au début, la manière détournée de mettre en circulation des 'locutions théopathiques', en les faisant remonter à des Écritures Saintes, où Dieu parlait à la première personne", *Essai*, p. 135.
11. *Ibid., loc. cit.*
12. *Ibid.*, p. 120.
13. The classical Muslim authorities on the Ḥadîth define the *mursal* as an ḥadîth with an *isnâd* traced only to a Follower, not a Companion, of the Prophet; i.e., there is no transmitting authority from the contemporaries of Muḥammad. See al-Ḥâkim an-Naysâbûrî, *Maʿrifah*, pp. 25–27, and Ibn aṣ-Ṣalâḥ, *ʿUlûm al-ḥadîth*, pp. 48–51.
14. *Essai*, pp. 120–122.
15. *Ibid.*, pp. 120–122.
16. Pp. 30ff.
17. *Ibid.*, p. 284.
18. III, 28–29, s. v. "ḥadīt̲h̲ ḳudsī".

19. "The Material of Tradition".
20. *Ibid.*, p. 266.
21. Concerning ʿUmar's disapproval of transmitting ḥadîths of the Prophet, see: Ibn Saʿd, VI, 2; Ibn Mâjah, *Muqaddimah*, 2:7; cf. Ibn Saʿd, V, 139–143. See also Azmi, *Studies*, pp. 56–57, and further references there.
22. *Papyri*, II, 7–8, n. 25.
23. On p. 6 of the published text of the *Mabânî*, its author, who is unknown because of the absence of the first folio of the only known MS, says that he began the work in this year.
24. *ʿAlá jihat at-tablîgh wa-r-risâlah lâ ʿalá jihat annahu qurʾân yutlá aw yuktabu* (*al-Mabânî*, p. 88).
25. Saying 61 in Part III of the present study.
26. Saying 12 in Part III.
27. *Al-Mabânî*, pp. 88–89.
28. In the present work the Arabic *ṣalât* and other derivatives of the second form of the root *Ṣ-L-Y* are rendered uniformly by derivatives of "to pray". While this does not allow easily for distinction between *ṣalât* as the ritual act of worship and *duʿâʾ* as personal, supplicatory prayer, it does allow the rendering of *ṣallá ʿalá* as "to pray for".
29. The Divine Saying is not treated, let alone given a special name, in the classical works of the *ʿulûm al-ḥadîth*: *Maʿrifat ʿulûm al-ḥadîth* and *al-Madkhal ilá maʿrifat al-iklîl* of al-Ḥâkim an-Naysâbûrî (d. 405/1014), *al-Kifâyah fî ʿilm ar-riwâyah* of al-Khaṭîb al-Baghdâdî (d. 463/1071), and *ʿUlûm al-ḥadîth* of Ibn aṣ-Ṣalâḥ (d. 643/1245). There is no mention of the Divine Saying under the words *ḥadîth*, *qudsî*, *ilâhî*, *rabbânî*, *waḥy*, or *ilhâm* in lexicographical works such as *Jamharat al-lughah* of Ibn Durayd (d. 321/933), *Tahdhîb al-lughah* of al-Azharî (d. 370/981), or *Maqâyîs al-lughah* of Ibn Fâris al-Qazwînî (d. ca. 390/1000).
30. The work is briefly described in Ahlwardt, *Verzeichnis*, VIII, 122–123 (MS no. 1297) [WE. 112]). I have not been able to see a copy of this MS, which would be important for a thorough study of Muslim interpretation of the Divine Saying. See also Appendix A.
31. *Mishkât*, p. 33, l. 14. Ibn al-ʿArabî otherwise refers to the Divine Sayings as ḥadîths "traced back to God" (*musnadah ilá Allâh*), rather than as *aḥadîth ilâhîyah*.
32. *GAL*, II, 64; *GAL*(S), II, 67 (which gives the name as aṭ-Ṭîbî). He is cited only by the *nisbah* in the later sources that quote him (see below, n. 33), but of the homonymous authors listed in *GAL* (see *GAL*(S), III, Index, s.v.), this Ṭayyibî is the only Ḥadîth authority.

33. Quoted by Abû al-Baqâ', *Kullîyât*, p. 288, and, quoting from him, by Râghib Pâshâ, *Safînah*, p. 162; by al-Qâsimî, *Qawâ'id at-taḥdîth*, p. 66; and in the afterword to al-Madanî, p. 188 [note that the author of the afterword is not al-Madanî, but one "al-Qâḍî Sharîfaddîn"].
34. The *Muqaddimah* was probably written for the most part in the last years before Ibn Khaldûn's move to Egypt in 784/1382, in all likelihood during his time in the castle of Ibn Salâmah in North Africa, in the mid-770's: cf. Muhsin Mahdi, *Ibn Khaldûn's Philosophy of History* (Chicago: University of Chicago Press, 1964), pp. 47–52.
35. *Muqaddimah*, I, 172 / *Muqaddimah* (Rosenthal), I, 192–193 (translation my own).
36. *GAS*, 119. Quoted by Râghib Pâshâ, *Safînah*, p. 162, and in Muḥammad Sharîfaddîn's afterword to al-Madanî, p. 188.
37. Râghib Pâshâ, *Safînah*, p. 162.
38. *GAL*, II, 216–217; *GAL*(S), II, 305–306.
39. *at-Taʿrîfât*, p. 88.
40. Quoted in Tahânawî, *Kashshâf*, pp. 280–281, and al-Qâsimî, *Qawâʿid at-taḥdîth*, pp. 64–65.
41. Tahânawî, *Kashshâf*, p. 280.
42. The following is not a word-for-word translation but a detailed resumé of the discussion of Ibn Ḥajar (Tahânawî, *Kashshâf*, pp. 280–281; al-Qâsimî, *Qawâʿid at-taḥdîth*, p. 65), much of which is given verbatim.
43. The *muḥdith* is a person in a state of minor ritual impurity or uncleanness (*ḥadath*), while the *junub* is one in a state of major impurity (*janâbah*). The former may not touch the Qur'ân (one among several prohibitions), but he *may* recite it, while the *junub* may do neither. The former may regain a state of ritual purity (*ṭahârah*) by performing the "minor ablutions" (*wuḍû'*), while the latter can do so only by performing the "major ablutions" (*ghusl*). On the subject, see G. H. Bousquet, "Ḥadath", *EI*², III, 19; Th. W. Juynboll, "Djanâba", *EI*², II, 440–441; Goldziher, *Ẓâhiriten*, pp. 48–52.
44. It is not clear how consciously the word *baqîyah*, "remainder", is used in the phrase *baqîyat al-aḥâdîth al-qudsîyah* here, but the point should be made that in the most general sense *any* word attributed to God, whether in the Qur'ân, previous "Books", or the Ḥadîth is as this phrase indicates, a "Divine Saying". Thus the *ḥadîth qudsî* so-called is but one instance of *ḥadîth qudsî* in a more general sense, which includes the Qur'ân.
45. *Al-âḥâd* in Muslim scholarship refers to that which has been transmitted by some authorities, but not by so many of them as to preclude the report's being false or deficient. Such a report is the opposite of a *mutawâtir* report,

which is guaranteed by so many independent chains of authorities that its authenticity and accuracy are assured. In the present instance, the intention is to indicate that the text of a Divine Saying is not absolutely guaranteed, as is that of the Qur'ân, which is *mutawâtir* through every generation since Muḥammad. On *âḥâd*, see Lane, *Lexicon*, I, 28a.

46. *Kalâm Allâh* is the normal theological predicate for the Qur'ân and the Qur'ân alone; here the Divine Saying is included in the *Kalâm Allâh*.
47. Cf. above, Chapter 2, n. 66.
48. See below, Chapter 4, B.
49. *Al-Aḥâdîth al-qudsîyah al-arbaʿînîyah*. On ʿAlî al-Qârî, see *GAL*, II, 394–398; *GAL*(S), II, 539.
50. In general, the proscriptions for the woman in menstruation (*ḥayḍ*) or the woman who has just given birth (and is in the state of *nifâs*) are the same as for the *junub*, or person in a state of major ritual impurity (cf. n. 43 above). On the subject, see G. H. Bousquet, "Ḥayḍ", *EI*², III, 315.
51. ʿAlî al-Qârî, p. 2.
52. *Kullîyât*, p. 288. On Abû al-Baqâ', see *GAL*, II, 454; *GAL*(S), II, 674.
53. *Kashshâf*, pp. 280–281. On Tahânawî, see *GAL*, II, 421; *GAL*(S), II, 628.
54. *Safînah*, p. 162. On Râghib, see *GAL*, II, 424; *GAL*(S), II, 632.
55. *Qawâʿid at-taḥdîth*, pp. 64–69.
56. *ʿUlûm al-ḥadîth* (1379/1959), pp. 122–125.
57. *Tetkikler* (1379/1959), pp. 13–16.
58. *ʿUlûm al-ḥadîth*, p. 11.
59. Aḥmad Hamzah, *et al.*, "Nadwat *Liwâ' al-Islâm*", p. 760.
60. *Ibid.*, p. 761.
61. *Ibid.*, p. 761; Muḥammad Afandî aṣ-Ṣaʿîdî, "al-Farq bayn al-Qur'ân wa-l-aḥâdîth al-qudsîyah", p. 499 (cf. p. 498, at the bottom).
62. "Al-Fatâwá wa-l-aḥkâm: al-aḥadîth al-qudsîyah", pp. 188–189.
63. The discussion is quoted at length by al-Qâsimî, *Qawâʿid at-taḥdîth*, pp. 66–69.
64. *Adh-Dhahab al-ibrîz min kalâm Sayyidî* [*fî manâqib ash-shaykh*] *ʿAbdalʿazîz b. Masʿûd ad-Dabbâgh*, as quoted in al-Qâsimî, *loc.cit.* On Aḥmad b. al-Mubârak as-Sijilmâsî al-Lamaṭî, see *GAL*, II, 463; *GAL*(S), II, 704.
65. This and the succeeding parenthetical page references in the discussion of the interpretation of Shaykh ʿAbdalʿazîz refer to al-Qâsimî, *Qawâʿid at-taḥdîth*.
66. The rendering of *al-Ḥaqq* as an epithet for God with "Divine Truth" is not entirely satisfactory; the term carries also the sense of "Divine Reality", or "Absolute Reality".

67. See above, p. 57.
68. *Al-Mabânî*, p. 88.
69. *Aḥsân al-ḥadîth*: Sûrah 39:23; Bukhârî 78:70.
70. I.e., that of an-Naysâbûrî: see Appendix A, no. 1.
71. The printed Shîʿî collection of al-Ḥurr al-ʿÂmilî is treated below in the discussion of Shîʿî Ḥadîth collections.
72. Sulaymân b. Aḥmad aṭ-Ṭabarânî: *GAS*, pp. 195–197; *GAL*(S), I, 279.
73. Abû al-Ḥasan ʿAlî b. ʿUthmân ad-Dâraquṭnî: *GAS*, pp. 206–209; *GAL*, I, 165; *GAL*(S), I, 275.
74. Abû Bakr Aḥmad b. al-Ḥusayn al-Bayhaqî: *GAL*, I, 363; *GAL*(S), I, 618; article, "al-Bayhaḳī", by James Robson, *EI*[2], s. v.
75. On the collections of "forty" ḥadîths, see A. Karahan, "Aperçu général sur les 'quarante hadiths' dans la littérature islamique", *Studia Islamica*, IV (1955), 39–55, and the same author's book on the subject, *İslâm-Türk edebiyatında Kırk Hadîs toplama, tercüme ve şerhleri* (Istanbul: İbrahim Horoz Basımevi, 1954).
76. *Mishkât*, pp. 2–3.
77. On al-Kulînî, see *GAS*, pp. 540–542.
78. *Jawâhir*, pp. 201 ff.
79. This is clearly different from the better known *Muṣḥaf Fâṭimah*, which is supposed to contain non-Qurʾânic material about all that will happen until the Last Day. According to the reports in the *Kitâb al-ḥijjah* of the *Kâfî*, the *Muṣḥaf* was written down by ʿAlî, who sat to one side while the angel Gabriel related its contents to Fâṭimah (cf. Eliash, "The Šīʿite Qurʾān", pp. 16, 23–24); the *Lawḥ*, on the other hand, is only a short text in which God speaks in the first person and proclaims the special place of Muḥammad among the Prophets and names the Imâms to follow him as his heirs (cf. *Jawâhir*, pp. 203–204). Eliash's article, while it does correct some of the grosser errors of previous scholarship, is disarmingly elementary, and only points toward the work that needs to be done on the Shîʿî notion of Qurʾânic and non-Qurʾânic revelation.
80. *GAS*, pp. 535–536.
81. *Ṣaḥîfat ar-Riḍâʾ* (1390/1970). There are no clear divisions between individual reports in many instances, which makes it impossible to arrive at a meaningful estimate of the total number of ḥadîths in the forty-eight-page booklet Divine Sayings are found on pp. 7, 9, 14, 17, 24, 26, 30, 34, 36, 40, 46.
82. See, for example, vol. VIII, pp. 198–199, 219, 233.
83. Van Ess, "Zwischen Ḥadīṯ und Theologie", p. 20. In particular, the rôle of the angels, especially Gabriel, in the transmission of the Divine Saying would

be an interesting topic for investigation. In many instances both in the "classical" Ḥadîth and in Ṣûfî and later sources, the *isnâd* for a Divine Saying goes in effect beyond the Prophet to Gabriel, who transmits God's word to Muḥammad. For a few such instances, see Suyûṭî, *Itqân*, p. 102; Tahânawî, V, 1162; al-Ḥurr al-ʿÂmilî, pp. 127, 128, 130, 136, 146, 168; *Ṣaḥîfat ar-Riḍâ*ʾ, p. 14; Ibn al-ʿArabî, *Mishkât*, p. 7. For examples from the "classical" Ḥadîth, see Part III below, Sayings 52, 68, 88.

84. *GAS*, pp. 304–305; Wolfensohn, *Kaʿb al-Aḥbâr*; Andrae, *Islamische Mystiker*, pp. 28–31; B. Chapira, "Légendes bibliques attribuées à Kaʿb al-Aḥbâr".
85. *GAS*, pp. 305–307; Andrae, *Islamische Mystiker*, pp. 31–35.
86. See above, Chapter 2, B, p. 47, n. 107.
87. In Part II of the *Mishkât*, Sayings 8, 10, 12, 14, 18, 19, 21, 25, 27, and 28 are cited on the authority of Kaʿb. Saying 7 in the same section is quoted from Wahb b. Munabbih.
88. *At-Tîjân li-maʿrifat mulûk az-zamân.*
89. *Murûj adh-dhahab.* Cf., for example, the Divine Sayings in the stories about Adam (I, 54, 56).
90. Notably the *Bad*ʾ *ad-dunyâ wa-qiṣaṣ al-anbiyâ*ʾ of al-Kisâʾî (fl. early fifth/eleventh century) (*GAL*, I, 350) and the *ʿArâʾis al-majâlis fî qiṣaṣ al-anbiyâ*ʾ of ath-Thaʿlabî (d. 427/1035) (*GAL*, I, 350–351). A book of this genre is also attributed to Wahb b. Munabbih (*GAS*, p. 306). Cf. the Ph.D. Dissertation of Tilman Nagel, "Die Qiṣaṣ al-Anbiyâʾ", and the older studies of Lidzbarski, *De Propheticis*, Sidersky, *Origines des légendes*, and Weil, *Biblische Legenden*. Many *qiṣaṣ* are also found in the *Taʾrîkh* of Ṭabarî, as well as in his and other *tafsîr* works (cf. Nagel, *op.cit.*, pp. 18–23, 26ff.).
91. On the *quṣṣâṣ*, see Goldziher, *M. Studien*, II, 161–170; Mez, *Renaissance*, 314ff.; J. Pedersen, "Masdjid", *SEI*, pp. 337–338, and "The Islamic Preacher"; and Ibn al-Jawzî, *Kitâb al-quṣṣâṣ*.
92. *Ideals and Realities*, p. 83.
93. These concerns are primarily those of personal devotion, devout and constant worship of and communion with God, fear and awe of Him, love for Him and one's fellows, trust in divine mercy and forgiveness, and direct experience of the divine presence. See below, Chapter 4, D.
94. See above, Section A of the present chapter.
95. *Qût*, II, 111. The final portion reads: ... *wa-lâkin li-yuʿṭiya ar-rubûbîyah ḥaqqahâ.* Numerous examples of such Divine Sayings to previous prophets from Ṣûfî sources are found in Andrae, *Islamische Mystiker*, pp. 25–37 (almost all from the *Ḥilyah* of Abû Nuʿaym), and Ritter, *Meer der Seele*, Index, s. v. "Mose", "David", etc.

96. See above, Section A of the present chapter, p. 53.
97. Kalâbâdhî, *Taʿarruf*, 153 / Arberry, *Doctrine*, p. 157 (translation my own).
98. This phenomenon is perhaps most pronounced in the famous *shaṭḥîyât* of al-Bistâmî (see Sarrâj, *al-Lumaʿ*, pp. 380–395); cf. also the *Riwâyât* of al-Ḥallâj.
99. I, 516.
100. See "Other References" under Saying 49 for numerous Ṣûfî citations of this Saying.
101. See below, Chapter 4, B, for discussion of the introductory phrases.
102. Kalâbâdhî, *Taʿarruf*, 104 / Arberry, *Doctrine*, 96 (translation my own). Cf. Ghazzâlî, I, 295.
103. Quoted by Ibn Khaldûn (from al-Farghânî), *Muqaddimah*, III, 69 / *Muqaddimah* (Rosenthal), III, 87–88. Rosenthal (III, 88, n. 495) gives further references to other occurrences, including several of the many occurrences of this Saying in Rûmî's *Mathnawî*. See also Ritter, *Meer der Seele*, p. 623.
104. Ibn al-ʿArabî, *Mishkât*, pp. 21–22, no. 32; also quoted in *Jawâhir*, p. 167. Note that the *isnâd* in the *Mishkât* version goes even beyond Muḥammad to Gabriel and then to Michael, then to God. Such "angelic" links in transmission chains are common especially in Ṣûfî materials. Cf. n. 83 above.
105. Kalâbâdhî, *Taʿarruf*, p. 87 / Arberry, *Doctrine*, p. 76 (translation my own). Here also the Prophet has the Saying from Gabriel, not directly from God.
106. ʿAṭṭâr, *Tadhkirat al-awliyâʾ*, II, 291.
107. *Mawdûʿât al-Harawî* (British Museum Or. Ms. 12, 853), fol. 17b. See also: al-Aflâkî, *Manâqib al-ʿârifîn*, ed. Tahsı Yafıcı (Ankara, 1959–61), I, 478, where it is quoted in connection with Abû Hurayrah's black cat. I have Yohanan Friedmann and Annemarie Schimmel, respectively, to thank for these two references.
108. Nasr, *Ideals and Realities*, p. 84.

4

The Divine Saying in Early Islam

The many instances in Islamic sources, and especially in Ṣûfî sources, of Divine Sayings that are deficient or wanting in *isnâd*s have clearly been a significant factor in the tendency of Western scholars to regard such Sayings as rather late (i.e., third/ninth-century) and basically adventitious phenomena in Islam. Those who have concentrated upon the Divine Saying as primarily the product of ecstatic mystical experience and those who have seen it as an accepted formal mechanism for "borrowing" from Jewish and Christian materials have, however, relied principally upon either Ṣûfî sources or the later collections of Divine Sayings for their data. Implicit in this have been the twin assumptions that relatively few Divine Sayings are to be found in the "classical" Ḥadîth sources and that these sources themselves contain in any event primarily third-century materials, which are hardly "early".

The present chapter and the collection of source material in Part III are based upon the premise that neither of the latter two assumptions is accurate. Not only can a considerable number of Divine Sayings be located in the "standard" Ḥadîth collections and also in earlier collections of Ḥadîth from the second/eighth century; it is also a mistake, as current investigations are showing,[1] to assume that the majority of the "classical" Ḥadîth is composed of third-century forgeries. It is possible to collect from early and "classical" Ḥadîth sources a variety of Divine Sayings, most of which in all probability date from the first century and a half of Islam. While it is not possible to trace particular reports back into the first century with any assurance, these texts can be assumed to represent materials preserved by Muslims from at least a few generations after the time of the Prophet. They are therefore a body of material relevant to the understanding of early Muslim attitudes towards revelation and prophet. The presentation of these texts as comparatively early Islamic documents raises specific questions about the validity of some general assumptions about the early Community's understanding of its sources. It reinforces the interpretation of a fundamentally unitive understanding of divine word and prophetic word, of revelation and prophetic activity, which was put forward in Part I. It offers further evidence of the lack of a rigid notion in the early *Ummah* of Ḥadîth as merely human word only and of the Qur'ân as the only acceptable source of divine word.

A. Early Sources of the Divine Saying

The Divine Saying is found in substantial numbers in even the earliest collections of Ḥadîth available. These collections, which date from the second/eighth century, vary in size, but are relatively small compared with the Ḥadîth collections of later centuries. They are described in early sources in various ways, but the names most commonly used for such a collection in the early period are *ṣaḥîfah*, *juz'*, or *nuskhah*.[2] Even though they now exist only in later manuscript copies, they were apparently originally written notebooks of particular individuals, some of which were "family" collections of Ḥadîth passed on from father to son.[3] In the present investigation, five such collections were consulted, and all except one contain Divine Sayings. This latter collection, the *Aḥâdîth* of Nâfiʿ (d. 117/735),[4] has some 128 hadiths, almost all of which deal primarily with matters of legal importance. This may account for the absence of any Divine Sayings here, as such Sayings tend almost without exception to be only marginally relevant to legal questions.[5]

Of the four remaining collections, the earliest is the *ṣaḥîfah* of Hammâm b. Munabbih (d. ca. 101–2/719–20).[6] It is a collection of 138 ḥadîths that dates from around the end of the first century A.H. and contains some eighteen Divine Sayings.[7] The next oldest of the four is a "family" collection, the *Nuskhah* of Suhayl b. Abî Ṣâliḥ (d. 138/754–5)[8] in the recension of ʿAbdalʿazîz b. al-Mukhtâr (d. ca. 175–200/791–815)[9] which reports ḥadîths from Abû Ṣâliḥ (d. 101/719).[10] It contains forty-nine ḥadîths, four of which have Divine Sayings in them.[11] The somewhat later *Mashyakhah* of Ibrâhîm b. Ṭahmân (d. 163/780)[12] has a smaller percentage of Divine Sayings, nine out of a total of 208 ḥadîths.[13] The last of the early *ṣaḥîfah*s consulted is the *Nuskhah* of Abû al-Yamân al-Ḥakam b. Nâfiʿ (d. 222/837),[14] which is probably derived from a written collection of Ibn Shihâb az-Zuhrî (d. 124/742)[15] as transmitted by Shuʿayb b. Abî Hamzah (d. 162/779).[16] In this collection, only two out of seventy-two ḥadîths report Divine Sayings.[17]

While the percentages of Divine Sayings in these early texts are admittedly small, it is also true that even in the larger, "classical" collections they are likewise numerically quite small relative to the entire corpus of Ḥadîth. What is significant is that they are found at all in these early *ṣaḥîfah*s, for these collections represent materials that in all likelihood go back to at least the end of the first century of Islam, even if not to the lifetime of Muḥammad.[18] It is clear from the evidence of these early collections that the Divine Saying has as venerable a lineage in Islamic tradition as any other kind of report preserved in the Ḥadîth. Their existence in these works is a confirmation of their essentially equal status as "authentic" segments of the Ḥadîth alongside other reports that entered likewise into the major collections.

The larger, and generally later, collections of Ḥadîth that have been so widely relied upon by later Islam that they can be called in some sense the "classical" works number at least nine:[19] the *Muwaṭṭa'* of Mâlik b. Anas (d. 179/795),[20] the *Musnad* of Ahmad b. Ḥanbal (d. 241/855),[21] the two famous *Ṣaḥîḥ*s of al-Bukhârî (d. 256/870)[22] and Muslim b. al-Ḥajjâj (d. 261/875),[23] the *Ṣaḥîḥ* of at-Tirmidhî (d. 279/892),[24] and the so-called *sunan* (plur. of *sunnah*) works of Abû Dâwûd (d. 275/888),[25] an-Nasâ'î (d. 303/915),[26] Ibn Mâjah (d. 273/886),[27] and ad-Dârimî (d. 255/869).[28] It is from these collections, along with the earlier *ṣaḥîfah*s, that the Divine Sayings presented in Part III have been drawn.

The first two of these major Ḥadîth sources are considered by Ḥadîth scholarship *per se* to be less authoritative and reliable in their reports than the later, "canonical" collections, primarily because the former are less scrupulous in their treatment of *isnâd*s.[29] Nevertheless, both the *Muwaṭṭa'* and the *Musnad* have played a major rôle in Muslim life to the present day as important sources of Ḥadîth. The *Muwaṭṭa'* in particular is of great value because of its antiquity (the version usually used is actually the recension of al-Maṣmûdî, who died in 234/848[30]). Despite its being, in Goldziher's words, a *corpus juris*[31] rather than a "pure" Ḥadîth collection, it contains a cross-section of Muslim tradition that is as broad as that of any of the six or seven so-called "canonical" collections. Thus it is no surprise that it contains a considerable number of Divine Sayings, as Part III demonstrates, even though few if any of these Sayings could be described as "juristic" in nature. The *Musnad* presents a different picture, in that it is generally considered to include, along with most of the ḥadîths found also in other collections, a great number of dubious ḥadîths, many of which might be described as representative of the more popular forms of Muslim religiosity. If the *Muwaṭṭa'* can be said to represent the tradition of Medinan jurists, the *Musnad* might well represent that of the folk-preachers (*quṣṣâṣ*) of the streets and marketplaces of dozens of Islamic cities.[32] Thus its preservation of a majority of the Divine Sayings attested to in the classical sources is already a possible indication of the general milieu in which this kind of Saying originally flourished.

With regard to the other seven of the aforementioned collections, the first six of these have come to be widely treated in Islam almost as "canonical" collections of Ḥadîth. They are usually referred to simply as "the six books" (*al-kutub as-sittah*), although the seventh, ad-Dârimî's *Sunan*, often replaces Ibn Mâjah's *Sunan* as the sixth of these generally authoritative collections.[33] The Divine Saying is much in evidence in all of these works, not least in the two most highly esteemed collections, those of Muslim and Bukhârî. If it can be taken as a reasonable assumption that in Bukhârî and Muslim, and also in the *Muwaṭṭa'*, the *Musnad*, and the other five works to some degree, there is a considerable body of Ḥadîth that dates from the mid-second century of Islam, then it is possible to seek at least the broad outlines of early Muslim piety and faith in the oft-maligned Ḥadîth literature. Aside from those ḥadîths that by their tendentious content or obviously deficient *isnâd*s are to be rejected as later forgeries, it is not unreasonable to look upon the Ḥadîth in general, as collected in the major sources, as an aggregate of traditions in circulation in the first century or century and a half of Islam. Moreover, on the basis of the present investigation, it appears that a firm element in this aggregate was the Divine Saying.

Part III of the present study represents an attempt to cull from the classical and the available earlier Ḥadîth collections the Divine Sayings to be found there, or at least a large and representative sample of them. In a few cases, Divine Sayings in other types of early and classical Islamic sources have been cited also, but systematic attention has been given only to those works mentioned above, all of which represent basically the same kind of material. In all, some ninety distinct Divine Sayings, or "families" of Divine Sayings, have been selected from these sources and presented in Part III.[34] Of these ninety, one-third are attested to by both Muslim and Bukhârî, and nearly three-fifths are cited by at least one of these two. No more than one-sixth of the whole are attested by only one of the classical sources other than Muslim and Bukhârî. Approximately one-third of the total are found in the early *ṣaḥîfah*s, and all of these are also reported in the major collections. From these figures, there can be little doubt of the "authenticity" of these Sayings as an early and generally accepted element in Islamic Tradition, whatever their origins or absolute, individual "authenticity" as reports of Muḥammad. The crucial fact is that these Divine Sayings were in general perceived in the early Community as authentic divine words transmitted by the Prophet himself.[35] It is in this sense that they may be described as "early Divine Sayings".

B. Forms of the Early Divine Saying

Identification of Divine Sayings in the Ḥadîth. The major question concerning the forms of the Divine Saying in the Ḥadîth sources is that of the identifying characteristics of this kind of tradition. When one searches the classical collections for Divine Sayings, it becomes rapidly apparent that here, as in later sources, no single criterion for a so-called *ḥadîth qudsî* exists. There are different kinds of Divine Sayings to be found in the Ḥadîth, and the only satisfactory identifying characteristic of all of them is that they are words ascribed to God.

In the Muslim discussions of the *ḥadîth qudsî* (treated above, Chapter 3, B), it is commonly stated that the primary *formal* earmark of this kind of tradition is the formula used to introduce the Divine Saying itself.[36] Two formulae are usually cited: (1) "the Apostle of God said in that which he related from his Lord",[37] and (2) "God said in that which the Apostle of God related from Him".[38] By contrast, a quotation from the Qur'ân is always introduced by "God said", and a Prophetic Tradition by "the Apostle of God said", or the like. Such neat scholastic distinctions notwithstanding, a glance at any page of even the later collections of Divine Sayings (e.g., those of Ibn al-ʿArabî, al-Madanî, ʿAlî al-Qârî, al-Ḥurr al-ʿÂmilî) indicates that no such formal rule for quoting Divine Sayings has actually been in use. The most common introductory formula in these collections is simply "God said/says", which is generally preceded by "the Prophet said", or the like.

Therefore, it is no surprise to find that in the classical and earlier collections of Ḥadîth there is no set formula or formulae for introducing non-

Qur'ânic words of God. The variations in the introductory phrases are considerable, as the following random sample from Sayings in Part III indicates:

"The Prophet said: 'Your Lord said ...'" (*qâla an-nabî qâla rabbukum*) (*Musnad*, II, 359; Saying 41 in Part III, below)
"From the Prophet; he reported it from his Lord ..." (*'an an-nabî yarwîhi 'an rabbihi*) (Bukhârî 97:50:1; Saying 12a)
"I heard the Apostle of God say on the authority of his Lord ..." (*sami'tu rasûl Allâh yaḥkî 'an rabbihi*) (*Musnad*, II, 232; Saying 48:iii)
"From the Prophet, in that which he related from God ..." (*'an an-nabî fîmâ rawá 'an Allâh*) (Muslim 45:55; Saying 80)
"I tell you on the authority of the Prophet, who traced [lit., raised] it to his Lord ..." (*uḥaddithuka 'an an-nabî yarfa'uhu ilá rabbihi*) (*Musnad*, V, 239; Saying 19a:vi)
"The Prophet – that is, the Lord – said ..." (*inna an-nabî qâla ya'nî ar-rabb*) (*Musnad*, II, 509; Saying 12a:x)
"From the Prophet: 'God said ...'" (*'an an-nabî qâla Allâh*) (Bukhârî 97:35:1; Saying 89)
"Gabriel said to me [i.e., Muḥammad], '... God says to you ...'" (*inna Jibrîl qâla lî ... inna Allâh yaqûlu laka*) (*Musnad*, I, 191; Saying 52)
"The Apostle of God said [concerning "one of the prophets"]: 'God revealed to him ...'" (*qâla rasûl Allâh ... fa-awḥá Allâh ilayhi*) (Muslim 39:150; Saying 25:ii)
"God said, [speaking] through the tongue of His Prophet ..." (*inna Allâh qâla 'alá lisân nabîyihi*) (Muslim 4:62; Saying 60)

By far the most common way in the classical sources of introducing the Divine Saying is simply with "the Apostle of God said: 'God said ...'" (*qâla rasûl Allâh qâla Allâh*), as the texts in Part III confirm. In a few cases, even the *Allâh* is left out, giving "the Apostle of God said: 'He said ...'" (*qâla rasûl Allâh qâla*), and it must be taken for granted that the subject of the *qâla* is God.[39] Not all Divine Sayings are introduced by verbs of speaking, for the word of God may also be a written word. One ḥadîth introduces such a word of God with "God wrote in His book [which is] above the Throne ..."[40] Another describes one particular Divine Saying as a verse from the Qur'ân that is also found (albeit in somewhat different form) in the Torah.[41] This identification of a Divine Saying as an extract from a previous "Book", or revelation, is also encountered in later works. For example, as-Sarrâj (d. 378/988) quotes a word of God that He revealed (*awḥá*) to Hell (*Jahannam*): "If you do not do what I command, I shall cause you to burn with My greatest fires (*bi-nirânî al-kubrá*)", a Saying that is said to be found in "some of the Books" (*baʿḍ al-kutub*).[42]

There are also many instances in which it is not immediately obvious that a particular statement in an ḥadîth is being quoted as a word of God rather than an ordinary word of the Prophet. In some cases, a Divine Saying may follow immediately upon the words, "the Prophet said", or the like, without any external indication that the Saying is to be understood as God's word.[43] Even more ambiguous are the numerous ḥadîths – primarily those describing the events on the Day of Resurrection – in which "a voice" (*ṣawt*)[44] or "a speaker" (*munâdin*)[45] addresses those gathered for Judgment, or the angels, or the prophets, or even a particular person. A variation on this is the use of an impersonal or passive verb which implies an unidentified speaker: "it is said" (*yuqâlu*) or "they are called to" (*nûdû*, from *nâdá*) are the words commonly used here.[46] Thus Saying 67:ii begins: "[The Prophet] said: 'When the people of Paradise enter Paradise, and the People of the Fire the Fire, they will be called to (*nûdú*): "O people of Paradise ..."'", and there follows a statement that is clearly meant to come from God. Later Islam also knows this kind of unnamed heavenly speaker: Ibn Ḥajar quotes an ḥadîth that says, "No group sits down together to remember God (through *dhikr*) without a 'speaker' (*munâdin*) from heaven calling out: 'Arise, for I have pardoned you and transformed your evil deeds into good ones.'"[47] It is also quite common among the Ṣûfîs.[48]

In both those cases where a possible Divine Saying is apparently cited as a word of Muḥammad and those where an unnamed heavenly voice is said to have uttered the words in question, the same question arises: How is it possible to say with reasonable certainty that the words were understood by the transmitters as divine rather than prophetic words or angelic words, respectively? In such instances, there is recourse to two criteria: the sense or content of the words in question and the testimony of parallel versions of the same ḥadîth. By the former means, for example, it can be assumed that if the saying in question speaks of men as "My servants" (*ʿibâdî*) or the like, it could only be God who is speaking.[49] By the latter method, it may be possible in ambiguous cases to find variants of the ḥadîth in question that include an introductory formula such as "God said", which will confirm the internal indications that the tradition involves a Divine Saying.[50]

There is, however, at least one example in which it is extremely difficult to determine by either of these criteria whether or not the ḥadîth is reporting God's words or the Prophet's. This is Saying 4 in Part III, which is quoted explicitly as a Divine Saying in the *Mishkât* of Ibn al-ʿArabî.[51] None, however, of the four versions that are found in the classical collections makes any mention of God being the speaker. The content in general appears more consonant with a divine than a prophetic word, although when it refers to people of faith as "my friends", or "those near to me" (*awliyâʾî*), it could conceivably be the Prophet speaking rather than God. Nevertheless, on the strength of Qurʾânic parallels for *awliyâʾ* as well as Ibn al-ʿArabî's assessment, it has been interpreted here as a Divine Saying.[52]

Sayings cited both as prophetic and as divine words. A more difficult problem is posed by certain traditions that are clearly quoted *both* as words of Muḥammad and *also* as words of God. In such cases, the question that naturally arises is what the relationship between the different versions is and why both are found in the early and classical sources. If the evidence of the *isnâd*s can be trusted, it appears that in many instances such Sayings circulated in both forms quite early and were incorporated thus into the classical collections later on. The *isnâd*s suggest that in some cases different chains of transmission carried different versions, some as prophetic, others as divine statements, as may be seen in the case of Saying 31, among others.[53] In the variants of Saying 31 it is possible to correlate the variance as to prophetic or divine speech with the variation of the *isnâd*s attached to the different versions. The text of this Saying is reported in three places as a first-person statement *by God* ("If My Servant desires to meet Me, I desire to meet him ..."), always *via isnâd* 5.[54] On the other hand, there are eleven occurrences of the same statement as a third-person word of the Prophet *about God* ("Whoever desires to meet God, God desires to meet him ..."), which are attested to by wholly different *isnâd*s (nos. 1, 151, 152, 210, 400). In such a case it is impossible to say that one transmission is anterior to the other.

In other cases, however, there are no correlations between *isnâd* variation and textual variation. There are numerous examples in which an ḥadîth occurs sometimes as a Prophetic Tradition and sometimes as a Divine Saying without there being any observable pattern in the *isnâd* variation.[55] In some instances the *isnâd*s for two variants of a single ḥadîth, one a divine and one a prophetic word, are the same to the third or fourth transmitter but diverge thereafter.[56] In such cases one may on the one hand conjecture that the *isnâd* divergence marks the point at which a later transmitter altered the text.[57] On the other hand, it is not possible to determine on the basis of such *isnâd*s alone whether this was actually the case or if the earlier transmitters common to both *isnâd*s had the report *both* as a Divine Saying *and* as a Prophetic Tradition from the outset.[58] Similarly, it is hard to assess the textual history of those ḥadîths that occur numerous times as Divine Sayings, yet appear also once or twice as Prophetic Traditions, and then without any observable pattern of *isnâd* divergence.[59]

In general, when one examines the relatively large number of early Divine Sayings that occur also one or more times as Prophetic Traditions only, one is struck by the almost casual willingness of a given compiler – be it Bukhârî or Muslim or whoever – to report the same statement as a word of God and also a word of Muḥammad, sometimes side by side. It is difficult to account in a satisfactory manner for this phenomenon, especially where both versions are reported via the same transmitters, as noted in the preceding paragraph. One plausible answer is that many of these Sayings could be quite primitive traditions that were popularly ascribed by the first generations of Muslims to the Prophet without excessive concern as to whether he was speaking in inspired, "prophetic" manner as the "mouthpiece" of God or was simply speaking as the ordinary man who had been chosen by God for an extraordinary task. Such an explanation would be, of course, in line with the early Muslim understanding of the fundamental inseparability of prophet and revelation that has been postulated in the present study. It is, however, admittedly conjectural and does lead into the vexed problem of the psychology of prophetic vocation. Nonetheless, it would appear that in most instances little distinction in relative authoritativeness was made between a simple prophetic word of Muḥammad and a divine word transmitted by him in non-qur'ânic form. Both would, after all, have been understood to have come from the Prophet, and this at a time when the dogmatic questions of revelation versus inspiration or direct divine authority versus prophet-mediated divine authority would hardly have been matters of major concern.

The suggestion that there is little evidence of an early Muslim notion that a tradition might carry more weight if ascribed to God rather than the Prophet is borne out by the relative absence of any legal, political, or theological material *per se* in the early Divine Sayings. One would expect that precisely in the most controversial issues, which certainly spawned a number of tendentious forgeries in the Ḥadîth, an attempt would have been made to lend greater force to a tradition by ascribing it to God. At least one instance of such an activity has been suggested by J. van Ess, but even this case is not unambiguous, as will be seen below.[60] In later Islam, specifically in the later collections of Divine Sayings, there are clear instances of statements that are given as divine words, but which are found solely as prophetic statements in the earlier "classical" sources.[61] There is, however, little concrete evidence of the existence of a similar tendency in early Islam.

There is, nevertheless, some indication that Divine Sayings may in a few cases represent modifications of older Prophetic Traditions. This is suggested primarily by a comparison of the early *ṣaḥîfah*s with the later, standard collections, for in some cases one can point to prophetic sayings in the former that appear in the latter not only as prophetic, but also as divine words. A good example of this is seen in Saying 28, which is reported by Suhayl as a Prophetic Tradition only. It is quoted five times in the later collections, and only one of these times as a Divine Saying. Even then, the Divine Saying proper amounts to no more than an appended three-word statement by God that underscores the Prophet's own words in the rest of the Ḥadîth. This, as well as the fact that *all* versions of this tradition are transmitted with Suhayl's *isnâd* at least as far as Suhayl himself, suggests that the divine word in the one version represents an insertion in the original Prophetic Tradition to strengthen the main point made by the ḥadîth. Such a change is still, however, relatively minor, and is better described as a rhetorical elaboration than a "forgery" of a divine word.[62] There are also other instances in which a similar textual amplification or elaboration of the material in a straightforward Prophetic Tradition may have produced variant versions that contain divine words. These, however, will be considered below in the discussion of those Divine Sayings that are part of a longer narrative.

On the other hand, such comparison between traditions in the early *ṣaḥîfah*s and in the later collections does not always yield the same results. In Saying 45 and the "family" of Sayings, 89–89a–89b, the evidence is much more equivocal. In each case, the same basic statement is recorded both by Hammâm and by Ibrâhîm b. Ṭahmân, as well as in numerous places in the classical collections. In the case of the former tradition, Hammâm has it as a Divine Saying, Ibrâhîm as a prophetic word, and the later collections in both forms. Since Hammâm's work is earlier than Ibrâhîm's, it becomes therefore very difficult to argue in this instance that the Divine Saying is a later modification of the "original" Prophetic Tradition, especially since the *isnâd* evidence is at best contradictory. The fact that Bukhârî reports the tradition as a statement of the Prophet through Hammâm's *isnâd* would even suggest that one of the transmitters after Hammâm changed the statement from a divine word into a prophetic word.

In the case of Sayings 89, 89a, and 89b, Hammâm gives the basic statement as a word of God (89a), while Ibrâhîm has it both as a word of God (89b:iii) and as a word of the Prophet (89:vi), and the later collections report both forms. The two variant versions in Ibrâhîm's work are each reported from Abû Hurayrah, but through two different pairs of intermediate transmitters to Ibrâhîm. This indicates that the variation is to be traced to the pupils of Abû Hurayrah or their pupils, and it is not possible to argue that one version is anterior to the other. In fact, the possibility cannot be ruled out that Abû Hurayrah transmitted it in different ways at different times – which would, if true, support the suggestion that there was little anxiety in the early Community about the absolute distinction between implicitly inspired words of Muḥammad and non-Qur'ânic revelations to him. There is in any event no internal evidence here that the Divine-Saying versions of this tradition are later modifications of an earlier Prophetic Tradition that were intended to "heighten" the form of that Tradition.[63] Any serious work on the textual history of such Sayings awaits much-needed progress in form-critical study of the Ḥadîth as a whole.

C. The Material of the Early Divine Saying

For the purpose of understanding the content of the Divine Saying as it is found in the early Ḥadîth literature, perhaps the most crucial factor is the relation of the actual Saying to the rest of the "text" (*matn*) of the ḥadîth in which it occurs. Since virtually all of these Sayings are related from God on the authority of Muḥammad, they are normally introduced by, set within, or "framed" by words attributed to him. Thus the Divine Saying generally occurs within the framework of a Prophetic Tradition, whether the latter amounts to only the words "God said ..." or is a full-blown story or discourse in which the Prophet quotes a Divine Saying. In addition, both the Saying and its prophetic frame-material may, in turn, be set within the larger frame of a Companion's narrative about the circumstances in which he heard Muḥammad relate the ḥadîth with the Divine Saying.[64] In a few cases there may even be a further frame-story for the Companion's report; that is, the second transmitter (after Muḥammad) in the *isnâd* may also tell of the circumstances in which *he* heard the first transmitter's, or Companion's story about the Prophet's words. Thus the chief object of the present study, the Divine Saying, can be visualized as the core unit of an ḥadîth in which one or a series of "frames" or frame-stories may enclose the Saying proper.[65]

Narrative-linked Divine Sayings. The early Divine Sayings that are collected in Part III may be broken down into two basic groups on the basis of the relation of the actual divine word quoted to its frame-material. There are first those ḥadîths that contain a narrative or story that includes a Divine Saying, and in which the Divine Saying is only an incidental adjunct to the narrative rather than the focal point of the ḥadîth. In these cases, the narrative usually takes a form that can be variously described as story, legend, myth, or moral fable,[66] and it is in every case ascribed to the Prophet. This kind of narrative is commonly a story that describes God's encounter with a previous prophet,[67] Gabriel or other angels,[68] Satan,[69] a hypothetical worshipper or "everyman",[70] or those gathered for Judgment on the Day of Resurrection.[71] In this type of tradition, the words of God that are quoted are subordinated to the thrust of the narrative as a whole. This is clearly seen in an example that belongs to the last category above, the story of the money-lender who is called to account at the Resurrection by his Lord (Saying 24). Only two of the nine instances of this ḥadîth quote direct words of God; the remaining seven consist entirely of a third-person narration of the story by the Prophet with no direct quotations. This is a case similar to that of Saying 28 discussed above, in that the Divine Saying appears to be a narrative embellishment inserted into a story to dramatize the moral or lesson of the account. It is in any case clear that the narrative itself and its point are the main concern, not the Divine Saying, and this is true of the other ḥadîths that fall within this general category of narrative traditions, which includes one-third of the total Sayings in Part III.[72] While it can be argued that such narrative traditions have no claim to the clear status of revelatory words of God reported on the Prophet's authority, they have been included in the present work both because they are reckoned as Divine Sayings in all of the Muslim collections that were used and because the dividing line between these traditions and the other main type of Divine Saying is not always clear.

Self-Contained Divine Sayings. The other, and larger, group of Ḥadîth are those in which the Divine Saying that is quoted is either wholly independent of any real frame-material or, if the ḥadîth contains other material, is itself still the focal point of the text and states a generally valid truth rather than something applicable only to a particular person or situation. The characteristic mark of this kind of Divine Saying is its basic intelligibility and self-containment completely aside from the context in which it happens to occur. Of the fifty Sayings in Part III that can be reckoned in this category, some two-thirds of these, unlike those in the narrative traditions described above, are actually introduced or "framed" by no more than the Prophet's words, "God said/says ..."[73] There are also a few instances in which a basically independent Divine Saying does need some further explanation as to the context in which God is speaking, but this usually takes the form of a simple introductory sentence, "God says on the Day of Resurrection ...", or the like.[74] A few others are set within a moral lesson given by the Prophet, as in Saying 60, where Muḥammad emphasizes the virtues of praising God by ascribing to God the apodictic proclamation: "God gives ear to him who praises Him".[75] Finally, there are a few independent Divine Sayings introduced by "God says/said ...", or the like, which are set within a Companion's frame-story that describes the occasion on which Muḥammad related them. A good example of this is seen in Saying 18, which is said to have been quoted by the Prophet after the early morning prayer at Ḥudabîyah, where the truce with the Meccans was signed.[76] Here, as in all of the various types of Ḥadîth that contain relatively independent Divine Sayings, the focus is not on the frame-story but on the specific words that are ascribed to God.

Other Divine Sayings. There are also a few traditions containing Divine Sayings that do not fall clearly into the category either of a divine word that is ancillary to the narrative of the ḥadîth or of an independent divine statement that is the focus of the ḥadîth.[77] In these intermediate cases, it is difficult to determine where the main emphasis of the tradition lies, since the frame-material is necessary to the Divine Saying but does not overshadow it. Such traditions could be placed in either category. A good example of this kind of tradition is seen in Saying 72, where the Prophet's description of the shepherd who, though alone, calls to Prayer and prays, provides the context for God's words about a faithful worshipper, but where those words themselves are the focus of the ḥadîth and would be intelligible to some extent even out of context.

In addition to this more or less "intermediate" group of ḥadîths containing Divine Sayings, there are also a number of instances where part or all of a Divine Saying is set in different frame-material in different versions. While such Sayings tend to belong to the category of self-contained, independent Divine Sayings, some of the narrative-linked Sayings are also involved. Thus a divine word may be found both with and without a frame-story,[78] in two or more *different* frame-stories,[79] inserted in a multiple, "sermon" ḥadîth along with other independent traditions,[80] or joined with another divine word or words to form a longer, composite Divine Saying.[81] Such variations are, however, a common facet of the Ḥadîth generally and in no way peculiar to the Divine Saying. Various units of traditional material are commonly reported in the Ḥadîth in different contexts or joined to different kinds of material, since different chains of reporters have transmitted essentially the same report in different ways. Such cases in the Divine Sayings treated here do, however, point to some of the difficulties and complexities in any scheme of classification for so diverse a group of reports.

If, however, the general outlines of this classification of early Divine Sayings are valid, there ensue certain consequences for the rôle or rôles of the Divine Saying as a special kind of material in early Islam. Of the two categories, the narrative-linked Saying would likely have been unconsciously accepted by the early Muslims as part of the Prophet's special fund of knowledge as God's chosen Apostle. This kind of Saying, as has been seen, normally occurs within a legend concerning previous prophets or peoples, a myth concerning heavenly happenings, or an eschatological vision of events on the Day of Resurrection – all of which are the kinds of material with which the Prophet might be expected to have instructed his people in the nature and scope of God's *Heilsgeschichte.* On the other hand, the more independent, self-contained Saying would more likely have represented a kind of "extra-Qur'ânic" word that God was thought to have revealed directly to His Prophet, especially where an apodictic pronouncement about God or His ways with men is involved. While there are many caveats to be made about such an interpretation, it is an hypothesis worthy of further consideration in future studies. It is at present only very imperfectly understood how materials such as those under discussion were compiled, functioned, or were understood in the early Community. In the absence of contrary evidence it is reasonable to suppose that some prophetic reports outside the Qur'ân should have been conceived of as accounts of direct divine words, while others would have been understood as didactic, authoritative accounts of God's previous, present, and future dealings and words with man, which only a prophet could know.

D. Themes of the Early Divine Saying

When one turns finally to the subject matter of the early Divine Saying, the striking feature of the corpus as a whole is that the same general concerns run throughout the entire group. It cannot be overemphasized that these Sayings are almost without exception material that is primarily relevant within the sphere of personal devotion, morality, and piety and very little concerned with questions of theological or juristic import. Almost all of the Sayings in Part III can be said to fall within the general category of what in classical and New-Testament scholarship would be called *paraenetic*,[82] or "sermonic", material: admonition, exhortation, and general didactic, moralistic, and pietistic teaching about religious life and spiritual values. Whether it takes the form of an eschatological, legendary, mythical, or apodictic pronouncement by God, the early Divine Saying is almost exclusively concerned with the practical religious life and its duties, the love of man for God and God for man, the need to seek God's aid and to ask His forgiveness, and the proper attitude of the worshipper towards his Lord. These concerns are not unlike the largely "sermonic" emphases of the Qur'ân, which contains a similar variety of material that constantly echoes the promise and threat of judgment at the hands of the living God.

Themes of narrative-linked Sayings. While both the narrative-linked and self-contained Divine Sayings share this general "sermonic" content, they do evidence some differences of emphasis that make it useful to treat each separately. As indicated in the previous section, the former Sayings occur primarily within historical legends, myths, eschatological accounts, or moral fables. The legends all deal with God's words to a previous prophet: with Moses' (and man's?) desire to put off death (Saying 35), with the origins of the peace greeting or *taslîm* formula of blessing (Saying 29), and in two instances with rather cryptic stories that apparently have to do with moral issues concerning rashness and anger (Saying 25) and man's greed and/or duty of gratitude to God (Saying 79).[83] In each of these legends the moral lesson is taught in the good or bad example of an earlier prophet.

The myths deal in one instance with God's answer to Satan, in which He promises to forgive man's sins (Saying 21), and otherwise with God's words in Heaven. He calls upon the angels to tell Him what His servants are doing (Saying 56); to summon those servants who say "There is no god but God" to their reward (Saying 33); to report to Him on the faithfulness of His servants in their performance of the Prayer (Saying 37); and to love a person because He loves him or her (Saying 68). In Saying 70, God is said to have asked Gabriel about Paradise and the Fire when He created them and then to have altered them both to make Paradise even more attractive and the Fire even more fearful. Finally, in Saying 90 God is described as adorning His Paradise every day and promising those who fast in Ramaḍân relief from all their cares. Thus all of these myths stress the religious observance and piety that is pleasing in the eyes of God.[84]

Most of the eschatological narratives that contain Divine Sayings deal with either the threat of Hell for the evildoers and the heedless (Sayings 7, 30) or the promise of Paradise for the faithful and God-fearing (Sayings 8, 24, 62, 71). Similar themes are evident also in those Divine Sayings whose frame-stories are eschatological but subordinated to the Saying itself, so that they do not fall in the present category of narrative-linked Sayings.[85] Whether narrative-linked or independent, all of the eschatological Sayings clearly aim at reminding the Muslim of the final reckoning.

To the last subcategory of the narrative-linked Sayings, that of the "moral fable", belong those ḥadîths that present God's words about moral behaviour in the context of a generalized story. God is depicted as promising to aid the just *imâm*, the person who fasts, and the person who has been wronged (Saying 20); telling a suicide that He has forbidden him Paradise (Saying 26); saying of the man who is faithful in the Prayer, "This is My servant in truth" (Saying 27); threatening those who say that others are damned (Saying 28); accepting the intercession of a Muslim's neighbors and forgiving him his sins (Saying 57); and telling the Muslim who visits the sick that he has acted well (Saying 66). In these as in the other narrative-linked Sayings, the Divine Saying proper is set in a story or framework that lends moralistic or didactic strength to the divine word quoted.

Themes of self-contained Sayings. The more independent Divine Sayings are similarly "sermonic" in nature, and the vast majority of the fifty Sayings included in this category involve specifically exhortation or admonition of man by God to, in the phraseology of later Muslim theology, "do good and refrain from evil". Fasting (Sayings 5, 61) and performance of the Prayer (Sayings 58, 85, 22) are especially enjoined, as are the praise and "remembrance" (*dhikr*) of God (Sayings 12c, 12, 60, 9) and proper conduct towards others (Sayings 64, 16, 54, 19, 34, 65). God says that He has forbidden evil to Himself and to man (Saying 80) and that the most beloved of His "friends" (*awliyâʾ*) are those who possess little, delight in prayer, serve God and obey Him unnoticed among men, and are satisfied with little (Saying 4). He reminds man that he should be grateful to Him for all that he has on earth (Saying 82), and He promises to supply his want so long as man devotes himself to His service and is obedient (Sayings 86, 41).

Throughout these Sayings, the promise of God's aid on earth and favour in Paradise and the threat of His enmity on earth and punishment in the Fire are held out as reminders of man's duty to God. The "promises", however, and not the "threats" take clear precedence in these more independent Sayings. God says that the soul of the faithful servant has a place of special honor with Him (Saying 1), and that those who suffer in this world will have reward in the next (Sayings 55, 32). He promises those who struggle "for God's sake" that He will either grant them booty from the enemy or give them Paradise (Saying 46). As for the joys and splendors of Paradise, they are such as "neither eye has seen, nor ear heard, nor have entered into the heart of man" (Saying 2).

The positive thrust of the Divine Saying in general, and that of the "self-contained" Saying in particular, is marked. One of the strongest themes of the latter is that of God's all-encompassing mercy and forgiveness. God is the All-Merciful (Saying 15); He forgives again and again and again, whatever man may do (Saying 3), even if his sins are so many as to fill the entire earth (Saying 83; cf. 51). If man does a good deed, it will be counted in Heaven as ten; if he only *intends* a good deed, it will still count as a good deed; if he commits an evil act, it will only be counted just as it is; and if he intends but does not commit it, it will be forgiven him (Saying 34; cf. 51). God's eternal promise is that His mercy always conquers His wrath (Saying 59), and those who dispute His forgiveness are confounded (Saying 50). God is said to descend each night to the lowest heaven just to ask who seeks His forgiveness or His aid so that He can forgive or aid him (Saying 53), for as long as man asks for His forgiveness or His assistance, God is ready to answer his supplication (Sayings 83, 75; cf. 51).

This emphasis upon God's forgiving mercy and concern for man in these Sayings has a natural counterpart in the theme of divine-human love. In several Sayings there is a pronounced stress upon the bond of love (*maḥabbah*) between man and God and the nearness (*qurb*) of God to man. Among these is the famous *ḥadîth an-nawâfil*, or "Saying on supererogatory works" (Saying 49), which has occupied a prominent place in Ṣûfî piety through the ages. In the central segment of this long Saying, God says that when His servant draws closer to Him through the performance of supererogatory acts, He loves him, so that He becomes the very ears, eyes, hands and feet of His *walî*, or "friend". God is thus "in" His servant and His servant "in" Him. This notion of being "in God" is found in even more explicit terms in another Divine Saying: "My love belongs by right to those who love one another in Me, sit together in Me, visit one another in Me, and give generously to one another in Me".[86]

The love between man and God is reciprocal: God's love necessarily precedes and conditions man's love for Him, but man must love God and draw near to Him to experience the divine love. Thus God says that if His servant desires encounter with Him, He also desires encounter with him; but if he shuns the encounter, God shuns it also (Saying 31). The servant's human love and effort to approach God are, however, always exceeded by the greater divine love and divine nearness. In another famous Saying, God proclaims that whoever draws closer by any amount to Him, He will draw twice as close to him (Sayings 12a, 51). God always more than meets his beloved servant halfway. Whatever the latter may expect of Him, God has already met that expectation (Saying 12b), for He always precedes and exceeds His servant in everything. Thus, if the servant draws nearer to Him by constantly "remembering" Him – even if only his lips move soundlessly with His name (Saying 12c) – God will "remember" the servant in Heaven just as the latter has remembered Him on earth (Saying 12). The recurring emphasis in all of these Sayings is upon God's readiness to show His love for man if man strives to show his love for God.

The counterpart of man's love for and nearness to God is his awe and reverence before Him and his consciousness of his own creatureliness and limitedness in the face of God's omnipotent and "wholly other" character – in sum, what Schleiermacher called "the sense of utter dependence".[87] Perhaps the most striking Divine Sayings, all but two of which may be classified as self-contained, independent Sayings, are those that stress God's omnipotence and majesty and, by implication, man's contingency and dependence upon God. These Sayings are in one sense "self-descriptions" or "self-revelations" in which God declares who He is and what His prerogatives are; yet these pronouncements are perhaps better described as "self-magnifications" or "self-glorifications", for they do not constitute self-revelations of a previously unknown God, as are found, for example, in Hellenistic mystery religion. There are both "I am ..." statements and declarations of God's activity or position *vis-à-vis* those of man, but they serve primarily as reminders to man of the praise and worship that are God's due. They do not establish God's identity, but rather drive home the overwhelming contrast between the Absolute and the contingent, the Infinite and the finite, the Creator and the created. As such, they complement and complete the other "sermonic" concerns of these Sayings.

The "I am ..." statements all involve epithets, words, or phrases that apply to God. Thus God proclaims, "I am the King", in several places (Sayings 13, 13a, 13b, 13c, 53a).[88] In one of these instances, He adds a whole series of epithets, "the All-Powerful", "the Self-magnifying", "the Mighty" and "the Beneficent" (Saying 13a); in another He adds "the Requiter" (Saying 13c), and in a third instance, He challenges man to compare His Kingship with the kingships of the earth (Saying 13). In one of the few Sayings that may reflect early theological issues, God declares that man should not curse fateful Time for its action, for He *is* Time (Saying 89). He warns man against the sin of "associating" other beings with Him (*shirk*) by stating: "I am the Associate most free to dispense with [all] association" (Saying 10). He reminds man, "I am to be feared ..." (Saying 11), "I am God" (Saying 15:v). Yet even in the midst of these declarations of omnipotence and majesty, there is also the comforting word: "I am the Merciful ..." (Saying 15).

Similar in content to the "I am ..." statements are Sayings such as the first-person paraphrase of the *Shahâdah*, "There is no God but I, and I am greatest ..." (Saying 43), and the ringing declaration, "Majesty is My cloak and grandeur My girdle ..." (Saying 39). In a Saying relevant to the early theological issue of predestination, God reminds man of His control over all creation: "A vow brings the son of Adam nothing that I have not [pre-] ordained for him" (Saying 45). Most other Sayings that declare God's omnipotence and majesty take the form of challenges or warnings to man. Thus God asks, "Who is more wicked than he who tries to create as I have created?" and challenges man to create even a tiny grain or seed (Saying 48). He admonishes His servant for accusing Him of being a liar about the resurrection of the dead and for blaspheming by saying that He has taken a son (Saying 36). Then, in one of the longer and more beautiful Divine Sayings, God catalogs all the ways in which man is dependent upon Him and reminds man that however much piety he might show or evil he might do, neither would improve or impair God's dominion in the least; and if all the creatures of Heaven and earth were to ask and receive whatever they desired, God's realm would be diminished not at all (Saying 80).

Other concerns. In addition to the narrative-linked and self-contained Sayings, there are other Divine Sayings in Part III that similarly evidence "sermonic" concerns, but which elude classification according to the previous categories. In one instance (Saying 40), a composite, or "sermon" ḥadîth gives several Divine Sayings on different topics, all of which are used by the Prophet to bolster the faith of the Muslims in his mission and in God's overarching concern for His worshippers. Two other Sayings are apparently warnings ascribed to God Himself about dissident Muslim factions or non-

Muslim adversaries of Islam who will arise in later ages (Sayings 18, 69). While it could be argued that these latter two are *ex post facto*, polemical forgeries, Saying 69 is at least a relatively early one, for it is found (albeit as a Prophetic Tradition and not a Divine Saying) in the *Ṣaḥîfah* of Hammâm b. Munabbih.

A number of Divine Sayings are either explanations or paraphrases of Qur'ânic verses, which amount to exegesis of the Qur'ân from God Himself.[89] In another case, a Divine Saying is described specifically as a quotation from the Torah (Saying 78). Both this and Saying 87, which is directed to Jesus, might be described as pre-Islamic divine words that were apparently accepted in early Islam as actual quotations from earlier revelations. In each case the Saying contains reassurance for the Muslims about their (and their Prophet's) special place in the divine plan for mankind.

In conclusion, it should be reiterated that in all of the different kinds of Divine Saying collected in Part III, the overriding concern is the life of faith. If a few can be construed as in some sense "legal" (e.g., Sayings 22, 85, concerning the number of daily Prayers and "bows" in the morning Prayer, respectively) or "dogmatic" (e.g., the aforementioned Sayings 45, 18, 74) in nature, there is still no evidence that these were specifically conjured up for doctrinaire purposes, even if they were later so used. This is true both of the narrative-linked Sayings in their legendary or fabulous settings and of the more independent, self-contained Sayings in which God exhorts and admonishes man, reminding him of his proper relationship to his Lord. Throughout these Sayings there is an informality and personal character to these Sayings that set them apart from the language of the Qur'ân and ally them with the reports of the Prophet's own words. They are addressed to the individual, and they call upon him or her for commitment and devotion to the stern and just, yet infinitely loving and forgiving God of Muslim piety. Even a rapid reading of these texts demonstrates that the Divine Sayings belong not to the scholars and theoreticians but to the popular devotion of the Muslim community.

Notes to Chapter 4: "The Divine Saying in Early Islam"

1. See Introduction, n. 2.
2. These three terms were apparently used almost synonymously for such early

"books". See Azmi, *Studies*, pp. 28–30; *GAS*, p. 84; Abbott, *Papyri*, II, 57–64.

3. Concerning the "family" *isnâd* (i.e., one attached to a report or collection of reports and passed on from father to son), see Abbott, *Papyri*, II, 36–39.
4. In the recension of ʿUbaydallâh b. ʿUmar (d. 145/762–3). Nâfiʿ was the client of ʿAbdallâh b. ʿUmar (d. 74/692–3), from whom the traditions in his collection are related. On Nâfiʿ, see *GAS*, p. 82, and Azmi, *Studies*, in the Index, s. v. The latter work also contains the edited text of the *Aḥâdîth* (pp. 109–132 of the texts in Part II of the book).
5. See below, Section C.
6. *GAS*, pp. 81, 86; Hamidullah, *Earliest Extant Work*, pp. 40–62. The latter book also includes the edited text of the *Ṣaḥîfat Hammâm* and was first published in 1953 in *RAAD* (see Bibliography, s. v. "Hammâm"). Hammâm's date of death is disputed in the sources, as the two works cited above indicate. The alternate date most often cited is 131/747–8.
7. Nos. 8, 13, 16, 17, 30, 39, 40, 46, 51, 53, 55, 58, 59, 65, 80, 105, 106, 117. These correspond to the following Divine Sayings in Part III: 37, 59, 61, 25, 2, 45, 16, 79, 17, 34, 63, 29, 35, 12b, 12a, 34a, 36, 89a, respectively.
8. *GAS*, p. 97 (where Suhayl is identified as "Sahl"); Azmi, *Studies*, pp. 269–275. The latter work also contains the edited text of the *Nuskhah* (Part II, pp. 13–24).
9. *GAS*, p. 97.
10. *GAS*, pp. 97, 790; Azmi, *Studies*, p. 65 (see also Index, s. v. "Abû Ṣâliḥ").
11. Nos. 8, 16, 22, 34, which correspond to the following Divine Sayings in Part III: 61c, 68, 53a, 56, respectively.
12. *GAS*, pp. 92–93; Azmi, *Studies*, pp. 264–265, 270 (where his date of birth is given as 168 A.H.); *Tahdhîb*, I, 129–131. The manuscript copy (Ẓâhirîyah, *Majallah* 107/10, ff. 236–255) was generously made available to me in photostat by M. Tahir Mallick at the Orientalisches Seminar in Tübingen in 1972, when he was preparing an edition and study of the *juzʾ*. The work is entitled in the MS: *al-Juzʾ al-awwal wa-th-thânî min mashyakhat Ibrâhîm b. Ṭahmân.*
13. Nos. 80, 102, 103, 104, 105, 107, 109, 116, 127, which correspond to the following Sayings in Part III below: 19, 83, 10, 34c, 89b, 61a, 17, 61b, 12, respectively.
14. *GAS*, 102–103; Azmi, *Studies*, pp. 277–278. The latter work also contains the edited text of the *Nuskhah* (Part II, pp. 137–162).
15. Azmi, *Studies*, pp. 277–278. Concerning Zuhrî, see *ibid.*, 278–292; *GAS*, pp. 280–283; Abbott, *Papyri*, II, Index, s. v.
16. *Tahdhîb*, IV, 351–352; Azmi, p. 278.
17. Nos. 49 and 59, which correspond to Sayings 53 and 15, respectively, in Part III.

18. Hamidullah, *Earliest Extant Work*, pp. 41, 46–55; Azmi, *Studies*, Part I, pp. 270–278; Part II, pp. 25–103, 134–136, 161–162.
19. Ten, if the *Musnad* of Abû Dâwûd aṭ-Ṭayâlisî (d. 203/818 or 204/819) is included. This work has been omitted from systematic consideration here because it is not accessible through Wensinck's *Concordance*.
20. *GAS*, pp. 457–464; cf. Goldziher, *M. Studien*, II, 213–226.
21. *GAS*, pp. 502–509.
22. *GAS*, pp. 115–134; cf. Goldziher, *M. Studien*, II, 234–245.
23. *GAS*, pp. 136–143; cf. Goldziher, *M. Studien*, II, 245–248.
24. *GAS*, pp. 154–159.
25. *GAS*, pp. 149–152.
26. *GAS*, pp. 167–169.
27. *GAS*, pp. 147–148.
28. *GAS*, pp. 114–115.
29. Anyone using these two very different works cannot, however, but note the agreement of "texts" and *isnâd*s in many cases with the same ḥadîths in Bukhârî and Muslim. Much of the *Musnad*'s variation from other collections comes in its multiple reports (with different *isnâd*s) of the same tradition in different versions, although it does present a number of ḥadîths not found elsewhere.
30. *GAS*, p. 459.
31. *M. Studien*, II, 213.
32. All too little is known about the actual social and religious provenance of these and other materials in the Ḥadîth and elsewhere. One does see, however, very different interests at work in the compilation of these two works. It is conceivable that serious study of *isnâd*s might be able to establish or at least suggest the kind of men who preserved particular genres of material and perhaps even uncover regional variations in the kind of material preserved.
33. Goldziher, *M. Studien*, II, 258–265.
34. See the Introduction to Part III, below, concerning the method of selection employed with these Sayings.
35. Albeit with some exceptions in which a Companion is quoted. See, for example, Sayings 33 and 78 in Part III. Cf. Sayings 13b, commentary; 75; 88.
36. Cf. the resumé of Ibn Ḥajar al-Haythamî's discussion above, Chapter 3, B, pp. 59–60. Note also aṣ-Ṣâliḥ's emphasis upon Muḥammad's [sic!] use of a special *ʿibârah* to set them apart from the rest of his words (above, *ibid.*).
37. *Qâla rasûl Allâh fîmâ yarwî ʿan rabbihi*, which Ibn Ḥajar identifies as the ancient traditional form of introduction for an *ḥadîth qudsî* (*ʿibârat as-salaf*). See above, p. 60.

38. *Qâla Allâh fîmâ rawâhu ʿanhu rasûl Allâh,* according to Ibn Ḥajar the later usage of the two (above, p. 60).
39. E.g., Saying 89b.
40. Saying 59.
41. Saying 78.
42. *Al-Lumaʿ*, p. 390. Note also Goldziher's observation that the mystics often cite words from previous "Books", "deren Namen nach ihrer Ansicht Termini für tief mystische Vorstellungen sind" ("Ueber muhammedanische Polemik gegen Ahl al-kitâb", p. 352). Cf. above, Chapter 3, C.
43. E.g., Sayings 12a:vii; 18:vi; 45; 61; 65:iii; 84.
44. Saying 7:ii.
45. E.g., Saying 7:vii; 10:v; 67:iii, iv; 77.
46. E.g., Sayings 63; 67:ii, v; 77:iv, v.
47. *Iṣâbah*, I, 744. The ḥadîth is not found in the standard collections. Goldziher cites it as a tradition influenced by Matt. 9:2–7 (*M. Studien*, II, 386).
48. E.g., Kalâbâdhî, *Taʿarruf*, 141, 151, 160 / Arberry, *Doctrine*, 142, 154, 165. Cf. Ibn Isḥâq, 1018 / Guillaume, *Life*, 688, for the original of the second of the three examples cited from Kalâbâdhî.
49. E.g., Sayings 12a:vii; 18; 36:ii; 65:iii; 84. Note, however, that some Divine Sayings use the third person even of God Himself, in much the same way that the Qur'ân, although the direct word of God, speaks of God in the third person. Cf. Saying 19b.
50. Cf. Sayings 12, 36, 65. Note also Saying 25, where *Allâh* must be supplied in the quoted version, but is present in the text of all the variants cited.
51. Pp. 4–5.
52. See the commentary to Saying 4 for a full discussion of the problem.
53. Cf. Sayings 22, 24, 34b, 55, 89, 89a.
54. The numbers given for *isnâd*s refer throughout to the list of *isnâd*s in Appendix B.
55. E.g., Sayings 12a, 15, 28, 45.
56. Note that the *isnâd*s in the present study have been catalogued only to the third transmitter or "rank" of the *isnâd*s: see the introductory note to Appendix B.
57. E.g., Sayings 15a and 15b.
58. It would in principle be possible for two different versions of the ḥadîth to have been handed down by the same three initial transmitters, but this seems unlikely.
59. E.g., Sayings 2a, 8, 12a, 60. The obverse also obtains: cf. Sayings 28 and 44, each of which occurs only once as a Divine Saying but several times as a

Prophetic Tradition in the classical collections.

60. "Zwischen Ḥadīṯ und Theologie", p. 21, with specific reference to the ḥadîth concerning *dahr*, which is treated as Saying 89 in Part III of the present study. He argues that this ḥadîth, which is germane to the theological discussion of *qadr* in early Islam, was given the form of a Divine Saying to make it a stronger proof-text for the anti-Qadarî position of the "determinists". Concerning this tradition, see below, p. 91.
61. E.g., al-Madanî, no. 82: "God said: 'My faithful servant is dearer to Me than some of My angels'." Ibn Mâjah reports the same tradition, but as the Prophet's words: "The Apostle of God said: 'The man of faith is more esteemed by God than some of the angels'" (36:6:3).
62. A similar case is presented by Saying 31, which was considered above, p. 88. As noted there, however, the two different versions have correspondingly different *isnâds*, unlike Saying 28. A further difference is that the Divine-Saying version represents an alteration of the entire text from a third-person to a first-person statement and not simply the addition of a phrase attributed to God.
63. Van Ess (n. 60, above) uses the term *hinaufsteigern* to describe the effect of the change that he postulates from a Prophetic Tradition to a Divine Saying. Such an interpretation of the reason for the existence of the same tradition both as divine and as prophetic statements is a logical one that one would expect to have obtained; however, as the evidence assembled here shows, the situation appears to have been more complex – or at least less straightforward – than this interpretation allows.
64. Cf. Saying 3a:ii.
65. E.g., Sayings 19a, 48:iii, 52. Eckart Stetter, in his Ph.D. dissertation (Tübingen, 1965), deals with the frame-story, or *Rahmengeschichte*, as a general structural phenomenon of the Ḥadîth. He uses it, however, primarily to designate the descriptive accounts by Companions that describe the circumstances in which particular reports of the Prophet were heard, and he does not treat the special case of the Divine Saying and its frame-material, to which the concept is applied here.
66. In the positive sense of these terms: see the discussion of myth and legend above, Introduction, n. 4.
67. Sayings 7, 25, 29, 35, 79.
68. Sayings 17 (to Paradise and the Fire rather than the angels), 33, 35, 37, 56, 68, 70, 90 (likewise to Paradise).
69. Saying 21.
70. Sayings 20, 26, 27, 28, 38, 57, 66.

71. Sayings 7, 8, 14, 17, 24, 26, 30, 47, 62, 71, 76, 77, 81.
72. According to the present scheme, this category contains thirty Sayings, as listed in nn. 67–71 above (note that some occur in more than one category).
73. Sayings 1, 2, 4, 5, 6, 9, 10, 11, 12, 15, 16, 22, 31, 32, 34, 36, 39, 41, 44, 45, 48, 49, 51, 55, 61, 65, 69, 80, 83, 84, 85, 86, 89; i.e., thirty-three out of the fifty that are classified here as self-contained or independent Sayings. The remaining seventeen in this category are listed below in the text and in nn. 74–76.
74. Cf. Sayings 13, 19, 50, 53 (53a), 54, 59, 82, 87. Cf. also 34a.
75. Other examples are Sayings 3, 40, 43, 46, 58.
76. Other examples are Sayings 64 and 78.
77. According to the present scheme, ten of the ninety Sayings in Part III fall into this category: nos. 23, 42, 52, 63, 67, 72, 73, 74, 75, and 88. This compares with thirty in the category of narrative-linked Sayings and fifty in that of self-contained Sayings, as indicated above.
78. Cf. Sayings 2, 3a, 10, 13–13a–13b, 15–15a, 18, 19a, 34b, 48, 76.
79. Sayings 3, 8, 13a–13b, 19a–19b.
80. E.g., Sayings 40 and 64 (cf. 16).
81. Sayings 12 (cf. 12a, 12b, 12c), 16:vi (cf. 45:x), 49 (see commentary).
82. The Greek noun is παραίνεσις, “advice, counsel, exhortation, admonishment”; the verb, παραινέω, “recommend, advise, urge, exhort, admonish”.
83. There is also a Divine Saying, no. 87, directed specifically to Jesus, which, because of its centrality in the ḥadîth in which it occurs, has been reckoned among the self-contained Sayings treated below.
84. Other mythic frame-stories are found also attached to independent, self-contained Sayings: e.g., Sayings 38, 56, 59, 88.
85. E.g., Sayings 2a:viii, 9, 13, 14, 17, 19, 42, 54, 63, 67, 82.
86. Saying 19a; cf. 19, 19b. Concerning the phrase “in God”, see commentary to 19a.
87. “Das schlechthinnige Abhängigkeitsgefühl”: *Der christliche Glaube*, 7th ed. (Berlin: Walter de Gruyter, 1960), p. 28.
88. Note also the “I am ...” statement in the narrative-linked Saying 85: “I am your Lord”.
89. Sayings 7, 11, 15a, 36, 38, 48 (see n. 1), 50, 58, 67:i, 75, 77, 88. There do not appear to be any obvious instances of abrogated or omitted Qur’ân verses among the early Divine Sayings, but the possibility cannot be ruled out that some of the Sayings that appear to be paraphrases of Qur’ân verses represent variant *qur’âns* that were passed over in favor of those that were included in the final Qur’ân text. See above, Chapter 2, A.

5

Conclusion: The Divine Saying as Divine Word and Prophetic Word

The present study has attempted to assess the early Muslim understanding of Revelation and Prophet in the light of a reinterpretation of the early Community's perception of the "source-materials" that it held to be its spiritual inheritances from the time of Muḥammad. This interpretation suggests that dividing lines between Qur'ân and Ḥadîth, scriptural revelation and prophetic inspiration, divine word and prophetic word, were not so absolute in the first century of Islam as would be indicated by later divisions of Islamic literature and scholarly disciplines and especially by Western scholarly work on the various categories of Islamic sources. Instead, a much more unitive notion of the prophetic mission and authority on the one hand and of the divine activity and revelation on the other hand is hypothesized. Such a "unitive" perception of their origins would mean that the early Muslims were less concerned with theological *categories* of religious guidance flowing from the prophetic-revelatory event than with seeking *all* possible guidance as to what *Islâm*, "submission" to God, involves in a post-prophetic, post-revelation world.

In such a view, the Qur'ân and all the other variegated sources, most of which eventually took on the form of Ḥadîth, would have been perceived as part of the same continuum of source-materials. The common relevance of these materials to communal and individual life would have united them more than their differences divided them. The most striking evidence of the lack of rigid lines separating even divine word and prophetic word is the existence of explicit words of God outside of the Qur'ân. The point here is not that there were from the outset no materials that were specifically set apart as *qur'âns* from God, but rather that divine authority and even divine revelation were not thought to be exhausted with the "recitations" received by Muḥammad. The Divine Saying is the most tangible evidence of this that has been preserved in Muslim Tradition, and it is in this context that the present study has approached this kind of Saying. While perhaps more questions have been raised than answered, it is possible to make some general assessments based upon the evidence presented.

There are first three preliminary observations that arise from the consideration of the Divine Saying as a general phenomenon in Islam: (1) the modern scholarly assessment of the Divine Saying has mistakenly placed it in the category of relatively late, even adventitious developments in Islamic, and specifically Ṣûfî, piety; (2) the Muslim treatment of it as a sub-genre of the formal Ḥadîth is apparently itself a late, post-fifth-century development that belies an earlier position for the Divine Saying as a special kind of report that was seen primarily in its relation to or differentiation from the Qur'ân, not the Ḥadîth; and (3) the Saying itself is not a homogeneous type of material: it takes various forms and appears in a variety of materials, most commonly in the Ḥadîth, although it is itself an ḥadîth only in the most general sense of the word.

When the Divine Sayings in the Ḥadîth literature are examined, two further observations can be made: (1) the Divine Saying is as ancient and venerable as any other of the varied materials that were reported as Ḥadîth; (2) the only viable criterion for distinguishing a Divine Saying from other materials is the attribution of it, usually by Muḥammad himself, to God. Thus the Divine Saying can be seen as an early element of traditional material in Islam that is reported on the Prophet's authority as a word of God. It is therefore both divine word and prophetic word. While the same can be said of the *qur'ân*s in the sense that they were "recited" by Muḥammad, this dual aspect of the Divine Saying is much more pronounced because it customarily occurs within the framework of a statement of the Prophet.

As it appears in the Ḥadîth, the Divine Saying takes in general one of two forms: either it is a divine word that is part and parcel of a legend or myth told by the Prophet for the instruction of the Muslims, or it is a relatively self-contained divine pronouncement that appears to be a unit unto itself, usually a divine pronouncement directed to man in general. The content of both kinds of Saying and the frame-material in which they occur tend to be almost exclusively "sermonic" in nature. The Divine Saying is primarily relevant to the spiritual life and religious observances of the individual: it involves most often the promise of reward for piety and the threat of punishment for sinfulness, and it recalls again and again various aspects of the proper relationship of man to God.

Contrary to what might be expected, there is little or no evidence that this kind of Saying was thought to carry a special authority (as a divine word analogous to a *qur'ân*) that was denied to words quoted from Muḥammad alone. It does not appear either to have been used to lend greater weight to statements otherwise cited as Prophetic Traditions, nor to have posed a "threat" to the authority of the Qur'ân that might have led ʿUmar and others to discourage the reporting of ḥadîths in general. Scarcely any of the Divine Sayings have direct relevance for juridical or doctrinal questions such as prompted many of the tendentious Ḥadîth "fabrications" (*mawḍûʿât*) of the second/eighth century especially, and this argues against any formal or recognized status for this type of Saying as a separate source of authoritative guidance.

On the basis of these observations concerning the early Divine Saying, three general conclusions suggest themselves. First, the Divine Saying appears to be an early, even "primitive" element in Islamic Tradition which belongs to the sphere of personal and popular piety. Whatever its "origins" or "authenticity" in every instance as a word from Muḥammad, the Divine Saying was evidently an accepted unit of traditional material. It was quoted either as a part of the religious legend and myth that Muḥammad and the early Community drew upon so vividly and to such effect that as a result the Muslim world-view has been immeasurably enriched and expanded ever since; or it was cited as an independent and direct divine revelation that admonishes or exhorts the Muslim, reminding him of his duty as a servant of God. This kind of Saying does not seem to have been used by jurists and theologians to support their arguments, but to have served the individual as a source of inspiration in the personal life of faith. It echoes the Qur'ânic motifs of a heightened eschatological awareness, a sense of continuity in the divine *Heilsgeschichte* leading up to the last and greatest prophetic-revelatory event, and the highly-charged ambivalence of the relationship between creature and Creator that encompasses awe and terror of God and loving communion with Him, fear of judgment and retribution and hope of forgiveness and mercy.

From these latter points about the content of the Divine Saying, the second conclusion emerges: the Divine Saying is one specific genre of early material that reflects those spiritual concerns that were at a later date subsumed under the rubric of *taṣawwuf*. Not only is the Divine Saying *not* a late blossom of some "movement" called "Sufism"; it is a strong argument for the deep roots of Ṣûfî piety in early Muslim spirituality and the prophetic-revelatory event itself. The Ṣûfîs' "free" approach to the "materials" of religiousness is but an extension of the "primitive", "naïve", and fresh awareness of the absolute dependence of man upon God and the inner relatedness of all things, including man and God. This awareness has been called mythopoeic; certainly it represents an existential stance in which truth does not reside in dogmatic propositions but in the proper relationship of man to God – a relationship that can only be expressed in non-rational, non-discursive symbols, in the language of legend and myth, through prophesying and "revealing".

Prophesying and "revealing" are the keys to the third and final conclusion from the present study: that divine word and prophetic word are in the last analysis congruent. The Prophet's authority cannot be effectively isolated from the divine authority that determines prophethood. The apparent unconcern with transmitting the same basic report both as a word of Muḥammad and as a Divine Saying does not argue *against* the importance of Divine Sayings so much as it argues *for* the sacred character of prophetic sayings. Even where a "Book" is revealed verbatim to a prophet, the prophet's own words are also a "revealing" by virtue of his divine office as God's appointed.

In the Divine Saying one sees perhaps most clearly that aspect of Muḥammad's mission that is most often ignored: his genuinely *prophetic* function as the ordinary man who is transformed by his "calling" to "rise and warn" – not only through his "Book", but in all his words and acts. In the Divine Sayings Muḥammad becomes the "mouthpiece" of God. Outside the scriptural Revelation, God's revealing goes on, and most vividly so in the action and speech of His messenger. In terms of religious authority, especially within the realm of personal faith and personal piety, the Qur'ân and the varied materials in the Ḥadîth form not two separate homogeneous bodies of material, but one continuum of religious truth that encompasses a heterogeneous array of materials. The question is not whether Divine Sayings were confused with *qur'âns* – they do not appear to have been – but whether Divine Sayings (and Prophetic Traditions) are not to be seen as early kinds of traditional material that mediated to the heirs of the Prophet the immediacy and power of "the Revealing", of what has been termed here *the prophetic-revelatory event*. The present study suggests that they are.

PART THREE

The Early Divine Saying: Texts, Translations, and Sources

Introduction to Part III

The following collection of Divine Sayings affords an overview of the form and content as well as the approximate extent of this genre of Ḥadîth as it exists in the standard Muslim collections and the available earlier compilations, or *ṣaḥîfah*s (see above, Chapter 4, A). The collection does not presume to be exhaustive, but it can be safely assumed that it does comprise the bulk of the independent or "self-contained" Divine Sayings and a representative selection of the "narrative-linked" Divine Sayings in the sources consulted (on the distinction between these types of Saying, see above, Chapter 4, C).

The compilation of the present group of Sayings was accomplished in various ways, primarily by tracing Sayings cited in later Muslim works (e.g., special collections of Divine Sayings such as Ibn al-ʿArabî's *Mishkât al-anwâr* and Ṣûfî texts such as al-Qushayrî's *Risâlah*) back to the classical Ḥadîth works. Wensinck's *Concordance* was the indispensable key to this process, although additional Sayings were found through selective reading in the major Ḥadîth compendia and through a search of the early *ṣaḥîfah*s.

The present collection comprises ninety distinct Sayings, or "families" of Sayings, arranged in English alphabetical order according to the specific words of God that are quoted. Details of the alphabetical arrangement are available in Appendix C, "Index of Sayings in Part III". Most of the Sayings occur more than once in the sources, usually in several slightly varying forms. In such cases, one version has been selected as the base text, and the remaining versions are cited as parallels or variants. Wherever possible, the base text has been drawn from an early *ṣaḥîfah*, or from Muslim or Bukhârî; in each case, however, the integrity of the text and the relative frequency of occurrence of a particular version have also been taken into consideration. In some instances several Sayings are clearly related but differ substantially in form and/or content. Such distinct but related texts have been treated as separate base texts belonging to a single "family" of Sayings, which shares a common number; the different base texts in such a family are distinguished by the addition of "a", "b", "c", etc. to the second and subsequent base texts cited (e.g., Sayings 12, 12a, 12b, 12c, etc.). Therefore, while the number of Sayings or "families" of Sayings is ninety, the actual number of separate texts given in full is 114.

The decision as to whether to cite two similar texts as (1) entirely separate Sayings, (2) related members of the same "family", or (3) simple variants of the same base text, has been based on a number of criteria. It has been dictated by the peculiarities of each case and the cumulative experience gained by working with the Divine Sayings over a long period of time, rather than by any hard and fast rules. As has been demonstrated in Chapter 4 above, the early Divine Saying is not a homogeneous body of Tradition. The variety of types and forms that it exhibits makes any single rule of discrimination among individual Sayings arbitrary at best. It will be seen from the Sayings below, for example, that many of what I have called "narrative-linked" Sayings (see Chapter 4, C) are marginal Divine Sayings in the strict sense. I have purposely included even some questionable examples (where the words of God that are quoted are very incidental parts of a sustained narrative), because later Muslim scholarship has considered these also to be Divine Sayings, and because, in a first attempt to deal with such a neglected genre of material, it is important not to prejudge the full range of that genre prematurely, thereby eliminating possibly relevant sources.

The information given for each of the 114 texts that follow has been divided under six rubrics (not including regular footnotes):

1. The number (or number and letter) of the Saying, followed by a transliteration of the first or major line of the Saying, which determines the place of the Saying in the alphabetical arrangement of the texts (see Appendix C);
2. The Arabic base text of the Saying and part or all of the ḥadîth (excluding the *isnâd*) that frames the actual words of God;
3. An English translation of the base text;
4. A list of references to the standard and early sources for the various occurrences of the Saying. Each of these is denoted by a lower-case Roman numeral, the number "i" referring in every case to the source of the base text. Each reference is followed by an *isnâd* number (which refers to the *isnâd* list in Appendix B) and the name of the first transmitter in the *isnâd*. After the *isnâd* information, any significant variations from the

base text "i" or other textual peculiarities are noted. Duplicate versions of the base text have no notation after the *isnâd* data;

5. A list of "Further References" to other, usually later, occurrences of the Saying (or parts of it) in Muslim sources;
6. Brief commentary on the text as a whole or explanation of any special problems associated with all or part of it.

Texts, Translations, and Sources

SAYING 1: *ʿabdî al-muʾmin ʿindî bi-manzilat kull khayr*

. . . سمعت رسول الله صلعم يقول : إنّ الله عزّ و جلّ يقول إنّ عبدى
المؤمن عندى بمنزلة كلّ خير يحمدني وأنا أنزع نفسه من بين جنبيه .

... I heard the Apostle of God say: "God says: 'My faithful servant is with Me in a place of complete goodness.[1] He praises Me, even as I take his soul from his body [lit., from between his two sides]'."

i. *Musnad*, II, 341, *isnâd* 34 (Abû Hurayrah).
ii. *Musnad*, II, 361, *isnâd* 34a (Abû Hurayrah).
Other References: al-Madanî, pp. 39, 76.

This Saying could also be interpreted in an eschatological rather than existential sense; i.e., as a promise of reward to the faithful in Paradise. Cf. Sayings 19, 19a, where the "places" promised the faithful are "upon platforms of light in the shadow of the Throne".

SAYING 2: *aʿdadtu li-ʿibâdî aṣ-ṣâliḥîn mâ lâ ʿayn raʾat*

وقال رسول الله صلعم إنّ الله عزّ وجلّ قال أعددت لعبادى الصالحين ما
لا عين رأت ولا أذن سمعت ولا خطر على قلب بشر .

The Apostle of God said: "God said: 'I have prepared for My upright servants what neither eye has seen, nor ear has heard, nor has entered into the heart of [any] man'."

i. Hammâm b. Munabbih, no. 30, *isnâd* 1 (directly from Abû Hurayrah).
ii. Bukhârî 97:35:8, *isnâd* 1 (Abû Hurayrah).
iii. *Musnad*, II, 313, *isnâd* 1.
iv. Muslim 51:3, *isnâd* 5 (Abû Hurayrah): adds at end: *dhukran balha mâ*

aṭlaʿakum Allâh ʿalayhi, "A treasure in addition to [lit., other than, aside from] that of which God has informed you".

v. Bukhârî 59:8:5, *isnâd* 5: adds at end, quoting from S. 32:17 [concerning the delights of Paradise]: "For no one knows what has been prepared for them as refreshment for [the] eyes".

vi. Bukhârî, *Tafsîr*, S. 32:17, no. 1, *isnâd* 5: same as version v.

vii. Muslim 51:2, *isnâd* 5: same as version v.

viii. Tirmidhî, *Tafsîr*, S. 32:17, no. 2, *isnâd* 5: same as version v.

ix. Tirmidhî, *Tafsîr*, S. 56, no. 1, *isnâd* 6a (Abû Hurayrah): same as version v. Note that S. 56 is concerned with the description of Paradise. There is no indication in this version that the Saying is meant to refer to one particular verse in the Sûrah; rather, it is adduced as confirmation of the whole Sûrah.

x. Bukhârî, *Tafsîr*, S. 32:17, no. 2, *isnâd* 3 (Abû Hurayrah): same as version v, with essentially the same additional sentence (inserted after *bashr* and before S. 32:17) as version iv.

xi. Ibn Mâjah 37:39:1, *isnâd* 3: same as version v.

xii. Muslim 1:312, *isnâd* 250 (al-Mughayrah b. Shuʿbah): variant of version v; set within a long story about God's answers to Moses's questions in Paradise concerning the rewards given there. S. 32:17 is quoted by the Prophet at the end of the story.

xiii. Muslim 51:5, *isnâd* 240 (Ṣahl b. Saʿd): *ḥadîth nabawî:* "In it [Paradise] is that which neither eye has seen, nor ear has heard, nor has entered into the heart of man". These words are said to have been uttered one day by Muḥammad from the pulpit[2] after he had given a description of Paradise. He closes his words with S. 32:17 as in version v.

xiv. *Musnad*, V, 334, *isnâd* 240: *ḥadîth nabawî*, same as version xiii.

Other References: Ibn al-ʿArabî, *Mishkât*, p. 14; al-Madanî, p. 5; *Jawâhir*, pp. 359, 362.

This particular Divine Saying has a long history in other religious traditions of the Near East as well. It is commonly found in connection with eschatological predictions (cf. its use in the *tafsîr* of S. 32:17 and S. 56 in versions vff.). Cf. Isaiah 64:4: "Never has ear heard nor eye seen ...", and Paul's use of the same traditional saying (I Cor. 2:9): "'Things beyond our seeing, things beyond our imagining, all prepared by God for those who love Him' – these it is that God has revealed to us through the Spirit." Almost the identical words of the Divine Saying are also found in the Coptic Gospel of Thomas: "Jesus said: 'I will give you what no eye has seen and what no ear has heard and no hand has touched and what has not come into the heart of man'" (*Sourcebook of Texts for the Comparative Study of the Gospels*, eds. and trans., David R. Cartlidge and David L. Dungan, Sources for Biblical Study, no. 1, 2nd ed., rev. [(Missoula, Montana?): Society of Biblical Literature, 1972], p. 115).

SAYING 3: *adhnaba ʿabdî dhanban*

... عن النبيّ صلعم فيما يحكى عن ربّه عزّ وجلّ قال أذنب عبد ذنبا فقال اللّهمّ اغفر لى ذنبى فقال تبارك وتعالى أذنب عبدى ذنبا فعلم أنّ له ربّا يغفر الذنب ويأخذ بالذنب ثمّ عاد فأذنب فقال أى ربّ اغفر لى ذنبى فقال تبارك وتعالى عبدى أذنب ذنبا فعلم أنّ له ربّا يغفر الذنب ويأخذ بالذنب ثمّ عاد فأذنب فقال أى ربّ اغفر لى ذنبى فقال تبارك وتعالى أذنب عبدى ذنبا فعلم أنّ له ربّا يغفر الذنب ويأخذ بالذنب اعمل ما شئت فقد غفرت لك .

... from the Prophet in that which he related from his Lord. He said: "A servant commits a sin, then says: 'O God! Forgive me my sin!' Then God says: 'My servant has committed a sin. He knows that he has a Lord who forgives sin and takes it [from him].' Thereupon he sins again and says: 'O my Lord, forgive me my sin!' Then God says: 'My servant has committed a sin. He knows that he has a Lord who forgives sin and takes it [from him].' Thereupon he sins again and says: 'O my Lord, forgive me my sin!' Then God says: 'My servant has committed a sin. He knows that he has a Lord who forgives sin and takes it [from him]. Do what you will, I have forgiven you.'"

i. Muslim 49:29, *isnâd* 28 (Abû Hurayrah).
ii. Muslim 49:30, *isnâd* 28.
iii. *Musnad*, II, 296, *isnâd* 28.
iv. *Musnad*, II, 492, *isnâd* 28.
v. *Musnad*, II, 405, *isnâd* 28: shorter version; the exchange between the sinner and God occurs only once, not three times as in version i; omits *iʿmal mâ shiʾta* entirely.

Other References: Ibn al-ʿArabî, *Mishkât*, p. 37; al-Madanî, p. 92; al-Makkî, *Qût*, II, 99; Ghazzâlî, I, 312.

SAYING 3a: *iʿmalû mâ shiʾtum fa-qad ghafartu lakum*

. . . عن رسول اللّه صلعم قال إنّ اللّه عزّ وجلّ اطّلع على أهل بدر فقال
اعملوا ما شئتم فقد غفرت لكم .

... from the Apostle of God. He said: "God looked down upon the people of Badr[3] and said: 'Do what you will, I have forgiven you'."[4]

i. *Musnad*, II, 295–296, *isnâd* 3f (Abû Hurayrah).

ii. Bukhârî, *Tafsîr*, S. 60:1, *isnâd* 301 (ʿAlî b. Abî Ṭâlib): set in the frame of a long story about a letter from one of the *muhâjirûn*, Ḥâṭib b. Abî Baltaʿah, to some of his kinsmen in Mecca while the Muslims were still in Madînah and at daggers-drawn with the Meccans. ʿUmar wants to execute Ḥâṭib at once, but Muḥammad reminds him that Ḥâṭib had been with the Muslims at Badr and then quotes the Divine Saying as in version i – not as words that he has heard directly from God, but as something he thinks God *might* have said (*laʿalla Allâh iṭṭalaʿa ... wa-qâla*) about the people who fought at Badr for the Muslims. The ḥadîth ends with the statement (by ʿAlî) that it was on this occasion that S. 60:1 was revealed: "O you who are faithful! Do not take My enemies and your enemies as friends ...".

iii. Bukhârî 64:9, *isnâd* 302 (ʿAlî b. Abî Ṭâlib): similar frame-story to version ii.

iv. Bukhârî 64:46:1, *isnâd* 301: same as version ii.

v. Muslim 44:161, *isnâd* 301: same as version ii.

vi. Bukhârî 78:74, *isnâd* missing: quoted by Bukhârî in the introductory remarks to *Bâb* 74, rather than among the "sound" ḥadîths in the body of the *bâb*; the full ḥadîth here reads: "ʿAmr told Ḥâṭib that he was a (religious) hypocrite (*munâfiq*), and the Prophet said: 'You do not realize that perhaps (*laʿalla*) God looked down upon the people of Badr and said: "I have forgiven you (*qad ghafartu lakum*)".'"

Other References: Ibn Isḥâq, pp. 809–810 / Guillaume, *Life*, p. 545; al-Madanî, p. 64; Kalâbâdhî, *Taʿarruf*, p. 77.

SAYING 4: *aghbaṭ awliyâʾî ʿindî la-muʾmin khafîf al-ḥâdh*

. . . عن النبيّ صلعم قال إنّ أغبط أوليائى عندى لمؤمن خفيف الحاذ ذو
حظّ من الصلاة أحسن عبادة ربّه وأطاعه فى السرّ وكان غامضا فى الناس لا
يشار اليه بالأصابع وكان رزقه كفافا فصبر على ذلك ثم نقر باصبعيه فقال عجلّت
منيّته قلّت بواكيه قلّ تراثه .

... from the Prophet. He said: "[God said:] 'The most blessed of My friends is a man of faith who has few possessions [lit., is light of back] and delights in the prayer, who performs well the service of his Lord and obeys Him in secret. He is unnoticed among men: they do not point to him with their fingers. His sustenance is just sufficient, and he is satisfied with that.'" Then he [Muḥammad] shook his finger and said: "His death is hastened, he is not wept over much, and the legacy that he leaves is small."

i. Tirmidhî 34:35:1, *isnâd* 260 (Abû Umâmah).
ii. *Musnad*, V, 252, *isnâd* 260.
iii. *Musnâd*, V, 255, *isnâd* 260.
iv. Ibn Mâjah 37:4:3, *isnâd* 261 (Abû Umâmah): shorter version; *aghbaṭ an-nâs ʿindî*, "the most blessed persons in My estimation", replaces *aghbaṭ awliyâʾî*.
Other References: Ibn al-ʿArabî, *Mishkât*, pp. 4–5.

The words "God said" in line 1 have been interpolated even though it is debatable whether this statement is to be understood as a Divine Saying or as words of the Prophet. Ibn al-ʿArabî clearly took it as a divine word rather than a statement of Muḥammad alone, as its inclusion in the *Mishkât* indicates. This is not, however, a conclusive argument for its having been originally understood in this fashion. The key to the problem is the word *awliyâʾ* (plur. of *walî*), which can mean "friends", "protectors", or "saintly persons". In Muslim usage, the word eventually came to have the almost technical meaning of "saints" – insofar as one may use the word to refer to Muslim heros of piety, asceticism, and special spiritual power. The development of this specific usage beyond the more general usage found in the Qurʾân (which is discussed below in the commentary to Saying 49) makes it more difficult to determine whether the Prophet (or the early generations of Muslims) would have spoken of "my *awliyâʾ*" in this fashion or could only have been quoting God. *Awliyâʾ an-nabî* does occur in the Ḥadîth (see *Concordance*, VII, 329ff.); however, in the context of the rest of the present Saying one would expect God to be the speaker in this case even aside from the question of *awliyâʾ*. The entire question needs further investigation (how little attention has been paid to the exact early use of the term is shown by the Carra de Vaux article, "walī", *SEI*, 629–631).

The content of this ḥadîth makes it likely that this Saying derives from ascetic circles in early Islam. From the Prophet or not, it must have been transmitted by people who took their *islâm* and its duties so seriously as to see the ascetic ideals of poverty (*faqr*), patient endurance (*ṣabr*), god-fearing piety (*taqwá*), and supererogatory works (*nawâfil*) as the norms for their lives. Cf. Tor Andrae's portrayal of early asceticism in Islam in his *Islamische Mystiker*, Chapter 2.

SAYING 5: *aḥabb ʿibâdî ilayya aʿjaluhum fiṭran*

... عن رسول اللّه صلعم قال يقول اللّه عزّ وجلّ إنّ أحبّ عبادى إلىّ أعجلهم فطرا .

... from the Apostle of God. He said: "God says: 'The most beloved of My servants is the one who is quickest in breaking the fast'."

i. *Musnad*, II, 237–238, *isnâd* 6 (Abû Hurayrah).
ii. Tirmidhî 6:13, *isnâd* 6.
iii. *Musnad*, II, 329, *isnâd* 6.
Other References: ʿAlî al-Qârî, no. 22; al-Madanî, p. 8.

This Saying may be directed against those who lengthen the time of fasting in order to ḍemonstrate their piety – thus committing the sin of pride (in their own righteousness). The Muslim who carefully observes the start of the fast and hastens to break the fast when it is time to do so is the truly pious one, who shows his gratitude to God just as much in the *fiṭr* as in the *ṣawm* itself.

SAYING 6: *aḥabb mâ taʿabbadanî bihi ʿabdî ilayya an-nuṣḥ lî*

... عن النبّى صلعم قال قال اللّه عزّ وجلّ أحبّ ما تعبّدنى به عبدى إلىّ النصح لى .

... from the Prophet. He said: "God said: 'The most desirable way in which My servant [can] serve Me is through sincerity[5] towards Me'."

i. *Musnad*, V, 254, *isnâd* 260 (Abû Umâmah).
Other References: ʿAlî al-Qârî, no. 24; al-Madanî, p. 8.

SAYING 7: *akhrij baʿth an-nâr*

... عن النبي صلّعم قال يقول اللّه تعالى يا آدم قال فيقول لبّيك وسعديك والخير في يديك قال فيقول أخرج بعث النار قال وما بعث النـار قال من كلّ ألف تسع مائة وتسع وتسعين فعنده يشيب الصغير "وتضع كلّ ذات حمل حملها وترى النّاس سكارى ولكنّ عذاب اللّه شديد " .

... from the Prophet. He said: "God says: 'O Adam!' And he says: 'I wait always and ever ready to serve and aid Thee. The good is in Thy hands'. Then He says: 'Let the company of the Fire come forth!' He [Adam] says: 'And what is the company of the Fire?' He [God] answers: 'From every thousand, nine hundred and ninety-nine!' And at [the aspect of] it, the young shall have their hair turn white [as if grown suddenly old], 'and every pregnant woman shall bring forth what she carries [before time], and you shall see men drunk, yet they are not [actually] drunk; but verily God's punishment is terrible!' [S. 22:2]"

i. Bukhârî 60:7:4, *isnâd* 120 (Abû Saʿîd al-Khudrî): the ḥadîth continues at the end of the quoted section with an account of how the Prophet was asked who the one in a thousand who will not enter the Fire will be. He answers at first that of those present, only one will be saved, even though a thousand from the vast population of Gog and Magog (on which, see S. 18:92–96 and A. J. Wensinck, "Yâdjûdj wa Mâdjûdj", *EI*, s. v.) will be saved. Then, however, he goes on to say that he hopes that his followers will make up as much as a fourth, or even a third, or even a half of those in Paradise. Finally he says that he in fact thinks that the Muslims are so special that they stand out among men who will be judged as the black hairs on the hide of a white bull, or the white hairs on a black one.

ii. Bukhârî, *Tafsîr*, S. 22:2, no. 1, *isnâd* 120: wording variations throughout; the command for the *baʿth an-nâr* to come forth is given by "a voice" (*yunâdá bi-ṣawt*), and not explicitly by God (see the discussion of this kind of usage in Chapter 4, B, p. 87, above).

iii. Muslim 1:379, *isnâd* 120.

iv. Bukhârî 81:46:1, *isnâd* 120: wording variations throughout.

v. *Musnad*, III, 32–33, *isnâd* 120.

vi. Bukhârî 97:32:3, *isnâd* 120: shorter version; omits the additional portion described under version i.

vii. Bukhârî 81:45:8, *isnâd* 44 (Abû Hurayrah): essentially the same as version vi.

viii. *Musnad*, I, 388, *isnâd* 192 (ʿAl. b. Masʿûd): essentially the same as version vi; the Divine Saying portions are cited here specifically as words of a *munâdin* sent by God (see above, Chapter 4,B, p. 87).

Other References: Ibn al-ʿArabî, *Mishkât*, p. 13; al-Madanî, pp. 32, 45.

SAYING 8: *akhrijûhu man kâna fî qalbihi mithqâl ḥabbah min khardal min îmân*

... عن النبىّ صلعم قال يدخل أهل الجنّة الجنّة وأهل النار النار ثمّ يقول
اللّه أخرجوا من كان فى قلبه مثقال حبّة من خردل من إيمان فيخرجون منها
قد اسودّوا فيلقون فى نهر الحيا أو الحيوٰة شكّ مالك فينبتون كما تنبت الحبّة
فى جانب السيل ألم تر أنّها تخرج صفراء ملتوية .

... from the Prophet. He said: "The people of Paradise will enter Paradise, and the people of the Fire, the Fire. Then God will say [addressing His angels]: 'Bring forth [from the Fire] him in whose heart there is the weight of a mustard seed of faith'. Thereupon they will be brought forth from it, having become black, and they will be cast into the river of rain water" – or, "of life" (Mâlik hesitated here)[6] – "then they will sprout forth just as wild seeds sprout beside the torrent. Have you not seen how they emerge, yellow [and] luxuriant?"

i. Bukhârî 2:15:1, *isnâd* 125 (Abû Saʿîd al-Khudrî).

ii. Bukhârî 81:51:12, *isnâd* 125.

iii. Muslim 1:304, *isnâd* 125: the specific words ascribed to God are: *unẓurû man wajadtum fî qalbihi mithqâl ḥabbah min khardal min îmân wa-akhrijûhu*, "look for him in whose heart you find [even] the weight of a mustard seed of faith, and bring him forth [from the Fire]".

iv. Muslim 1:302, *isnâd* 121 (Abû Saʿîd al-Khudrî): a variant of the Divine Saying in version i (*dînâr min khayr*, "a dinar of goodness", replaces *ḥabbah min khardal min îmân*) is set within a longer frame-story about the intercession of the Muslims for their brethren in the Fire on the Day of Resurrection. This story is in turn one of a series of eschatological descriptions ascribed to Muḥammad on the authority of Abû Saʿîd and contained in the single long multiple tradition of Muslim 1:302. This tradition also contains two further Divine Sayings, nos. 62:i and 76:iv.

v. Bukhârî 97:24:5, *isnâd* 121: essentially the same as version iv.

vi. *Musnad*, III, 16–17, *isnâd* 121: essentially the same as version iv.

vii. *Musnad*, III, 11–12, *isnâd* 126 (Abû Saʿîd al-Khudrî): set within a longer tradition similar to that of version iv but in the third person as an *ḥadîth nabawî* rather than as a Divine Saying. There are numerous similar versions: e.g., Muslim 1:148, 149, 185; Abû Dâwûd 31:26; *Musnad*, I, 412, 451; Tirmidhî 37:10:3 (further references at *Concordance*, I, 294b, "mithqâl").

viii. Bukhârî 97:36:2, *isnâd* 104a (Anas b. Mâlik): set within a long tradition known as the *ḥadith ash-shafâʿah*, "ḥadîth of intercession", to which are also joined some of the materials contained in the longer traditions from which versions iv–vii are drawn. The *ḥadîth ash-shafâʿah* (concerning which, see Ritter, *Meer*, pp. 19–20) tells how each of the prophets will be asked in turn on the Last Day to intercede for mankind at the Judgment, but only Muḥammad is able to do so. Cf. Sayings 62, 76.

ix. *Musnad*, I, 295–296, *isnâd* 140 (Abn ʿAbbâs): same as version viii.

x. *Musnad*, I, 281–282, *isnâd* 140: same as version viii.

SAYING 9: *akhrijû min an-nâr man dhakaranî yawman*

... عن النبىّ صلعم قال يقول اللّه أخرجوا من النار من ذكرنى يوما أو خافنى فى مقام .

... from the Prophet. He said: "God says: 'Bring forth from the Fire him who has remembered Me [even] a day or feared Me somewhere'."

i. Tirmidhî 37:9:3, *isnâd* 103 (Anas b. Mâlik).
Other References: al-Madanî, p. 30.

This Saying has a form very similar to that of Saying 8: "Let him depart from the Fire in whose heart there is the measure of a mustard seed of faith." Cf. also Saying 12 on *dhikr*.

SAYING 10: *anâ aghná ash-shurakâʾ ʿan ash-shirk*

..إنّ رسول اللّه صلعم قال قال اللّه عزّ وجلّ أنا أغنى الشركاء عن الشرك فمن عمل لى عملا أشرك فيه غيرى فأنا منه برئ وهو للّذى أشرك .

... the Apostle of God said: "God said: 'I am the Associate most free to dispense with association.[7] As for him who carries out an action in which he has someone other than Me participate, with it [the action] I have nothing to do. It is [the action] of him who ascribes partners [to Me]'."

i. Ibrâhîm b. Ṭahmân, no. 103 (fol. 247a), *isnâd* 13 (Abû Hurayrah).

ii. Ibn Mâjah 37:21:1, *isnâd* 13.

iii. Muslim 53:46, *isnâd* 13: *taraktuhu wa-shirkahu*, "I abandon him and his *shirk* [association of others with God]", replaces *fa-anâ minhu bariʾ wa-huwa li-lladhî ashraka*.

iv. *Musnad*, II, 301 (two almost identical versions with *isnâds* that vary only in their final transmitter), *isnâd* 13: *anâ khayr ash-shurakâʾ*, "I am the best of associates", replaces *anâ aghná ash-shurakâ ʿan ash-shirk*.

v. Ibn Mâjah 37:21:2, *isnâd* 340 (Abû Saʿd): slightly different version; occurs within an eschatological frame-story in the third person as the words of a "caller" or "herald" *(munâdin)* addressed to those assembled for the Last Judgment (see above, Chapter 4, B, p. 87).

Other References: Ibn al-ʿArabî, *Mishkât*, p. 4; al-Madanî, pp. 7, 10, 12, 74; ʿAlî al-Qârî, no. 16; *Jawâhir*, pp. 167, 169; al-Muḥâsibî, *Riʿâyah*, pp. 90, 92, 138.

The entire Saying is built up upon varying forms of the Arabic root *Sh-R-K*, the basic sense of which is *association*, *participation*, or *sharing*. It is impossible satisfactorily to render all the various forms of this root in the present text with the same English root without losing much of the stylistic force of the original; hence *association*, *participate*, and *ascribe partners to* have all been used to translate the same basic root in its several forms in the passage.

SAYING 11: *anâ ahl an uttaqá*

. . . إنّ رسول اللّه قرأ أو تلا هذه الآية "هو أهل التقوى وأهل المغفرة"
فقال قال اللّه عز وجل أنا أهل أن اتّقى فلا يجعل معى اله آخر فمن
اتّقى أن يجعل معى الها آخر فأنا أهل أن أغفر له .

... the Apostle of God recited this *âyah*: "His it is to be feared; His it is to forgive."[8] Then he said: "God said: 'Mine it is to be feared. No other God is to be placed beside Me. Whoever fears to place another god beside Me, him it is Mine to forgive'."

i. Ibn Mâjah 37:35:7a, *isnâd* 104 (Anas b. Mâlik).

ii. *Musnad*, III, 142, *isnâd* 104: *kâna ahl an aghfira lahu*, "he is worthy to be forgiven by Me", replaces *fa-anâ ahl an aghfira lahu*.

iii. *Musnad*, III, 243, *isnâd* 104: same as version ii.

iv. Ibn Mâjah 37:35:7b, *isnâd* 104: *fa-lâ yushraka bî ghayrî wa-anâ ahl li-man ittaqá an yushrika bî an aghfira lahu*, "Nothing else is to be associated with Me as a partner; Mine it is to forgive him who fears to associate anything with Me as a partner", replaces *fa-lâ yujʿalu* … (to the end).

Other References: ʿAlî al-Qârî, no. 33; al-Madanî, p. 20; *Jawâhir*, p. 169.

SAYING 12: *anâ ʿind ẓann ʿabdî bî … in taqarraba ilayya shibran*

... قال النبيّ صلعم يقول اللّه تعالى أنا عند ظنّ عبدى بى وأنا معه اذا ذكرنى فإن ذكرنى فى نفسه ذكرته فى نفسى وان ذكرنى فى ملاء ذكرته فى ملاء خير منهم وان تقرّب إلىّ شبرا تقرّبت إليه ذراعا وان تقرّب إلىّ ذراعا تقرّبت إليه باعا وان أتانى يمشى أتيته هرولة .

… the Prophet said: "God says: 'I fulfill My servant's expectation of Me,[9] and I am with him when he remembers Me. If he remembers Me in his heart, I remember him in My heart; and if he remembers Me in public, I remember him before a public [far] better than that.[10] And if he draws nearer to Me by a handsbreadth, I draw nearer to him by an armslength; and if he draws nearer to Me by an armslength, I draw nearer to him by a fathom; and if he comes to Me walking, I come to him running'."[11]

i. Bukhârî 97:15:3, *isnâd* 3 (Abû Hurayrah).

ii. Ibrâhîm b. Ṭahmân, no. 127 (fol. 249a), *isnâd* 3 (directly from al-Ḥasan b. ʿImârah from al-Aʿmash, etc.): *ʿabdî ʿind ẓannihi bî*, "My servant is right in what he thinks about Me" [?], replaces *anâ ʿind ẓann ʿabdî bî; wa-in dhakaranî waḥdahu dhakartuhu waḥdî*, "and if he remembers Me alone, I shall remember him alone", is added after *fî nafsî*.

iii. Muslim 48:21, *isnâd* 3.

iv. Muslim 48:1, *isnâd* 3: also adds a second version (same *isnâd* to 4th transmitter) which omits *wa-in taqarraba ilayya dhirâʿan taqarrabtu ilayhi bâʿan*.

v. Tirmidhî 45:31:1, *isnâd* 3.

vi. Ibn Mâjah 33:58:2, *isnâd* 3.

vii. *Musnad*, II, 251, *isnâd* 3.

viii. *Musnad*, II, 413, *isnâd* 3.

ix. *Musnad*, II, 482, *isnâd* 28a (Abû Hurayrah).

x. *Musnad*, II, 480, *isnâd* 3b (from Abû Hurayrah): first sentence same as version ii; *wa-aṭyab* inserted after *malaʾ khayr minhum*, so that the entire phrase reads: "a public better and finer than those".

xi. *Musnad*, II, 524, *isnâd* 3a (Abû Hurayrah): same as version x.

xii. *Musnad*, II, 534–535, *isnâd* 3a: same as version x.

xiii. Muslim 49:1, *isnâd* 3a: the middle portion, *in dhakaranî fî nafsihi … mala' khayr minhum*, is replaced by *wa-llâhi la-llâh afraḥ bi-tawbat ʿabdihi min aḥadikum yajidu ḍâllatahu bi-l-falât*, "and God is truly more delighted with the pious fear/repentance of His servant than one of you [would be] who finds his stray camel in the desert".

Other References: Ibn al-ʿArabî, *Mishkât*, 19; al-Madanî, pp. 11, 13, 16, 20, 34; Ghazzâlî, I, 295.

Dhakara, "remember", is here to be understood so as to include both the *dhikr bi-l-qalb*, the "remembrance in the heart" of God, and the *dhikr bi-l-lisân*, the "remembrance with the tongue" or "making [constant] mention" of God. While the *dhikr* as a particular form of prayer or personal devotional practice (involving the repetition of the *shahâdah* or other words of praise) did develop in many Ṣûfî circles into a ritualized group practice, the basic idea of the rhythmic, repetitive litany of praise as a means of drawing closer to God began quite early in Islam and continues in many forms to the present day. In the text here, it is impossible to say how much of a technical, ritualistic sense is to be attached to the word, but the probability of some degree of antiquity for the Saying (based upon its occurrence in the *juz'* of Ibrâhîm b. Ṭahmân as well as in most of the major collections) argues for a general interpretation rather than a very specific one (as a group ritual). On *dhikr*, see L. Gardet, "dhikr", *EI*², II, 223–227; Ritter, *Meer*, p. 82; Hartmann, *Ḳuschairī*, pp. 35–38; and K. Nakamura, *Ghazali on Prayer*, pp. 33–59. The practice of repeating the name of God or a formula of praise is almost universal. A salient example from another tradition is the Nembutsu (*namu-amida-butsu*), or "calling the name of Amida", practiced among the Pure Land sects in Japan. (For a comparison of *dhikr* and Nembutsu, see K. Nakamura, "A Structural Analysis of *Dhikr* and *Nembutsu*", *Orient*, VII (1971), 75–96.) The idea of the efficacy of such a practice in lifting one into contact with the Divine probably rests not only upon its inherent value as a spiritual discipline for concentration on God, but also on the likely far more ancient sense of the inherent power of the spoken word; see Frazer, *The Golden Bough*, pp. 283–304, and Van der Leeuw, *Religion in Essence and Manifestation*, I, 224–226, 381; II, 403–413.

SAYING 12a: *idhâ taqarraba al-ʿabd ilayya shibran*

... عن النبىّ صلعم يرويه عن ربّه قال إذا تقرّب العبد إلىّ شبرا تقرّبت
إليه ذراعا واذا تقرّب منّى ذراعا تقرّبت منه باعا واذا أتانى مشيا أتيته هرولة.

... from the Prophet, reporting from his Lord. He said: "'If [My] servant draws nearer to Me by a handsbreadth, I draw nearer to him by an armslength, and if he draws nearer to Me by an armslength, I draw nearer to him by a fathom. And if he comes to Me walking, I come to him running.'"

i. Bukhârî 97:50:1, *isnâd* 100 (Anas b. Mâlik).
ii. *Musnad*, III, 122 (in two places), *isnâd* 100.
iii. *Musnad*, III, 130, *isnâd* 100.
iv. Hammâm b. Munabbih, no. 80, *isnâd* 1 (directly from Abû Hurayrah): *talaqqânî*, "comes to meet Me", replaces *taqarraba ilayya* (and so throughout the Saying, *L-Q-Y* for *Q-R-B*); final sentence reads: *wa-idha talaqqânî bi-bâʿin jiʾtuhu (aw qâla ataytuhu) bi asraʿ*, "and if he comes a fathom's length to meet Me, I come [even] faster to meet him".
v. Muslim 48:2, *isnâd* 1 (Abû Hurayrah).
vi. Bukhârî 97:50:2, *isnâd* 25 (Abû Hurayrah): no mention of *yarwîhi ʿan rabbihi* or any other indication that God is speaking; a second *isnâd*, 102 (Anas b. Mâlik), is also given by Bukhârî, with the notation that the text is spoken by God.
vii. Muslim 48:20, *isnâd* 25.
viii. *Musnad*, II, 435, *isnâd* 25.
ix. *Musnad*, II, 509, *isnâd* 25.
x. *Musnad*, III, 40, *isnâd* 123 (Abû Saʿîd al-Khudrî): in third person as an *ḥadîth nabawî* (*idhâ taqarraba al-ʿabd ilá Allâh* ... [etc.]).
xi. *Musnad*, V, 155, *isnâd* 136 (Abû Dharr): *ḥadîth nabawî*, same as version x.
Other References: al-Muḥâsibî, *Riʿâyah*, p. 20 (from Abû Hurayrah); al-Madanî, pp. 6, 10, 27–28, 33; ʿAlî al-Qârî, no. 19.

This Saying also occurs as one segment of a longer, composite Saying (other than Saying 12): see Saying 51.

SAYING 12b: *anâ ʿind ẓann ʿabdî bî*

... إنّ رسول الله صلعم قال قال الله أنا عند ظنّ عبدى بى .

... the Apostle of God said: "God said: 'I fulfill My servant's expectation of Me'."[12]

i. Bukhârî 97:35:14, *isnâd* 5 (Abû Hurayrah).
ii. Hammâm b. Munabbih, no. 65, *isnâd* 1 (directly from Abû Hurayrah).
iii. *Musnad*, II, 516, *isnâd* 3 (Abû Hurayrah): adds at end: *wa-anâ maʿahu ḥaythu yadhkurunî* (cf. Saying 12).
iv. *Musnad*, II, 517, *isnâd* 3: same as version iii.
v. Muslim 48:19, *isnâd* 27 (Abû Hurayrah): adds at end, *wa-anâ maʿahu idhâ daʿânî*, "and I am with him when he entreats Me".
vi. Tirmidhî 34:50, *isnâd* 27: same as version v.
Other References: Ibn al-ʿArabî, *Mishkât*, p. 10; al-Madanî, pp. 10, 17, 29, 72; *Jawâhir*, pp. 359, 363; *Mabânî*, p. 89 (This version, like one of the four citations on p. 10 of al-Madanî, adds: *fa-l-yaẓanna bî mâ shâʾa*, "let him think what he will about Me". This variation does not seem to be attested to in the standard Ḥadîth sources).

SAYING 12c: *anâ maʿ ʿabdî ḥaythumâ dhakaranî*

... عن النبىّ صلعم قال الله تعالى أنا مع عبدى حيث ما ذكرنى وتحرّكت بى شفتاه .

... from the Prophet: "God said: 'I am with My servant whenever he remembers Me and his lips move [in mention of Me]'."[13]

i. Bukhârî 97:43 (in the Introduction to *Bâb* 43), *isnâd* directly from Abû Hurayrah and therefore *maqtûʿ*, wanting in intermediate authorities (this is presumably the reason for its being mentioned only in the section heading by Bukhârî, and not in the body of the section with the "sound" ḥadîths there).
ii. *Musnad*, II, 540, *isnâd* 38 (Abû Hurayrah).
iii. Ibn Mâjah 33:53:3, *isnâd* 38.
Other References: Ibn al-ʿArabî, *Mishkât*, p. 9; ʿAlî al-Qârî, no. 37; al-Madanî, pp. 19, 21, 71, 74; Ghazzâlî, I, 294; cf. *Jawâhir*, p. 362.

Saying 13: *anâ al-malik ayn mulûk al-arḍ*

...عن النبيّ قال يقبض اللّه الأرض يوم القيامة ويطوى السماء بيمينه ثمّ يقول
أنا الملك أين ملوك الأرض .

... from the Prophet. He said: "God will take hold of the earth on the Day of Resurrection and roll up the sky in His right hand.[14] Then He will say: 'I am the King! Where are the kings of the earth?'"

i. Bukhârî 97:6, *isnâd* 2 (Abû Hurayrah).
ii. Muslim 50:23, *isnâd* 2.
iii. Ibn Mâjah, *Muqaddimah*, 13:16, *isnâd* 2.
iv. *Musnad*, II, 374, *isnâd* 2.
v. Bukhârî 81:44:1, *isnâd* 2: *yawm al-qiyâmah* omitted.
vi. Bukhârî 97:19:3, *isnâds* 6 (Abû Hurayrah), 173 (ʿUbaydallâh from Nâfiʿ from ʿAl. b. ʿUmar), 174 (ʿUmar b. Ḥamzah from Sâlim b. ʿAl. from ʿAl. b. ʿUmar): omits *ayn mulûk al-arḍ*.
vii. Bukhârî, *Tafsîr*, S. 39:67, *isnâd* 6: omits *yawm al-qiyâmah*.
viii. Muslim 50:24, *isnâd* 174 (ʿAl. b. ʿUmar): substantial variations: God's words are: "I am the King! Where are the arrogant in power (*ayn al-jabbârûn*)? Where are the prideful (*ayn al-mutakabbirûn*)?" Cf. Saying 13a:iii.

Saying 13a: *anâ al-jabbâr anâ al-mutakabbir anâ al-malik*

...إنّ رسول اللّه صلعم قرأ هذه الآية ذات يوم على المنبر " وما قدروا
اللّه حقّ قدره والأرض جميعا قبضته يوم القيامة والسّموات مطويّات بيمينه سبحانه
وتعالى عمّا يشركون" ورسول اللّه صلعم يقول هكذا بيده ويحرّكها يقبل بها
ويدبر يمجّد الربّ نفسه أنا الجبّار أنا المتكبّر أنا الملك أنا العزيز أنا الكريم
فرجف برسول اللّه صلعم المنبر حتّى قلنا ليخرّنّ به .

... the Apostle of God recited this *âyah* one day from the pulpit:[15] "And they have not estimated God properly. The earth will be [held] entirely in His grasp on the Day of Resurrection, and the heavens will be rolled up in His right hand. Glory be to Him! He transcends that which they associate [with Him]!"[16] The Apostle of God, [gesturing] thus with his hand, moving it forward and then back, said: "The Lord glorifies Himself: 'I am the

All-Powerful, I am the Self-Magnifying, I am the King, I am the Mighty, I am the Beneficient'."[17] And the pulpit shook with the Apostle of God so that we said, "It will surely fall with him!"

i. *Musnad*, II, 72, *isnâd* 170 (ʿAl. b. ʿUmar).
ii. *Musnad*, II, 88, *isnâd* 170: *anâ al-mutaʿâlî*, "I am the Transcendent", replaces *anâ al-ʿazîz anâ al-karîm*.
iii. Ibn Mâjah 37:33:4, *isnâd* 170a (ʿAl. b. ʿUmar): the Divine Saying proper reads: *anâ al-jabbâr anâ al-malik ayn al-jabbârûn ayn al-mutakabbirûn*, "I am the All-Powerful, I am the King! Where are those who are arrogant in their power, where are the prideful?" Cf. Saying 13:viii.
iv. Muslim 50:25, *isnâd* 170a: the Divine Saying proper reads: *anâ Allâh anâ al-malik*, "I am God, I am the King".
Other References: al-Madanî, p. 64.

SAYING 13b: *anâ al-malik*

... جاء حبر الى رسول اللّه صلعم فقال يا محمّد إنّ اللّه يضع السماء على إصبع والأرض على إصبع والجبال على إصبع والشجر والأنهار على إصبع وسائر الخلق على إصبع ثمّ يقول بيده أنا الملك فضحك رسول اللّه صلعم وقال "ما قدروا اللّه حقّ قدره".

... a Jewish man of learning[18] came to the Apostle of God and said: "O Muḥammad, God puts the sky upon a finger, the earth upon a finger, the mountains upon a finger, the trees and rivers upon a finger, and the rest of creation upon a finger. Then He says with [a gesture of] His hand, 'I am the King!'" Thereupon the Apostle of God laughed and said [quoting S. 39:67], "'And they have not estimated God properly....'"

i. Bukhârî 97:26, *isnâd* 190 (ʿAl. b. Masʿûd).
ii. Muslim 50:21, *isnâd* 190: *anâ al-malik* is repeated once.
iii. Bukhârî 97:19:4, *isnâd* 191 (ʿAl. b. Masʿûd).
iv. Bukhârî 97:36:5, *isnâd* 191: same as version ii.
v. Muslim 50:19, *isnâd* 191: same as version ii.
vi. *Musnad*, I, 429, *isnâd* 191.
vii. *Musnad*, I, 457, *isnâd* 191.

The remainder of the Qurʿânic verse at the end of this Saying must be supplied (for which, see Saying 13a) in order to understand Muḥammad's response. His citation of this verse indicates that he is confirming the correctness of what the Jewish scholar has quoted as a word of God rather than denying that it is accurate. A variant reading in version iv substantiates this interpretation: it describes Muḥammad as responding to the Jew's words by "laughing until his side teeth showed, being astonished at and confirming the truth of his [the Jew's] statement" (*yaḍḥaku ḥattá badat nawâjidhuhu taʿajjuban wa-taṣdîqan li-qawlihi*). This and the association of S. 39:67 with the *anâ al-malik* statement in Divine Sayings 13 and 13a indicate that this word of God, even though it is quoted by a non-Muslim, is meant to be understood as an authentic Divine Saying.

SAYING 13c: *anâ al-malik ad-dayyân*

... سمعت النبىّ صلعم يقول يحشر اللّه العباد فيناديهم بصوت يسمعه من بعد كما يسمع من قرب أنا الملك الديّان .

... I heard the Prophet say: "God will collect the worshippers [on the Last Day], and then He will call to them in a voice that those who are far away will hear just [as clearly] as those who are close at hand: 'I am the King, the Requiter!'"[19]

i. Bukhârî 97:32, *isnâd* 200 (directly from Jâbir b. ʿAl. from ʿAl. b. Unays, and therefore a deficient *isnâd*, wanting in intermediate authorities [*maqtûʿ*]. In this instance, as in Saying 12c:i, Bukhârî places the Saying not among the ḥadîths in the body of the chapter, but in his own introductory remarks to the chapter, apparently because he has no proper *isnâd* for it).

ii. *Musnad*, 495, *isnâd* 200 (ʿAl. b. Unays).

SAYING 14: *ạnâ rabbukum*

... فقال رسول اللّه ... يجمع اللّه الناس يوم القيامة فيقول من كان يعبد شيئا فليتّبعه فيتّبع من كان يعبد الشمس الشمس ويتّبع من كان يعبد القمر القمر ويتّبع من كان يعبد الطواغيت الطواغيت وتبقى هذه الأمّة فيها منافقوها فيأتيهم اللّه تبارك وتعالى فى صورة غير صورته الّتى يعرفون فيقول أنا ربّكم فيقولون نعوذ باللّه منك هذا مكاننا حتّى يأتينا ربّنا فإذا جاء

ربّنا عرفناه فيأتيهم الله تعالى فى صورته الّتى يعرفون فيقول أنا ربّكم فيقولون أنت ربّنا فيتّبعونه ويضرب الصراط بين ظهرى جهنّم فأكون أنا وأمّتى أوّل من يجيز ....

... the Apostle of God said: "... God gathers the people together on the Day of Resurrection and then says: 'He who used to serve and worship something, let him now follow it'. Thereupon, he who used to serve and worship the sun follows the sun; he who used to serve and worship the moon follows the moon; and he who used to serve and worship the idols follows the idols. In this community there are still hypocrites. God comes to them in a form other than His form that they know. Then He says: 'I am your Lord'. Then they say: 'We take refuge in God from Thee! This is our place until our Lord comes to us! If our Lord were to come, we would know Him.' So God comes to them in His form that they know. Then He says: 'I am your Lord'. Thereupon they follow Him, and He sets up the bridge between the two halves of Hell. Then I and my community shall be the first to cross over...."

i. Muslim 1:299, *isnâd* 41 (Abû Hurayrah): the text quoted is a segment of a much longer ḥadîth that deals with the Prophet's answer to questions about "seeing God" in the next world and other aspects of the Day of Resurrection.
ii. Bukhârî 81:52, *isnâd* 41: set in same longer ḥadîth as version i.
iii. Bukhârî 97:24:4, *isnâd* 41: set in same longer ḥadîth as version i.
Other References: Ibn al-ʿArabî, *Mishkât*, p. 18.

SAYING 15: *anâ ar-raḥmân wa-anâ khalaqtu ar-raḥim*

... أنّه سمع رسول الله صلعم يقول قال الله أنا الرحمٰن وأنا خلقت الرحم شققت لها من اسمى فمن وصلها وصلته ومن قطعها قطعته وثبّته [وبتّته].

... he heard the Apostle of God say: "God said: 'I am the All-Merciful, and I created the tie of (blood) kinship.[20] I have derived its name from My name.[21] Whoever strengthens [lit., makes close] it, him I strengthen; whoever severs it, him I sever and cut off'."[22]

i. Abû al-Yamân, no. 59, *isnâd* 273 (ʿAr. b. ʿAwf).
ii. *Musnad*, I, 191, *isnâd* 274 (ʿAr. b. ʿAwf): *battattuhu*, "him I sever", replaces *qaṭaʿtuhu wa-battattuhu*.

iii. Abû Dâwûd 9:45:6, *isnâds* 273 and 275 (ʿAr. b. ʿAwf): *wa-hiya ar-raḥim*, "it is the tie of kinship", replaces *wa-anâ khalaqtu ar-raḥim; battattuhu* same as version ii.

iv. *Musnad*, II, 498, *isnâd* 6 (Abû Hurayrah): same as version iii.

v. Tirmidhî 25:9:1, *isnâd* 272 (ʿAr. b. ʿAwf): same as version iii; *anâ Allâh wa-*, "I am God, and ..." precedes *anâ ar-raḥmân*.

vi. *Musnad*, I, 194, *isnâd* 273: same as version ii.

Other References: al-Madanî, pp. 7, 9, 35; ʿAlî al-Qârî, no. 20; al-Ḥasan al-ʿAskarî, *Tafsîr*, p. 15.[23]

Raḥim is a feminine noun in Arabic. It is found in the Qur'ân only in the plural, *arḥâm*, but with both of its two possible meanings, *womb* (S. 6:144, 145; 13:8) and *blood-tie* (S. 47:22; 60:3). An argument could be made in the present Saying and subsequent variants, in which the *raḥim* is personified, for using the feminine pronoun instead of the neuter form for it in translation, especially if one wishes to emphasize the connection of the "tie" with Woman (who is herself in a patriarchical society above all the "tie of kinship", since all members of the society are interrelated through her womb alone). Such a usage in the English seems, however, somewhat artificial, especially since the neuter pronoun is the natural form to use for such a personified concept. It is not clear whether the *blood-tie* here refers to only the familial relations or to the common tie of humanity among all men, but the former appears to be more likely. This is borne out by the interpretation of Qâḍî ʿÎyâḍ as quoted in the commentary of ʿAbdalbâqî to Muslim 45:16 (IV, 1981). For a Shîʿî interpretation, see n. 23 above.

SAYING 15a: *man waṣalaki waṣaltuhu wa-man qaṭaʿaki qaṭaʿtuhu*

... عن النبىّ صلعم قال إنّ الرحم شجنة من الرحمٰن فقال اللّه لها من وصلك وصلته ومن قطعك قطعته .

... from the Prophet. He said: "The tie of (blood) kinship is derived from the All-Merciful [as a branch from a tree]. God said of it: 'Whoever strengthens [lit., makes close] you, him shall I strengthen; and whoever severs you, him shall I sever'."

i. Bukhârî 78:13:2, *isnâd* 3d (Abû Hurayrah).

ii. Bukhârî 78:13:3, *isnâd* 150 (ʿÂ'ishah): omits *qâla Allâh lahâ*, but the final statement is still a first-person word of God.

Other References: al-Madanî, pp. 8, 28, 79.

Concerning the translation of the key words in this Saying, see the notes and commentary to Saying 15.

SAYING 15b: *a-mâ tarḍayna an aṣila man waṣalaki*

. . . عن النبيّ صلعم قال إنّ الله خلق الخلق حتّى إذا فرغ من خلقه قالت الرحم هذا مقام العائذ بك من القطيعة قال نعم أما ترضين أن أصل من وصلك وأقطع من قطعك قالت بلى يا رب قال فهو لك قال رسول الله صلعم فاقرؤا إن شئتم "فهل عسيتم إن تولّيتم أن تفسدوا في الأرض وتقطّعوا أرحامكم".

... from the Prophet. He said: “God created the creatures. Then, when He had completed His creatures, the tie of (blood) kinship said: ‘This is the place of refuge from the severing of kindred ties.’ He [God] said: ‘Yes, are you not happy that I strengthen [lit., make close] whomever strengthens you, and that I sever whomever severs you?’ It [the tie of kinship] said: ‘Certainly, O Lord’. He said: ‘Then it is yours’.” The Apostle [then] said: “So recite, if you wish, ‘Would you, if you turned away, work corruption in the earth and sever your ties of kinship?’ ”[24]

i. Bukhârî 78:13:1, *isnâd* 16a (Abû Hurayrah).
ii. Bukhârî 97:35:11, *isnâd* 16a.
iii. Muslim 45:16, *isnâd* 16a.
iv. *Musnad*, II, 330, *isnâd* 16a.
Other References: Ibn al-ʿArabî, *Mishkât*, p. 36.

SAYING 15c: *a-mâ tarḍayna an aṣila man waṣalaki*

. . . عن النبيّ صلعم أنه قال إنّ الرحم شجنة من الرحمٰن تقول يا ربّ انّي قطعت يا ربّ إنّي ظلمت يا ربّ إنّي أسيئ إليّ يا ربّ يا ربّ فيجيبها ربّها عزّ وجلّ فيقول أما ترضين أن أصل من وصلك وأقطع من قطعك .

... from the Prophet. He said: “The tie of (blood) kinship is derived from the All-Merciful (as a branch from a tree). It [the tie of kinship] says: ‘O Lord, I have been severed! O Lord, I have been wronged! O Lord, evil has been done to me! O Lord ...', and so on. Thereupon, its Lord answers it, saying: 'Are you not happy that I strengthen [lit., make close] whomever strengthens you, and sever whomever severs you?'"[25]

i. *Musnad*, II, 455, *isnâd* 19 (Abû Hurayrah).
ii. *Musnad*, II, 383, *isnâd* 19.
iii. *Musnad*, II, 406, *isnâd* 19.
iv. *Musnad*, II, 295, *isnâd* 19: ends with *yâ rabbi yâ rabbi*, "O my Lord, O my Lord", omitting the words of God: hence an *ḥadîth nabawî*.

SAYING 15d: *irḥamû ahl al-arḍ yarḥamukum ahl as-samâ'*

... يبلغ به النبىّ صلعم قال الراحمون يرحمهم الرحمٰن ارحموا أهل الأرض يرحمكم أهل السماء والرحم شجنة من الرحمٰن من وصلها وصلته ومن قطعها بتّته .

... the Prophet informed him, saying: "As for those who are merciful, God is merciful to them: [He says:] 'Be merciful to the people of the earth, and the people of heaven will be merciful to you. The tie of (blood) kinship is derived from the All-Merciful.[26] Whoever strengthens [lit., makes close] it, him shall I strengthen; whoever severs it, him shall I sever'."

i. *Musnad*, II, 160, *isnâd* 181 ('Al. b. 'Amr).
ii. Tirmidhî 25:16:3, *isnâd* 181: completely in the third person, an *hadîth nabawî*. The parallel versions of this tradition as well as the final sentence in the text indicate that the quoted pronouncement is to be understood as a Divine Saying.

SAYING 16: *anfiq yâ ibn Âdam unfiq 'alayka*

... انّ رسول الله صلعم قال قال الله أنفق يا ابن آدم أنفق عليك .

...the Apostle of God said: "God said: 'Give generously, O son of Adam, [and] I shall give generously to you'."

i. Bukhârî 69:1:2, *isnâd* 5 (Abû Hurayrah).
ii. Bukhârî 97:35:5b, *isnâd* 5: omits *yâ ibn Âdam*.
iii. *Musnad*, II, 464, *isnâd* 5.

iv. Muslim 12:36, *isnâd* 5: following the Divine Saying, Muḥammad adds: *yamîn Allâh malʾá saḥḥâʾ lâ yaghîḍuhâ shayʾ al-layl wa-n-nahâr*, "the right hand of God is full, ever-flowing [with bounty]; nothing diminishes it by day or by night".

v. *Musnad*, II, 242, *isnâd* 5: same as version iv.

vi. Ibn Mâjah 11:15:2, *isnâd* 5: joined to an *ḥadîth nabawî* concerning the vow, or *nadhr* (see Saying 45).

vii. Bukhârî, *Tafsîr*, S. 11:7, *isnâd* 5: similar to version iv, but with an expanded statement of the Prophet at the end. See version ix.

viii. Hammâm b. Munabbih, no. 40, *isnâd* 1 (directly from Abû Hurayrah): adds at end: *wa-sammá al-ḥarb khudʿah*, "and he [Muḥammad] called war 'a deception'". The meaning of this added phrase is not wholly clear. It might represent an admonition to those Arabs who would depend upon the spoils of war gained in their tribal raids for their sustenance, rather than upon God's bounty alone. Cf. S. 8:1: "They ask you about the spoils of war. Say: 'Spoils belong to God and the Apostle. So fear God and set things right among you....'" Note, however, the apparently different intent of the Divine Saying in another context: see Saying 40, where it is integrated into another, longer word of God.

ix. Muslim 12:37, *isnâd* 1 (Abû Hurayrah): similar to version iv; the Prophet's words are slightly expanded and include a paraphrase of the statement in S. 11:7: *wa-kâna arshuhu ʿalá al-mâʾ*, "and His throne was upon the water [at the creation]".

x. *Musnad*, II, 314, *isnâd* 1: same as version viii.

Other References: Ibn al-ʿArabî, *Mishkât*, p. 9; ʿAlî al-Qârî, no. 17; al-Madanî, pp. 5, 19. A similar Divine Saying is quoted by al-Jâḥiẓ, *al-Kitâb al-musammâ bi-l-maḥâsîn wa-l-aḍdâd* (ed. G. Van Vloten, Leiden, E. J. Brill, 1898), p. 168, and al-Bayhaqî, *al-Maḥâsîn wa-l-masâwî* (ed. F. Schwally, Giessen, 1902), p. 310, although in a slightly different form: *yâ ibn Âdam aḥdith lî safar uḥdith laka rizq*, "O son of Âdam, make a journey to Me, and I shall make sustenance for you". This version is evidently not found in the standard Ḥadîth collections (see Nöldeke-Schwally, I, 258).

The form of address used here, *yâ ibn Âdam*, "O son of Adam", is one that occurs often in the Ḥadîth. As a form of address for man in general, it is especially evident as an introductory formula in Divine Sayings (see Appendix C, s.v.). The exact provenance and relation of this formula to similar forms of address in other Near Eastern literatures has yet to be studied. For a brief consideration, see Nöldeke-Schwally, I, 242, n. 1.

The Qurʾânic text that bears the greatest similarity in content to this Saying is S. 92:18–21: "Whoever gives his wealth to purify himself, and does not do a favor for someone for its [own] reward, but seeking only the face of his Lord, the Transcendent – he will surely be satisfied [with his reward]."

SAYING 17: *anti raḥmatî arḥamu biki man ashâ'u min ʿibâdî*

. . . وقال رسول اللّه صلعم تحاجّت الجنّة والنار فقالت النار أوثرت بالمتكبّرين والمتجبّرين وقالت الجنّة فمالى لا يدخلنى إلّا ضعفاء الناس وسقطهم وغرّتهم فقال اللّه للجنّة إنّما أنت رحمتى أرحم بك من أشاء من عبادى وقال للنار إنّما أنت عذابى أعذّب بك من أشاء من عبادى ولكل واحدة منكما ملؤها فأما النار فلا تمتلئ حتّى يضع اللّه تعالى فيها رجله فتقول قطّ قطّ فهنالك تمتلئ ويزوى بعضها إلى بعض ولا يظلم اللّه من خلقه أحدا وأما الجنّة فإنّ اللّه عزّ وجلّ ينشئ لها خلقا .

The Apostle of God said: "Paradise and the Fire were arguing with each other, and the Fire said: 'I have been honored with the proud and the haughty'. Paradise said: 'And what falls to me except the weakest and the lowly and the naïve?' Thereupon God said to Paradise: 'Truly, you are My mercy. Through you I show mercy to whomever of My servants I will.' And He said to the Fire: 'You are My punishment. Through you I punish whomever of My servants I will. And each of you will have its fill.' [But] as for the Fire, it will not be filled up until God puts His foot into it; then [the Fire] will say: 'Enough! Enough!' At that point it will be filled, and one corner will close in upon the other.[27] God does not wrong any one of His creatures. And as for Paradise, God will produce creatures for it."

i. Hammâm b. Munabbih, no. 51, *isnâd* 1 (directly from Abû Hurayrah).

ii. Bukhârî, *Tafsîr*, S. 50:30, *isnâd* 1 (Abû Hurayrah): S. 50:30 reads: *yawma naqûlu li-jahannam hal imtala'tu wa-taqûlu hal min mazîd*, "[this happens] on a day when We shall say to Hell: 'Are you filled?' And it will say: 'Are there still more [for me]?'"

iii. Ibrâhîm b. Ṭahmân, no. 109 (fol. 247b), *isnâd* 8 (directly from Hishâm b. Ḥassân from Muḥ. b. Sîrîn from Abû Hurayrah): only the initial statements of Paradise and the Fire are given, followed by "al-ḥadîth" (= *et cetera*, indicating that the rest of the Saying is well-enough known not to need repeating in its entirety).

iv. Bukhârî 97:25:3, *isnâd* 5b (Abû Hurayrah): variant wording and some rearrangement of the segments.

v. Muslim 51:34, *isnâd* 5 (Abû Hurayrah): ends with *wa-li-kull wâḥidah minkumâ mil'uhâ.*

vi. Muslim 51:35, *isnâds* 5 and 8c (Abû Hurayrah): ends with *yuzwá baʿḍuhâ ilá baʿḍ.*

vii. Muslim 51:36a, *isnâd* 1.

viii. Muslim 51:36b, *isnâd* 120 (Abû Saʿîd al-Khudrî): ends with *li-kull waḥidah minkumâ milʾuhâ*, same as version v.

ix. *Musnad*, II, 314, *isnâd* 1.

x. *Musnad*, II, 450, *isnâd* 6a (Abû Hurayrah): ends with God's words to Paradise and the Fire.

xi. *Musnad*, II, 507, *isnâd* 8: essentially the same as version iv.

xii. *Musnad*, II, 276, *isnâd* 8c: essentially the same as version iv.

xiii. *Musnad*, III, 13, *isnâd* 127 (Abû Saʿîd al-Khudrî): variant version, same story.

xiv. *Musnad*, III, 78, *isnâd* 127: variant version, same story.

xv. *Musnad*, III, 79, *isnâd* 120: same as version viii.

Other References: al-Madanî, p. 47.

SAYING 18: *aṣbaḥa min ʿibâdî muʾmin bî wa-kâfir bî*

... صلّى لنا رسول اللّه صلعم صلاة الصبح بالحديبية على إثر السماء كانت من اللّيل فلمّا انصرف أقبل على الناس فقال أتدرون ماذا قال ربّكم قالوا اللّه ورسوله أعلم قال قال أصبح من عبادى مؤمن بى وكافر بى فأمّا من قال مطرنا بفضل اللّه ورحمته فذلك مؤمن بى كافر بالكوكب وأما من قال مطرنا بنوء كذا وكذا فذلك كافر بى مؤمن بالكوكب .

... the Apostle of God led us in the early morning prayer at Ḥudaybîyah after the rain, when it was still dark.[28] When he turned around [at the end of the Prayer], he approached the people and said, "Do you know what your Lord said?" They said: "God and His Apostle know best." He said: "[God] said: 'There will arise among My servants some [lit., one] who have faith in Me and some who refuse to be faithful to Me. As for the one who says, "It rains upon us through God's bounty and His mercy", that is one who has faith in Me and rejects Venus. As for the one who says, "It rains upon us through such and such a setting star", that is one who rejects Me and has faith in Venus'."[29]

i. *Muwaṭṭa'* 13:4, *isnâd* 230 (Zayd b. Khâlid).
ii. Muslim 1:125, *isnâd* 230.
iii. Abû Dâwûd 27:22, *isnâd* 230.
iv. Bukhârî 64:35:1, *isnâd* 230: minor variants in the frame-story and the wording of the Divine Saying: e.g., *najm* replaces *naw'* (meaning: *star*).
v. Bukhârî 97:35:12, *isnâd* 230: shorter version: the entire ḥadîth reads: *muṭira an-nabî ṣlʿm fa-qâla qâla Allâh aṣbaḥa min ʿibâdî kâfir bî wa-mu'min bî*, "It rained on the Prophet, and he said: 'God said: "There will arise among My servants some [lit., one] who are ungrateful to and reject Me and some who have faith in Me".'"
vi. Bukhârî 10:156:2, *isnâd* 230: minor wording variants; *qâla Allâh* is omitted, but the Saying is clearly a word of God.
vii. Muslim 1:26, *isnâd* 20 (Abû Hurayrah): no frame-story at all; the entire ḥadîth reads: *qâla rasûl Allâh ṣlʿm a-lam taraw ilá mâ qâla rabbukum qâla mâ anʿamtu ʿalá ʿibâdî min niʿmah illâ aṣbaḥa farîq minhum bihâ kâfirûn yaqûlûna al-kawâkib wa-bi-l-kawâkib*, "The Apostle of God said: 'Have you not noticed what your Lord said? He said: "I have not bestowed any favor upon My servants without a group of them coming to reject it, saying, 'the stars' and 'through the stars'".'"
Other References: Ibn al-ʿArabî, *Mishkât*, pp. 19–20; *Jawâhir*, p. 170.

The idea of rain as a testimony to the bounty of God and His power is attested to in the Qur'ân, where natural phenomena generally are spoken of as the "signs" (*âyât*) of God (cf. 2:22, 159; 6:95–99; 41:37; 42:29, 33; 50:6). The stress upon God as rain-giver plays a prominent rôle here: "And among His signs is [this], that you see the earth brought low; then when We send water down upon it, it comes to life and grows. He who revives it can also revive the dead. Verily, He has power over all things" (41:39).

SAYING 19: *ayn al-mutaḥâbbûn li-jalâlî*

. . . قال رسول اللّه صلعم : إنّ اللّه تبارك وتعالى يقول يوم القيامة
أين المتحابّون لجلالى اليوم أظلّهم في ظلّي يوم لا ظلّ إلّا ظلّي .

... the Apostle of God said: "God will say on the Day of Resurrection: 'Where are those who have loved one another for [the sake of] My majesty?[30] Today I shall shade them in My shade,[31] a day in which there is no shade but My shade'."

i. Muslim 45:37, *isnâd* 16 (Abû Hurayrah).

ii. Ibrâhîm b. Ṭahmân, no. 80, *isnâd* 34c (directly from Mâlik from Saʿîd al-Maqbarî from Abû Hurayrah).

iii. *Muwaṭṭa'* 51:13, *isnâd* 16: *bi-jalâlî* replaces *li-jalâlî.*

iv. *Musnad,* II, 237, *isnâd* 16.

v. *Musnad,* II, 338, *isnâd* 16

vi. *Musnad,* II, 370, *isnâd* 16.

vii. *Musnad,* II, 523, *isnâd* 16.

viii. *Musnad,* II, 535, *isnâd* 16.

ix. *Dârimî* 20:44, *isnâd* 16.

Other References: Ibn al-ʿArabî, *Mishkât*, p. 10; al-Madanî, pp. 8, 9, 11, 13, 14, 37, 38, 71, 74; ʿAlî al-Qârî, no. 40.

SAYING 19a: *wajabat maḥabbatî li-l-mutaḥâbbîn fîya*

... فإنّى سمعت رسول الله صلعم يقول قال الله تبارك وتعالى وجبت محبتى للمتحابّين فىّ والمتجالسين فىّ والمتزاورين فىّ والمتباذلين فىّ .

... I heard the Apostle of God say: "God said: 'My love belongs by right to those who love one another in Me, to those who sit together (in fellowship) in Me, to those who visit one another in Me, and to those who give generously to one another in Me'."

i. *Muwaṭṭa'* 51:16, *isnâd* 220 (Muʿadh b. Jabal): the Divine Saying is set within a long frame-story in which Abû Idrîs, the second transmitter, tells how, when visiting the mosque in Damascus, he encounters the young Muʿadh b. Jabal, who is already known for his piety and learning. Muʿadh tells him that he loves him "for God's sake" (*li-llâh*) and then explains this usage by quoting the Divine Saying.

ii. Ibn Saʿd, III, ii, 123, *isnâd* 220: *raḥmatî*, "My mercy", replaces *maḥabbatî.*

iii. *Musnad,* V, 233, *isnâd* 220.

iv. *Musnad,* V, 247, *isnâd* 220c (Muʿadh b. Jabal): the Divine Saying stands alone, without any frame-story; *al-mutazâwirûn* is omitted.

v. *Musnad,* V, 237, *isnâd* 211 (ʿUbâdah b. aṣ-Ṣâmit): set within the same basic frame-story as version i, but related by ʿUbâdah to Abû Idrîs at the mosque *after* the latter has heard a *different* Divine Saying (no. 19b) from Muʿadh in the mosque; *wajabat maḥabbatî* is replaced by *ḥaqqat mahabbatî*, "My love has been assured ...", which is repeated before each of the groups of people named; *al-mutajâlisûn* is omitted; after quoting the Divine Saying, ʿUbâdah then repeats the same Saying that Muʿadh has already related to Abû Idrîs (i.e., Saying 19b).

vi. *Musnad,* V, 239, *isnâd* 211: same basic frame-story as version v, although it is set in the mosque at Ḥims (Homs) rather than Damascus; *ḥaqqat* replaces *wajabat,* as in version v; *al-mutawâṣilûn,* "those who join together", replaces *al-mutajâlisûn.*

vii. *Musnad,* V, 328, *isnâd* 211*a* (ʿUbâdah b. aṣ-Ṣâmit): same as version vi.

Other References: Ibn al-ʿArabî, *Mishkât,* p. 37; ʿAlî al-Qârî, no. 25; *Jawâhir,* pp. 166, 191; Ghazzâlî, I, 313.

The use of *fî Allâh* (or, here, *fîya*) and similar phrases such as *li-llâh, li-jalâl Allâh, bi-jalâl Allâh* (cf. Sayings 19, 19b, 54, 65, 66) deserves some comment. Their use in Muslim sources has been noted by Goldziher (*M. Studien,* II, 392–393), who points out that classical Muslim commentators usually gloss the usage with *fî sabîl Allâh,* "in the cause [lit., way] of God", and notes that the origin of the phrases is to be found in New Testament usage. Cf. Nöldeke's comment on this: "Das ist eine spezifisch-christliche, schon im Neuen Testament überaus häufige Ausdrucksweise, die sich aber in der muhammedanischen Literatur ganz eingebürgert hat" (Nöldeke-Schwally, I, 257). The latter goes on to say that such usages are strange to the Qurʾân and to maintain that the phrases, *jâhadû fî Allâh* (S. 22:78) and *jâhadû fînâ* (S. 29:69), are to be glossed with *fî sabîl* for *fî* (*ibid.,* I, 257–258), as Goldziher had already suggested. This does not, however, seem to be an entirely satisfactory explanation even for the Qurʾânic "striving in God" (*jihâd fî Allâh*), and it is even less so for the "loving one another in God", "visiting one another in God", and the like in the present Saying. There appears rather to be a conscious effort here to express something more subtle – one might even say, more mystical – than "in the cause of God". And if the phrase did have Christian antecedents, this interpretation would be all the more reasonable. The phrases *bi-jalâl Allâh* and *li-jalâl Allâh* indicate an action done "for the sake of" or "because of" God, which is indicative of a more personal relationship between the servant and his Lord than the *fî sabîl* gloss expresses; however, it is the simple *fî Allâh* or *bi-llâh* (*fîya* or *bî* in the Divine Saying here) that points towards the "participation in God" that later receives so much development and elaboration at the hands of the mystics concerned with the *fanâʾ* ("extinction", "dissolving") and *baqâʾ* ("abiding") "in God", and even the identification of the creature with the Divine (as in the thought of Ibn al-ʿArabî). In these Sayings, there is no apparent intention of suggesting elaborate doctrines of mystic union with the Divine; yet they do convey a sense of the possibility of life "for", "in", "out of", and "with" God. This sense of participation in and sustenance from the Divine is in fact very close to the New Testament sense of being "in Jesus Christ" (ἐν Χριστῷ, ἐν Χριστῷ Ἰησοῦ, ἐν κυριῳ) as found especially in Pauline usage (Rom. 6:11, 23; 8:39; I Cor. 1:4; II Cor. 3:14; Gal. 2:4; 3:14, 26, 28, *inter alia*) and in the Gospel of John (14:20; 15:4–10). Still closer a New Testament parallel is the concept of being "in God" (ἐν τῷ θεῷ, ἐν τῷ πατρί) as found in the first of the Johannine epistles (I Jn. 3:24; 4:13–16). The entire question of the Arabic usage, its non-Arabic analogues and antecedents, and the meaning or meanings read out of it in Qur'ânic and later writings deserves a systematic study.

SAYING 19b: *al-mutaḥâbbûn fî Allâh ʿalá manâbir min nûr*

... سمعت رسول الله صلعم يحكى عن ربّه يقول المتحابّون فى الله على منابر من نور فى ظلّ العرش يوم لا ظلّ إلّا ظلّه .

... I heard the Apostle of God say, relating from his Lord: "'Those who love one another in God shall be upon platforms of light in the shadow of the Throne on a day in which there will be no shade except His [its[32]] shade.'"

i. *Musnad*, V, 236–237, *isnâd* 220a (Muʿadh b. Jabal): set in same frame-story as Saying 19a:v; after Muʿadh tells this Saying to Abû Idrîs, ʿUbâdah also relates it to him as an addition to another Divine Saying (19a:v [*isnâd* 211]).

ii. *Musnad*, V, 239, *isnâd* 220a: set in the same frame-story as Saying 19a:vi; the text of the Saying is: *al-mutaḥâbbûn fî jalâlî lahum manâbir min nûr yaghbituhum an-nabîyûn wa-sh-shuhadâ'*, "Those who love one another in My majesty have [places upon] platforms of light; the prophets and the martyrs delight in them".

iii. Tirmidhî 34:53:1, *isnâd* 220a: no frame-story; text as version ii.

iv. *Musnad*, V, 328, *isnâd* 220b (Muʿadh b. Jabal): set in the same frame-story as Saying 19a:vii; *bi-jalâl Allâh*, "in God's majesty", replaces *fî Allâh*; the saying is cited as an *ḥadîth nabawî*, not a Divine Saying.

Other References: Ibn al-ʿArabî, *Mishkât*, p. 22; al-Madanî, p. 8; ʿAlî al-Qârî, no. 23.

The "platforms of light" (*manâbir min nûr*) spoken of in the text are evidently positions of special honor in Paradise, perhaps those raised up closer to God (perhaps with the Qur'ânic image of the *aʿrâf* of S. 7:46 in mind?). There may be also a reference to the elevated or special rôle that the loving faithful will have (after the angels and prophets) as intercessors before God on behalf of their sinner brethren on the Day of Resurrection (cf. Saying 62).

The singular of *manâbir* is *minbar*, which is the standard word for the "pulpit" or raised platform from which the sermon, or *khuṭbah*, is given in the mosque. It is said to have been introduced in the time of the Prophet himself so that the people could still hear his words even after the Community in Medina had grown quite large. As an institution in the Islamic cultus, the use of the *minbar* by the Prophet appears to have carried associations from the ancient Near Eastern practice of seating the judge or ruler upon an elevated platform as a sign of his office. Thus the word "pulpit" is ordinarily not an entirely accurate rendering of the Arabic original, even though the *minbar* has come to serve the same function as the pulpit. On the subject, see the important study of C. H. Becker, "Die Kanzel im Kultus des alten Islam", *Orientalische Studien Theodor Nöldeke zum siebzigsten Geburtstag* (Giessen, 1906), I, 331–351, and the resumé of work on the subject by J. Pedersen in Section D:2:d of his article, "Masdjid", *SEI*, pp. 343–345. Cf. also Widengren, *Muḥammad the Apostle*, pp. 154–161.

The plural form, *manâbir*, is also found in other traditions about Paradise with the same apparently special sense; e.g., Ibn Mâjah 37:39:9: *manâbir min nûr*, *min lu'lu'* (pearl), *min yâqût* (sapphire), *min zabarjad* (topaz or light-colored emerald), *min dhabab* (gold), etc. For other occurrences, see *Concordance*, VI, 353a.

Saying 20: *bi-ʿizzatî la-anṣurannaka wa-law baʿd ḥîn*

... قال رسول الله صلعم ثلاثة لا يردّ دعاؤهم الإمام العادل والصائم حتّى يفطر ودعوة المظلوم يرفعها الله فوق الغمام يوم القيامة ويفتح لها أبواب السماء ويقول الربّ عزّ وجلّ بعزّتي لأنصرنّك ولو بعد حين .

... the Apostle of God said: "There are three persons whose prayers are not turned away: the just *imâm* [religious leader], the one who fasts – until he breaks the fast, and the person who has been wronged, whose prayer God raises above the clouds on the Day of Resurrection, when He will open[33] the gates of Heaven for him. The Lord says: 'By My glory, I shall aid you, even if at a later time'."

i. *Musnad*, II, 445, *isnâd* 32 (Abû Hurayrah).
ii. *Musnad*, II, 304–305, *isnâd* 32: minor variations in wording.

iii. Ibn Mâjah 7:48:1, *isnâd* 32: *tuftaḥu* for *yuftaḥu* (see n. 33).
iv. Tirmidhî 36:2, *isnâd* 33 (Abû Hurayrah): same as version iii.

SAYING 21: *bi-ʿizzatî wa-jalâlî lâ abraḥu aghfiru lahum*

... سمعت رسول اللّه صلعم يقول إنّ ابليس قال لربّه عزّ وجلّ وعزّتك
وجلالك لا أبرح أغوى بنى آدم ما دامت الأرواح فيهم فقال له ربّه عزّ وجلّ
فبعزّتى وجلالى لا أبرح أغفر لهم ما استغفرونى .

... I heard the Apostle of God say: "Iblîs[34] said to his Lord: 'By Thy glory and majesty, I shall continue to seduce the sons of Adam so long as their souls remain in them!' Then his Lord said to him: 'Then by My glory and majesty, I shall continue to forgive them as long as they seek My forgiveness!'"

i. *Musnad*, III, 41, *isnâd* 124 (Abû Saʿîd al-Khudrî).
ii. *Musnad*, III, 29, *isnâd* 126a (Abû Saʿîd al-Khudrî).
Other References: al-Madanî, pp. 25, 79.

SAYING 22: *faraḍtu ʿalá ummatika khams ṣalawât*

... قال رسول اللّه صلعم قال اللّه تعالى إنّى فرضت على أمّتك خمس
صلوات وعهدت عندى عهدا أنّه من جاء يحافظ عليهنّ لوقتهنّ أدخلته الجنّة
ومن لم يحافظ عليهنّ فلا عهد له عندى .

... the Apostle of God said: "God said: 'I have established five Prayers as a duty for your [Muḥammad's] community, and I have pledged Myself to [this], that whoever tries to observe them at their proper times, him shall I cause to enter Paradise. And whoever does not observe them has no pledge from Me.'"

i. Abû Dâwûd 2:9:6, *isnâd* 410 (Abû Qatâdah b. Ribʿî).
ii. Ibn Mâjah 5:194:5, *isnâd* 410.
iii. Abû Dâwûd 2:9:1, *isnâd* 213 (ʿUbâdah b. aṣ-Ṣâmit): the same basic idea is

expressed in the third person as an *ḥadîth nabawî*; additional mention of the prescribed ablutions, prostrations, and the proper state of humility in the Prayer is included in the condition set forth by God for His "pledge".

iv. Ibn Mâjah 5:194:3, *isnâd* 212 (ʿUbâdah b. aṣ-Ṣâmit): essentially the same content as versions i and ii, but in the third person as an *ḥadîth nabawî*.

Other References: ʿAlî al-Qârî, no. 27; al-Madanî, pp. 8, 43.

SAYING 23: *ghafartu lahum mâ khalâ aẓ-ẓâlim*

... انّ النبىّ صلعم دعا لأمّته عشيّة عرفة بالمغفرة فأجيب انّى قد غفرت
لهم ما خلا الظالم فانّى آخذ للمظلوم منه قال أى ربّ ان شئت أعطيت
المظلوم من الجنّة وغفرت للظالم فلم يجب عشيّته فلمّا أصبح بالمزدلفة أعاد
الدعاء فاجيب الى ما سأل قال فضحك رسول اللّه صلعم أو قال تبسّم فقال
له أبو بكر وعمر بأبى أنت وأمّى انّ هذه لساعة ما كنت تضحك فيها فما الّذى
أضحكك أضحك اللّه سنّك قال انّ عدوّ اللّه ابليس لمّا علم أنّ اللّه عزّ وجلّ
قد استجاب دعائى وغفر لأمّتى أخذ التراب فجعل يحثوه على رأسه ويدعو
بالويل والثبور فأضحكنى ما رأيت من جزعه .

... the Prophet prayed for forgiveness for his community on the evening of ʿArafah, and he was answered: "I have forgiven them, except the evildoer, and I shall exact from him for the one whom he has wronged."[35] He [Muḥammad] said: "O my Lord, if You wished, You could give the one who has been wronged [a share in] Paradise and forgive the evil-doer." He was not answered that evening; then, when it was morning at Muzdalifah, he repeated the entreaty and was granted what he asked. Thereupon the Apostle of God laughed – or [in another version] smiled, and Abû Bakr and ʿUmar said to him: "May my father and mother be ransomed for you![36] Truly, this was [always] an-hour in which you were not wont to laugh! What is it that makes you laugh? May God [continue to] make you laugh!" He said: "When the enemy of God, Iblîs [Satan], learned that God had answered my prayer and forgiven my community, he took dust and began to pour it over his head, crying out in lamentation and woe. And what I saw of his anguish made me laugh."

i. Ibn Mâjah 25:56:1, *isnâd* 330 (ʿAbbâs b. Mirdâs).
ii. *Musnad*, IV, 14, *isnâd* 330.

The frame-story in which the Divine Saying here occurs is set during the Ḥajj, or Pilgrimage ritual, and probably during the last or "Farewell" Pilgrimage of Muḥammad. God's quoted words are given on the 9th Dhû al-Ḥijjah, the "Day of ʿArafah [or: ʿArafât], during which the Pilgrims halt on the plain by the sacred hill at ʿArafah. Two afternoon *khuṭbahs* [see commentary to Saying 40] are delivered at the hill, and at sunset the pilgrims run to nearby Muzdalifah, where the 10th of the month begins at sunset.

Muzdalifah, the scene of the sunset and evening Prayers after ʿArafah, lies on the Meccan side of ʿArafah. Here, after the evening Prayer, the pilgrims spend the night and arise to perform an early Prayer that is followed by a *khuṭbah*, after which they set out for Mînâ for the ritual of stoning the evil satans. See A. J. Wensinck, "Ḥadjdj", *EI*², III, 31–37.

SAYING 24: *hal ʿamilta khayr qaṭṭu*

... عن رسول الله صلعم قال إنّ رجلا لم يعمل خيرا قطّ وكان يداين
الناس فيقول لرسوله خذ ما تيسّر واترك ما عسر تجاوز لعلّ الله تعالى أن
يتجاوز عنّا ولمّا هلك قال الله عزّ وجلّ له هل عملت خيرا قطّ قال لا إلاّ أنه
كان لى غلام وكنت أداين الناس فإذا بعثته ليتقاضى قلت له خذ ما تيسّر
واترك ما عسر وتجاوز لعلّ الله يتجاوز عنّا قال الله تعالى قد تجاوزت عنك .

... from the Prophet. He said: "A man who has never done any good and who used to loan money to people says to his messenger, 'Take what is easy [to collect] and leave what is hard. Pass over [the latter]; perhaps God will pass us over without punishment.' Then when he perishes, God will say: 'Have you ever done any good?' He says: 'No, except that I had a servant when I loaned money to people, and when I sent him to claim payment, I told him: "Take what is easy and leave what is hard. Pass over [the latter]; perhaps God will pass us over without punishment".' Then God says: 'I have passed you over without punishment'."

i. Nasâʾî 44:104:1, *isnâd* 3a (Abû Hurayrah).
ii. *Musnad*, II, 361, *isnâd* 3a.

iii. Bukhârî 60:54:17, *isnâd* 20 (Abû Hurayrah): same basic story as versions i, ii, but only as an *ḥadîth nabawî*, without any words of God being quoted. Other instances of the ḥadîth in the same form (all with *isnâd* 20) are: Bukhârî 34:18; Muslim 22:31; Nasâʾî 44:104:2; *Musnad*, II, 263, 332, 339.

Other References: al-Madanî, p. 91.

SAYING 25: *hal lâ namlah wâḥidah*

وقال رسول اللّه صلعم نزل نبىّ من الأنبياء تحت شجرة فلدغته نملة فأمر بجهازه فأخرج من تحتها فأمر بها فأحرقت فى النار فأوحى [اللّه] اليه فهلاّ نملة واحدة .

The Apostle of God said: "One of the prophets made camp beneath a tree. An ant stung him, whereupon he had his things removed from under it and had it [the tree (and the ant colony)] burned. Thereupon God revealed to him: 'Why not [burn just the] one ant [that was at fault]?'"

i. Hammâm b. Munabbih, no. 17, *isnâd* 1 (directly from Abû Hurayrah): The *Allâh* supplied by the editor of the text is present in other versions.

ii. Muslim 39:150, *isnâd* 1 (Abû Hurayrah).

iii. Muslim 39:149, *isnâd* 5 (Abû Hurayrah).

iv. Bukhârî 59:16:6, *isnâd* 5.

v. Abû Dâwûd 40:164, *isnâd* 5.

vi. *Musnad*, II, 313, *isnâd* 5.

vii. *Musnad*, II, 449, *isnâd* 5.

viii. Nasâʾî 42:38, *isnâds* 2 (Abû Hurayrah) and 6 (Abû Hurayrah): the Divine Saying reads: *in qad qaraṣatka namlah ahlakta ummah min al-umam tusabbiḥu*, "If an ant has stung you, you have [still] destroyed one of the communities [i.e., that of the ants] that praise [God]". Similar versions are also cited with *isnâd* 8b (Abû Hurayrah) and two faulty *isnâds* through al-Ḥasan al-Baṣrî that do not go back to the Prophet.

SAYING 26: *ḥarramtu ʿalayhi al-jannah*

... سمعت الحسن يقول إنّ رجلا ممّن كان قبلكم خرجت به قرحة فلمّا آذته انتزع سهما من كنانته فنكأها فلم يرقأ الدم حتّى مات قال ربّكم قد حرّمت عليه الجنّة ثمّ مدّ يده إلى المسجد فقال أى واللّه لقد حدّثنى بهذا الحديث جندب عن رسول اللّه صلعم فى هذا المسجد .

... I heard al-Ḥasan say: “A man who lived before you developed a boil [on his body]. Then, when it bothered him, he drew out an arrow from his quiver and lanced it [the boil]. Then the blood continued flowing until he died. Your Lord said: ‘I have forbidden Paradise to him’.” Then he [al-Ḥasan] stretched out his hand toward the mosque and said: “By God, Jundab related this ḥadîth to me from the Apostle of God in this mosque!”

i. Muslim 1:180, *isnâd* 361 (Jundab).

ii. Bukhârî 23:84:1b, *isnâd* 361a (Jundab): wording of frame-story varies; text of Divine Saying proper reads: *badaranî ʿabdî bi-nafsihi ḥarramtu ʿalayhi al-jannah*, “My servant acted hastily with his own life. I have forbidden Paradise to him”.

iii. Bukhârî 60:50:11, *isnâd* 361a: essentially the same as version ii, but has preferable reading *bâdaranî* for *badaranî*.

Other References: Ibn al-ʿArabî, *Mishkât*, p. 27; al-Madanî, p. 90.

This ḥadîth occurs often without any first-person word of God: Bukhârî 93:8:2; Muslim 33:21, 1:227, 228 (*isnâd* 320); Muslim 1:218; Ibn Mâjah 13:8:2; Nasâʾî 49:30; *Muwaṭṭaʾ* 36:11 (*isnâd* 262), *inter alia.*

SAYING 27: *hâdhâ ʿabdî ḥaqqan*

... قال رسول اللّه صلعم إنّ العبد إذا صلّى فى العلانية فأحسن وصلّى فى السرّ فأحسن قال اللّه عزّ وجلّ هذا عندى حقّا .

... the Apostle of God said: “The servant [of] God, when he performs the Prayer publicly, does a good thing. And if he performs it in private, he does a good thing. God says: ‘This is My servant in truth!’ ”

i. Ibn Mâjah 37:20:3, *isnâd* 5 (Abû Hurayrah).

Other References: al-Madanî, p. 80.

SAYING 28: *huwa hâlik*

... قال رسول اللّه صلعم إذا سمعتم رجلا يقول قد هلك الناس فهو أهلكهم يقول اللّه إنّه هو هالك .

... the Apostle of God said: "When you hear a man say, 'People are doomed to perish',[37] he is the one of them most doomed. God says: 'Verily, he is one who is [already] perishing!'"

i. *Musnad*, ii, 272, *isnâd* 3c (Abû Hurayrah).

ii. *Muwaṭṭa*ʾ 56:2, *isnâd* 3c (directly from Suhayl from Dahkwân from Abû Hurayrah): has only the *ḥadîth nabawî* segment, omitting the *yaqûlu Allâh* ... portion entirely.

iii. *Muslim* 45:139, *isnâd* 3c: *ḥadîth nabawî*, same as version ii.

iv. Abû Dâwûd 40:77, *isnâd* 3c: *ḥadîth nabawî*, same as version ii.

v. *Musnad*, II, 342, *isnâd* 3c: *ḥadîth nabawî*, same as version ii.

vi. Suhayl b. Abî Ṣâliḥ, no. 11, *isnâd* 3c (directly from Dhakwân from Abû Hurayrah): *ḥadîth nabawî*, same as version ii, with minor variations.

The intended meaning of this ḥadîth is not entirely clear. It is perhaps directed against pessimism and/or self-righteousness; or it may be a warning to those who fancy themselves as harbingers of the apocalypse; or it may have been intended as a rebuke to the man who presumes to judge others (thus arrogating to himself the prerogative that rightfully belongs only to God). For discussion of the transmission of this ḥadîth, see Azmi, *Studies*, p. 228.

SAYING 29: *idhhab fa-sallim ʿalá ûlâʾika an-nafar*

وقال رسول اللّه صلعم خلق اللّه آدم على صورته طوله ستّون ذراعا فلمّا خلقه قال اذهب فسلّم على أولئك النفر وهم نفر من الملائكة جلوس فاستمع ما يحيّونك فإنّها تحيّتك وتحيّة ذريّتك قال فذهب فقال السلام عليكم فقالوا وعليكم السلام ورحمة اللّه فزادوا ورحمة اللّه قال فكلّ من يدخل الجنّة على صورة آدم طوله ستّون ذراعا فلم يزل الخلق ينقص بعد حتّى الآن .

The Apostle of God said: "God created Adam in His own form. His height was sixty armslengths. Then, when He had created him, He said: 'Go and greet those people there with peace' – and they were a group of angels who were seated [there] – 'Then listen how they greet you; it will be your greeting formula and that of your descendants likewise.' So he went and said: 'Peace be upon you', and they said: 'And upon you be peace and the mercy of God' – and they added, 'and the mercy of God'. And everyone who enters Paradise will be in the form of Adam and have a height of sixty armslengths. And men have continued to diminish in height from that time to the present."

i. Hammâm b. Munabbih, no. 58, *isnâd* 1 (directly from Abû Hurayrah).
ii. Bukhârî 60:1:1, *isnâd* 1 (Abû Hurayrah).
iii. *Musnad*, II, 315, *isnâd* 1.
Other References: Ibn al-ʿArabî, *Mishkât*, p. 16.

At least the first part of the ḥadîth seems to be an explanation of the origin of the practice of the *taslîm*, or "greeting with peace", which has continued through the centuries to be one of the most universal outward marks of social life in Islam. It is attested to numerous times in the Qur'ân and specifically enjoined upon the Muslims in what is generally considered to be a late Meccan revelation, S. 6:54: "And when those who have faith in Our signs come to you, say, 'Peace be upon you'. Your Lord has written down mercy [as a pledge] for Himself", and also in two Medinan passages, 24:27 and 24:61. See article, "Salām", by C. van Arendonck, *SEI*, pp. 489–491. Cf. also S. 4:86.

SAYIṆG 30: *idhhabû ilá alladhîna kuntum tarâ'ûna fî ad-dunyâ*

. . . إنّ رسول اللّه صلعم قال إنّ أخوف ما أخاف عليكم الشرك الأصغر قالوا وما الشرك الأصغر يا رسول اللّه قال الرياء يقول اللّه عزّ وجلّ لهم يوم القيامة اذا جزى الناس بأعمالهم اذهبوا إلى الّذين كنتم تراءون فى الدنيا وانظروا هل تجدون عندهم جزاء .

... the Apostle of God said: "The most dreadful thing that I fear for you [i.e., the Muslims] is the 'lesser *shirk*'." They said: "And what is the 'lesser *shirk*', O Apostle of God?" He said: "Hypocrisy! God will say to people on the Day of Resurrection, when they are rewarded for their actions: 'Depart to those [with whom] you practiced hypocrisy in the world. And look! Do you find reward with them?'"

i. *Musnad*, V, 428, *isnâd* 350 (Maḥmûd b. Labîd).

ii. *Musnad*, V, 429, *isnâd*s 350a (Maḥmûd b. Labîd) and 351 (Maḥmûd b. Labîd): minor wording variations.

Other References: al-Muḥâsibî, *Riʿâyah*, p. 91.

The *Shirk* spoken of in this text is the sin of "associating" or "ascribing" to God other gods or anything else "as partners" – i.e., placing anything else on the same plane with Him (cf. Saying 10). The definite elative form, *al-aṣgharu*, would normally be translated as a superlative, but here the comparative form is better, because the intent is not to call *riyâ*ʾ ("hypocrisy", "lip-service") the "smallest" or "least" *shirk*, but to show its seriousness by labeling it a form of the most heinous sin in Muslim eyes, the ascription of equals to God. *Shirk* remains *shirk*, however "small".

SAYING 31: *idhâ aḥabba ʿabdî liqâʾî aḥbabtu liqâʾahu*

... إنّ رسول الله صلعم قال قال الله إذا أحبّ عبدى لقائى أحببت لقاءه
واذا كره لقائى كرهت لقاءه .

... the Apostle of God said: "God said: 'If My servant longs to meet Me, I long to meet him. And if he abhors meeting Me, I abhor meeting him.'"

i. *Muwaṭṭa*ʾ 16:50, *isnâd* 5 (Abû Hurayrah).

ii. Bukhârî 97:35:12, *isnâd* 5.

iii. Nasâʾî 21:10, *isnâd* 5.

iv. Hammâm b. Munabbih, no. 20, *isnâd* 1 (directly from Abû Hurayrah): in the third person, as an *ḥadîth nabawî* ("He who longs to meet God, God longs to meet him ...", etc.). The saying is attested to in this form in numerous places (i.e., as an *ḥadîth nabawî* rather than a Divine Saying): Bukhârî 81:41:1, 2, *isnâds* 210, 151, 400; Muslim 48:14, 15, 16, 17, 18, *isnâd*s 210, 151, 152, 23, 400, respectively; *Musnad*, II, 313, *isnâd* 1; Nasâʾî 21:10, *isnâd*s 23, 210, 151; and Ibn Mâjah 37:31:7, *isnâd* 151.

Other References: al-Madanî, p. 6; ʿAlî al-Qârî, no. 14; Qushayrî, *Risâlah*, p. 246 (as an *ḥadîth nabawî*).

The verb *aḥabba* in this Saying could be translated simply as "desires", but its sense in Arabic is stronger than "desires" indicates. This ḥadîth has been interpreted generally by Ṣûfî writers within the context of the passionate longing of man for God (cf. Hujwîrî, *Kashf*, p. 310; Hartmann, *Ḳuschairī*, p. 63).

SAYING 32: *idhâ ibtalaytu ʿabdî bi-habîbatayhi*

. . . سمعت النبيّ صلعم يقول إنّ الله تعالى قال إذا ابتليت عبدى بحبيبتيه فصبر عوضته منهما الجنّة .

... I heard the Prophet say: "God said: 'If I put My servant to the test by [taking away] his eyes,[38] and he endures it with patience, I shall indemnify him for them by [granting him] Paradise'."

i. Bukhârî 75:7,*isnâds* 107 (Anas b. Mâlik) and 108 (Anas b. Mâlik).

ii. *Musnad*, III, 144, *isnâd* 107.

iii. Tirmidhî 34:58:1, *isnâd* 109 (Anas b. Mâlik): variant: *idhâ akhadhtu karîmatay ʿabdî fî ad-dunyâ lam yakun lahu jazâʾ ʿindî illá al-jannah*, "If I take away the eyes of My servant in the world, he will have no other reward than Paradise from Me".

iv. *Musnad*, III, 283, *isnâd* 108a (Anas b. Mâlik): essentially the same as version iii.

v. Tirmidhî 34:58:2, *isnâd* 3 (Abû Hurayrah): variant: *man adhhabtu ḥabîbatayhi fa-ṣabara wa-iḥtasaba lâ arḍ lahu thawâban dûn al-jannah*, "Whoever, if I take from him his eyes, endures patiently and remains content, shall inherit no land short of Paradise".

vi. *Musnad*, II, 265, *isnâd* 3: same as version v.

vii. *Musnad*, V, 258, *isnâd* 260a (Abû Umamah): variant of version v; *karîmatayhi* replaces *ḥabîbatayhi*; the Divine Saying is addressed to man (*ibn Âdam*) in the second person ("... if I take your eyes ...").

Other References: Ibn al-ʿArabî, *Mishkât*, p. 22; al-Madanî, pp. 4, 10, 11, 16, 20, 21, 35, 74; ʿAlî al-Qârî, no. 5.

According to Margoliouth (*Early Development*, p. 156), Abû Ṭâlib al-Makkî credits some of the Companions of the Prophet with desiring to lose their eyesight. Among the more ascetically inclined Ṣûfîs generally the idea existed that bodily infirmities are often a way to spiritual health.

SAYING 33: *idhâ qâlû lâ ilâh illâ Allâh istajâbû*

... ذكر لنا أنّ الله تعالى قال لملائكته أدعوا إلىّ عبادى قالوا يا ربّ
كيف والسموات السبع دونهم والعرش فوق ذلك قال إنّهم إذا قالوا لا اله إلاّ
الله استجابوا ...

... he ['Abdallâh b. 'Amr] told us that God said to His angels: "Summon My servants to Me!" They said: "O Lord, how [shall we do that], when the seven heavens are in between and the Throne is above that?" He said: "Truly, if they say, 'There is no god but God',[39] they will answer [to your call]".[40]

i. *Musnad*, II, 197, *isnâd* 184 ('Al. b. 'Amr): the ḥadîth is not raised to Maḥammad, but is quoted directly by 'Abdallâh b. 'Amr. It is followed by a separate ḥadîth with the same *isnâd*, which also includes a Divine Saying (no. 74:iii).

SAYING 34: *idhâ taḥaddatha 'abdî bi-an ya'mala ḥasanah*

وقال رسول الله صلعم : قال الله تعالى إذا تحدّث عبدي بأن يعمل حسنة
فأنا أكتبها له حسنة ما لم يعملها فإذا عملها فأنا أكتبها له بعشر
أمثالها واذا تحدّث بأن يعمل سيّئة فأنا أغفرها له ما لم يعملها
فإذا عملها فأنا أكتبها له بمثلها .

The Apostle of God said: "God said: 'If My servant intends a good deed, then I count it for him as a good deed [even if] he does not carry it out. And if he does carry it out, then I count it for him as ten like unto it. And if he plans to do an evil deed, then I forgive him for it so long as he does not carry it out. And if he carries it out, I count it for him as it is.'"

i. Hammâm b. Munabbih, no. 53, *isnâd* 1 (directly from Abû Hurayrah).
ii. Muslim 1:205a, *isnâd* 1 (Abû Hurayrah).
iii. *Musnad*, II, 315, *isnâd* 1.
Other References: Ibn al-'Arabî, *Mishkât*, p. 29; al-Madanî, p. 25.

Compare this Saying with Sayings 51 and 56, which contain segments that are almost identical with parts of the present Saying.

SAYING 34a: *irqubûhu fa-in ʿamalahâ fa-ktubûhâ lahu bi-mithlahâ*

وقال رسول اللّه صلعم قالت الملائكة يا ربّ ذاك عبد يريد أن يعمل سيّئة
وهو أبصر به فقال ارقبو فإن عملها فاكتبوها له بمثلها وان تركها فاكتبوها له
حسنة إنّما تركها من جرّاى .

The Apostle of God said: "The angels say: 'O Lord, there is a servant here who wants to commit an evil act'. And God knows better about it [than they]. He says: 'Wait for him, and if he does it, reckon it to him as it is. And if he does not do it, then reckon it to him as a good deed. Truly, he abandons it only for My sake.'"

i. Hammâm b. Munabbih, no. 105, *isnâd* 1 (directly from Abû Hurayrah).
ii. Muslim 1:205b, *isnâd* 1 (Abû Hurayrah).
iii. *Musnad*, II, 317, *isnâd* 1.
Other References: Ibn al-ʿArabî, *Mishkât*, p. 31.

SAYING 34b: *man hamma bi-ḥasanah fa-lam yaʿmalhâ*

... عن النبيّ صلعم فيما يروى عن ربّه عزّ وجلّ قال قال إنّ اللّه كتب
الحسنات والسيئات ثم بيّن ذلك فمن همّ بحسنة فلم يعملها كتبها اللّه عنده
حسنة كاملة فان همّ بها فعملها كتبها اللّه عنده عشر حسنات الى سبعمائة
ضعف الى أضعاف كثيرة ومن همّ بسيئة فلم يعملها كتبها اللّه له عنده حسنة
كاملة فإن همّ بها فعملها كتبها اللّه له سيئة واحدة .

... from the Prophet, in that which he related from his Lord. He said: "Truly, God writes down good deeds and evil deeds". Then he explained the difference: "Whoever intends a good deed and then does not do it, God writes it down for him as a wholly good deed. And if he intends it and does it, God writes it down for him as ten good deeds, [or] up to seven hundred, or many more. And if he intends an evil deed and then does not do it, God writes it down for him as a wholly good deed. And if he intends it and does it, God writes it down as a single evil deed."

i. Bukhârî 81:31, *isnâd* 143 (Ibn ʿAbbâs): not a direct quotation of God's words: see commentary below.

ii. Muslim 1:207, *isnâd* 143.

iii. *Musnad*, I, 310, *isnâd* 143.

iv. *Musnad*, I, 361, *isnâd* 143.

v. Muslim 1:259, *isnâd* 104b (Anas b. Mâlik): shorter version, given as direct words of God; set within the much longer ḥadîth concerning Muḥammad's *miʿrâj* (see above, pp. 28–29) and quoted as God's words to Muḥammad on that occasion, along with the prescription of the five daily Prayers.

vi. *Musnad*, III, 148–149, *isnâd* 104b: same as version v.

vii. *Musnad*, I, 227, *isnâd* 143a (Ibn ʿAbbâs): shorter version, *ḥadîth nabawî.* The ḥadîth occurs in this form as a simple *ḥadîth nabawî* also at: Muslim 1:206; *Musnad*, II, 234, 411, 498. All of the latter instances are attested by *isnâd* 8 (Abû Hurayrah).

Other References: al-Madanî, p. 5; *Mabânî*, p. 88; *Jawâhir*, p. 168; Nawawî, *Arbaʿûn*, no. 37.

This ḥadîth is presented as words that Muḥammad reported on God's authority; i.e., words that he heard from God and is reporting in his own words. In this kind of indirect Divine Saying, one is at the borderline between the Prophetic ḥadîth and the Divine Saying. Thus it is no surprise that in the various classical citations of this tradition the main portion of the ḥadîth is quoted sometimes as God's words and sometimes as Muḥammad's words only.

SAYING 34c: *idhâ hamma ʿabdî bi-ḥasanah wa-lam yaʿmalhâ*

... عن رسول الله قال يقول الله عزّ وجلّ إذا همّ عبدى بحسنة ولم يعملها كتبتها له حسنة فإن عملها كتبت له عشر حسنات إلى سبعمائة ضعف وان همّ عبدى بسيّئة فلم يعملها لم أكتبها عليه فإن عملها كتبتها له سيّئة واحدة .

... from the Apostle of God. He said: "God says: 'If My servant intends a good deed and does not do it, I write it down for him as a good deed. Then if he does it, I write it down for him as ten good deeds, or up to seven hundred times that. And if My servant intends an evil deed and does not do it, I do not write it down against him. And if he does it, I write it down for him as [only one] evil deed.'"

i. Ibrâhîm b. Ṭahmân, no. 104 (fol. 247a), *isnâd* 13 (directly from al-ʿAlâʾ b. ʿAr. from ʿAr. b. Yaʿqûb from Abû Hurayrah).

ii. Muslim 1:204, *isnâd* 13.

iii. Muslim 1:203, *isnâd* 5 (Abû Hurayrah): variant wording throughout.

iv. Bukhârî 97:35:10, *isnâd* 5: similar to version iii.

v. *Musnad*, II, 242, *isnâd* 5: similar to version iii.

Other References: ʿAlî al-Qârî, no. 13.

Saying 35: *irjaʿ ilá ʿabdî fa-taqul lahu al-ḥayât turîdu*

وقال رسول اللّه صلعم جاء ملك الموت إلى موسى فقال له اجب ربّك قال
فلطم موسى عين ملك الموت ففقأها قال فرجع الملك إلى اللّه عزّ وجلّ فقال
إنّك أرسلتنى إلى عبد لك لا يريد الموت وقد فقأ عينى قال فردّ اللّه إليه
عينه قال ارجع إلى عبدى فقل له الحياة تريد فإن كنت تريد الحياة فضع
يدك على متن ثور فما وارت يدك من شعرة فإنّك تعيش بها سنّة قال ثمّ
مه قال ثمّ تموت قال فالآن من قريب قال ربّ ادننى من الأرض المقدّسة
رمية بحجر وقال رسول اللّه صلعم لو أنّى عنده لأريتكم قبره إلى جانب الطريق
عند الكثيب الأحمر .

The Apostle of God said: "The angel of death came to Moses and said to him, 'Answer your Lord'. Whereupon Moses struck the angel of death in the eye and put it out. Then the angel returned to God and said: 'Thou has sent me to a servant of Thine who does not want to die, and he put out my eye!' Thereupon God returned his eye to him and said: 'Return to My servant and say to him, "Is it life that you want? If you want life, put your hand upon the back of a bull; as many hairs as your hand covers, so many years will you live."' [When this was communicated, Moses] said: 'And then what?' He said: 'Then you will die'." He [Muḥammad] said: "Then the time [of death] drew near, and [Moses] said: 'O my Lord, [only] bring me closer to the Holy Land by a stone's throw.'" And the Apostle of God said: "If I were there, I would show you his grave by the side of the road at the red sand-ridge."

i. Hammâm b. Munabbih, no. 59, *isnâd* 1 (directly from Abû Hurayrah).

ii. Muslim 43:158, *isnâd* 1 (Abû Hurayrah).

iii. *Musnad*, II, 315, *isnâd* 1.
iv. *Musnad*, II, 269, *isnâd* 26 (Abû Hurayrah).
v. Bukhârî 23:69, *isnâd* 26.
vi. Tirmidhî 21:121, *isnâd* 26.
vii. *Musnad*, II, 351, *isnâd* 22 (Abû Hurayrah).
viii. *Musnad*, II, 533, *isnâd* 42 (Abû Hurayrah).
Other References: Ṭabarî, *Ta'rîkh*, I, 503.

M. Grünbaum, "Beiträge zur vergleichenden Mythologie aus der Hagada", pp. 182–185, provides a wealth of examples of the permutations of the story of Moses and the angel of death in Jewish haggadic material (see esp. p. 183). The most interesting example relevant to the present ḥadîth is that found in the Midrash Debarum, where Moses strikes Sammael (the angel sent to collect his soul) blind, but does so not with a blow of his fist; instead, he blinds him with his radiant countenance (clearly a reference to the brilliance of Moses' countenance after the Sinai experience: see Exodus 34:29ff.), whereupon God Himself descends and takes his servant's soul with a kiss (Grünbaum, p. 184).

SAYING 36: *kadhdhabanî ʿabdî ... wa-shatamanî ʿabdî*

وقال رسول اللّه صلعم قال اللّه عزّ وجلّ كذّبنى عبدى ولم يكن ذلك له
وشتمنى عبدى ولم يكن ذلك له أمّا تكذيبه إياى أن يقول لن يعيدنا كما
بدأنا وأمّا شتمه إياى أن يقول اتخذ اللّه ولدا وأنا الصمد لم ألد ولم
أولد ولم يكن لى كفؤا أحد .

The Apostle of God said: "God said: 'My servant has accused Me of lying,[41] and it is not his [to do]. My servant has cursed Me, and it is not his [to do].[42] As for his calling Me a liar, he says, "He will not bring us back[43] as He created us";[44] and as for his cursing Me, he says, "God has taken a child".[45] [Yet] I am the Eternal [Refuge]. I have not begotten, nor am I begotten, and there has [never] been one equal to me.'"[46]

i. Hammâm b. Munabbih, no. 106, *isnâd* 1 (directly from Abû Hurayrah).
ii. Bukhârî, *Tafsîr*, S. 112, no. 2, *isnâd* 1 (Abû Hurayrah): omits *qâla Allâh*, but the text is clearly a statement of God, not the Prophet. Concerning S. 112, see n. 46.

iii. Bukhârî, *Tafsîr*, S. 112, no. 1, *isnâd* 5 (Abû Hurayrah): inserts additional sentence after *kamâ bada'anî*: *wa-laysa awwal al-khalq bi-ahwan ʿalayya min iʿâdatihi*, "And the first of creation was no easier for Me than its repetition" (i.e., I can resurrect all creatures as easily as I originally created them).

iv. Bukhârî 59:1:3, *isnâd* 5: shorter version; omits paraphrase of S. 112 entirely.

v. Nasâ'î 21:17, *isnâd* 5: same as version iii.

vi. Bukhârî, *Tafsîr*, S. 2:116, no. 8, *isnâd* 142 (ʿAl. b. ʿAbbâs): minor wording variations.

vii. *Musnad*, II, 350–351, *isnâd* 22 (Abû Hurayrah): same as version iii.

Other References: Ibn al-ʿArabî, *Mishkât*, pp. 7–8; ʿAlî al-Qârî, no. 2; al-Madanî, pp. 5, 17, 38.

Saying 37: *kayf taraktum ʿibâdî*

... وقال رسول اللّه صلعم الملائكة يتعاقبون فيكم ملائكة بالليل وملائكة بالنهار ويجتمعون فى صلاة الفجر وصلاة العصر ثمّ يعرج إليه الّذين باتوا فيكم فيسألهم وهو أعلم بهم كيف تركتم عبادى قالوا تركناهم وهم يصلّون وأتيناهم وهم يصلّون .

... and the Apostle of God said: "The angels take turns with you, some angels during the night and other angels during the day. They assemble during the Prayer at dawn and the Prayer in the afternoon. Then those who were with you during the night ascend to Him, and He asks them – and He knows better than they: 'How [i.e., in what state] did you leave My servants?' They say: 'We left them while they were praying [just as] we came to them while they were praying'."

i. Hammâm b. Munabbih, no. 8, *isnâd* 1 (directly from Abû Hurayrah).

ii. *Muwaṭṭa'* 9:82, *isnâd* 5 (directly from ʿAl. b. Dhakwân from al-Aʿraj from Abû Hurayrah).

iii. Bukhârî 97:23:1, *isnâd* 5.

iv. Bukhârî 9:16:2, *isnâd* 5.

v. Bukhârî 59:6:17, *isnâd* 5.

vi. Nasâ'î 5:21:1, *isnâd* 5.

vii. *Musnad*, II, 357, *isnâd* 40 (Abû Hurayrah).

viii. *Musnad*, II, 344, *isnâd* 10a (Abû Hurayrah): wording variations: God's first words to the angels are: *min ayn ji'tum*, "Whence do you come?" (cf. Saying 56). God questions first the angels of the day and then the angels of the night, and in both instances they answer: *ji'nâka min ʿind ʿibâdika ataynâhum wa-hum yuṣallûna wa-ji'nâka wa-hum yuṣallûna*, "We have come from among Thy servants. We came to them, and they were praying; and we came to Thee, and they were [still] praying".

Compare this Saying with the similar tradition of Saying 56 below.

SAYING 38: *khalaqtu hâ'ulâ' li-l-jannah*

... انّ عمر بن الخطّاب سئل عن هذه الآية "واذ أخذ ربّك من بني آدم من ظهورهم ذرّيتهم وأشهدهم على أنفسهم ألست بربّكم قالوا بلى شهدنا أن تقولوا يوم القيامة إنّا كنّا عن هذا غافلين" فقال عمر بن الخطّاب سمعت رسول الله صلعم يسأل عنها فقال رسول الله صلعم إنّ الله تبارك وتعالى خلق آدم ثمّ مسح ظهره بيمينه فاستخرج منه ذرّية فقال خلقت هؤلاء للجنة وبعمل أهل الجنّة يعملون ثمّ مسح ظهره فاستخرج منه ذرّيّة فقال خلقت هؤلاء للنار وبعمل أهل النار يعملون فقال رجل يا رسول الله ففيم العمل قال فقال رسول الله صلعم إنّ الله إذا خلق العبد للجنّة استعمله بعمل أهل الجنّة حتى يموت على عمل من أعمال أهل الجنّة فيدخله به الجنّة واذا خلق العبد للنار استعمله بعمل أهل النار حتّى يموت على عمل من أعمال أهل النار فيدخله به النار .

... ʿUmar b. al-Khaṭṭâb was asked about this *âyah*: "And when your Lord took from the sons of Adam, from their loins [lit., backs], their seed and made them testify against themselves, [He said:] 'Am I not your Lord?' They said: 'Certainly, we testify [to it]' – [this was done] that you might not say on the Day of Resurrection, 'We were unaware of this!'" [S. 7:172]. Then ʿUmar b. al-Khaṭṭâb said: "I heard the Apostle of God being asked about this, and he said: 'God created Adam and then touched his loins with His right hand and brought forth from them [his] progeny. Thereupon He said: "I have created these for Paradise, and they shall act in the manner of the people of Paradise". Then He touched his loins and brought forth from them [other] progeny. He said: "I have created these for the Fire, and they shall act in the manner of the people of the Fire".' Then a man said: 'O Apostle of God, then what is action for?' The Apostle of God said: 'God, when He creates the servant for Paradise, causes him to act in the manner of the people of Paradise until he dies in the manner of the people of Paradise, whereupon He causes him to enter Paradise with that act. And if He creates the servant for the Fire, He causes him to act in the manner of the people of the Fire until he dies in the manner of the people of the Fire, whereupon He causes him to enter the Fire with that act.'"

i. *Muwaṭṭâ'* 46:1:2, *isnad* 280 (ʿUmar b. al-Khaṭṭâb).
ii. Tirmidhî, *Tafsîr*, S. 7:172, no. 3, *isnâd* 280.
iii. Abû Dâwûd 39:16:13, *isnâd* 280.
Other References: Ṭabarî, *Tafsîr*, S. 7:172 (IX, 113) (from Mâlik b. Anas, with the same *isnâd* back to ʿUmar); al-Madanî, pp. 65–66.

This ḥadîth would appear to be one of the few instances of traditions involving Divine Sayings that are concerned with specific theological issues that were important in the early doctrinal disputes in Islam. The question of *qadar*, or God's "[pre-]determination" of human acts, was one of the earliest issues of a dogmatic nature that divided Muslim religious scholars. On the subject, see Watt, *Free Will*; Ringgren, *Arabian Fatalism.* Cf. Sayings 45, 89.

SAYING 39: *al-kibriyâ' ridâ'î*

... قال رسول الله صلعم يقول الله سبحانه الكبرياء ردائى والعظمة إزارى من نازعنى واحدا منهما ألقيته فى جهنم .

... the Apostle of God said: "God says: 'Majesty is My cloak, and grandeur My girdle. Whoever contends with Me in either one of these, him shall I cast into Jahannam.'"

i. Ibn Mâjah 37:16:2, *isnâd* 12 (Abû Hurayrah).
ii. *Musnad*, II, 248, *isnâd* 12: *ʿizzah*, "glory", replaces *ʿaẓamah*; *an-nâr*, "the Fire", replaces *jahannam.*
iii. *Musnad*, II, 414, *isnâd* 12: *an-nâr*, "the fire", replaces *jahannam.*
iv. *Musnad*, II, 427, *isnâd* 12.

v. *Musnad*, II, 442, *isnâd* 12.

vi. Abû Dâwûd 31:25, *isnâd* 12: *an-nâr*, "the Fire", replaces *jahannam.*

vii. Muslim 45:136, *isnâds* 12a (Abû Hurayrah) and 122 (Abû Saʿîd al-Khudrî): part in the third person, part in the first person: *al-ʿizzah izâruhu wa-l-kibriyâʾ ridâʾuhu fa-man yunâzuʿunî ʿadhdhabtuhu*, "Glory is His girdle, and majesty His cloak; whoever contends with Me, him shall I punish".

viii. *Musnad*, II, 376, *isnâd* 5a (Abû Hurayrah): *adkhaltuhu*, "I cause him to enter", replaces *alqaytuhu.*

ix. Ibn Mâjah 37:16:3, *isnâd* 141 (ʿAl. b. al-ʿAbbâs): *an-nâr*, "the Fire", replaces *jahannam.*

Other References: Ibn al-ʿArabî, *Mishkât*, p. 11; ʿAlî al-Qârî, no. 21; al-Madanî, pp. 7, 8, 28, 37, 76; al-Muḥâsibî, *Riʿâyah*, pp. 232, 233.

Compare S. 45:37: *wa-lahu al-kibriyâʾ fî as-samawât wa-l-ard*, "And His is the majesty in the heavens and the earth". *Al-ʿaẓamah* does not occur in the Qurʾân, but *ʿizzah* (cf. Sayings 20, 21) is found frequently, e.g., S. 10:35: *fa-li-llâh al-ʿizzah jamîʿan*, "And to God belongs the glory entirely". Other Qurʾânic references at *Muʿjam*, p. 409b. ʿAbdalbâqî, in his commentary on the version of the Saying cited by Muslim (version vii), notes the similarity of the whole first statement to an Arabian saying: *fulân shiʿâruhu az-zuhd wa-dithâruhu at-taqwá*, "So-and-so's emblem is abstemiousness, and his wrap is piety/fear of God", where *shiʿâr* and and *dithâr*, like *ridâʾ* and *izâr*, can be glossed as *sifât*, "characteristic traits", or "qualities" (Muslim, IV, 2023).

SAYING 40: *kull mâl naḥaltuhu ʿabdan ḥalâl*

... أنّ رسول الله صلعم قال ذات يوم فى خطبته ألا انّ ربّى أمرنى أن أعلّمكم ما جهلتم ممّا علّمنى يومى هذا· كلّ مال نحلته عبدا حلال وانّى خلقت عبادى حنفاء كلّهم وانّهم أتتهم الشياطين فاحتالتهم عن دينهم وحرّمت عليهم ما أحللت لهم وأمرتهم أن يشركوا بى ما لم أنزل به سلطانا وانّ الله نظر الى أهل الأرض فمقتهم عربهم وعجمهم إلاّ بقايا من أهل الكتاب وقال إنّما بعثتك لأبتليك وأبتلى بك وأنزلت عليك كتابا لا يغسله الماء تقرؤه نائم ويقظان وانّ الله أمرنى أن أحرّق قريشا فقلت ربّ اذا يثلغوا رأسى فيدعوه خبزة قال استخرجهم كما استخرجوك واغزهم نغزك وأنفق فسننفق عليك وابعث جيشا نبعث خمسة مثله وقاتل بمن أطاعك من عصاك ...

... the Apostle of God said one day in his sermon: "My Lord commanded me to teach you what you did not know of that which He taught me this day. [God said:] 'All wealth that I have freely given [any] servant is permitted. Truly, I have created all of My servants *ḥanîf*s [i.e., true worshippers of the one God]. The satans have come to them and scattered [and turned] them away from their religious practice. They have forbidden them what I have allowed them and commanded them to associate [as a partner] with Me that with regard to which no authority has been sent by Me.' Then God looked down upon the people of the earth, and He despised them [for their evil ways], the Arabs and non-Arabs among them, save for a remnant of the people of the Book. And He said: 'Truly, I sent you that I might test you and test others through you. And I sent down to you a book that water does not wash away, which you recite sleeping and waking.' Then God commanded me to rouse Quraysh. So I said, 'My Lord, surely they will break my skull and leave it like a [flat] piece of bread!' He [God] said: 'Drive them out just as they drive you out;[47] make raids against them, and We shall support your raids;[48] give freely, and We shall give freely to you;[49] send forth an army, and We shall send forth five like it;[50] and fight beside him who obeys you against him who disobeys you.'"

i. Muslim 51:63, *isnâd* 310 ('Iyâḍ b. Ḥimâr): occurs as the initial and principal portion of a *khuṭbah* of Muḥammad; followed in the text by a long tradition from the Prophet concerning those who will be in Paradise and those who will be in the Fire.

ii. Muslim 51:64a, *isnâd* 310: set in the same sermon of Muḥammad as version i, but in this instance a second Divine Saying (no. 64) is inserted after this tradition and before that concerning those who will be in Paradise and the Fire.

iii. *Musnad*, IV, 162, *isnâd* 310: set in the same sermon as version i.

Other references: al-Madanî, pp. 64–65.

This Saying is a "sermon ḥadîth", that is, a report of various individual statements (any of which alone would be an ḥadîth as well) that are said to have been uttered by Muḥammad in the course of a "sermon", or *khuṭbah*. It clearly provides a useful vehicle for stringing together words of the Prophet into a more or less coherent composite narrative. One might well imagine that just such reports as those collected here might actually have been preserved from *khuṭbahs* of the Apostle of God on diverse occasions. (For the early development of the *khuṭbah*, its form, and its political associations, as well as the differing scholarly opinions as to its forerunners and models, see A. J. Wensinck, "Khuṭba", *SEI*, pp. 258–259.)

Note the statement attributed to God concerning His creation of all of those who serve Him as *ḥanîf*s, i.e., as "natural monotheists". The term *ḥanîf* is widely attested in the Qur'ân, where it is applied primarily to those pre-Islamic prophets and other people who, in contradistinction to the polytheists (and even to the later Jews and Christians who distorted their revelations), held to the worship and service of the one God. Abraham is traditionally the first *ḥanîf*, and the religion of Abraham is often considered to be the *ḥanîfîyah*. In the Qur'ân and later Muslim usage, *ḥanîf* is also used broadly to designate anyone who is a true *muslim* – one who submits to God – and hence applied to pre-Islamic as well as Islamic "submitters". Thus the usual definition, "pre-Islamic monotheist", is not adequate, as the sense of the present Saying shows. In this case, it seems to be implied that all men are created as *ḥunafâ'*, i.e., in the state of *fiṭrah*, or natural faithfulness to God. There is also implied a clear historical progression, even a *Heilsgeschichte*, which begins with the first men and moves forward to the sending of the Qur'ân and the calling of the Prophet and the struggle to found the (re)new(ed) community of the faithful. So while God's words about creating all men *ḥanîf*s are just as valid yesterday, today, or at any time, it is also a statement of how things were done at the beginning of time: God says this as he looks upon the evil ways of men before Islam by way of explanation as to why the Qur'ân and the Prophet's mission are necessary.

Saying 41: *law anna ʿibâdî aṭâʿûnî la-asqaytuhum*

... أنّ النبى صلعم قال : قال ربكم عزّ وجلّ : لو أنّ عبادى أطاعونى لأسقيتهم المطر بالليل وأطلعت عليهم الشمس بالنهار ولما أسمعتهم صوت الرعد .

... the Prophet said: "Your Lord said: 'If My servants obey Me, I shall send down rain by night and cause the sun to shine upon them by day, and I shall not let them hear the voice of the thunder'."

i. *Musnad*, II, 359, *isnâd* 37 (Abû Hurayrah): set within a longer tradition of the Prophet, which has to do with faith and true service of God.

Other References: al-Madanî, p. 88; ʿAlî al-Qârî, no. 32; *Mabânî*, p. 89.

SAYING 42: *law anna laka mâ fî al-arḍ min shay² a-kunta taftadî bihi*

... عن النبى صعلم قال يقول اللّه تعالى لأهون أهل النار عذابا يـــوم
القيامة لو أنّ لك ما فى الأرض من شئ أكنت تفتدى به فيقول نعم فيـــقول
أردت منك أهون من هذا وأنت فى صلب آدم أن لا تشرك بى شيئا فأبيت
إلاّ أن تشرك بى .

... from the Prophet. He said: "God will say to the one among the people of
the Fire with the lightest punishment on the Day of Resurrection: 'If you had
everything on earth, would you then ransom yourself with it?' Thereupon he
will say, 'Yes'. Then God will say: 'I desired of you that which is easier than
that [desired of you] when you were [still] in the loins of Adam: that you not
associate anything as a partner with Me. [But] you then refused [to do
anything else] but to associate partners with me.'"

    i. Bukhârî 81:51:9, *isnâd* 105 (Anas b. Mâlik).
    ii. Bukhârî 60:1:9, *isnâd* 105.
    iii. Muslim 50:51, *isnâd* 105.
    Other References: Ibn al-'Arabî, *Mishkât*, p. 11; 'Alî al-Qârî, no. 39; al-Madanî,
p. 73.

SAYING 43: *lâ ilâh illâ anâ*

... انّه قال من قال لا اله إلاّ اللّه واللّه أكبر صدّقه ربّه فقال لا اله إلاّ
أنا وأنا أكبر واذا قال لا اله إلاّ اللّه وحده قال يقول اللّه لا اله إلاّ أنــا
وحدى واذا قال لا اله إلاّ اللّه وحده لا شريك له قال لا اله إلاّ أنا وحدى
لا شريك لى واذا قال لا اله إلاّ اللّه له الملك وله الحمد قال اللّه لا الــه
إلاّ أنا لى الملك ولى الحمد واذا قال لا اله إلاّ اللّه ولا حول ولا قوّة إلاّ
باللّه قال اللّه لا اله إلاّ أنا ولا حول ولا قوّة إلاّ بى وكان يقول من قــالها
فى مرضه ثمّ مات لم تطعمه النار .

... he [Muḥammad] said: "Whoever says, 'There is no god but God, and
God is greatest', his Lord counts him trustworthy and says: 'There is no god

but I, and I am most great'. And if he says, 'There is no god but God alone', God says: 'There is no god but I, and I alone'. And if he says, 'There is no god but God alone; He has no partner', He says: 'There is no god but I, and I have no partner'. And if he says, 'There is no god but God. His is the kingdom and the praise', God says: 'There is no god but I. Mine is the kingdom and Mine is the praise'. And if he says, 'There is no god but God, and no power and no might except with God', God says: 'There is no god but I, and no power and no might except with Me'." And he [Muḥammad] used to say: "Whoever says this in his illness and then dies, him shall the Fire not consume".

i. Tirmidhî 45:36, *isnâds* 12a (Abû Hurayrah) and 122 (Abû Saʿîd al-Khudrî).
Other References: al-Madanî, pp. 51, 153; cf. al-Makkî, *Qût*, II, 81; Ghazzâlî, I, 300–301.

SAYING 44: *lâ yanbaghî li-ʿabdî an yaqûla innahu khayr min Yûnus*

. . . عن النبىّ صلعم فيما يرويه عن ربّه قال لا ينبغى لعبدى أن يقول
إنّه خير من يونس بن متّى ونسبه إلى أبيه .

... from the Prophet, in that which he related from his Lord. He said: "'My servant [i.e., Muḥammad] ought not to say that he is better than Jonah, son of Mattá,'"[51] and he [Muḥammad] mentioned his father by name.[52]

i. Bukhârî 97:50:4, *isnâd* 144 (Ibn ʿAbbâs).
ii. Bukhârî 60:24, *isnâd* 144: *ḥadîth nabawî.*
iii. Muslim 43:167, *isnâd* 144: *ḥadîth nabawî.*
iv. Bukhârî, *Tafsîr*, S. 6:86, no. 1, *isnâd* 144: *ḥadîth nabawî*; final sentence (from *wa-nasabahu*) is omitted. S. 6:86 mentions Jonah as one of those whom God has guided rightly in the past.
v. Bukhârî 60:35, *isnâd* 145 (Ibn ʿAbbâs): *ḥadîth nabawî*; wording varies; final sentence omitted.
vi. Bukhârî, *Tafsîr*, S. 4:163, no. 26:1, *isnâd* 145: *ḥadîth nabawî*; final sentence omitted. S. 4:163 mentions Jonah among the leaders of other peoples who have received a revelation from God.
vii. Bukhârî, *Tafsîr*, S. 6:86, no. 2, *isnâd* 36 (Abû Hurayrah): *ḥadîth nabawî*; final sentence omitted.

viii. *Musnad*, II, 405, *isnâd* 36: *ḥadîth nabawî*; final sentence omitted.

ix. Bukhârî, *Tafsîr*, S. 4:163, no. 26:2, *isnâd* 7b (Abû Hurayrah): *ḥadîth nabawî*; wording varies: *man qâla anâ khayr min Yûnus b. Mattá fa-qad kadhaba*, "Whoever says, 'I am better than Jonah, son of Mattá', has lied".

Other References: al-Madanî, p. 6; an-Nawawî, *Tahdhîb al-asmâ'* (pt. 1, ed. Wüstenfeld, Göttingen, 1842–1847), p. 641 (as an *ḥadîth nabawî*).

Saying 45: *lâ ya'tî ibn Âdam an-nadhr bi-shay' lam akun qad qadartuhu*

وقال رسول اللّه صلعم لا يأتى ابن آدم النذر بشىء لم أكن قد قدرته
ولكن يلقه النذر وقد قدرته له استخرج به من البخيل ويؤتينى عليه ما
لم يكن آتانى من قبل .

The Apostle of God said: "[God said:][53] 'A vow brings the son of Adam nothing that I have not [pre]ordained for him. Rather, a vow meets it [i.e., that which has been ordained],[54] and I have already [pre]ordained it for him. I extract by it [i.e., the vow] from the miserly, and he gives Me that which he would not have given Me before.'"

i. Hammâm b. Munabbih, no. 39, *isnâd* 1 (directly from Abû Hurayrah).

ii. *Musnad*, II, 314, *isnâd* 1 (Abû Hurayrah): the *qâla Allâh* is included in the text here (see n. 53).

iii. *Musnad*, II, 242, *isnâd* 5 (Abû Hurayrah): *qâla Allâh* included in the text; the last half of the Saying (from *wa-lâkin yalqâhu*) reads: *wa-lakinnahu shay' astakhriju bihi min al-bakhîl yu'tînî 'alayhi mâ lâ yu'tînî 'alá al-bukhl*, "Rather, it is something that I extract from the miserly that he gives Me [when he makes a vow, but] does not give Me when he is miserly".

iv. Ibrâhîm b. Ṭahmân, no. 88 (fol. 246a), *isnâd* 13 (directly from al-'Alâ' b. 'Ar. b. Ya'qûb from 'Ar. b. Ya'qûb from Abû Hurayrah): in third person as an *ḥadîth nabawî*; *lâ tandhirû*, "do not make vows", is inserted at the beginning.

v. Ibrâhîm b. Ṭahmân, no. 90 (fol. 246a), *isnâd* 172 (directly from Manṣûr from 'Al. b. Murrah from 'Al. b. 'Umar): in third person as an *ḥadîth nabawî*.

vi. Bukhârî 82:6:2, *isnâd* 1: in third person as an *ḥadîth nabawî*.

vii. Bukhârî 83:26:3, *isnâd* 5: in third person as an *ḥadîth nabawî*.

viii. Nasâ'î 35:25, *isnâd* 13: in third person as an *ḥadîth nabawi*.

ix. *Musnad*, II, 373, *isnâd* 5c (Abû Hurayrah): the last part of the ḥadîth (from *wa-lâkin yalqâhu*) reads: *wa-lâkinna an-nadhr muwâqif al-qadar fa-yukhraju bi-dhâlika min al-bakhîl mâ lam yakun al-bakhîl yurîdu an yukhraja*, "Rather, a vow is in agreement with predetermination, and by it is extracted from the miserly what the miserly does not want extracted".

x. Ibn Mâjah 11:15:2, *isnâd* 5: in third person as an *ḥadîth nabawî*; adds at end a separate Divine Saying (no. 16). This seems to be a case where two distinct traditions have been written down together as one by a later transmitter or scribe (see above, p. 94).

Other References: al-Madanî, p. 6.

Josef van Ess, in a conversation in June, 1972, noted that the discussion of the vow probably entered the *qadar* disputes in Islam only in the second century of the Hijrah. If it does in fact belong to a later stage in the predestinarian disputes, the presence of this Saying in the early collection of Hammâm may indicate that it was a "primitive" ḥadîth that was later adapted for use in the *qadar* debates, rather than a later forgery manufactured specifically as an anti-Qadarî weapon.

SAYING 46: *lâ yukhrijuhu illâ îmân bî aw taṣdîq bi-rasulî*

... عن النبيّ صلعم قال انتدب اللّه عزّ وجلّ لمن خرج فى سبيله لا يخرجه إلاّ إيمان بى أو تصديق برسلى أن أرجعه بما نال من أجر أو غنيمة أو أدخله الجنّة ولولا أن أشقّ على أمّتي ما قعدتّ خلف سريّة ولوددتّ أنى أقتل فى سبيل اللّه ثمّ أحيا ثمّ أقتل ثمّ أحيا ثمّ أقتل .

... from the Prophet. He said: "God answers him who goes forth [as a warrior] in His cause: 'Only faith in Me and complete trust in the veracity of My Apostles causes him to go forth. I shall send him back with what he has gained in the way of reward or booty, or [else] I shall cause him to enter Paradise.' [Muḥammad said:] If it were not that I would cause my community hardship, I would not remain behind the troops, and I would wish that I might be killed in God's cause. Then I would live, then be killed; then live, then be killed!"

i. Bukhârî 2:26, *isnâd* 11 (Abû Hurayrah).
ii. Muslim 33:103, *isnâd* 11: longer version, different wording.
iii. Ibn Mâjah 24:1:1, *isnâd* 11: same as version ii.
iv. *Musnad*, II, 231, *isnâd* 11: same as version ii.
v. *Musnad*, II, 384, *isnâd* 11: same as version ii.
vi. *Musnad*, II, 399, *isnâd* 3c (Abû Hurayrah): the Divine Saying is essentially the same; the words of the Prophet differ.

vii. *Musnad*, II, 494, *isnâd* 17a (Abû Hurayrah): wording of the Divine Saying varies somewhat; Muḥammad's final words are omitted.

viii. Nasâ'î 25:14:2, *isnâd* 17a: essentially the same as version vii.

ix. Nasâ'î 47:24:1, *isnâd* 17a: essentially the same as version vii.

x. Nasâ'î 47:24:2, *isnâd* 11: variant of version vii.

xi. Nasâ'î 25:15:2, *isnâd* 175 (ʿAl. b. ʿUmar): variant of version vii; ends with *wa-in qabaḍtuhu ghafartu lahu waraḥimtuhu*, "If I take his soul, I must forgive him and show him mercy".

xii. Tirmidhî 20:1:2, *isnâd* 100a (Anas b. Mâlik): shorter, variant version of no. vii.

xiii. Nasâ'î 25:14:1, *isnâd* 5 (Abû Hurayrah): in third person as an *ḥadîth nabawî*.

xiv. *Muwaṭṭa'* 21:2, *isnâd* 5: *ḥadîth nabawî*, same as version xiii.

Other References: Ibn al-ʿArabî, *Mishkât*, pp. 33–34; al-Madanî, pp. 8, 30, 32, 62; ʿAlî al-Qârî, no. 26.

The *khurûj fî sabîl Allâh* that is spoken of in this Saying need not, at least in later Islam, be only a "going out" in war for God (*jihâd*). It does, however, seem clear here that the more literal sense of the expression is intended, and not the metaphorical interpretation of *jihâd* as moral striving alone (often called "the greater *jihâd*"). The references to the spoils of war and to being killed indicate in particular that it is the willingness to die in the cause of God rather than a more spiritual striving that is being encouraged. This is further substantiated by the specific mention of *ghazá*, "to go out on raids, to raid", in version ii and other variants. Similarly, the apparent meaning of Muḥammad's final statement is that he would gladly be killed again and again by his enemies to gain fulfillment of God's promises. Here the physical *jihâd* itself takes on a larger significance: it becomes the martyr's rapid road into the presence of God.

SAYING 47: *lima faʿalta hâdhâ*

... انّ رسول اللّه صلعم قال قال رجل لم يعمل حسنة قطّ لأهله إذا مات فحرّقوه ثمّ أذروا نصفه فى البرّ ونصفه فى البحر فواللّه لئن قدر اللّه عليه ليعذّبنّه عذابا لا يعذّبه أحدا من العالمين فلمّا مات الرجل فعملوا ما أمرهم به فامر اللّه البرّ فجمع ما فيه وأمر البحر فجمع ما فيه ثمّ قال لم فعلت هذا قال من خشيّتك يا ربّ وأنت أعلم قال فغفر له .

... the Apostle of God said: "A man who had never done anything good said to his family that when he died, they should cremate him and then sprinkle half [of his ashes] on land and half of them on the sea; for, [so said he,] by God, if indeed God should get hold of him [whole], He would set him a punishment more severe than any punishment administered by Him to any other earthly creature. When the man died, they did what he had ordered them to do. Then God commanded the earth, and it gathered up [that part of him] that was in it; He commanded the sea, and it gathered up [that part of him] that was in it. Then He said: 'Why did you do that?' He [the man] said: 'Out of fear of Thee, O Lord. Thou knowest better'. Then He forgave him."

i. *Muwaṭṭa'* 16:51, *isnâd* 5 (Abû Hurayrah).
ii. Bukhârî 97:35:15, *isnâd* 5: omits *fa-lamma mâta ar-rajul fa-ʿamalû mâ amarahum bihi.*
iii. Muslim 49:24, *isnâd* 5.

SAYING 48: *man aẓlam mimman dhahaba yakhluqu ka-khalqî*

... سمعت النبىّ صلعم يقول قال اللّه عزّ وجلّ ومن أظلم ممّن ذهب
يخلق كخلقى فليخلقوا ذرّة أو ليخلقوا حبّة أو شعيرة .

... I heard the Prophet say: "God said: 'Who is more wicked than he who sets out to create as I have created? Let them create a tiny particle,[55] or let them create a seed or a grain of barley!'"

i. Bukhârî 97:56:6, *isnâd* 11 (Abû Hurayrah).
ii. *Musnad*, II, 391, *isnâd* 11: final sentence reads: *fa-l-yakhluqû mithla khalqî dharrah aw dhubâbah aw ḥabbah*, "Let them create as I have created, [even] a speck, or a fly, or a tiny seed!" *Qâla Allâh* is omitted, but the Saying is clearly understood to be God's word.
iii. *Musnad*, II, 232, *isnâd* 11: the Divine Saying proper is set within a frame-story about the Prophet, which is in turn set within a frame-story about Abû Hurayrah. It is said to have been related by Muḥammad just before he demonstrated the permissible limits of the *ḥilyah* ablutions (washing the shanks and forearms as well as the hands and feet). Abû Hurayrah is said to have related this to Abû Zurʿah when the two of them came upon a man sketching a picture one day. While the

latter frame-story or situational account clearly links the Saying to the question of iconoclasm in Islam, there is no apparent internal connection between the Saying and the *ḥilyah*: thus the latter is probably drawn in only to pinpoint the occasion on which Muḥammad told the Saying. This is a common method in the Ḥadîth of strengthening the veracity of a report (the additional situational details serving to confirm the accurate memory of the transmitter and the authenticity of his account). See above, pp. 91 ff. (Chapter 4, C).

iv. Bukhârî 77:90:2, *isnâd* 11: same as version iii, with minor variations in wording. *Qâla Allâh* is omitted, as in version ii.

v. Muslim 37:101, *isnâd* 11: set in the frame-story of the artist, as in version iii, but without mention of the *ḥilyah*-demonstration episode.

vi. *Musnad*, II, 259, *isnâd* 6a (Abû Hurayrah): *baʿûḍah*, "gnat", replaces *dharrah*; *dharrah* replaces *ḥabbah aw shaʿîrah*. See n. 55.

vii. *Musnad*, II, 527, *isnâd* 6a: same as version vi.

viii. *Musnad*, II, 451, *isnâd* 6a: same as version vi.

Other References: al-Madanî, pp. 6, 21.

This Saying echoes at least two different Qurʾânic motifs. The initial interrogative phrase, *man aẓlam mimman* ..., "who is more wicked than he who ...", occurs fifteen times in the Qurʾân (see *Muʿjam*, p. 438) in similar contexts as a challenge-formula of God to man. It is most often completed by ... *iftará ʿalá Allâh al-kadhib*, "... fabricates a lie against God". See, *inter alia*, S. 6:93, 144; 11:18; 18:15; 29:28; 39:32; 61:7. On lying about God and calling Him a liar, see Saying 36 above.

The last part of this Saying recalls very clearly the Qurʾânic challenge to all those who would deny that the Qurʾân comes from God alone, imagining that a human being could create such a sublime work. Cf. S. 52:35–36: *am khuliqû min ghayr shayʾ am hum al-khâliqûn am khalaqû as-samawât wa-l-arḍ bal lâ yûqinûn*, "Or were they created out of nothing? Or are they the creators? Or did they create the heavens and the earth? Certainly not! They are without sure knowledge!" The verses here are addressed to those who mock the Qurʾân and say that it is a contrivance of Muḥammad.

SAYING 49: *man ʿâdá lî walîyan ... kuntu samʿahu alladhî yasmaʿu bihi*

... قال رسول الله صلعم إنّ الله قال من عادى لى وليّا فقد آذنته بالحرب
وما تقرّب إلىّ عبدى بشئ أحبّ إلىّ ممّا افترضته عليه وما يزال عبدى
يتقرّب إلىّ بالنوافل حتّى أحبّه فإذا أحببته كنت سمعه الّذى يسمع به
وبصره الّذى يبصر به ويده الّتى يبطش بها ورجله الّتى يمشى بها وان
سألنى لأعطينّه ولئن استعاذنى لأعيذنّه وما تردّدت عن شئ أنا فاعله
تردّدى عن نفس المؤمن يكره الموت وأنا أكره مساءته .

... the Apostle of God said: "God said: 'Whoever treats a friend of Mine as an enemy, on him I declare war. My servant draws near to Me by means of nothing dearer to Me than that which I have established as a duty[56] for him. And My servant continues drawing nearer to Me through supererogatory acts[57] until I love him; and when I love him, I become his ear with which he hears, his eye with which he sees, his hand with which he grasps, and his foot with which he walks. And if he asks Me [for something], I give it to him. If indeed he seeks My help, I help him. I have never hesitated to do anything as I hesitate [to take] the soul of the man of faith who hates death, for I hate to harm him.'"

i. Bukhârî 81:38:2, *isnâd* 7 (Abû Hurayrah).

ii. *Musnad*, VI, 256, *isnâd*s 153, 153a (ʿÂʾishah): variant wording throughout; the entire second segment (*kuntu samʿahu ... wa-rijlahu allatî yamshî bihâ*) is not present in this version, however (see commentary).

Other References: The two citations above are apparently the only occurrences of this ḥadîth in full or nearly full form in the standard and early sources. Nonetheless it ranks as perhaps the most famous and most frequently quoted of all Divine Sayings among later Muslim writers, especially theorists of mysticism (*taṣawwuf*). Ritter, *Meer*, p. 559, gives numerous references. Other instances occur in the following: Ibn al-ʿArabî, *Mishkât*, p. 38; Ibn al-ʿArabî, *Rûḥ al-bayân* (in Massignon, *Receuil*, p. 118); al-Madanî, pp. 18–19, 36, 68, 75; al-Muḥâsibî (in an unidentified quotation in Massignon, *Essai*, pp. 127, 252, where Massignon says that Muḥâsibî identifies the Saying as a revelation to John the Baptist reported by Ibrâhîm b. Adʹham); al-Makkî, *Qût*, II, 109; as-Sarrâj, *Lumaʿ*, p. 383; al-Ghazzâlî, *Iḥyâʾ*, IV, 327, 328; ʿAṭṭâr, *Musîbatnâme* (quoted in Ritter, *Meer*, p. 28); Nawawî, *Arbaʿûn*, no. 38; Ibn Taymîyah, *Muʿjizât*, p. 15 (where it is attributed to

Tirmidhî); Qushayrî, *Risâlah*, p. 157 (one of the few instances cited here in which the entire ḥadîth as cited by Bukhârî in the text above is quoted, rather than only one portion of it: see the commentary below on the composite nature of this Saying); Kalâbâdhî, pp. 121, 123, 136, 149.

The use of *walî*, "friend", with respect to either God or man in the Divine-human relationship goes back to the Qurʾân: "His [God's] friends (*awliyâʾuhu*) are only the god-fearing (*al-muttaqûn*)" (8:34), and "Surely the friends of God (*awliyâʾ Allâh*) shall have no fear [weigh] upon them, neither shall they sorrow" (10:62). Note that in the former passage, the translation depends upon construing the pronominal suffix as the referent of the antecedent *Allâh* in the previous verse (so Ṭabarî), not *masjid al-ḥarâm*, which would yield "its [the mosque's] protectors" (so Arberry, *Koran*, p. 201), not "His friends" (numerous references in Paret, *Kommentar*, p. 188). Most of the numerous occurrences of *walî* and *awliyâʾ* in the Qurʾân refer to man having no other friend save God. Some refer to the friend(s) of the faithful or the unfaithful (*kâfirs*); others speak of the friends of the devils, or *shayṭâns*; and still others state simply that God is the *walî* of the faithful (see *Muʿjam*, pp. 766–767). Cf. the discussion of *walî* in the commentary to Saying 4 above.

Note that this Saying appears to be a composite one with several identifiable segments that could stand independently of the others: (1) "Whoever treats a friend of Mine as an enemy, on him I declare war"; (2) "My servant draws near to Me ... I become ... his foot with which he walks"; (3) "And if he asks Me ... I help him"; and (4) I have never hesitated ... for I hate to harm him". Of all these segments, the second is the one most often found alone in the later sources that are listed under "Other References" above. Here it is interesting to note that this segment is precisely the one that is missing in the version cited in the *Musnad*, which may indicate that it was the portion most frequently quoted as a separate tradition from early on. Segment 3 is also found alone or in combination with other material as a separate Divine Saying in the classical sources: cf. Sayings 53, 67, 75, and 80 below. However, since only the two cited occurrences of the full or nearly full form of the composite Saying have been found in the classical collections, it is impossible to determine with any precision the textual history of this tradition and its various segments.

SAYING 50: *man dhâ-lladhî yataʾallá ʿalayya an lâ aghfiru li-fulân*

... إنّ رسول اللّه حدّث أنّ رجلا قال واللّه لا يغفر اللّه لفلان وانّ اللّه
تعالى قال من ذا الّذى يتألّى علىّ أن لا أغفر لفلان فإنّى قد غفرت لفلان
وأحبطت عملك أو كما قال .

... the Apostle of God related: "A man said: 'By God, God will not forgive so-and-so!' God said: 'Who is it who swears an oath by Me that I will not forgive so-and-so? I have indeed forgiven so-and-so, and I have made your action fruitless'" (or words to that effect).

i. Muslim 45:137, *isnâd* 360 (Jundab).
Other References: al-Madanî, p. 90.

The final phrase of God's words, *wa-aḥbaṭtu ʿamalaka*, echoes similar words in the Qurʾân: *fa-aḥbaṭa Allâh aʿmâlahum*, "So God has made their works fruitless" (33:19); *fa-aḥbaṭa aʿmâlahum*, "So He has made their works fruitless" (47:9, 28); *wa-sa-yuḥbiṭu aʿmâlahum*, "And He will make their works fruitless" (47:32).

SAYING 51: *man jâʾa bi-l-ḥasanah fa-lahu ʿashr amthâlihâ*

... قال رسول اللّه صلعم يقول اللّه عزّ وجلّ من جاء بالحسنة فله عشر
أمثالها وأزيد ومن جاء بالسيّئة فجزاؤه سيّئة مثلها أو أغفر ومن تقرّب منّى
شبرا تقرّبت منه ذراعا ومن تقرّب منّى ذراعا تقرّبت منه باعا ومن أتانى يمشى
أتيته هرولة ومن لقينى بقراب الأرض خطيئة لا يشرك بى شيئا لقيته بمثلها
مغفرة .

... the Apostle of God said: "God says: 'Whoever does a good deed, to him belong ten like it, and I increase [even this]. Whoever does an evil deed, his requital is an evil deed like it, or I forgive [it]. Whoever draws nearer to Me by a handsbreadth, I draw nearer to him by an armslength; whoever draws nearer to Me by an armslength, I draw nearer to him by a fathom; and whoever comes to meet Me walking, I come to him running. Whoever meets

Me with sins such as to fill the earth but does not associate anything with Me [as partner],[58] him I shall meet with the same measure of forgiveness.'"

i. Muslim 48:22, *isnâd* 130 (Abû Dharr).
ii. Ibn Mâjah 33:58:1, *isnad* 130.
iii. *Musnad*, V, 153, *isnâd* 130.
iv. *Musnad*, V, 169, *isnâd* 130.
v. *Musnad*, V, 148, *isnâd* 130a (Abû Dharr): omits the *man taqarraba ... harwalatan* segment entirely.
vi. *Musnad*, V, 155, *isnâd* 130a: same as version v.
vii. *Musnad*, V, 180, *isnâd* 130a: same as version v.
Other References: al-Madanî, p. 32.

Several segments of this Saying occur alone or in other contexts also. The first sentence is similar to Saying 34 and its variants. The central portion (as far as ... *ataytuhu harwalatan*, "I come to him running") is found also as a separate Divine Saying (see Saying 12a) and in combination with other material (see Saying 12). The final statement concerning God's forgiveness to those who do not commit the sin of *shirk* (see n. 58 above) is also included in a different Divine Saying, no. 83, below.

SAYING 52: *man ṣallá ʿalayka ṣallaytu ʿalayhi*

... عن عبد الرحمن بن عوف قال خرج رسول اللّه صلعم فاتّبعته حتّى دخل نخلا فسجد فأطال السجدة حتّى خفت أو خشيت أن يكون اللّه قد توفّاه أو قبضه فجئت أنظر فرفع رأسه فقال مالك يا عبد الرحمن قال فذكرت ذلك له فقال إنّ جبريل عليه السلام قال لى ألا ابشّرك إنّ اللّه عزّ وجلّ يقول لك من صلّى عليك صلّيت عليه ومن سلّم عليك سلّمت عليه .

... from ʿAr. b. ʿAwf. He said: "The Apostle of God went out and I followed him until he entered the palm trees. Then he prostrated himself and remained prostrate for so long a time that I feared that God had caused him to die" – or: "taken his soul". "So I went to see, and then he raised his head and said: 'What is the matter with you, ʿAbdarraḥmân?' So I mentioned that [which I had feared] to him, and he said: 'Gabriel said to me: "Truly, I bring you good news! God says to you: 'He who prays for you, for him shall I pray;

and he who greets you with peace [i.e., pronounces the benediction of peace upon you], him shall I greet with peace [i.e., upon him shall I pronounce the benediction of peace]'".'"

i. *Musnad,* I, 191, *isnâd* 270 (ʿAr. b. ʿAwf).
ii. *Musnad,* I, 191, *isnâd* 270: minor variations in frame-story.
iii. *Musnad,* I, 191, *isnâd* 271 (ʿAr. b. ʿAwf): minor variations in frame-story.
Other References: Ibn al-ʿArabî, *Mishkât*, 24.

Saying 53: *man yadʿûnî fa-astajîba lahu*

... أنّ رسول الله صلعم قال ينزل ربّنا تبارك وتعالى كلّ ليلة إلى السماء الدنيا حين يبقى ثلث الليل الآخر فيقول من يدعونى فأستجيب له من يسألنى فأعطيه من يستغفرنى فأغفر لـه .

... the Apostle of God said: "Our Lord descends each night to the nearest heaven when the last third of the night remains. Then He says: 'Who entreats Me, that I may answer him? Who asks [something] of Me, that I may give to him? Who asks My forgiveness, that I may forgive?'"

i. *Muwaṭṭa'* 15:30, *isnâds* 4 (directly from az-Zuhrî from al-Agharr from Abû Hurayrah) and 6 (directly from az-Zuhrî from Abû Salamah from Abû Hurayrah).
ii. Abû al-Yamân, no. 49, *isnâds* 4 and 6 (directly from az-Zuhrî in both instances): minor wording variations.
iii. Bukhârî 19:14, *isnâd* 4.
iv. Bukhârî 80:14, *isnâds* 4, 6.
v. Bukhârî 97:35:4, *isnâd* 4.
vi. Muslim 6:168, *isnâds* 4, 6.
vii. Tirmidhî 45:80:1, *isnâds* 4, 6.
viii. *Musnad,* II, 464, *isnâds* 4, 6.
ix. *Musnad,*II, 267, *isnâds* 4, 6.
x. Abû Dâwûd 39:19, *isnâds* 4, 6.
xi. Ibn Mâjah 5:182:3, *isnâds* 4, 6: adds *hattá yaṭluʿa al-fajr fa-li-dhâlika kânû yastaḥibbûna ṣalât âkhir al-layl ʿalá awwalihi*, "... until dawn breaks. Therefore they used to prefer the Prayer at the end of the night to [that at] the first of it".
xii. Ibn Mâjah 5:182:4, *isnâd* 390 (Rifâʿah al-Juhanî): wording variations.

xiii. Muslim 6:170, *isnâd* 6b (Abû Hurayrah): minor wording variations.

xiv. Muslim 6:171, *isnâd* 31 Abû Hurayrah): slightly shorter version; adds at end: *man yuqriḍu ghayr ʿadîm wa-lâ ẓalûm*, "Whoever lends to the destitute and is not unjust", apparently a reference to the man whose prayers will be answered by God.

xv. Muslim 6:172, *isnâd*s 4a (Abû Hurayrah) and 122 (Abû Saʿîd al-Khudrî): minor wording variations.

xvi. *Musnad*, II, 258, *isnâd* 18 (Abû Hurayrah): *man yastaghfirunî fa-aghfira lahu* is replaced by *man dhâ-lladhî yastarziqunî fa-urziqahu man dhâ-lladhî yastakshifu aḍ-ḍurr fa-ukshifahu ʿanhu*, "He who asks Me for sustenance, for him shall I provide. He who asks Me to relieve him in his distress, him shall I rescue from it".

Other References: al-Madanî, pp. 49, 55, 57, 77, 78, 93.

This tradition as a whole is known as the *ḥadîth an-nuzûl*, "the tradition concerning the descent [of God]", according to Shâkir, commentary on *Musnad*, II, 258, (version xvi in the present list), *Musnad*, XIII, 251.

SAYING 53a: *anâ al-malik anâ al-malik man dhâ-lladhî yadʿûnî*

... عن رسول اللّه صلعم قال ينزل اللّه الى السماء الدنيا كلّ ليلة حين يمضى ثلث الليل الأول فيقول أنا الملك أنا الملك من ذا الّذى يدعونى فأستجيب له من ذا الّذى يسألنى فأعطيه من ذا الّذى يستغفرنى فأغفر له فلا يزال كذلك حتّى يضئ الفجر .

... from the Apostle of God. He said: "God descends each night to the nearest heaven when the first third of the night has passed. Then He says: 'I am the King! I am the King![59] He who entreats Me, him shall I answer. He who asks [something of] Me, to him shall I give. He who asks My forgiveness, him shall I forgive.' And He continues thus until the dawn breaks."

i. Muslim 6:169, *isnâd* 3c (Abû Hurayrah).

ii. Suhayl b. Abî Ṣâliḥ, no. 22, *isnâd* 3c (directly from Dhakwân from Abû Hurayrah).

iii. *Musnad*, II, 258, *isnâd* 3c.

iv. *Musnad*, II, 282, *isnâd* 3c.

v. *Musnad*, II, 419, *isnâd* 3c.
viii. Tirmidhî 2:211, *isnâd* 3c.
Other References: Ibn al-ʿArabî, *Mishkât*, p. 29; Ghazzâlî, I, 304.

SAYING 54: *mariḍtu fa-lam taʿudnî*

... قال رسول اللّه صلعم انّ اللّه عزّ وجلّ يقول يوم القيامة يا ابن آدم مرضت فلم تعدنى قال يا ربّ كيف أعودك وأنت ربّ العالمين قال أما علمت أنّ عبدى فلانا مرض فلم تعده أما علمت أنّك لو عدته لوجدتنى عنده يا ابن آدم استطعمتك فلم تطعمنى قال يا ربّ وكيف أطعمك وأنت ربّ العالمين قال أما علمت أنّه استطعمك عبدى فلان فلم تطعمه أما علمت أنّك لو أطعمته لوجدت ذلك عندى يا ابن آدم استسقيتك فلم تسقنى قال يا ربّ كيف أسقيك وأنت ربّ العالمين قال استسقاك عبدى فلان فلم تسقه أما إنك لو سقيته وجدت ذلك عندى .

... the Apostle of God said: "God says on the Day of Resurrection: 'O son of Adam, I was sick and you did not visit Me'. He says: 'O my Lord, how could I visit You, when you are the Lord of all beings?' He says: 'Did you not know that My servant so-and-so was sick, and you did not visit him? Did you not know that if you had visited him, you would have found Me with him? – O son of Adam, I sought food from you, and you did not feed Me.' He [man] says: 'O my Lord, how could I feed you, when you are the Lord of all beings?' He says: 'Did you not know that My servant so-and-so sought food from you, and you did not feed him? Did you not know that if you had fed him, you would have found that to have been for Me? – O son of Adam, I asked you for drink, and you did not give Me to drink.' He says: 'O my Lord, how could I give you to drink, when You are the Lord of all beings?' He says: 'My servant so-and-so asked you for drink, and you did not give him to drink. [Did you not know] that if you had given him to drink, you would have found that to have been for Me?'"

i. Muslim 45:43, *isnâd* 10a (Abû Hurayrah).
ii. *Musnad*, II, 404, *isnâd* 39 (Abû Hurayrah): much shorter version; note in particular the use of *lî* in God's answer to man's questions: *fa-law ʿâdahu kaʾanna*

mâ yaʿûduhu lî, "If he had visited him [who was sick], [it would have been] as if he had visited him in [or: because of, for the sake of, etc.] Me": see the commentary to Saying 19a concerning the *fî* usage.

Other References: Ibn al-ʿArabî, *Mishkât*, p. 40; ʿAlî al-Qârî, no. 4; al-Madanî, pp. 74–75.

This entire Saying of God parallels closely the well-known passage of Matthew 25: 41–45, and thus may conceivably represent a text that Muslims were ready to accept as a pre-Qurʾânic revelation that Muḥammad quoted for the benefit of his community.

SAYING 55: *mâ li-ʿabdî al-muʾmin ʿindî jazâʾ ... illâ al-jannah*

... ان رسول اللّه صلعم قال يقول اللّه تعالى ما لعبدى المؤمن عندى
جزاء إذا قبضت صفيّه من أهل الدنيا ثمّ أحتسبه إلاّ الجنّة .

... the Apostle of God said: "God says: 'My faithful servant has nothing less than Paradise as a reward from Me, should I take away his truest friend among the people of the world, and he ask reparation for him'."

i. Bukhârî 81:6:2, *isnâd* 34 (Abû Hurayrah).
ii. *Musnad*, II, 417, *isnâd* 34.
iii. Nasâʾî 21:23, *isnâd* 182 (ʿAl. b. ʿAmr b. al-ʿÂṣ): variant version, in third person as an *ḥadîth nabawî*.

Other References: al-Madanî, p. 32.

SAYING 56: *mâ yaqûlu ʿibâdî ... ushhidukum annî qad ghafartu lahum*

... قال رسول اللّه صلعم إنّ للّه ملائكه يطوفون فى الطرق يلتمسون أهل
الذكر فإذا وجدوا قوما يذكرون اللّه تنادوا هلمّوا إلى حاجتكم قال فيحفّونهم
بأجنحتهم الى سماء الدنيا قال فيسألهم ربّهم عزّ وجلّ وهو أعلم منهم ما يقول
عبادى قال يقولون يسبحّونك ويكبّرونك ويحمدونك ويمجّدونك قال فيقول هل
رأونى قال فيقولون لا واللّه ما رأوك قال فيقول وكيف لو رأونى قال يقولون لو
رأوك كانوا أشدّ لك عبادة وأشدّ لك تمجيدا وأكثر لك تسبيحا قال يقول فما

يسألونى قال يقولون يسألونك الجنّة قال يقول وهل رأوها قال يقولون لا واللّه
يا ربّ ما رأوها قال يقول فكيف لو أنّهم رأوها قال يقولون لو انّهم رأوها
كانوا أشدّ عليها حرصا وأشدّ لها طلبا وأعظم فيها رغبة قال قال فممّ يتعوّذون
قال يقولون من النار قال يقول وهل رأوها قال يقولون لا واللّه يا ربّ ما
رأوها قال يقول فكيف لو رأوها قال يقولون لو رأوها كانوا أشدّ منها فرارا
وأشدّ لها مخافة قال فيقول فأشهدكم أنّى قد غفرت لهم قال يقول ملك من
الملائكة فيهم فلان ليس منهم إنّما جاء لحاجة قال قال هم الجلساء لا
يشقى بهم جليسهم .

… the Apostle of God said: "God has angels who roam about seeking those who remember and make mention [of God].[60] When they find a group making mention of God, they call to one another, 'Come to that which you have been seeking!' And they beat their wings [and fly up] to the nearest heaven. Then their Lord questions them – and He knows better than they: 'What do my servants say?' They say: 'They glorify and magnify Thee, praise Thee and laud Thee'. Then He says: 'Have they seen Me?' Then they say: 'No, by God, they have not seen Thee'. Thereupon He says: 'And how [would it be] if they saw Me?' They say: 'If they were to see Thee, they would be the stronger in service to Thee, the stronger in glorifying Thee, and the stronger in praising Thee'. He says: 'And what do they ask of Me?' They say: 'They ask Thee for Paradise'. He says: 'And have they seen it?' They say: 'No, by God, they have not seen it'. He says: 'Then how would it be if they were to see it?' They say: 'If they were to see it, they would be the stronger in their striving for it, the stronger in their seeking it, and the stronger in their desire for it'. He says: 'Then from what do they seek deliverance?' They say: 'From the Fire'. He says: 'And have they seen it?' They say: 'No, by God, they have not seen it'. He says: 'Then how [would it be] if they were to see it?' They say: 'They would be the stronger in their flight from it and the stronger in their fear of it'. He says: 'I call you to witness that I have forgiven them'. One of the angels says: 'Among them is so-and-so, who is not one of them. He has come only for something he needs'. He [God] said: 'They are companions with whom no one who is their companion will be wretched'."

i. Bukhârî 80:66:2, *isnâds* 3 (Abû Hurayrah) and 3c (Abû Hurayrah): cf. Saying 37.

ii. Tirmidhî 45:129, *isnâds* 3 and 120 (Abû Sa'îd al-Khudrî): essentially the same ḥadîth; God's first words to the angels are: *ayy shay' taraktum 'ibâdî yaṣna-'ûna*, "What did you leave My servants doing?" Cf. Saying 37.

iii. *Musnad*, II, 251–252, *isnâds* 3, 3c, 120, and 3b (Abû Hurayrah).

iv. Suhayl b. Abî Ṣâliḥ, no. 34, *isnâd* (directly from Dhakwân from Abû Hurayrah): a different version of the same basic story; God's first words to the angels are: *min ayn ji'tum*, "Whence do you come?" Cf. Saying 37:viii.

v. *Musnad*, II, 358–359, *isnâd* 3c: essentially the same as version iv.

vi. *Musnad*, II, 382–383, *isnâd* 3c: essentially the same as version iv.

Other References: Ibn al-'Arabî, *Mishkât*, p. 35; al-Madanî, pp. 93, 94; Ghazzâlî, I, 296.

SAYING 57: *qabiltu shahâdat 'ibâdî 'alá mâ 'alimû*

... عن النبيّ صلعم يرويه عن ربّه عزّ وجلّ قال ما من عبد مسلم يموت يشهد له ثلاثة أبيات من جيرانه الأدنين بخير إلاّ قال الله عزّ وجلّ قد قبلت شهادة عبادى على ما علموا وغفرت له ما أعلم .

... from the Prophet, relating from his Lord. He said: "No Muslim worshipper for whom three households from among his closest neighbors testify to the good [ever] dies without God saying: 'I have accepted the testimony of My worshippers according to that which they knew, and I have forgiven him that which I know'."

i. *Musnad*, II, 384, *isnâd* 29 (Abû Hurayrah).

ii. *Musnad*, II, 408, *isnâd* 29.

Other References: al-Madanî, p. 51.

SAYING 58: *qasamtu aṣ-ṣalât baynî wa-bayn 'abdî*

... عن أبى هريرة عن النبيّ صلعم قال من صلّى صلاة لم يقرأ فيها بأمّ القرآن فهى خداج ثلاثا غير تمام فقيل لأبى هريرة إنّا نكون وراء الامام فقال اقرأ بها فى نفسك فإنّى سمعت رسول الله صلعم يقول قال الله تعالى

قسمت الصلاة بينى وبين عبدى نصفين ولعبدى ما سأل فإذا قال العبد
"الحمد لله ربّ العالمين" قال الله تعالى حمدنى عبدى واذا قال "الرّحمٰن
الرّحيم" قال الله تعالى أثنى علىّ عبدى واذا قال "مالك يوم الدّين" قال
مجّدنى عبدى وقال مرّة فوّض إلىّ عبدى فإذا قال "إيّاك نعبد وايّاك نستعين"
قال هذا بينى وبين عبدى ولعبدى ما سأل فإذا قال "اهدنا الصّراط
المستقيم صراط الّذين أنعمت عليهم غير المغضوب عليهم ولا الضّالّين" قال
هذا لعبدى ولعبدى ما سأل .

... from Abû Hurayrah, from the Prophet. "He [Muḥammad] said: 'Whoever performs a Prayer in which he does not recite the "Mother of the Qur'an",[61] [his Prayer] is thrice[62] deficient; it is incomplete'." Then someone said to Abû Hurayrah, "But we are behind the *imâm* [when we pray]". He said: "[Then] recite it to yourselves, for I heard the Apostle of God say: 'God said: "I have divided the Prayer in two halves between Me and My servant, and My servant shall have what he asks". When the servant says, "Praise be to God, Lord of all beings", God says, "My servant praises Me". And when he says, "The All-Merciful, the All-Compassionate", God says, "My servant extols Me". And when he says, "Master of the Day of Judgment", He says, "My servant glorifies Me" (one time he said: "My servant gives full power to Me"). And when he says, "Thee do we serve, and Thee do we ask for help", He says, "This is between Me and My servant, and My servant shall have what he asks". And when he says, "Lead us on the straight path, the path of those whom Thou hast guided, not of those against whom Thou art angry, nor of those who are astray", He says, "This belongs to My servant, and My servant shall have what he asks".'"

i. Muslim 4:38, *isnâd* 13 (Abû Hurayrah).
ii. Muslim 4:41, *isnâd* 13.
iii. *Musnad*, II, 241, *isnâd* 13.
iv. Tirmidhî, *Tafsîr*, S. 1, no. 1, *isnâd* 13.
v. Ibn Mâjah 33:52:6, *isnâd* 13: introductory frame-story omitted.
vi. Muslim 4:39, *isnâd* 24 (Abû Hurayrah).
vii. Muslim 4:40, *isnâd* 24.
viii. *Muwaṭṭa'* 3:39, *isnâd* 24.
ix. Nasâ'î 11:23, *isnâd* 24.
x. Abû Dâwûd 2:132, *isnâd* 24.

xi. *Musnad*, II, 285, *isnâd* 24.

xii. *Musnad*, II, 460, *isnâd* 24.

Other References: Ibn al-ʿArabî, *Mishkât*, pp. 20–21; ʿAlî al-Qârî, no. 1; al-Madanî, p. 6.

SAYING 59: *raḥmatî ghalabat ghaḍabî*

. . . قال رسول اللّه صلعم لمّا قضى اللّه الخلق كتب في كتابه فهو عنده فوق العرش أنّ رحمتي غلبت غضبي .

... the Apostle of God said: "When God finished the creation, He wrote in His book, which is there with Him, above the Throne: 'Verily, My mercy overcomes My wrath'."

i. Bukhârî 59:1:4, *isnâd* 5 (Abû Hurayrah).

ii. Hammâm b. Munabbih, no. 13, *isnâd* 1 (directly from Abû Hurayrah): *kitâban* replaces *fî kitâbihi*, which would seem to carry a different sense from that of version i: i.e., "He wrote down a [particular] writing that is with Him ...", meaning that it is specifically this writing ("My mercy overcomes My wrath") that is above the Throne rather than a larger book containing *inter alia* this particular statement.

iii. *Musnad*, II, 313, *isnâd* 1 (Abû Hurayrah): *sabaqat*, "precedes, takes precedence over", replaces *ghalabat*.

iv. Bukhârî 97:22:5, *isnâd* 5: same as version iii.

v. Bukhârî 97:28:1, *isnâd* 5: same as version iii.

vi. *Musnad*, II, 242, *isnâd* 5: same as version iii; Divine Saying only, without any frame-story.

vii. *Musnad*, II, 258, *isnâd* 5: same as version iii.

viii. *Musnad*, II, 260, *isnâd* 5: same as version iii.

ix. *Musnad*, II, 358, *isnâd* 5.

x. Muslim 49:14, *isnâd* 5.

xi. *Muslim* 49:15, *isnâd* 5: Divine Saying only, without any frame-story.

xii. Bukhârî 97:15:2, *isnâd* 3 (Abû Hurayrah): inserts after *kitâbihi*, *wa-huwa yaktubu ʿalá nafsihi wa-huwa waḍʿ ʿindahu ʿalá al-ʿarsh*, "and He writes it for [i.e., as an obligation upon] Himself, and it is with Him upon the Throne".

xiii. *Musnad*, II, 466, *isnâd* 3: *ʿalá ʿarshihi*, "upon His Throne", replaces *fî kitâbihi ... fawq al-ʿarsh*; *sabaqat* replaces *ghalabat*.

xiv. *Musnad*, II, 397, *isnâd* 3: *kataba kitâban bi-yadihi li-nafsihi qabl an yakhluqa as-samawât wa-l-arḍ fa-waḍaʿahu taḥt ʿarshihi fihi raḥmatî sabaqat ghaḍabî*, "He wrote down a writing with His own hand for Himself before He created the heavens and earth. Then He put it beneath His Throne. In it [is]: 'My mercy takes precedence over My wrath'".

xv. *Musnad,* II, 433, *isnâd* 15 (Abû Hurayrah): *bi yadihi ʿalá nafsihi* replaces *fî kitâbihi*: see version xiv.

xvi. Ibn Mâjah, *Muqaddimah,* 13:13, *isnâd* 15: same as version xv, with the addition of *qabl an yakhluqa al-khalq* as in version xiv.

xvii. Ibn Mâjah 37:35:3, *isnâd* 15.

xviii. Bukhârî 97:55:1, *isnâd* 10 (Abû Hurayrah): gives *ghalabat aw sabaqat*, "overcomes *or* precedes".

xix. *Musnad,* II, 381, *isnâd* 10: same as version xviii.

xx. Muslim 49:16, *isnâd* 17 (Abû Hurayrah): *fî kitâbihi* is replaced by *fî kitâbihi ʿalá nafsihi,* "in His book, for [?] Himself": cf. versions xii, xiv, and xv.

Other References: al-Madanî, pp. 6, 65, 69; ʿAlî al-Qârî, no. 18.

SAYING 60: *samaʿa Allâh li-man ḥamidahu*

...[فقال رسول اللّه صلعم]... واذا قال سمع اللّه لمن حمده فقولوا اللّهمّ ربّنا لك الحمد يسمع اللّه لكم فإنّ اللّه تبارك وتعالى قال على لسان نبيّه صلعم سمع اللّه لمن حمده ....

... [then the Apostle of God said:] "If [the leader of the Prayer] says, 'God gives ear to him who praises Him', then [you worshippers should] say: 'O God, our God, to Thee be praise!' God gives ear to you. Indeed, God said, through the tongue of His Prophet, 'God gives ear to him who praises Him!'"

i. Muslim 4:62, *isnâd* 401 (Abû Mûsá al-Ashʿarî): occurs in the course of a long ḥadîth that deals with the correct way to perform the Prayer and respond to the *imâm*, or leader of the Prayer.

ii. Muslim 4:63, *isnâd* 401: minor variations in the frame-story only.

iii. Muslim 4:64, *isnâd* 401: set in same frame story; *qaḍá ʿalá lisân* replaces *qâla ʿalá lisân.*

iv. Muslim 4:86, *isnâd* 5 (Abû Hurayrah): *ḥadîth nabawî.* This saying is found in numerous instances with many different *isnâd*s as a word of Muḥammad rather than of God: e.g., Muslim 4:25, 28, 54, 71, 77, 88, 89, 196, 198, 199, 202, 6:202, 203; 10:3, 6; Bukhârî 16:4, 5, 19; 18:17; 64:21, etc. Other references at *Concordance*, II, 536 ("samiʿa").

Other References: Ibn al-ʿArabî, *Mishkât*, p. 20.

SAYING 61: *aṣ-ṣawm lî wa-anâ ajzî bihi*

. . . قال رسول اللّه صلعم إنّ اللّه عزّ وجلّ يقول إنّ الصوم لى وأنا أجزى
به إنّ للصائم فرحتين إذا أفطر فرح واذا لقى اللّه فرح والّذى نفس محمّد
بيده لخلوف فم الصائم أطيب عند اللّه من ريح المسك .

... the Apostle of God said: "God says: 'Fasting is Mine, and I reward it'.[63] The one who fasts has two joys: when he breaks the fast, he rejoices, and when he meets God, he rejoices. By Him in whose hands is the soul of Muḥammad, the smell of the mouth of the one who fasts is more delectable to God than the scent of musk."[64]

i. Muslim 13:165, *isnâd*s 3i (Abû Hurayrah) and 120a (Abû Saʿîd al-Khudrî).
ii. *Musnad*, III, 5, *isnâd*s 3i, 120a.
iii. *Musnad*, II, 232, *isnâd* 3i.
iv. Nasâʾî 22:42:1, *isnâd* 120a.
v. Nasâʾî 22:41:1, *isnâd* 300 (ʿAlî b. Abî Ṭâlib).
vi. Nasâʾî 22:42:2, *isnâd* 3g (Abû Hurayrah).
Other References: al-Madanî, p. 73; *Jawâhir*, p. 363.

SAYING 61a: *yadharu shahwatahu wa-ṭaʿâmahu wa-sharâbahu min ajlî*

. . . وقال رسول اللّه صلعم والّذى نفس محمّد بيده لخلوف فم الصائم
أطيب عند اللّه من ريح المسك يذر شهوته وطعامه وشرابه من أجلى فالصيام
لى وأنا أجزى به .

... the Apostle of God said: "By Him in whose hand is the soul of Muḥammad! The smell of the one who fasts is more delectable to God than the scent of musk. [God says:][65] 'He abstains from his desire[s], his food, and his drink for My sake. Fasting is Mine, and I reward it'."

i. Hammâm b. Munabbih, no. 16, *isnâd* 1 (directly from Abû Hurayrah).
ii. *Musnad*, II, 313, *isnâd* 1 (Abû Hurayrah).
iii. *Muwaṭṭaʾ* 18:58, *isnâd* 5 (Abû Hurayrah): adds at end, *kull ḥasanah bi-ʿashr amthâlihâ ilá sabʿimîʾah ḍiʿf*, as in Saying 61e, which see.

iv. Bukhârî 30:2, *isnâd* 5: same as version v, with addition of one segment at the beginning: *aṣ-ṣawm junnah ... innî ṣâ'im*, as in Saying 61d.
v. *Musnad*, II, 465, *isnâd* 5: essentially the same as version iv.
vi. *Musnad*, II, 395, *isnâd* 8a (Abû Hurayrah): *qâla rabbukum*, "Your Lord said", is inserted before *yadharu*.
vii. *Musnad*, III, 40, *isnâd* 123 (Abû Saʿîd al-Khudrî): minor wording variations.
Other References: al-Madanî, p. 20; Kalâbâdhî, *Taʿarruf*, p. 143.

SAYING 61b: *al-ḥasanah li-ʿashr amthâlihâ wa-ṣ-ṣawm lî*

. . . عن رسول الله صلعم قال يقول الله عزّ وجلّ الحسنة لعشر أمثالها
والصوم لى وأنا أجزى به انّه يذر طعامه وشرابه من أجلى ولخلوف فم الصائم
أطيب عند الله من ريح المسك .

... from the Apostle of God. He said: "God says: 'A good deed is [reckoned] as ten like it.[66] Fasting is Mine, and I reward it. He [the one who fasts] abstains from his food and his drink for My sake. The smell of the mouth of the one who fasts is more delectable to God than the scent of musk.'"[67]

i. Ibrâhîm b. Ṭahmân, no. 107 (fol. 247b), *isnâd* 8 (directly from Hishâm b. Ḥassân from Muḥ. b. Sîrîn from Abû Hurayrah).
ii. *Musnad*, II, 234, *isnâd* 8.
iii. *Musnad*, II, 410–411, *isnâd* 8.
iv. *Musnad*, II, 516, *isnâd* 8: omits *innahu yadharu ... min ajlî.*
Other References: al-Madanî, pp. 14, 20, 65, 88.

SAYING 61c: *li-kull ʿamal kaffârah wa-ṣ-ṣawm lî*

. . . عن النبىّ صلعم يرويه عن ربّكم قال لكلّ عمل كفّارة والصوم لى وأنا
أجزى به ولخلوف فم الصائم أطيب عند الله من ريح المسك .

... from the Prophet, relating from your Lord. He said: "'For every action there is reparation. Fasting is Mine, and I reward it. The smell of the mouth of the one who fasts is more delectable to God than the scent of musk.'"[68]

i. Bukhârî 97:50:3, *isnâd* 9a (Abû Hurayrah).

ii. *Musnad*, II, 504, *isnâd* 9a.

iii. Ibrâhîm b. Ṭahmân, no. 116 (fol. 248a), *isnâd* 9 (directly from Muḥ. b. Ziyâd from Abû Hurayrah): *li-kull ʿamal* is replaced by *kull ʿamal*, which presents some difficulties in sense and translation: it seems most likely that this is simply an error in the text.

iv. *Musnad*, II, 457, *isnâd* 9a: same as version iii.

v. *Musnad*, II, 467, *isnâd* 9b (Abû Hurayrah): the final sentence is clearly given as words of Muḥammad.

SAYING 61d: *kull ʿamal ibn Âdam lahu illá aṣ-ṣawm fa-innahu lî*

... قال رسول اللّه صلعم قال اللّه عزّ وجلّ كلّ عمل ابن آدم له إلاّ الصيام
فانّه لى وأنا أجزى به والصيام جنّة واذا كان يوم صوم أحدكم فلا يرفث ولا
يصخب فان سابه أحد أو قاتله فليقل إنّى صائم والّذى نفس محمّد بيده
لخلوف فم الصائم أطيب عند اللّه من ريح المسك للصائم فرحتان يفرحهما إذا
أفطر فرح واذا لقى ربّه فرح بصومه .

... the Apostle of God said: "God said: 'Every action of the son of Adam is his except fasting. It is Mine, and I reward it. Fasting is a protection. When one of you has a day of fasting, he should then speak neither obscenely nor too loudly; and if someone seeks to curse him or fight with him, let him say, "I am fasting".'[69] By Him in whose hands is the soul of Muḥammad, the smell of the mouth of the one who fasts is more delectable to God than the scent of musk. The one who fasts has two joys in which to delight: when he breaks the fast, he rejoices; and when he meets his Lord, he rejoices, because of his fasting."

i. Bukhârî 30:9, *isnâd* 3h (Abû Hurayrah).

ii. Muslim 13:163, *isnâd* 3h: inserts *yawm al-qiyâmah*, "on the Day of Resurrection", before *min rîḥ al-misk*, and *bi-fiṭrihi*, "[rejoices] in his fast breaking", before *wa-idhâ laqiya rabbahu*.

iii. Nasâʾî 22:42:4, *isnâd* 3h: same as version ii.

iv. Nasâʾî 22:42:5, *isnâd* 3h: ends with *min rîḥ al-misk*.

v. *Musnad*, II, 273, *isnâd* 3h: same as version ii.

vi. Bukhârî 77:78, *isnâd* 2 (Abû Hurayrah): has only two segments of version i: (1) *kull ʿamal ... ajzî bihi*, and (2) [*wa-*]*khulûf fam aṣ-ṣâʾim ... min rîḥ al-misk*.

vii. *Musnad*, II, 281–282, *isnâd* 2: essentially the same as version vi.

viii. Nasâʾî 22:42:6, *isnâd* 2: essentially the same as version vi.

ix. Suhayl b. Abî Ṣâliḥ, no. 8, *isnâd* (directly from Dhakwân from Abû Hurayrah): same basic elements as version i, but in different order, with some wording variations; also inserts a variant version of the same segment found in the middle of Saying 61b, "He abstains from ... for My sake".

Other References: ʿAlî al-Qârî, no. 12; al-Madanî, p. 4.

Saying 61e: *illâ aṣ-ṣawm fa-innahu lî wa-anâ ajzî bihi*

... قال رسول اللّه صلعم كلّ عمل ابن آدم يضاعف الحسنة عشر أمثالها إلى سبعمائة ضعف قال اللّه عزّ وجلّ الاّ الصوم فإنه لى وأنا أجزى به يدع شهوته وطعامه من أجلى للصائم فرحتان فرحة عند فطره وفرحة عند لقاء ربّه ولخلوف فيه أطيب عند اللّه من ريح المسك .

... the Apostle of God said: "Every action of the son of Adam will be multiplied: a good deed [will be counted] as from ten like it up to seven hundredfold. God said: 'Except fasting, for it is Mine, and I reward it. He [who fasts] abstains from his desires and his food for My sake.[70] The one who fasts has two joys: joy when breaking the fast, and joy when meeting his Lord. The smell of his mouth is more delectable to God than the scent of musk.'"

i. Muslim 13:164, *isnâd* 3 (Abû Hurayrah).

ii. Ibn Mâjah 33:58:3, *isnâd* 3: ends with *wa-anâ ajzî bihi*.

iii. Nasâʾî 22:42:3, *isnâd* 3: inserts *aṣ-ṣiyâm junnah*, "fasting is a protection", after *min ajlî*; minor wording variations in the first part.

iv. *Musnad*, II, 480, *isnâd* 3b (Abû Hurayrah): basically the same as version iii.

v. Bukhârî 97:35:2, *isnâd* 3: omits the initial words of the Prophet (*kull ʿamal ...* etc.); the Divine Saying proper begins: *aṣ-ṣawm lî wa-anâ ajzî bihi*, "Fasting is Mine, and I reward it"; *aṣ-ṣawm junnah*, as in version iii.

vi. *Musnad*, II, 393, *isnâd* 3: same as version v.

vii. *Musnad,* I, 446, *isnâd* 192 (ʿAl. b. Masʿûd): omits *yadaʿu shahwatahu wa-taʿâmahu min ajlî.*

Other References: al-Madanî, pp. 14, 20, 65, 88.

SAYING 62: *shafaʿat al-malâʾikah wa-shafaʿa an-nabîyûn*

...[عن النبىّ صلعم] فيقول اللّه عزّ وجلّ شفعت الملائكة وشفع النبيّـــون
وشفع المؤمنون ولم يبق إلاّ أرحم الراحمين ....

... [from the Prophet:] "God says: 'The angels have interceded, the prophets have interceded, and the faithful have interceded; there remains only the Most Merciful of the merciful'...."

i. Muslim 1:302, *isnâd* 121 (Abû Saʿîd al-Khudrî): one of a number of Divine Sayings that occur in the collection of eschatological accounts that make up the multiple-tradition in Muslim 1:302. Cf. Sayings 8:iv and 76:iv.

ii. Bukhârî 97:24:5, *isnâd* 121: set in the same multiple-tradition as version i.

iii. *Musnad,* III, 94–95, *isnâd* 121: set in the same multiple-tradition as version i.

Other References: Ibn al-ʿArabî, *Mishkât,* pp. 11–12.

This Saying stresses what so many of the Divine Sayings do, God's unbounded mercy. It emphasizes this idea by stating that even after the intercession of the most pious beings in creation, man will still be thrown at last upon the mercy of God alone, "the Most Merciful of the merciful".

SAYING 63: *tamanna ... fa-inna laka mâ tamannayta wa-mithlahu maʿahu*

وقال رسول اللّه صلعم إنّ أدنى مقعد أحدكم من الجنّة ان هيئ له أن
يقال له تمـــنّ فيتمنّى ويتمنّى فيقال له هل تمنّيت فيقول نعم فيقول له فان
لك ما تمنّيت ومثله معـــه .

The Apostle of God said: "If one of you were to have prepared for him a lowly dwelling in Paradise, it will be said to him [by God]: 'Wish!' And he will wish and wish. Then he will be asked, 'Have you wished?' He will say, 'Yes', and [God] will say to him: 'You shall have what you wished for and similar things as well'."

i. Hammâm b. Munabbih, no. 55, *isnâd* 1 (directly from Abû Hurayrah).
ii. Muslim 1:301, *isnâd* 1 (Abû Hurayrah).
iii. *Musnad*, II, 315, *isnâd* 1.
iv. *Musnad*, II, 450, *isnâd* 6a (Abû Hurayrah): wording varies.

The final statement by God is found in numerous traditions that have to do with the promise of Paradise to man. It is sometimes quoted by Abû Hurayrah, and sometimes by Abû Saʿîd al-Khudrî. Cf. Muslim 1:299, 309; Bukhârî 10:129; 81:52; 97:24; *Musnad*, II, 276, 294, 534; III, 27, 70, 74.

Saying 64: *tawâḍaʿû ḥattá lâ yafkharu aḥad*

... قام فينا رسول الله صلعم ذات يوم خطيبا .... وزاد فيه وانّ اللّه أوحى اليّ أن تواضعوا حتّى لا يفخر أحد ولا يبغى أحد على أحد .

... the Apostle of God gave a sermon in our company one day.... In it, he added: "Truly, God revealed to me: 'You should humble yourselves, so that none of you considers himself superior to another and none of you oppresses another'."

i. Muslim 51:64b, *isnâd* 310 (ʿIyâḍ b. Ḥimâr): set within a longer tradition that is described as a sermon (*khuṭbah*) of the Prophet (see commentary below and Saying 40:ii).
ii. Abû Dâwûd 40:40, *isnâd* 311 (ʿIyâḍ b. Ḥimâr): occurs alone, without any further material or reference to a longer sermon, as a separate Divine Saying.
iii. Ibn Mâjah 37:16:7, *isnâd* 310: occurs alone, as version ii; omits the final clause, *wa-lâ yabghî aḥad ʿalá aḥad.*
iv. Ibn Mâjah 37:23:4, *isnâd* 106 (Anas b. Mâlik): occurs alone, as version ii; omits *ḥattá lâ yafkharu aḥad ʿalá aḥad.*

The portion of the ḥadîth indicated by the ellipsis is a separate Divine Saying, which is cited as Muslim 51:64a and given as Saying 40:ii, which see.

SAYING 65: *thalâthah anâ khaṣmuhum yawm al-qiyâmah*

... عن النبىّ صلعم قال قال الله ثلاثة أنا خصمهم يوم القيامة رجل أعطى بى ثمّ غدر ورجل باع حرّا فأكل ثمنه ورجل استأجر أجيرا فاستوفى منه ولم يعط أجره .

... from the Prophet. He said: "God said: 'There are three persons whose foe I shall be on the Day of Resurrection: the man who gives [something] in Me[71] and then betrays [his gift]; the man who sells a free man and then feasts upon his [illicit] gain; and the man who hires a laborer, receives full measure from him, and then does not pay his wage.'"

i. Bukhârî 34:106, *isnâd* 34b (Abû Hurayrah).
ii. Bukhârî 37:10, *isnâd* 34b.
iii. Ibn Mâjah 16:4:1, *isnâd* 34b: omits *qâla Allâh*, but still clearly a Divine Saying.
iv. *Musnad*, II, 358, *isnâd* 34b: *aʿtá bî* is replaced by *uʿṭiyá bihi*, "to whom [something] is given".
Other References: al-Madanî, p. 5.

SAYING 66: *ṭibta wa-ṭâba mamshâka*

... انّ رسول الله صلعم قال إذا عاد المسلم أخاه أو زاره قال الله عزّ وجل طبت وطاب ممشاك وتبوّات فى الجنّة منزلا .

... the Apostle of God said: "If the Muslim pays frequent sick cells to his brother or visits him, God says: 'You have acted kindly and well, and your going there has been deemed good. And you shall have your abode in Paradise'."

i. *Musnad*, II, 344, *isnâd* 21 (Abû Hurayrah).
ii. *Musnad*, II, 326, *isnâd* 21: minor wording variations.
iii. *Musnad*, II, 354, *isnâd* 21: *fî Allâh* is inserted after *aw zârahu* in the portion of the ḥadîth that reports Muḥammad's words, according to one version attested to by one of a pair of transmitters who form the fifth link or rank in *isnâd* 21 here. On this usage, see the commentary to Saying 19a above.

There are also a number of Prophetic Traditions that do not contain Divine Sayings which assure the Muslim who calls upon the sick of a place in Paradise: cf. Muslim 45:41; Tirmidhî 8:2; *Musnad*, V, 276, 279, 283, 284; other references at *Concordance*, IV, 409b ("ʿâda").

Saying 67: *turîdûna shay'an azîdukum*

... عن النبيّ صلعم قال إذا دخل اهل الجنّة الجنّة قال يقول الله تبارك
وتعالى تريدون شيئا أزيدكم فيقولون ألم تبيض وجوهنا ألم تدخلنا الجنّة
وتنجّنا من النار قال فيكشف الحجاب فما أعطوا شيئا أحبّ إليهم من النظر
إلى ربّهم عزّ وجلّ .

... from the Prophet. He said: "When the people of Paradise enter Paradise, God will say: 'Do you want for anything more that I may give?' Then they will say: 'Hast Thou not caused our faces to light up [with joy]?[72] Hast Thou not caused us to enter Paradise and rescued us from the Fire?' Then He will lift the veil, and they [could] not be given anything that they would love more than the vision of their Lord."

i. Muslim 1:297, *isnâd* 380 (Ṣuhayb): a variant version with the same *isnâd* is also cited as no. 298: in it, the Prophet adds at the end a recitation of S. 10:26: *li-lladhîna aḥsanû al-ḥusná wa-ziyâdah wa-lâ yarhaqu wujûhahum qatar wa-lâ dhillah* ..., "To those who are righteous [belongs] the very best and more; and neither dust nor abasement will cover their faces ...".

ii. *Musnad*, IV, 332, *isnâd* 380: minor wording variations; *qâla Allah* is replaced by the passive verb *nûdû*, "they [the people of Paradise] are addressed/called to". S. 10:26 recitation also included. See p. 87 above.

iii. *Musnad*, IV, 333, *isnâd* 380: minor wording variations; *qâla Allâh* is replaced by *nâdá munâdin*, "a crier/speaker cried out/called out". S. 10:26 recitation also included. See p. 87 above.

iv. Tirmidhî, *Tafsîr*, S. 10:26, no. 1, *isnâd* 380: same as version iii. Concerning S. 10:26, see version i above.

v. *Musnad*, VI, 16, *isnâd* 380: minor wording variations; *nûdû* replaces *qâla Allâh* as in version ii; S. 10:26 is not mentioned.

Other References: Ibn al-ʿArabî, *Mishkât*, 12–13; al-Madanî, p. 49.

SAYING 68: *uḥibbu fulânan fa-aḥibbahu*

... عن النبيّ صلعم قال إذا أحبّ الله عبدا دعا جبريل فقال إنّي أحببت
فلانا فاحبّه فيحبّه جبريل ثمّ ينادى فى السماء إنّ الله قد أحبّ فلانا فأحبّوه
ثمّ يوضع له القبول فى الأرض واذا أبغض فمثل ذلك .

... the Prophet said: "God, if He loves a servant, calls Gabriel and says: 'I love so-and-so; therefore love him!' So Gabriel loves him, and then he calls forth in Heaven: 'Verily, God loves so-and-so; so love him!' Thereupon acceptance is accorded him on earth.[73] And if He hates [him], it transpires accordingly."

i. Suhayl b. Abî Ṣâliḥ, no. 16, *isnâd* 3c (directly from Dhakwân Abû Ṣâliḥ from Abû Hurayrah).

ii. *Musnad*, II, 267, *isnâd* 3c (Abû Hurayrah): minor wording variations.

iii. *Musnad*, II, 341, *isnâd* 3c: minor wording variations.

iv. *Muwaṭṭa'* 51:15, *isnâd* 3c (directly from Suhayl): *wa-idhâ abghaḍa* portion is expanded to read: *wa-idhâ abghaḍa Allâh al-ʿabd qâla Mâlik lâ aḥsibuhu illâ annahu qâla fî al-bughḍ mithla dhâlik*, "'And if God hates the servant', Mâlik said, 'I do not think otherwise than that He said something similar concerning hatred'".

v. Muslim 45:157, *isnâd* 3c: the *abghaḍa* portion is expanded to parallel the first portion concerning love ("And if He hates a servant, He calls Gabriel and says, 'I hate so-and-so; hate him also ...'", etc.).

vi. Tirmidhî, *Tafsîr*, S. 19:96, no. 7, *isnâd*s 3c and 3d (Abû Hurayrah): same as version v. S. 19:96 reads: "Verily those who have faith and act righteously, to them the All-Merciful shall give (lit., make, give: *yajʿalu*) love (*wudd*)".

vii. *Musnad*, II, 413, *isnâd* 3c: same as version v.

viii. *Musnad*, II, 509, *isnâd* 3c: same as version v.

ix. Bukhârî 97:33:1, *isnâd* 3d: the ḥadîth ends with *al-qabûl fî al-arḍ*, without any mention of *abghaḍa* at all.

x. Bukhârî 78:41, *isnâd* 14 (Abû Hurayrah): same as version ix.

xi. Bukhârî 59:6:3, *isnâd* 14: same as version ix.

xii. *Musnad*, II, 514, *isnâd* 14: same as version ix.

Other References: Ibn al-ʿArabî, *Mishkât*, p. 37; Qushayrî, *Risâlah*, p. 157.

SAYING 69: *ummatuka lâ yazâlûna yaqûlûna mâ kadhâ*

... عن رسول الله صلعم قال قال الله عزّ وجلّ إنّ أمّتك لا يزالون يقولون
ما كذا ما كذا حتّى يقولوا هذا الله خلق الخلق فمن خلق الله .

... from the Apostle of God: "God said: 'Verily, your community will not cease saying, "Not so! Not so!" until they [go so far as to] say, "God created creatures, but who created God?"'"

i. Muslim 1:217, *isnâd* 110 (Anas b. Mâlik): two further *isnâd*s are also given for the Saying as an *ḥadîth nabawî*, both to Anas through Mukhtâr.

ii. Hammâm b. Munabbih, no. 93, *isnâd* 1 (directly from Abû Hurayrah): *ḥadîth nabawî*.

Other References: al-Madanî, p. 16.

This Saying sounds like a tendentious ḥadîth aimed at speculators and/or doubters in religious matters; if so, it is an early one, for it is attested in Hammâm's *ṣaḥîfah* as indicated.

SAYING 70: *unẓur ilayhâ wa-ilá mâ aʿdadtu li-ahlihâ fîhâ*

... عن رسول الله صلعم قال لمّا خلق الله الجنّة والنار أرسل جبريل عليه
السلام الى الجنّة فقال انظر اليها والى ما أعددت لأهلها فيها فنظر اليها
فرجع فقال وعزّتك لا يسمع بها أحد إلاّ دخلها فأمر بها فحفّت بالمكاره فقال
اذهب اليها فانظر اليها والى ما أعددت لأهلها فيها فنظر اليها فإذا هى
قد حفّت بالمكاره فقال وعزّتك لقد خشيت أن لا يدخلها أحد قال اذهب
فانظر الى النار والى ما أعددت لأهلها فيها فنظر اليها فإذا هى يركب
بعضها بعضا فرجع فقال وعزّتك لا يدخلها أحد فأمر بها فحفّت بالشهوات
فقال ارجع فانظر اليها فنظر اليها فإذا هى قد حفّت بالشهوات فرجع وقال
وعزّتك لقد خشيت أن لا ينجو منها أحد إلاّ دخلها .

... from the Prophet. He said: "When God created Paradise and the Fire, He sent Gabriel to Paradise and said: 'Look at it and at that which I have prepared in it for its people'. So he [went and] looked at it; then he returned and said: 'By Thy glory, no one will hear of it without [doing all that is necessary for] getting in!' So God ordered that it be surrounded with trials. Then He said: 'Go to it and look at it and at that which I have prepared in it for its people'. So he [went and] looked at it, and lo, it had been set about with trials. Then he said: 'By Thy glory, [now] I fear that no one will [be able to] get into it!' He [God] said: 'Go and look at the Fire and at that which I have prepared in it for its people'. So he [went and] looked at it, and lo, one part of it was jammed up [hideously] upon another. Then he returned and said: 'By Thy glory, no one will [want to] enter it!' So He ordered that it be surrounded with lusts [to entice men], and He said: 'Return and look at it'. So he [went and] looked at it, and lo, it was set about with lusts. Then he returned and said: 'By Thy glory, [now] I fear that no one will be [able to be] saved from entering it!'"

i. Nasâ'î 35:3, *isnâd* 6a (Abû Hurayrah).
ii. Abû Dâwûd 39:22, *isnâd* 6a.
iii. Tirmidhî 36:21, *isnâd* 6a.
iv. *Musnad*, II, 333, *isnâd* 6a.
v. *Musnad*, II, 354, *isnâd* 6a.
vi. *Musnad*, II, 373, *isnâd* 6a.
Other References: Ibn al-ʿArabî, *Mishkât*, pp. 6–7.

This Saying is etiological in that it gives an explanation as to how Heaven and Hell came to be as wonderful and terrible, respectively, as they are. Paradise must be made difficult to attain; its people must win entry into it by their own striving to surmount the many obstacles that bar the way in. Similarly, Hell must be set about with lusts and desires that will lure the unfaithful in. Each place is entered only by a path that appears to be the opposite of the place at its end: by enduring trials, one gains the ease of Paradise; by succombing to one's lusts and passions, one ends by being sent to the Fire. The passage is a metaphorical explanation of these two possible fates of man.

SAYING 71: *unẓurû hal tajidûna lahu min taṭawwuʿ*

... أنّ النبىّ صلعم قال انّ أول ما يحاسب به العبد يوم القيامة صلاته
فان وجدت تامّة كتبت تامّة وان كان انتقص منها شيئ قال انظروا هل
تجدون له من تطوّع يكمّل له ما ضيّع من فريضة من تطوّعه ثمّ سائر الأعمال
تجرى على حسب ذلك .

... the Prophet said: "The first thing for which the servant will be called to account on the Day of Resurrection will be his [performance of the] Prayer. If it is found to have been carried out completely, it will be written up to him as complete. If anything was lacking in it, [God] will say: 'Look to see if you [the angels] find any *taṭawwuʿ* on his part [i.e., that he prayed out of a spontaneous desire to do so].' [If so], that part of his obligation which he neglected will be completed for him because of his *taṭawwuʿ*. Then the rest of [his] works will be reckoned in the same manner."

i. Nasâ'î 5:9:2, *isnâd* 10b (Abû Hurayrah).

ii. Nasâ'î 5:9:3, *isnâd* 45 (Abû Hurayrah): slightly shorter version; wording varies somewhat.

iii. Nasâ'î 5:9:1, *isnâd* 47 (Abû Hurayrah): wording varies.

iv. Abû Dâwûd 2:145, *isnâd*s 46 (Abû Hurayrah) and 420 (Tamîm ad-Dârî): longer version, essentially the same.

v. *Musnad*, II, 425, *isnâd* 46: same as version iv.

vi. Ibn Mâjah 5:202:2, *isnâd* 420: same as version iv.

vii. Ibn Mâjah 5:202:1, *isnâd* 46a (Abû Hurayrah).

Other References: Ibn al-ʿArabî, *Mishkât*, p. 31; al-Madanî, pp. 87–88.

Taṭawwuʿ is normally used to designate the voluntary performance of a religious duty; i.e., a spontaneous act done out of personal motivation rather than a sense of imposed duty. In the present context, the emphasis is upon the good intention and willingness of the worshipper in performing the religious duty (here the Ṣalât), as contrasted with the perfect (but perhaps perfunctory) performance of the duty in the prescribed manner. Such *taṭawwuʿ* can make up for imperfect performance of the details of the Prayer ritual, for any impairment (*intiqâṣ*) in its completeness or correctness. Cf. S. 2:158: *wa-man taṭawwaʿa khayran fa-inna Allâh shâkir ʿalîm*, "and when a person does a good work voluntarily, God is All-Grateful, All-Knowing [with respect to that work as to all else]." Cf. also S. 2:184.

SAYING 72: *unẓurû ilá ʿabdî hâdhâ yuʾadhdhinu wa-yuqîmu aṣ-ṣalât*

... سمعت رسول اللّه صلعم يقول يعجب ربّكم من راعى غنم فى رأس شظيّة بجبل يؤذن بالصلاة يصلّى فيقول اللّه عزّ وجلّ انظروا إلى عبدى هذا يؤذّن ويقيم الصلاة يخاف منى فقد غفرت لعبدى وأدخلته الجنّة .

... I heard the Apostle of God say: "Your Lord delights in a shepherd on top of a remote mountain peak who gives the call to Prayer and performs the Prayer. Thereupon God says: 'Look at this servant of Mine! He gives the call to Prayer and performs the Prayer. He fears Me. So I forgive My servant, and I shall cause him to enter Paradise.'"

i. Abû Dâwûd 4:3, *isnâd* 370 (ʿUqbah b. ʿÂmir).
ii. Nasâʾî 7:26, *isnâd* 370.
iii. *Musnad*, IV, 157, *isnâd* 370a (ʿUqbah b. ʿÂmir).
iv. *Musnad*, IV, 158, *isnâd* 370.

SAYING 73: *unẓurû ilá ʿabdî rajaʿa raghbatan fîmâ ʿindî*

... قال رسول اللّه صلعم عجب ربّنا من رجل غزا فى سبيل اللّه فانهزم يعنى أصحابه فعلم ما عليه فرجع حتّى أهريق دمه فيقول اللّه تعالى لملائكته انظروا إلى عبدى رجع رغبة فيما عندى وشفقة ممّا عندى حتّى أهريق دمه.

... the Apostle of God said: "Our Lord is well-pleased with [lit., wonders at][74] a man who goes to fight in the cause of God and then is put to flight – that is, his companions [are put to flight] – and, knowing what is incumbent upon him, returns [to fight] until his blood is shed. God says to his angels: 'Behold My servant! He returned out of desire for what is with Me [alone][75] and out of fear of what is with Me [alone],[76] until his blood was shed'."

i. Abû Dâwûd 15:36:1, *isnâd* 193 (ʿAl. b. Masʿûd).
ii. *Musnad*, I, 416, *isnâd* 193: same Divine Saying is set in slightly different frame-story.
Other References: Ibn al-ʿArabî, *Mishkât*, p. 34.

SAYING 74: *unẓurû ilá ʿibâdî qad qaḍaw farîḍah wa-hum yantaẓirûna ukhrá*

... عن عبد اللّه بن عمر وقال صلّينا مع رسول اللّه صلعم صلاة المغرب
فرجع من رجع وعقّب من عقّب فجاء رسول اللّه صلعم مسرعا قد حفزه النفس
وقد حسر عن ركبتيه فقال أبشروا هذا ربّكم قد فتح بابا من أبواب السماء
يباهى بكم الملائكة يقول انظروا إلى عبادى قد قضوا فريضة وهم ينتظرون أخرى.

... from ʿAbdallâh b. ʿAmr. He said: "We performed the late afternoon Prayer with the Apostle of God. [After it] some people left and some stayed [i.e., until the evening Prayer]. [At the evening Prayer] the Apostle of God hurried [so that] his breath came quickly and he uncovered both his knees [in haste to get there]. Then he said: 'Rejoice! Behold, your Lord has opened one of the gates of Heaven. He boasts of you before the angels, saying: "Behold My servants! They have performed the duty [of the Prayer at sunset], and they await another [opportunity to perform a duty – i.e., the evening Prayer]!"'"

i. Ibn Mâjah 4:19:3, *isnâd* 183 (ʿAl. b. ʿAmr).

ii. *Musnad*, II, 187–188, *isnâd* 183.

iii. *Musnad*, II, 197, *isnâd* 184 (ʿAl. b. ʿAmr): preceded by an ḥadîth concerning the virtue of reciting the *shahâdah* (Saying 33); minor wording variations throughout; the Divine Saying proper reads: *unẓurû ilá ʿibâdî addaw ḥaqqan min ḥaqqî thumma hum yantaẓirûna adâʾa ḥaqqin âkhara yuʾaddûnahu*, "Behold My servants! They have performed one of My rightful claims [on them], and then they await the performance of another such claim that they will carry out".

iv. *Musnad*, II, 188, *isnâd* 185 (ʿAl. b. ʿAmr): minor wording variation in the frame-story.

v. *Musnad*, II, 208, *isnâd* 185: same as version iv.

vi. *Musnad*, II, 224, *isnâd* 186 (ʿAl. b. ʿAmr): variant version: no frame story about the occasion for the Prophet's telling of the Divine Saying at all.

vii. *Musnad*, II, 305, *isnâd* 43 (Abû Hurayrah): same as version vi.

SAYING 75: *yâ ʿabdî tamanna ʿalayya uʿtika*

... سمعت جابر بن عبد اللّه يقول لمّا قتل عبد اللّه بن عمرو بن حرام
يوم أحد قال رسول اللّه صلعم يا جابر ألا أخبرك ما قال اللّه عزّ وجلّ لأبيك
قلت بلى قال ما كلّم اللّه إلاّ من وراء حجاب وكلّم أباك كفاحا فقال يا عبدى
تمنّ علىّ أعطك قال يا ربّ تحيينى فأقتل فيك ثانية قال إنّه سبق منّى أنّهم
اليها لا يرجعون قال يا ربّ فابلغ من ورائى فأنزل اللّه عزّ وجلّ هذه الآية
"ولا تحسبنّ الّذين قتلوا فى سبيل اللّه أمواتا" الآية كلها .

... I heard Jâbir b. ʿAbdallâh say: "When ʿAbdallâh b. ʿAmr b. Ḥarâm [Jâbir's father] was killed on the day of Uḥud,[77] the Apostle of God said: 'O Jâbir, shall I tell you what God said to your father?' I said, 'Yes'. He said: 'God does not speak to any one except from behind a veil, and [yet] He spoke to your father face to face. He said, "O My servant, ask what you want of Me, and I shall give [it] to you". He [i.e., ʿAbdallâh] said: "O my Lord, do Thou give me life, that I may be slain in Thee a second time". He said: "It has already been decreed by Me: 'They shall not return to life'." He said: "O my Lord, then inform those who are left behind". And God revealed this *âyah*: "You must not reckon those killed in the cause of God as dead; rather, they are alive [in the next world], and they are fed [a heavenly sustenance] with their Lord" [S. 3:169].'"

i. Ibn Mâjah 24:16:3, *isnâd* 290 (Jâbir b. ʿAl.).
ii. Ibn Mâjah, *Muqaddimah*, 13:14, *isnâd* 290.
iii. Tirmidhî, *Tafsîr*, S. 3:169, no. 18, *isnâd* 290.
Other References: Ibn Isḥâq, p. 605 / Guillaume, *Life*, p. 400; Ghazzâlî, I, 303.

God's final declaration, "They shall not return to life", may be intended as a quotation of S. 36:31, which is identical except for the single word *ilayhim*, "to them", rather than the Saying's *ilayhâ*, "to it [life]". The sense is certainly the same: in the Qurʾân the return is to the living, while in the Divine Saying the return is to life. The point is here to stress the continuing life in Paradise for the faithful, even as life in this world is brought to an end.

SAYING 76: *yâ ahl al-jannah ... uḥillu ʿalaykum riḍwânî*

. . . قال النبىّ صلعم إنّ الله يقول لأهل الجنّة يا أهل الجنّة يقولون لبّيك ربّنا وسعديك والخير فى يديك فيقول هل رضيتم فيقولون وما لنا لا نرضى يا ربّ وقد أعطيتنا ما لم تعط أحدا من خلقك فيقول ألا أعطيكم أفضل من ذلك فيقولون يا ربّ وأىّ شئ أفضل من ذلك فيقول أحلّ عليكم رضوانى فلا أسخط عليكم بعده أبدا .

... the Prophet said: "God says to the people of Paradise: 'O people of Paradise!' They say: 'We wait always and ever at Thy service, always and ever ready to aid Thee. The Good is in Thy hands'.[78] Then He says: 'Are you satisfied?' They say: 'What do we have that does not please us, O Lord, since Thou hast given us that which Thou hast given no one [else] of Thy creatures?' Then He says: 'Shall I give [or: Do I not give] you [something] better than that?' They say: 'O Lord, what thing is better than that?' Then He says: 'I shall accord you My pleasure and never afterwards be displeased with you'."

i. Bukhârî 97:38:1, *isnâd* 121 (Abû Saʿîd al-Khudrî).

ii. Bukhârî 81:51:4, *isnâd* 121: omits *wa-l-khayr fî yadayka; anâ uʿṭîkum*, "I shall give you", for *a-lâ uʿṭîkum.*

iii. Muslim 51:9, *isnâd* 121.

iv. Muslim 1:302, *isnâd* 121: a similar Divine Saying is set within a long eschatological frame-story related by Abû Saʿîd. In the story, God heeds the plea of the Muslims to save some of their earthly brethren who have been cast into the Fire, but who have even as much as a grain of a mustard seed of faith. When He has taken them from the flames and rejuvenated their scorched forms with "the water of life", He says to them: "Enter Paradise; whatever you see, it is yours!" They reply: "O Lord, Thou hast given us that which Thou hast given no other creature". He says: "I have for you what is better than that" (*lakum ʿindî afḍal min hâdhâ*). They then ask what is better than that, and He says: "My pleasure; and I shall never afterwards be displeased with you" (*riḍwânî fa-lâ askhaṭu ʿalaykum baʿdahu abadan*). See Sayings 8:iv and 62:i, which overlap this Saying in the long composite eschatological account of 1:302.

v. *Musnad*, III, 94–95, *isnâd* 121: same composite ḥadîth as version iv.

Other References: Ibn al-ʿArabî, *Mishkât*, p. 12; ʿAlî al-Qârî, no. 38; al-Madanî, pp. 71, 75; Abû Nuʿaym, *Ḥilyah*, VI, 342.

SAYING 77: *yâ ahl al-jannah khulûd wa-lâ mawt*

... قال رسول اللّه صلعم يوتى بالموت كهيئه كبش أملح فينادى مناد يا
أهل الجنّة فيشرئبّون وينظرون فيقول هل تعرفون هذا فيقولون نعم هذا
الموت وكلّهم قد رآه ثمّ ينادى يا أهل النار فيشرئبّون وينظرون فيقول هل
تعرفون هذا فيقولون نعم هذا الموت وكلّهم قد رآه فيذبح ثمّ يقول
يا أهل الجنّة خلود ولا موت ويا أهل النار خلود ولا موت ثمّ قرأ "وأنذرهم
يوم الحشرة إذ قضى الأمر وهم فى غفلة" وهؤلاء فى غفلة أهل الدنيا وهم
لا يؤمنون .

... the Apostle of God said: "Death is brought in in the guise of a black- and white-spotted ram.[79] Then a caller calls:[80] 'O people of Paradise!' And they crane their necks and look, and He says:[81] 'Do you recognize this [figure]?' They say: 'Yes, that is Death'. And each of them sees him. Then He calls: 'O people of the Fire!' And they crane their necks and look, and He says: 'Do you recognize this [figure]?' They say: 'Yes, that is Death'. And each of them sees him. Thereupon he is slaughtered. Then He says: 'O people of Paradise! Eternity, without death [is yours]! O people of the Fire, Eternity, without death [is yours]!'" Then he [Muḥammad] recited: "'And warn them of the Day of Anguish, when the matter will have been decided, while they are neglectful ...' – Those who are neglectful are the people of this world[82] – '... and they do not have faith! [S. 19:39]'"

i. Bukhârî, *Tafsîr*, S. 19:39, no. 1, *isnâd* 120 (Abû Saʿîd al-Khudrî).

ii. Bukhârî 81:51:3, *isnâd* 171 (ʿAl. b. ʿUmar): slightly shorter version; minor wording variations.

iii. *Musnad*, II, 118, *isnâd* 171: same as version ii.

iv. *Musnad*, III, 9, *isnâd* 120: minor wording variations; *yuqâlu*, "it [will] be said", replaces *yunâdî munâdin*.

v. Muslim 51:40, *isnâd* 120: minor variations; *yuqâlu* as in version iv.

vi. Dârimî 20:90, *isnâd* 3f (Abû Hurayrah): much shorter version.

vii. *Musnad*, II, 261, *isnâd* 6a (Abû Hurayrah): variant wording and arrangement.

viii. Ibn Mâjah 37:38:10, *isnâd* 6a: essentially the same as version vii.

ix. Bukhârî 81:50:5, *isnâd* 5 (Abû Hurayrah): has only the Divine Saying proper, in shorter form also.

The story of the sacrifice of Death at the end of time has parallels in Jewish legend, where there is also the motif of man's regret and anguish when he realizes his past heedlessness (the *ghaflah* of the present ḥadîth). See M. Grünbaum, "Beiträge", pp. 266–267.

SAYING 78: *yâ ayyuhâ an-nabî*

... عن عبد اللّه بن العاص أنّ هذه الآية التّى فى القرآن "يا أيّها النبىّ انّا أرسناك شاهدا ومبشّرا ونذيرا" قال فى التوريّة يا أيّها النبىّ إنّا أرسلناك شاهدا ومبشّرا وحرزا للأمّيّين أنت عبدى ورسولى سمّيتك المتوكّل ليس بفظّ ولا غليظ ولا سخّاب بالأسواق ولا يدفع السيّئة ولكن يعفو ويصفح ولن يقبضه حتّى يقيم الملّة العوجاء بأن يقولوا لا اله إلاّ اللّه فيفتح به أعينا عميا وآذانا صمّا وقلوبا غلفا .

... according to ʿAmr b. al-ʿÂṣ, this *âyah* that is in the Qurʾân, "O Prophet, verily We sent you as a witness and a proclaimer and a warner", is in the Torah: "O prophet, verily We sent you as a witness and a proclaimer and a refuge for the gentiles.[83] You are My servant and My apostle; I called you 'him who trusts wholly [in Me], who is neither harsh nor rough, who does not speak loudly in the marketplaces, and who does not return evil for evil, but is indulgent and forgiving.' God will not recall him until He has straightened through him the crooked nation so that they say: 'There is no god but God'; then through him He opens blind eyes, deaf ears, and sealed hearts."

i. Bukhârî, *Tafsîr*, S. 48:8, no. 3, *isnâd* 187 (ʿAl. b. ʿAmr b. al-ʿÂṣ).
ii. Bukhârî 34:50, *isnâd* 187.
iii. *Musnad*, II, 174, *isnâd* 187.

The initial Qurʾânic quotation in this text is from S. 48:8. There is no single passage in Jewish or Christian scripture that corresponds in its entirety to this text as it stands. There are, however, numerous verses in both that seem to have provided material or models for what purports to be an earlier revealed word of God that has a close Qurʾânic parallel. In the commentary that follows, an attempt is made to identify Biblical material that is similar to the various parts of this ḥadîth.

The first and longest portion of the Saying (to "is indulgent and forgiving") bears striking resemblance to the first of the four "Servant songs" of Deutero-Isaiah: "Behold my servant, whom I uphold,/ my chosen, in whom my soul delights;/ I have put my Spirit upon him,/ he will bring forth justice to the nations./ He will not cry or lift up his voice,/ or make it heard in the street;/ a bruised reed he will not break,/ and a dimly burning wick he will not quench;/ he will faithfully bring forth justice./ He will not fail or be discouraged/ till he has established justice in the earth;/ and the coastlands wait for his law" (Is. 42:1–4 [R.S.V.]; also quoted in Matt. 12:18–21). Cf. Is. 43:10: "'You are my witnesses', says the Lord, 'and my servant whom I have chosen....'" Cf. also Is. 41:8, 9; 44:1–2, 21; 49:3; 55:4. Concerning the Servant-songs in general, see: S. Mowinckel, *He That Cometh*, trans. G.W. Anderson (Nashville: Abingdon Press, [1954?]), pp. 187–257.

The next segment of the Saying, "God will not recall him until He has straightened through him the crooked nation ...", recalls the promise of Isaiah 40:4, as quoted in Luke 3:5 (R.S.V.): "Every valley shall be filled and every mountain and hill shall be brought low, and the crooked shall be made straight, and the rough ways shall be made smooth."

The initial part of the *Shahâdah*, "there is no god but God", which follows at this point, has numerous parallels in Deutero-Isaiah: "I am the Lord, and there is no other, besides me there is no God" (Is. 45:5 [R.S.V.]). Cf. Is. 44:6, 45:6, 18, 21, 22; 46:9.

Finally, the last clause of the Saying, "then through Him He opens blind eyes, deaf ears, and sealed hearts", echoes similar motifs in Isaiah again. Cf. Is. 42:6–7 (R.S.V.): "I am the Lord ..."; also Is. 6:10 (R.S.V.): "Make the heart of this people fat,/ and their ears heavy,/ and shut their eyes;/ lest they see with their eyes, and hear with their ears,/ and understand with their hearts,/ and turn and be healed" (also quoted in Matt. 13:15). There are many other Biblical references to blind eyes, deaf ears, etc. (e.g., Is. 42:18–20; 43:8; 61:1; Luke 4:18). The threefold series of eyes, ears, and heart used to represent man's capacity for true understanding is also evident in Saying 2 and its variants.

SAYING 79: *yâ Ayyûb a-lam akun aghnaytuka ʿamma tará*

وقال رسول اللّه صلعم بينما أيّوب يغتسل عريانا خرّ عليه رجل جراد من ذهب فجعل أيّوب يحثى فى ثوبه قال فناداه ربّه يا أيّوب ألم أكن أغنيتك عمّا ترى قال بلى يا ربّ ولكن لا غنى لى عن بركتك .

... from the Prophet. He said: "While Job was bathing in the nude, a swarm of golden locusts began to fall upon him, and Job set about throwing handfuls [of them] into his cloak. Thereupon his Lord summoned him: 'O Job, have I not made you rich enough to have no need of what you see [there]?' Job said: 'Certainly, O Lord, but I am never without need of Thy blessing'."

i. Hammâm b. Munabbih, no. 46, *isnâd* 1 (directly from Abû Hurayrah).
ii. Bukhârî 97:35:3, *isnâd* 1 (Abû Hurayrah).
iii. Bukhârî 5:20, *isnâd* 1.
iv. Bukhârî 60:20, *isnâd* 1.
v. *Musnad*, II, 314, *isnâd* 1.
vi. Nasâ'î 4:7:4, *isnâd* 7a (Abû Hurayrah).

SAYING 80: *yâ ʿibâdî innî ḥarramtu aẓ-ẓulm ʿalá nafsî*

... عن النبىّ صلعم فيما روى عن الله تبارك وتعالى آنّه قال يا عبادى إنّى حرّمت الظلم على نفسى وجعلته بينكم محرّما فلا تظالموا يا عبادى كلّكم ضالّ إلاّ من هديته فاستهدونى أهدكم يا عبادى كلّكم جائع إلاّ من أطعمته فاستطعمونى أطعمكم يا عبادى كلّكم عار إلاّ من كسوته فاستكسونى أكسكم يا عبادى إنّكم تخطئون بالليل والنهار وأنا أغفر الذنوب جميعا فاستغفرونى أغفر لكم يا عبادى إنّكم لن تبلغوا ضرّى فتضرّونى ولن تبلغوا نفعى فتنفعونى يا عبادى لو أنّ أوّلكم وآخركم وانسكم وجنّكم كانوا على أتقى قلب رجل واحد منكم ما زاد ذلك فى ملكى شيئا يا عبادى لو أنّ أوّلكم وآخركم وانسكم وجنّكم كانوا على أفجر قلب رجل واحد ما نقص ذلك من ملكى شيئا يا عبادى لو أنّ أوّلكم وآخركم وانسكم وجنّكم قاموا فى صعيد واحد فسألونى فأعطيت كلّ إنسان مسألته ما نقص ذلك ممّا عندى إلاّ كما ينقص المخيط اذا أدخل البحر يا عبادى إنّما هى أعمالكم أحصيها لكم ثمّ أوفّيكم ايّاها فمن وجد خيرا فليحمد الله ومن وجد غير ذلك فلا يلومنّ إلاّ نفسه .

... from the Prophet, in that which he related from his Lord. He said: "'O My servants, I have forbidden wrong to Myself and made it forbidden among you. So do not wrong one another. O My servants, each of you goes astray, save him whom I guide. So seek My guidance, and I shall guide you. O My servants, each of you is hungry, save him whom I feed. So ask Me for food, and I shall feed you. O My servants, each of you is naked, save him whom I clothe. So ask Me for clothing, and I shall clothe you. O My servants, you sin by day and by night, and I forgive sins. So seek My forgiveness, and I shall forgive you. O My servants, you are not capable of harming Me at all, and you are not capable of benefiting Me at all.[84] O My servants, if the first and the last of you and the men and *jinn* of you had hearts like that of the most god-fearing single man of you, that would not increase My dominion at all. O My servants, if the first and the last of you and the men and *jinn* of you had hearts like that of the most profligate single man of you, that would not diminish My dominion at all. O My servants, if the first and the last of you and the men and *jinn* of you were to stand all in one elevated place [of prayer][85] and ask something of Me, and I were to give every man of you what he asked, that would not diminish at all that which is Mine, no more than a needle stuck into the sea would diminish it.[86] O My servants, truly it is your actions that I reckon for you and then requite. So whoever found good, let him praise God; whoever found otherwise, let him blame only himself.'"

i. Muslim 45:55, *isnâd*s 134 (Abû Dharr) and 135 (Abû Dharr): the version transmitted by the second *isnâd* is slightly shorter.

ii. *Musnad*, V, 160, *isnâd* 135: slightly shorter version, as in version i, also with *isnâd* 135.

iii. Ibn Mâjah 37:30:11, *isnâd* 133 (Abû Dharr): slightly shorter version; minor wording variations.

iv. *Musnad*, V, 154, *isnâd* 133.

v. *Musnad*, V, 177, *isnâd* 133.

Other References: Ibn al-ʿArabî, *Mishkât*, pp. 3–4; ʿAlî al-Qârî, no. 15; al-Madanî, pp. 18, 31, 71; Nawawî, *Arbaʿûn*, no. 24; Ṣubḥî aṣ-Ṣâliḥ, pp. 123–124.

SAYING 81: *yâ ibn Âdam hal ra'ayta khayran qaṭṭu*

...قال رسول الله صلعم يؤتى بأنعم أهل الدنيا من أهل النار يوم القيامة فيصبغ فى النار صبغة ثمّ يقال يا ابن آدم هل رأيت خيرا قطّ هل مرّ بك نعيم قطّ فيقول لا والله يا ربّ ويؤتى بأشدّ الناس بؤسا فى الدنيا من أهل الجنّة فيصبغ صبغة فى الجنّة فيقال له يا ابن آدم هل رأيت بؤسا قطّ هل مرّ بك شدّة قطّ فيقول لا والله يا ربّ ما مرّ بى بؤس قطّ ولا رأيت شدّة قطّ .

... the Apostle of God said: "The most well-off one of the people of this world who are in the Fire is brought in on the Day of Resurrection and wholly immersed in the Fire. Thereupon it is said: 'O son of Adam, have you ever seen any good? Have you ever experienced any pleasure and ease?' Then he says, 'By God, no, O my Lord!' And the one person of those in Paradise who was in the most wretched circumstances in this world is brought in and wholly immersed in Paradise. Thereupon it is said to him: 'O son of Adam, have you ever seen any wretchedness? Have you ever experienced any hardship?' Then he says: 'By God, no, my Lord! I have never experienced any wretchedness, nor have I ever seen any hardship!'"

i. Muslim 50:55, *isnâd* 104b (Anas b. Mâlik).
ii. *Musnad*, III, 203, *isnâd* 104b.
iii. *Musnad*, III, 253, *isnâd* 104b.
Other References: Ibn al-ʿArabî, *Mishkât*, p. 28.

SAYING 82: *yâ ibn Âdam ḥammaltuka ʿalá al-khayl wa-l-ibl*

...عن النبىّ صلعم قال يقول الله عزّ وجلّ ... يوم القيامة يا ابن آدم حمّلتك على الخيل والابل وزوّجتك النساء وجعلتك تربع وترأس فأين شكر ذلك .

... from the Prophet. He said: "God will say ... on the Day of Resurrection: 'O son of Adam, I enabled you to ride horseback and camelback; I married you to women;[87] and I caused you to take the fourth part of the spoils [of war] and become chief.[88] Where is [your] gratitude for that?'"

i. *Musnad*, II, 492, *isnâd* 3e (Abû Hurayrah).
Other References: al-Madanî, p. 28.

SAYING 83: *yâ ibn Âdam innaka mâ daʿawtanî wa-rajawtanî*

... قال رسول اللّه صلعم فيما يذكر عن ربّه يقول اللّه يا ابن آدم إنّك ما
دعوتنى ورجوتنى أغفر لك كلّما كان فيك ولو لقيتنى بقراب الأرض خطيئة لقيتك
بقرابها مغفرة بعد أن لا تشرك بى شيئا ولو أذنبت تبلغ ذنوبك عنان السماء
ثمّ تستغفرنى غفرت لك ولا أبالى .

... the Prophet of God said, in that which he mentioned from his Lord: "God says: 'O son of Adam, so long as you entreat Me and fear Me, I forgive you all that which is in you [of sin]. And if you should meet Me with sins such as to fill the earth, I meet you with the same measure of forgiveness, so long as [lit., after] you have not associated anything with Me [as a partner].[89] And if you sinned such that your sins were to reach the skies [lit., the visible part of the sky (above the horizon)], and you were then to ask Me for forgiveness, I would forgive you and not be concerned.'"

i. Ibrâhîm b. Ṭahmân, no. 102 (fol. 247a), *isnâd* 132 (Abû Dharr).
ii. Dârimî 20:72, *isnâd* 132.
iii. *Musnad*, V, 167, *isnâd* 132.
iv. *Musnad*, V, 172, *isnâd* 132.
v. *Musnad*, V, 148, *isnâd* 131 (Abû Dharr): composed of only the one segment, "If My servant meets Me (*istaqbalanî*) with sins such as to fill the earth, I meet him with the same measure of forgiveness".
vi. *Musnad*, V, 147, *isnâd* 130b (Abû Dharr): composed of only the one segment, "O son of Adam, if you commit (*law ʿamilta*) sins such as to fill the earth, but do not associate anything with Me [as a partner], I shall prepare (*jaʿaltu*) for you the same measure of forgiveness".
vii. *Musnad*, 154, *isnâd* 133 (Abû Dharr): omits final portion (from *law adhnabta ...*).

viii. Tirmidhî 45:98:6, *isnâd* 101 (Anas b. Mâlik): somewhat different, slightly amplified version.

Other References: Ibn al-'Arabî, *Mishkât*, p. 19; 'Alî al-Qârî, no. 31; al-Madanî, pp. 10, 16, 21, 72; an-Nawawî, *Arba'ûn*, no. 42.

SAYING 84: *yâ ibn Âdam ithnatân lam takun laka*

... قال رسول الله صلعم يا ابن آدم اثنتان لم تكن لك واحدة منهما
جعلت لك نصيبا من مالك حين أخذت بكظمك لأطهّرك به وأزكّيك وصلاة
عبادى عليك بعد انقضاء أجلك .

... the Apostle of God said: "[God said:] 'O son of Adam! Two things are not yours [but Mine]. One of them I made a portion of your fortune [for your heirs], when death takes you [lit., when I seize you by the throat], in order to cleanse and purify you by that. [The second is] the Prayer of My servants on your behalf after your days are ended.'"

i. Ibn Mâjah 22:5:3, *isnâd* 173a ('Al. b. 'Umar).

Other References: al-Madanî, p. 11.

The meaning of this passage is not entirely clear. Despite the absence of "God said" in the text, the Saying is clearly a Divine Saying from its content. God is apparently telling man here that things beyond his mortal life are not in his hands, but God's. Out of His mercy God allows a fair share of a man's wealth to pass on to his (or, also, in the case of a woman, to her) heirs: cf. S. 4:7. Also out of His mercy, God has ordained prayers for the dead (*ṣalât al-janâ'iz*?) to which He will respond favorably.

SAYING 85: *yâ ibn Âdam lâ ta'jiz 'an arba' raka'ât*

...سمعت رسول الله صلعم يقول يقول الله عزّ وجلّ يا ابن آدم لا تعجز
عن أربع ركعات من أوّل نهارك أكفك آخره .

... I heard the Apostle of God say: "God says: 'O son of Adam, Do not fail [to perform] four bows at the beginning of your day; I shall suffice you for the rest of it [i.e., your day]'."

i. *Musnad,* V, 286, *isnâd* 430 (Nuʿaym b. Himâr al-Ghaṭfânî).
ii. *Musnad,* V, 286–287, *isnâd* 431 (Nuʿaym b. Himâr al-Ghaṭfânî).
iii. Tirmidhî 3:15, *isnâd* 161 (Abû ad-Dardâʾ): minor wording variations.
Other References: Ibn al-ʿArabî, *Mishkât,* p. 30; al-Madanî, pp. 3, 42, 76.

This Saying has reference to the performance of the four *rakaʿât* of the second Ṣalât of the day, the *ṣalât aẓ-ẓuhr.*

Saying 86: *yâ ibn Âdam tafarragh li-ʿibâdatî*

. . . عن النبيّ صلّعم قال : إنّ اللّه تعالى يقول يا ابن آدم تفرّغ لعبادتي
أملأ صدرك غنىً وأسدّ فقرك والاّ تفعل ملأت يديك شغلا ولم أسدّ فقرك .

... from the Prophet. He said: "God says: 'O son of Adam, if you devote yourself to My service, I shall amply satisfy you [lit., fill your breast] and allay your want. If you do not do [this], I shall fill your hands with labor and not allay your want.'"

i. Tirmidhî 35:30:3, *isnâd* 35 (Abû Hurayrah).
ii. Ibn Mâjah 37:2:3, *isnâd* 35: *ṣadraka,* "your breast", for *yadayka.*
iii. *Musnad,* II, 358, *isnâd* 35: same as version ii.
Other References: Ibn al-ʿArabî, *Mishkât,* p. 25; ʿAlî al-Qârî, no. 35; al-Madanî, p. 73.

Saying 87: *yâ ʿÎsâ innî bâʾith min baʿdika ummah*

. . . سمعت ابا القاسم صلعم يقول ما سمعته يكنيه قبلها ولا بعدها يقول
إنّ اللّه عزّ وجلّ يقول يا عيسى إنّى باعث من بعدك أمّة إن أصابهم ما
يحبون حمدوا اللّه وشكروا وان أصابهم ما يكرهون .احتسبوا وصبروا ولا حلم
ولا علم قال يا رب كيف هذا لهم ولا حلم ولا علم قال أعطيهما من حلمى
وعلمى .

... I heard Abû al-Qâsim – and I did not hear him called that before or after this[90] – say: "God says: 'O Jesus, I will send a community after you. If they are fortunate in what befalls them, they will praise God and be thankful.

And if they are unfortunate in what befalls them, they put it to account with God[91] and endure it with patience. There will be no understanding[92] and no knowledge [in them].' Jesus said: 'O my Lord, how can that be, when they have no understanding and no knowledge?' God says: 'I shall give them of My understanding and My knowledge'."

i. *Musnad*, VI, 450, *isnâd* 160 (Abû ad-Dardâ').
Other References: ʿAlî al-Qârî, no. 28; al-Madanî, p. 11.

SAYING 88: *yâ Jibrîl idhhab ilá Muḥammadan*

... انّ النبىّ صلّعم تلا قول اللّه عزّ وجلّ فى ابراهيم "ربّ إنّهنّ أضللن كثيرا من النّاس فمن تبعنى فإنّه منّى" الآية وقال عيسى عليه السلام "إن تعذّبهم فإنّهم عبادك وان تغفر لهم فإنّك أنت العزيز الحكيم" فرفع يديه وقال اللّهمّ أمّتى وبكى فقال اللّه عزّ وجلّ يا جبريل اذهب الى محمّد وربّك أعلم فسله ما يبكيك فأتاه جبريل عليه الصلاة والسلام فسأله فأخبره رسول اللّه صلّعم بما قال وهو أعلم فقال اللّه يا جبريل اذهب الى محمّد فقل انّا سنرضيك فى أمّتك ولا نسوءك .

... the Prophet recited God's word concerning Abraham: "'O my Lord! They [the idols][93] have led many of mankind astray; [but] when one of them follows me, he is one of mine...'", etc., the entire *âyah*.[94] And Jesus said: "'If Thou dost punish them, they are Thy servants [to do with as Thou wilt]. And if Thou dost forgive them [they are also Thine]. Thou art the Mighty, the Wise.'"[95] Thereupon he [Muḥammad] raised his hands and said: "Dear God! My people! My people!" And he wept. And God said: "O Gabriel, go to Muḥammad. Your Lord knows better, [but] ask him, 'Why are you weeping?' So Gabriel came to him and asked him. And the Apostle of God related to him – and He [God] knows better – what he [Muḥammad] had said. God said: "O Gabriel, go to Muḥammad and say: 'Truly We shall satisfy you concerning your people and shall do you no ill'."

i. Muslim 1:346, *isnâd* 180 (ʿAl. b. ʿAmr b. al-ʿÂṣ).

SAYING 89: *yu'dhînî ibn Âdam yasubbu ad-dahr wa-anâ ad-dahr*

. . . عن النبيّ صلعم قال اللّه تعالى يؤذيني ابن آدم يسبّ الدهر وأنا
الدهر بيدى الأمر أقلّب الليل والنهار .

... from the Prophet: "God said: 'The son of Adam vexes Me when he curses Time, for I am Time! In my hand is the command [of all things]. I cause the night and day to follow one upon the other.'"[96]

i. Bukhârî 97:35:1, *isnâd* 2 (Abû Hurayrah).

ii. Bukhârî, *Tafsîr*, S. 45:24, *isnâd* 2: S. 45:24 speaks of those who do not have faith in God but claim that blind Fate rules all existence: *wa qâlû mâ hiya illá ḥayâtunâ ad-dunyâ namûtu wa-naḥyâ wa-mâ yuhlikunâ illá ad-dahr*, "And they say, 'There is only our worldly [lit., nearer] life. We die and live, and it is Time alone that destroys us'." This verse, like the Divine Saying, is clearly aimed at the so-called "fatalism" of the pre-Islamic *Jâhilîyah*. See commentary below.

iii. Muslim 40:2, *isnâd* 2.

iv. *Musnad*, II, 238, *isnâd* 2.

v. Bukhârî 78:101:1, *isnâd* 6 (Abû Hurayrah): shorter, variant version: *yasubbu banû Âdam ad-dahr wa-anâ ad-dahr bi-yadî al-layl wa-n-nahâr*, "The sons of Âdam curse Time, and I am Time. In my hand is the night and the day".

vi. Ibrâhîm b. Ṭahmân, no. 108 (fol. 247b), *isnâd* 8 (Abû Hurayrah): shorter version, in third person as an *ḥadîth nabawî*: *lâ tasubbû ad-dahr fa-inna Allâh huwa ad-dahr*, "Do not curse Time, for truly, God is Time".

vii. *Musnad*, II, 395, *isnâd*s 8a (Abû Hurayrah) and 30 (Abû Hurayrah): same as version vi.

viii. *Musnad*, II, 496, *isnâd* 3a (Abû Hurayrah): variant version: *anâ ad-dahr al-ayyâm wa-l-layâlî lî ujaddiduhâ wa-ubâlîhâ wa-âtî bi-mulûk baʿd mulûk*, "I am Time. The days and the nights belong to Me. I renew them and bring them to an end. And I destroy kings after kings".

Other References: Ibn al-ʿArabî, *Mishkât*, p. 33; ʿAlî al-Qârî, no. 3; al-Madanî, pp. 5, 6.

This and the two additional texts (89a, 89b) in the same "family" of Sayings are clearly relevant to the early theological issue of predestination. Here we see the pre-Islamic concept of *dahr*, "all-devouring time", "fate", reinterpreted within an Islamic Weltanschauung: *God* is *dahr*; *He* it is Who creates, sustains, and has disposition over all things.

Concerning *dahr*, for which there is no one satisfactory term in English, see:

Ringgren, *Arabian Fatalism*, pp. 30–60 (esp. pp. 46, 48), 86–87, 130, 142–146, 154, 199–203; Watt, *Free Will and Predestination*, pp. 21–24, and *passim*; Ritter, *Meer*, pp. 43–44; and Shâkir, commentary to *Musnad*, II, 238 (Shâkir edition: XII, 238).

SAYING 89a: *lâ yaqul ibn Âdam yâ khaybat ad-dahr fa-innî anâ ad-dahr*

وقال رسول اللّه صلعم قال اللّه تعالى لا يقل ابن آدم يا خيبة الدهر فإنّى أنا الدهر أرسل الليل والنهار فإذا شئت قبضتهما .

The Apostle of God said: "God said: 'The son of Adam should not say, "Curse Time!" For I am Time! I send the day and the night, and if I wished, I would take them away [lit., seize them].'"

i. Hammâm b. Munabbih, no. 117, *isnâd* 1 (directly from Abû Hurayrah).
ii. *Musnad*, II, 275, *isnâd* 2 (Abû Hurayrah): *aḥadukum*, "one of you" replaces *ibn Âdam*; *uqallibu laylahu wa-nahârahu*, as in Saying 89, replaces *ursilu al-layl wa-n-nahâr*.
iii. *Musnad*, II, 272, *isnâd* 2: *yu'dhînî ibn Âdam yaqûlu*, "The son of Adam annoys Me, saying ...", replaces *lâ yaqul ibn Âdam*; *uqallibu laylahu wa-nahârahu* replaces *ursilu al-layl wa-n-nahâr* (see Saying 89).
iv. Muslim 40:3, *isnâd* 2: same as version iii.
v. *Musnad*, II, 259, *isnâd* 6 (Abû Hurayrah): shorter version, in third person as an *ḥadîth nabawî*.
vi. Bukhârî 78:101:2, *isnâd* 6: *ḥadîth nabawî*, essentially the same as version v.

SAYING 89b: *istaqraḍtu ʿabdî fa-lam yaqriḍnî ... wa-anâ ad-dahr*

... عن النبىّ صلعم قال يقول [اللّه] استقرضت عبدى فلم يقرضنى ويشتمنى عبدى وهو لا يدرى يقول وادهراه وادهراه وأنا الدهر .

... from the Prophet. He said: "[God][97] says: 'I have asked a favor of [lit., I have asked a loan of] My servant, and He has not given [it] to Me. My servant curses Me,[98] and he is not aware [how things really are]. He says, "O Time! O Time!"[99] and I am Time!'"

i. *Musnad*, II, 300, *isnâd* 13 (Abû Hurayrah).

ii. *Musnad*, II, 506, *isnâd* 13.

iii. Ibrâhîm b. Ṭahmân, no. 105 (fol. 247a–247b), *isnâd* 13 (directly from al-ʿAlâʾ from ʿAr. b. Yaʿqûb from Abû Hurayrah): *wa-huwa lâ yadrî* is replaced by *wa-lam yanbaghî lahu shatamanî*, "And it is not appropriate for him to curse Me" (see Saying 41); the Saying closes as follows: *yaqûlu wâ-dahrâhu wa-anâ ad-dahr thalâthan*, "He says, 'O Time!' and I am Time" (three times [this is said]).

SAYING 90: *yûshiku ʿibâdî aṣ-ṣâliḥûn an yulqû ʿanhum al-muʾnah wa-l-adhá*

. . . قال رسول الله صلعم أعطيت أمّتى خمس خصال فى رمضان لم يعطها أمّة قبلهم خلوف فم الصائم أطيب عند الله من ريح المسك وتستغفر لهم الملائكة حتّى يفطروا ويزيّن الله عزّ و جلّ كلّ يوم جنّته ثمّ يقول يوشك عبادى الصالحون أن يلقوا عنهم المؤنة والأذى ويصيروا اليك ويصفّد فيه مردة الشياطين فلا يخلصوا الى ما كانوا يخلصون اليه فى غيره ويغفرلهم فى آخر ليلة قيل يا رسول الله أهى ليلة القدر قال لا ولكن العامل إنّما يوفّى أجره إذا قضى عمله .

... the Apostle of God said: "My people have been given five good things [lit., qualities] during Ramaḍân which have not been given to any people before them: the smell of the mouth of the one who fasts is more delectable to God than the scent of musk,[100] and the angels ask for forgiveness for them until they break their fast; God adorns His Paradise each day, and then He says [to it]: 'My upright servants are about to have [all] care and hardship cast from them, and they will come to you [i.e., Paradise]'; the rebellious satans will be fettered during it [i.e., Ramaḍân], and they will not achieve what they [are able to] achieve in other months; and forgiveness will be theirs [i.e., the Muslims'] on the last night [of Ramaḍân]. Someone then asked: "O Apostle of God, is that the night of *qadr*?"[101] He said: "No, but the laborer is paid his wages when he completes his work".[102]

i. *Musnad*, II, 292, *isnâd* 6c (Abû Hurayrah).

NOTES TO: "TEXTS, TRANSLATIONS, AND SOURCES"

1. Or: "has a place of complete goodness with Me".
2. *Minbar*. Cf. below, commentary to Saying 19b.
3. I.e., those who fought with the Prophet in the battle against the Meccan caravan and reinforcements at Badr during Ramaḍân, 2/624. Although unimportant in purely military terms, the battle, in which a smaller Muslim contingent routed a large Meccan force, was taken as a sign of God's support of the Muslim cause and marked the first step in the campaign that eventually brought Mecca under Muslim sway. Cf. the references to the divine help given the Muslims at Badr in Sûrah 8.
4. The final words of this Saying are almost identical to those of Saying 3, and for that reason the two have been placed in the same "family". They belong, however, clearly to two different cycles of material, as both the *isnâd*s and the frame-stories indicate.
5. *Nuṣḥ* denotes here sincerity of faith in God, uprightness in thought, word, and deed according to the requirements of God.
6. This refers to Mâlik b. Anas, the fourth transmitter in the *isnâd* of this text and the author of the *Muwaṭṭa'*. Wensinck's *Concordance* does not, however, give any reference to an occurrence of this ḥadîth in the *Muwaṭṭa'* (cf. *Concordance*, I, 544a, s.v. "ḥayât").
7. Cf. S. 39:7: *in takfirû fa-inna Allâh ghanî ʿankum*, "If you are ungrateful [i.e., reject God], God has no need of you". Concerning *kufr* as ingratitude, see S. 31:11 (further references to other relevant Qur'ân passages in Paret, *Mohammed*, p. 74). *Shirk* is of course the worst kind of ingratitude, for it is the explicit refusal to recognize that God "has no need of" associates or anything else.
8. S. 74:56. The translation of the word *ahl* in this passage and in the Divine Saying is problematic, especially if the word is to be rendered in any uniform manner. Arberry translates the verse, "He is worthy to be feared, worthy to forgive" (*Koran*, II, 312); Pickthall has "He is the fount of fear; He is the fount of mercy" (*Glorious Koran*, p. 421); and Paret renders it "Ihm steht es zu, dass man ihn fürchtet. Und ihm steht es zu, (den Menschen ihre Sünden) zu vergeben" (*Koran*, p. 490). The last translation is the best, but there is no satisfactory similar construction in English. One possibility would be to use "He is ready to forgive", but this is not possible when the *ahl* is used with "to be feared". In the present translation, the use of "His it is ..." has been adopted as a consistent translation for *huwa ahl an* ... and its variations,

even though it is somewhat archaic and even awkward (especially in the final clause of the Saying).

9. I.e., "I am as good, as great, as merciful, etc., as man is capable of imagining Me to be." God so transcends man's ability to comprehend Him that man is incapable of a conception of God or His activity that exceeds or overestimates Him. Cf. also version ii.
10. Literally, "... better than those [in his 'public']." I.e., I remember him before the company of Heaven if he remembers ("mentions") Me in the company of men.
11. Cf. Saying 12a. Note that this latter portion and part of the earlier segment of the present Saying are also found by themselves as separate Divine Sayings (e.g., Sayings 12a, 12b).
12. On the translation of this Saying, see Saying 12, n. 9, above.
13. Concerning *dhikr*, see commentary to Saying 12 above.
14. This is apparently a reference to S. 39:67, which is quoted in full in Saying 13a. All but two of the Sayings containing *anâ al-malik* seem to be closely associated with this Qur'ân verse (cf. Sayings 13a, 13b); the two exceptions are Sayings 13c and 53a.
15. *Minbar*. Cf. below, commentary to Saying 19b.
16. S. 39:67. See also Saying 13 and n. 14 above.
17. Many of these same epithets of God are found also in S. 59:22–24: *viz. al-malik* [*al-quddûs*], *al-ʿazîz*, *al-jabbâr*, and *al-mutakabbir*.
18. The term *ḥabr* is used generally to designate a learned religious scholar or authority, usually a Jewish scholar, but also a Christian one. Even individual Muslims appear to have been called *aḥbâr* on occasion; e.g., Zayd b. Thâbit (Ibn Saʿd, II, ii, 117, 119). Ibn ʿAbbâs was called the *ḥabr* of the *Ummah* or even of the Arabs (see Goldziher, *Richtungen*, pp. 65, 73). In the present ḥadîth, four of the variant versions listed specify that the man here was a Jew: versions iii and vi have *yahûdî*, "a Jew", for *ḥabr*, and versions iv and v have *ḥabr min al-yahûd*, "a religious scholar [rabbi] of the Jews". Of the two remaining variants, version vii has only *ḥabr*, and version ii has *rajûl min ahl al-kitâb*, "a man of the People of the Book".
19. *Ad-dayyân*, "He who requites [good and evil]", i.e., "the Judge [of all]", or "He who rules over, has disposition over [all]", is an epithet of God that is not found in the Qur'ân.
20. On *raḥim* and its translation, see commentary to Saying 15.
21. This refers to the fact that *raḥim* and *ar-raḥmân* are derived from the same Arabic root.

22. Since most of the other versions of this Saying and its variants have *battattuhu* as a variant reading and synonym for *qaṭaʿtuhu*, it seems clear that *thabbattuhu* here in Azmi's text is an incorrect reading of the orthographic form that could be either without pointing.
23. In this version of the Saying, the *raḥim* is interpreted in specific terms as the tie of kinship joining Fâṭimah to the blood-line of the Shîʿî Imâms. I am indebted to Mahmoud Ayoub for this reference. It is taken from a bound lithograph edition of an Iranian manuscript that is undated and otherwise unmarked as to place or date of origin. The text is part of the general shelf collection of Widener Library, Harvard University.
24. S. 47:22. "Ties of kinship" translates *arḥâm*, plur. of *raḥim* (see the commentary to Saying 15).
25. On the translation of the key words in this Saying, see above, Saying 15, its commentary, and nn. 21–23.
26. See Saying 15 (n. 21).
27. The clause, *wa-yuzwá baʿḍuhâ ilá baʿḍ*, is not easily translated nor itself entirely clear. M. Rahimuddin, in Hamidullah, *Earliest Extant Work*, p. 79, translates this: "and one end of it will be joined to the other". Al-Qastallânî, in his commentary on the sentence as it occurs in Bukhârî, glosses it as follows: "it comes together and closes over whomever is inside, and God does not produce any [more] creatures for it" (*Irshâd*, VII, 339). The idea seems to be that the sides of Hell will be drawn together as a sack is drawn up, so that no one further may enter.
28. Ḥudaybîyah was the site of the Muslim encampment near Mecca in the sixth year of the Hijrah where the armistice with the Meccans was signed by Muḥammad and Suhayl b. ʿAmr (Ibn Isḥâq, 740–751 / Guillaume, *Life*, 499–507).
29. Or simply "the constellation". The sense is that such a one trusts in the stars (i.e., astrology).
30. This translation of *li-jalâlî* (or *bi-jalâlî*, in version iii) is substantiated by the gloss given for the phrase by Aḥmad Shâkir: *min ajl ʿaẓamatî taʿẓîman li-ḥaqq Allâh ... wa-lâ li-ʿaraḍ min ad-dunyâ*, "on account of My greatness, for the sake of God's Absolute [i.e., noumenal] Reality ... and not for the sake of any worldly thing [i.e., any superficial accident (*ʿaraḍ*)]" (*Musnad* [Shâkir], XII, 221). ʿAbdalbâqî gives a similar interpretation in his note to *Muwaṭṭaʾ* 51:13 (II, 952). Compare, however, this usage to the similar phrases in Sayings 19a, 54:ii, and 66:iii, where the locative sense of the preposition appears to be stronger (see especially the commentary to Saying 19a).

31. *Ẓill* carries much the same connotations as the English *shield* or the German *Schirm* in the sense of a protective covering (e.g., *unter dem Schirm des Höchsten stehen*; "But thou, O Lord, art a shield about me" [Psalms 3:3]). In the context of the searing heat of the Arabian peninsula, the metaphorical picture of the Last Judgment as a time when all except those whom God shields in His shade will be exposed as travelers on the desert are exposed is a compelling image. The notion of shade is found often in eschatological material in the Ḥadîth. Note, for example, the mention of a tree in Paradise so vast that a horseman would ride for a thousand years without leaving its shade (*ẓill*) (Hammâm b. Munabbih, no. 5; *Musnad*, II, 257). Still others are found at *Muwaṭṭa'* 51:14 ("God will shade seven people ...") and Ibn Mâjah 15:14:3 ("God will shade him who loves Him ..."). Cf. Goldziher, *M. Studien*, II, 384, for further references; see also *Concordance*, IV, 77, "*ẓill*".
32. In strict grammatical terms, the antecedent of *-hu* here is *al-ʿarsh*, the Throne; the probable intended antecedent is, however, God. The two are in any case closely linked. Cf. Saying 19 (n. 31).
33. The reading *tuftaḥu*, found in versions iii and iv below, seems preferable to the *yuftaḥu* of this text. The ḥadîth would then read: "... when the gates of Heaven will be opened for him, and the Lord will say...."
34. Satan. There are several instances of words spoken by Satan himself in the Ḥadîth literature. Examples of such *aḥâdîth ash-shayṭân* are found at *Musnad*, V, 71, and Muslim 1:133.
35. The *ẓâlim* is a perpetrator of evil and/or a tyrant or oppressor, and the *maẓlûm* is one who is evilly used and/or oppressed in a tyrannical fashion. The use of the English "evil-doer" and "one who has been wronged" does not convey the strength of the Arabic terms, but *oppressor* or *tyrant* and *the oppressed* would have too specific connotations in English for the meaning of the original here.
36. A standard oath or swear-formula in classical Arabic; see Lane, *Lexicon*, I, 11b.
37. Lit., "have perished", "have been doomed, damned"; construed here as an historical present. See the commentary note.
38. Bukhârî glosses *ḥabîbatan* as *ʿaynân*, "two eyes" (at the end of his citation of this text in 75:7). Likewise Ibn Athîr, *Nihâyah*, IV, 17.
39. The opening words of the *shahâdah*, or witness of faith.
40. *Istajâbû*, "they [will] answer", is perhaps an echo of the similar usage in S. 2:186.

41. *Takdhîb* in this context is the act of rejecting as a lie what is true – rather, what one *knows* to be true. Thus the man who calls God a liar is lying himself by saying what he knows to be a lie. Cf. W. C. Smith, "A Human View of Truth", *Studies in Religion*, I (1971), 8–10. The idea of lying about God in this fashion is found in a number of places in the Qur'ân, usually in conjunction with the challenge-formula, *man aẓlam mimman* ..., "who is more wicked than he who ...?" (See below, Saying 48 and the commentary to it.)
42. Cf. Saying 89b: iii, where God accuses man of "cursing" Him.
43. I.e., will not resurrect us on the Last Day, as He promises.
44. A reference to S. 21:104 *inter alia*: *kamâ bada'anâ awwâl khalqanâ nu'îduhu wa'd 'alaynâ innâ kunnâ fâ'ilîn*, "... as We originated a first creation, We shall bring it back again – a promise binding upon Us; so shall We do". Cf. S. 10: 4; *Mu'jam*, 493; Paret, *Kommentar*, p. 217.
45. Refers to S. 2:116: *qâlu ittakhadha Allâh waladan subḥanahu bal lahu mâ fî as-samawât wa-l-arḍ*, "They say, 'God has taken to Himself a child'. Glory be to Him! No! To Him belongs all that is in Heaven and earth ...". Other references at *Mu'jam*, p. 763b. Those who are said to make this accusation may be either Meccans who described certain goddesses as "daughters" of God or Christians, who recognize Jesus as the Son of God (see Paret, *Kommentar*, pp. 26–27).
46. A paraphrase in the first person of the third-person statement of S. 112: *qul huwa Allâh aḥad Allâh aṣ-ṣamad lam yalid wa-lam yûlad wa-lam yakun lahu kufu'an aḥad*, "Say, He is God, One! God is the Eternal [Refuge]. He has not begotten, not is He begotten, and there is no one equal to Him!" Some of the versions listed include also *aḥad* as well as *ṣamad* in their paraphrase of this Sûrah.
47. A reference to Muḥammad's forced emigration, or *hijrah*, from Mecca and his eventual victory over his persecutors there.
48. A reference to God's support to the Muslims in Madînah in their forays against the caravans and forces of the Meccans.
49. This segment of the tradition occurs also as a separate Divine Saying (no. 16).
50. Perhaps a reference to the battle of Badr, which was so critical for the Prophet and his followers. The Qur'ân describes how God sent ranks of His angels to aid the faithful in the conflict and thus assured the victory (S. 8: 9–14; cf. the discussion in Andrae, *Person Muhammeds*, pp. 17–18). See also Ibn Isḥâq's accounts of how the angels helped the Muslims at Badr (pp. 444, 474, 477 / Guillaume, *Life*, pp. 300, 320–322). See Saying 3a (n. 3) concerning Badr.

51. Jonah is mentioned several times in the Qur'ân as a previous prophet (4:161; 6:86; 10:98; 37:139), but never with the added *kunyah, Ibn Mattá.* It is unclear what the source for this is.
52. As Nöldeke-Schwally, I, 257, n. 2, indicates, this final statement is unclear. It could also be read, "and he traced his lineage to his father". In any case, the pronominal referents are unclear; they have been taken here to refer to Muḥammad, not Jonah.
53. Both the content and the parallel versions ii and iii show that this is to be understood as God's word. So Hamidullah, in his edition of the text (*Earliest Extant Work*, p. 78).
54. The defectively written [without the long *alif mamdûdah*] phrase *yalqâhu* is taken here in the sense of "correspond to", agree with": a vow is in agreement with God's preordination when it is fulfilled; it is not man's doing that it is fulfilled.
55. *Dhabbah* might also mean "ant" or "ant-larvae" here, if the variant *baʿûḍah*, "gnat", in version vi represents a correct synonym usage. In either case, whether as "tiny particle" or "ant", the sense is clear: no one can create even the tiniest thing in God's creation except God Himself, who alone is Creator of all things.
56. Concerning the *farâʾiḍ*, see Th. W. Juynboll, "Farḍ", s. v., *EI*². The most prominent of these are the duties described as the five *arkân*, or "members" (usually translated "pillars", but incorrectly so: cf. Ibn Mâjah, *Muqaddimah*, 9:9 and the note of ʿAbdalbâqî, which gives *jawâriḥ* as the explanation of *arkân*) of Islam. These are: profession of faith, Prayer (*ṣalât*), almsgiving, fasting, and pilgrimage, which are the responsibilities of the individual (*farâʾiḍ al-ʿayn*) as opposed to the responsibilities of the community as a whole (*farâʾiḍ al-kifâyah*). Cf. also Levy, *The Social Structure of Islam* (1962), p. 155.
57. These are the acts of piety beyond those prescribed by the Qur'ân, *sunnah*, or communal consensus (*ijmâʿ*) as obligatory. The *nawâfil* begin where the *farâʾiḍ* leave off. They include such acts as the *tarâwîḥ*, or additional prayers during Ramaḍân (cf. A. J. Wensinck, "Tarāwīḥ", *SEI*, p. 573), and the *tahajjud*, or night-vigil prayer (cf. A. J. Wensinck, "Tahadjdjud", *SEI*, p. 559; cf. S. 76:25–26; 50:40; 52:49).
58. Cf. S. 4:48: "God does not forgive it that partners should be ascribed to Him. He forgives [everything] up to that as He will. Whoever ascribes partners to God commits a mighty sin." Cf. also Saying 42 above.
59. Cf. Sayings 13–13c, which also contain this same declaration.
60. Concerning *dhikr*, "making mention of", "remembering", see the commentary to Saying 12 above.

61. I.e., the *Fâtiḥah,* or opening Sûrah of the Qur'ân, which is recited by each worshipper during every Prayer, or Ṣalât.
62. *Thalâthan* could also be construed to mean "three times [Muḥammad said]" (that his prayer is deficient).
63. There is no indication that God's words end here except the sense of the rest of the passage. The same question arises in the other texts in the present "family" of Sayings, nos. 61–61e.
64. The final segment of this Saying is found in many other ḥadîths: cf. Saying 90 and *Concordance*, II, 69b, s.v. "khulûf". See also Azmi, *Studies*, pp. 226f.
65. Both the sense of the passage and the testimony of version vi indicate that the following words are to be understood as words of God, not Muḥammad.
66. Cf. similar statements in Sayings 34, 76.
67. It would be possible to interpret the final statement ("The smell of the mouth ...") as words of Muḥammad rather than God, since God is mentioned in the third person. This is not, however, an uncommon mode of divine speech in either Divine Sayings or the Qur'ân itself: cf. above, p. 104, n. 49.
68. See Saying 61b (n. 67) above. Cf. version v of the present Saying.
69. This appears to be the point at which God's words end, but as in the previous Sayings in this "family", there is no external indication as to where the words of God end and the words of Muḥammad begin. Cf. n. 67 above.
70. It is also possible to read the text so that God's words end at this point; this would be in line with the readings of the previous Sayings in this "family" (cf. Sayings 61–61d above). However, in this instance it seems clearer and more logical to understand the entire statement as a divine word.
71. For a discussion of this phrase and similar usages concerning acting and being "in God", see the commentary to Saying 19a.
72. Possibly a reference to the phrase in S. 3:106: *tabyaḍḍu wujûh*, "[some] faces will be lightened", referring to those who enter Paradise on the Day of Resurrection.
73. *Qabûl* (or *qubûl*) could refer to acceptance either by one's fellow or by God (while one is on earth). In a sense, the former is the concomitant of the latter acceptance in any case, the divine love being the initiating force in all love among men. The latter notion is further borne out by the use of this verse by Tirmidhî (version vi) to explain S. 19:96 (see version vi). ʿAbdalbâqî (commentary to *Muwaṭṭa'* 51:15) glosses *qabûl* as *al-maḥabbah wa-r-riḍá wa-mayl an-nafs fî ahl al-arḍ*, "love and pleased acceptance and sympathy of people among the inhabitants of the earth", laying stress on the human acceptance accorded the person loved by God.
74. See Lane, *Lexicon*, V, 1956b–c.

75. I.e., Paradise.
76. I.e., the Fire, or Hell.
77. Inconclusive battle between the Prophet and his Madînan forces on the one hand and the Meccans on the other, in the month of Shawwâl, 3/625.
78. These words are known as the *talbiyah* (infinitive of *labbá*) from the initial phrase, *labbayka* (lit., "at your service"). The formula is used on various occasions in Muslim ritual, notably on the Pilgrimage. See A. J. Wensinck, "Talbiya", *SEI*, p. 571. *Labbayka* and *saʿdayka* are dual forms used as intensives: see Wright, *Grammar*, II, 74.
79. I.e., as a sacrificial animal.
80. This is a common formula in eschatological ḥadîths which is used to express words spoken on divine authority in Heaven, if not by God Himself. See above, Chapter 4, B, p. 87.
81. The unnamed speaker is referred to here as God, since the words spoken are clearly those of God's mouthpiece, if not of God Himself.
82. An explanation of the Qur'ânic quotation, S. 19:39. The interjected statement is Muḥammad's.
83. The *ummîyûn* (lit., unlettered, ignorant) are to be understood not as "Gentiles" in the narrow sense (i.e., as non-Jews only), but as "foreign peoples not worshipping the one true God" – which is the basic meaning of the concept for the Jews and is equally comprehensible in the Muslim or Christian context. In the quotation of the similar passage from Isaiah (see commentary) in the Gospel of Matthew, the Greek equivalent is instructive: τοῖς ἔθνεσιν, "for the gentiles", or "for the pagan peoples"!
84. Lit., "... you cannot reach the point of doing Me harm so that you harm Me; and you cannot reach the point of benefiting Me so that you benefit Me" The repetitive style of the Arabic gives an emphasis to the declarations that cannot be reproduced in English well.
85. On *ṣaʿîd* as a special place for the Prayer, cf. S. 4:43. The word normally refers simply to any elevated piece of ground.
86. I.e., God's realm is infinite, while man's realm is infinitesimal; cf. S. 47:38: "God is the [absolutely] Rich; you [men] are the poor".
87. Lit., "paired/joined you with women". The verb is used in the Qur'ân with respect to God's pairing men with houris in Paradise (S. 44:54; 52:20). See Lane, *Lexicon*, III, 1266a–b.
88. The "taking the fourth part of the spoils" is in fact the pre-Islamic prerogative of the chieftain among the Arabs; thus the two verbs here both refer to the same thing. "Being chief" is ranked here along with other characteristic major aspects of the life of the male Arab, all of which stand for all of the

things in human life for which man should be grateful to God. Lane, *Lexicon*, III, 1015a, cites a slightly different variant of this ḥadîth in explanation of this meaning of *R-B-*ʿ.

89. Cf. Saying 51 (n. 58) above.
90. Abû al-Qâsim is the *kunyah* of the Prophet.
91. I.e., they reckon with the fact that God will recompense them in the next world for their sufferings in this world.
92. *Ḥilm* could in this instance have its usual meaning of "clemency" or "compassion", but the sense is clearly somewhat more general here. In keeping with its other principal meaning, "intelligence", and its association with *ʿilm*, "knowledge", in this text, the apparent sense is "intelligent indulgence/understanding" or "compassionate wisdom".
93. The subject of the verb is understood as *aṣnâm*, "idols", from the preceding *âyah*, which is not quoted here. The feminine plural is used here, although *aṣnâm* are referred to elsewhere in the Qurʾân with the feminine singular pronominal suffix, *-hâ* (26:71), with the masculine plural of the verb, *yasmaʿûna* (26:72), and with the masculine plural pronominal suffix, *-hum* (21:58).
94. The *âyah* is S. 14:36, which is part of a speech of Abraham to God, a kind of complaint about the vagaries of men, who ought to join him in the service of God. The remainder of the verse reads: *wa-man ʿaṣânî fa-innaka ghafûr raḥîm*, "and whoever rebels against me [is at Thy mercy, yet] surely Thou art All-Forgiving, All-Compassionate".
95. S. 5:118.
96. The final sentence is a paraphrase of the opening words of S. 24:44: *yuqallibu Allâh al-layl wa-n-nahâr*, "God causes the night and the day to follow one upon the other".
97. It is clear from the text itself and corroborated by the variants of this Saying that *Allâh* is to be supplied here. Aḥmad Shâkir (*Musnad*, XV, 146) notes that Ṭabarî, *Tafsîr*, 2207, cites the same Saying with *yaqûlu Allâh*, as it should be.
98. Concerning the "cursing of God", see Saying 36.
99. This is an exclamation of dismay concerning the inexorable and inescapable march of "all-devouring time", which is difficult to render in English with the same succinctness and force. The sense is: "Woe is me, because of fateful Time!"
100. Cf. Saying 61 and its variants, 61a–61e.
101. The *la*ʾ*lat al-qadr*, or "night of power", is identified in the Qurʾân as the night in which the Qurʾân came down to Muḥammad (see above, p. 9). This

"blessed night" (S. 44:2) is normally reckoned as falling on the 27th of Ramaḍân, but it can be placed on and one of the last ten days of the month, especially the odd-numbered days. In any case, it is not necessarily nor even normally the last night of the month, which may account for the Companion's question here.

102. I.e., the servant who observes the fast and is sincere in his devotion during Ramaḍân will receive forgiveness on the last night of the month, when his "work" is done: i.e., when his penance, fasting, and worship are done.

Appendices

Muslim Collections of Divine Sayings

The following is a chronological list of fifteen collections of Divine Sayings that exist either in manuscript or in printed form. The list includes only those Arabic collections the authors and dates of which can be accurately identified. A few further collections, principally Turkish, are also cited by M. Tayyib Okiç in his *Tetkikler*.[1] Okiç gives a reasonably complete list of known Arabic and Turkish collections from the major Islamic bibliographical sources, but to date there has been no detailed list presented in any Western-language publication. Any study of later aspects of the Divine Saying in Islam would have to begin with the books and manuscripts given here:

1. Ẓâhir b. Ṭâhir b. Muḥammad ash-Shaḥḥâmî an-Naysâbûrî (d. 533/1138), *Kitâb al-aḥâdîth al-ilâhîyah*.[2]
2. Muḥyîddîn Muḥammad b. ʿAlî Ibn al-ʿArabî (d. 638/1240), *Mishkât al-anwâr fîmâ ruwiya ʿan Allâh min al-akhbâr*.[3]
3. Taqîyaddîn Abû al-Fatḥ Muḥammad b. ʿAlî b. Wahb Ibn Daqîq al-ʿÎd al-Manfalûṭî (d. 702/1302), *al-Arbaʿûn fî ar-riwâyah ʿan rabb al-ʿâlamîn*.[4]
4. ʿAlâʾaddîn Abû al-Qâsim ʿAlî b. Balabân b. ʿAbdallâh an-Numayrî al-Fârisî (d. 881/1476), *al-Maqâṣid as-sanîyah fî al-aḥâdîth al-ilâhîyah*.[5]
5. Shamsaddîn Abû ʿAbdallâh Muḥammad b. Aḥmad al-Mâlikî al-Madanî [or: al-Madyanî] (d. 881/1476), *al-Itḥâfât as-sanîyah fî al-aḥâdîth al-qudsîyah*.[6]
6. Muḥammad b. Maḥmûd Jamâl al-Millah wa-d-Dîn al-Âqsarâʾî (wrote during reign of Bâyazîd II, 886/1481–918/1512), *Arbaʿûn ḥadîthan* (a selection of forty traditions from Ibn al-ʿArabî's *Mishkât*).[7]
7. ʿAlî b. Sulṭân Muḥammad al-Qârî al-Harawî (d. 1014/1605), *al-Aḥâdîth al-qudsîyah al-arbaʿînîyah*.[8]
8. ʿAbdarraʾûf Muḥammad b. Tâj al-ʿÂrifîn b. ʿAlî b. Zayn al-ʿÂbidîn al-Ḥaddâdî al-Munâwî (d. 1031/1621), *al-Itḥâfât as-sanîyah bi-l-aḥâdîth al-qudsîyah*,[9] and *al-Maṭâlib al-ʿâlîyah az-zahîyah al-muntakhabah bi-l-aḥâdîth al-qudsîyah*.[10]

9. ʿAbdassalâm b. Muḥammad b. Aḥmad an-Nuzaylî, a collection of *aḥâdîth qudsîyah* compiled in 1045/1635.[11]
10. Muḥammad b. al-Ḥasan al-Ḥasanî al-Ḥurr al-ʿÂmilî (d. 1104/1692), *al-Jawâhir as-sanîyah fî al-aḥâdîth al-qudsîyah*, a Shîʿî collection.[12]
11. Jamâladdîn ʿAlî b. Ṣalâḥaddîn b. ʿAlî al-Kawkabânî (d. 1104/1692), *Manhaj al-kamâl wa-simṭ al-laʾâl fîmâ jâʾa fî al-ḥadîth min kalâm al-jalâl.*[13]
12. Muḥammad aṭ-Ṭarabzûnî al-Madanî (d. 1191/1777), *al-Itḥâfât as-sanîyah fî al-aḥâdîth al-qudsîyah.*[14]
13. ʿAbdarraḥmân b. as-Sayyid Muṣṭafá Wajîhaddîn al-ʿAydarûsî (d. 1192/1778), *an-Nafḥat al-unsîyah fî baʿḍ al-aḥâdîth al-qudsîyah.*[15]
14. Ṣâliḥ b. Muḥammad b. Nûḥ b. ʿAbdallâh b. ʿUmar al-ʿUmarî al-Fulânî (d. 1218/1803), *al-Aḥâdîth al-qudsîyah.*[16]
15. ʿAbdalmajîd b. ʿAlî al-ʿIdwî az-Zaynabî al-Miṣrî (d. 1303/1884–85), *at-Tuḥfah al-marḍîyah fî al-aḥâdîth al-qudsîyah wa-l-aḥâdîth an-nabawîyah.*[17]

Notes to Appendix A: "Muslim Collections of Divine Sayings"

1. Pp. 15–16.
2. *GAL*, I, 365, where this work is described as containing "traditions with precise *isnâd*s in nine sections; in the tenth, two chapters (*nawʿ*) from the work [presumably *at-Taqâsîm wa-l-anwâʿ*] of Ibn Ḥibbân (d. 354/965)". It would be useful to know if the two parts from Ibn Ḥibbân deal with or contain Divine Sayings. On Ibn Ḥibbân, see *GAL*, I, 164; *GAL*(S), I, 273.
3. Printed, Aleppo, 1346/1927. *GAL*, I, 442; *GAL*(S), I, 791–792. This work exists not only as a collection of 101 traditions, but also in a smaller collection [an extract? see example of such a selection in the sixth collection in the present list, that of al-Âqsarâʾî], as indicated by Brockelmann in the places cited above. Some MSS of this collection are also entitled simply *al-Aḥâdîth al-qudsîyah* (*GAL*, *GAL*(S), *loc.cit.*; *Kashf az-zunûn*, I, 14, 58). Such title variations are another example of the phenomenon mentioned above (Chapter 3, B, p. 57), the common practice of giving titles to manuscripts when they are copied even if the original titles were different. The *Kashf az-zunûn* also gives a further

reference to a collection of Ibn al-ʿArabî entitled *ar-Riyâḍ al-firdawsîyah fî al-aḥâdîth al-qudsîyah* (I, 937), which is probably another MS of the *Mishkât* (or a portion of it), again with a different title.

4. Ismâʿîl Pâshâ, I, 54, where the author is identified as Ibn Daqîq al-Miṣrî. The work is cited by Karahan, *Kırk Hadîs*, p. 340. Ibn Daqîq is treated in *GAL*, II, 63, and *GAL*(S), I, 605, 683; II, 66, but this work is not given.
5. *GAL*(S), II, 80.
6. Second edition printed Hyderabad, 1358/1939; first edition, Hyderabad, 1323/1905. *GAL*(S), II, 151 (N.b. that index references for al-Madanî in *GAL*[S], III, are incorrect).
7. *GAL*, II, 232, where the work is described as including "Ṣûfî explanations and commentary".
8. Printed, Aleppo, 1346/1927 (with the *Mishkât* of Ibn al-ʿArabî). Also published in Istanbul, 1316/1897–8, according to *GAL*, II, 394. *GAL*(S), II, 539, adds to the title ... *wa-l-kalimât al-insîyah.*
9. *GAL*, II, 306 (where this work of al-Munâwî is mistakenly confused with the 1323/1905 edition of al-Madanî's book of the same title [cf. collection no. 5 above]); *GAL*(S), II, 417.
10. *GAL*, II, 306, where the work is described as a "Ṣûfî collection of prayers and traditions as an addition to *al-aḥâdîth al-qudsîyah* of Ibn ʿArabî".
11. *GAL*(S), II, 553, where the collection given as number 11 in the present list is described as an amplification of this work, for which apparently no separate MS exists.
12. Printed edition, Baghdâd, 1384/1964. *GAL*, II, 412; *GAL*(S), II, 579, where this work is cited and said to have been written in 1056/1646. Note that *GAL*(S), II, 418, ascribes this work (including the same MS reference) incorrectly to another al-ʿÂmilî (d. 1073/1662).
13. *GAL*(S), II, 553: "An alphabetical collection of Ḥadîth Qudsî, an amplification and rearrangement of a work composed in 1045/1635 by ʿAbdassalâm an-Nuzaylî." Cf. n. 11 above.
14. Ismâʿîl Pâshâ, I, 13.
15. Ismâʿîl Pâshâ, *Hadîyah*, I, 554–555.
16. *GAL*(S), II, 523 (no MS reference given).
17. Ismâʿîl Pâshâ, I, 258; *GAL*, II, 490: *GAL*(S), II, 747 (title varies slightly in each reference).

B

Isnâds to the Divine Sayings in Part III

The following catalog of early transmitters of the Divine Saying was compiled originally to serve as the basis for determining whether this kind of Saying might have been early associated with a particular group (e.g., the *quṣṣâṣ*, or popular preachers; or Christian or Jewish converts to Islam) or a particular area (e.g., Baṣrah). The magnitude of any adequate study of such questions eventually precluded its inclusion in the present work, but the list of Divine-Saying *isnâd*s to the third transmitters is offered here as a possible resource for such an investigation and as an overview of the principal transmitters for these Sayings.

The following list has been compiled directly from the sources of the Sayings in Part III with the aid of several of the standard Arabic works on the early Ḥadîth authorities, primarily *Tahdhîb at-tahdhîb* and *al-Iṣâbah fî tamyîz aṣ-ṣaḥâbah* of Ibn Ḥajar, and *Usd al-Ghâbah fî maʿrifat aṣ-ṣaḥâbah* of Ibn al-Athîr. While particular attention has been paid to correct identification of the first transmitting authority in each *isnâd*, many of the names of subsequent transmitters cited have not been positively identified.

The numerical arrangement of the *isnâd*s is according to the earliest transmitter: numbers 1–99 have been assigned to *isnâd*s going back to Abû Hurayrah; 100–119 to Anas b. Mâlik; 120–129 to Abû Saʿîd al-Khudrî; and so on, each subsequent first transmitter being assigned ten numbers (130–139, 140–149, etc.). Within the *isnâd*s going back to a single first transmitter, all *isnâd*s with the same second transmitter are given a single number and the differing third transmitters are denoted by adding "a", "b", "c", etc., to the number: e.g., all *isnâd*s going back through Dhakwân as second authority to Abû Hurayrah as first authority carry the number *3*: *isnâd* 3 has al-Aʿmash as third authority; *isnâd* 3a, Zayd b. Aslam; *isnâd* 3b, Sulaymân at-Taymî, and so forth. Thus a glance at the *isnâd*s cited for versions of a given Saying in Part III gives an immediate idea of the distribution of transmitting authorities for that particular Saying.

First transmitter	Second transmitter	Third transmitter
Abû Hurayrah (*isnâds* 1–99)		
isnâd		
1	Hammâm b. Munabbih	Maʿmar b. Râshid
2	Saʿîd b. al-Musayyab al-Makhzûmî al-Qarshî	Ibn Shihâb az-Zuhrî
3	Dhakwân Abû Ṣâliḥ az-Zayyât as-Sammân	al-Aʿmash
3a		Zayd b. Aslam
3b		Sulaymân [at-Taymî?]
3c		Suhayl b. Abî Ṣâliḥ
3d		ʿAl. b. Dînâr
3e		Isḥâq b. ʿAl.
3f		ʿÂṣim b. Abî an-Najjûd
3g		al-Mundhîr b. ʿUbayd
3h		ʿAṭâʾ [b. Abî Rabâḥ?]
3i		Ḍirâr b. Murrah Abû Sinân
4	Abû ʿAl. al-Agharr	Ibn Shihâb az-Zuhrî
4a		Abû Isḥâq
5	ʿAr. al-Aʿraj	ʿAl. b. Dhakwân Abû az-Zinâd
5a		ʿAṭâʾ b. as-Sâʾib
5b		Ṣâliḥ b. Kaysân
5c		ʿAmr
6	Abû Salamah b. ʿAr.	Ibn Shihâb az-Zuhrî
6a		Muḥ. b. ʿAmr b. ʿAlqamah
6b		Yaḥyá b. Abî Kathîr
6c		Muḥ. b. al-Aswad
7	ʿAṭâʾ b. Yasâr al-Hilâlî al-Madanî al-Qâṣṣ	Sharîk b. ʿAl. b. Abî Namir al-Qarshî
7a		Ṣafwân b. Salîm
7b		Hilâl
8	Muḥammad b. Sîrîn	Hishâm b. Ḥassân al-Azadî al-Baṣrî
8a		ʿAwf b. Abî Jamîlah al-Baṣrî al-Aʿrâbî
8b		al-Ashʿath
8c		Ayyûb

First transmitter	Second transmitter	Third transmitter
Abû Hurayrah (continued)		
isnâd		
9	Muḥammad b. Ziyâd	Ibrâhîm
9a		Shuʿbah
9b		Ḥammâd b. Salamah
10	Abû Râfiʿ	Qatâdah
10a		Thâbit
10b		al-Ḥasan b. Ziyâd
11	Abû Zurʿah b. ʿAmr b. Jarîr	ʿUmârah b. al-Qaʿqâʿ
12	Abû Muslim al-Agharr al-Madanî [al-Kûfî]	ʿAṭâʾ b. as-Sâʾib
12a		Abû Isḥâq as-Sabîʿî
13	ʿAr. b. Yaʿqûb	al-ʿAlâʾ b. ʿAr. b. Yaʿqûb
14	Nâfiʿ [b. Jubayr?]	Mûsá b. ʿUqbah
15	ʿAjlân Mawlá Fâṭimah al-Madanî	Muḥ. b. ʿAjlân
16	Saʿîd b. Yasâr Abû Ḥubâb	ʿAr. b. ʿAr. b. Maʿmar Abû Ṭawâlah
16a		Muʿâwiyah b. Abî Muzarrid
17	ʿAṭâʾ b. Mînâʾ	al-Ḥârith b. ʿAr.
17a		Saʿîd
18	Abû Jaʿfar al-Anṣârî al-Madanî	Yaḥyá b. Abî Kathîr
19	Muḥ. b. Kaʿb [al-Quraẓî]	Muḥ. b. ʿAbdaljabbâr
20	ʿUbaydallâh b. ʿAl.	Ibn Shihâb az-Zuhrî
21	ʿUthmân b. Abî Sawdah	ʿÎsâ Abû Sinân
22	Abû Yûnus	Ibn Lahîʿah
23	Shurayḥ b. Hâniʾ	ʿÂmir
24	Abû Sâʾib Mawlá Hishâm b. Zuhrah	al-ʿAlâʾ b. ʿAr. b. Yaʿqûb
25	Anas b. Mâlik	Sulaymân at-Taymî
26	Ṭâwûs	ʿAl. b. Ṭâwûs al-Yamânî
27	Yazîd b. al-Aṣamm	Jaʿfar b. al-Burqân
28	ʿAr. b. Abî ʿAmrah	Isḥâq b. ʿAl. b. Abî Ṭalḥah
28a		Hilâl b. ʿAlî b. Usâmah
29	"Shaykh min ahl al-Baṣrah"	ʿAbdalḥamîd b. Jaʿfar az-Ziyâdî
30	Khilâs b. ʿAmr al-Baṣrî	ʿAwf b. Abî Jamîlah al-Baṣrî al-Aʿrâbî

First transmitter	Second transmitter	Third transmitter
Abû Hurayrah (continued)		
isnâd		
31	Sa'îd b. 'Al. Ibn Marjânah	Sa'd b. Sa'îd
32	Abû Mudillah Mawlá 'Â'ishah	Sa'd Abû Mujâhid aṭ-Ṭâ'î
33	Ziyâd aṭ-Ṭâ'î	Ḥamzah az-Zayyât
34	Sa'îd b. Abî Sa'îd al-Maqbarî	Yazîd b. al-Hâd
34a		'Amr b. Abî 'Amr
34b		Ismâ'îl b. Umayyah
34c		Mâlik
35	Abû Khâlid al-Wâlibî al-Kufî	Zâ'idah b. Nashîṭ al-Kûfî
36	Ḥumayd b. 'Ar. b. 'Awf	Sa'd b. Ibrâhîm
37	Shatîr b. Nahâr	Muḥ. b. Wâsi'
38	Umm ad-Dardâ'	Ismâ'îl b. 'Ubaydallâh
39	Abû Sa'îd [al-Khudrî?]	Sa'îd b. Abî Sa'îd
40	Mûsá b. Yasâr	Muḥammad
41	'Aṭâ' b. Yazîd al-Laythî	Ibn Shihâb az-Zuhrî
42	'Ammâr b. Abî 'Ammâr	Ḥammâd b. Salamah
43	Mujâhid b. Jabr Abû al-Hajjâj al-Makhzûmî	Yûnus
44	Abû al-Ghayth	Thawr
45	Yaḥyá b. Ya'mur	al-Azraq b. Qays
46	Anas b. Ḥakîm aḍ-Ḍabbî	al-Ḥasan [b. Ziyâd?]
46a		'Alî b. Zayd
47	Ḥurayth b. Qabîṣah	al-Ḥasan [b. Ziyâd?]
Anas b. Mâlik (*isnâds* 100–119)		
100	Qatâdah	Shu'bah
100a		Marzûq Abû Bakr
101	Bakr b. 'Al. al-Mazanî	Sa'îd b. 'Ubayd
102	[Abû Mu'tamir]	Mu'tamir
103	'Ubaydallâh b. Abî Bakr b. Anas	Mubârak b. Faḍâlah
104	Thâbit al-Bunânî	Suhayl b. 'Al.
104a		Ma'bad b. Hilâl
104b		Ḥammâd b. Salamah
105	Abû 'Imrân al-Jawnî	Shu'bah

First transmitter	Second transmitter	Third transmitter
Anas b. Mâlik (continued)		
isnâd		
106	Sinân b. Saʿd	Yazîd b. Abî Ḥabîb
107	ʿAmr Mawlá al-Muṭṭâlib	[Zayd] Ibn Hâd
108	al-Ashʿath b. Jâbir	[Zayd] Ibn Hâd
108a		Nûḥ. b. Qays
109	Hilâl Abû Zilâl	ʿAz. b. Muslim
110	Mukhtâr b. Fulful	Muḥ. b. Fuḍayl
Abû Saʿîd al-Khudrî (*isnâds* 120–129)		
120	Dhakwân Abû Ṣâlih az-Zayyât	al-Aʿmash
120a		Ḍirâr b. Murrah Abû Sinân
121	ʿAṭâʾ b. Yasâr al-Hilâlî	Zayd b. Aslam
122	Abû Muslim al-Agharr al-Madanî [al-Kûfî]	Abû Isḥâq
123	ʿAtîyah	Firâs
124	ʿAmr	Yazîd b. al-Hâd
125	Yaḥyá b. ʿUmârah	ʿAmr b. Yaḥyá al-Mâzinî
126	Sulaymân b. ʿUmar Abû al-Haytham	Abû ʿAr.
126a		Darrâj b. Samʿân
127	ʿUbaydallâh b. ʿAl. b. ʿUtbah	ʿAṭâʾ b. as-Sâʾib
Abû Dharr (*isnâds* 130–139)		
130	al-Maʿrûr b. Suwayd	al-Aʿmash
130a		ʿÂṣim
130b		Rabʿî b. Jirâsh
131	Abû Maʿrûf	ʿAlî b. Zayd
132	[ʿAmr b.?] Maʿdî Karab	Shahr b. Ḥawshab al-Ashʿarî
133	ʿAr. b. Ghanam	Shahr b. Ḥawshab al-Ashʿarî
134	Abû Idrîs al-Khawlânî	Rabîʿah b. Yazîd
135	ʿAmr Abû Asmâʾ ar-Raḥbî	Abû Kilâbah
136	Yazîd b. ʿAmr	Ibn Lahîʿah
ʿAl. Ibn ʿAbbâs (*isnâds* 140–149)		
140	Abû Naḍrah al-Baṣrî	ʿAlî b. Zayd

First transmitter	Second transmitter	Third transmitter
ʿAl Ibn ʿAbbâs (continued)		
isnâd		
141	Saʿîd b. Jubayr	ʿAṭâʾ b. as-Sâʾib
142	Nâfiʿ b. Jubayr	ʿAl. b. Abî Ḥusayn
143	Abû Rajâʾ al-ʿUṭâridî	Jaʿd Abû ʿUthmân
143a		al-Ḥasan b. Dhakwân
144	Abû al-ʿÂlîyah	Qatâdah
145	Shaqîq b. Salamah Abû Wâʾil al-Kûfî al-Asadî	al-Aʿmash
ʿÂʾisnah (*isnâds* 150–159)		
150	ʿUrwah [b. az-Zubayr]	Yazîd b. Rûmân
150a		Ibn Shihâb az-Zuhrî
151	Saʿd b. Hishâm	Zurârah b. Awfá
152	Shurayḥ b. Hâniʿ	ash-Shaʿbî
153	ʿAbdalwâḥid (Mawlá ʿUrwah)	Hammâd
153a		Abû al-Mundhir
Abû ad-Dardâʾ (*isnâds* 160–169)		
160	Umm ad-Dardâʾ	Yazîd b. Maysarah
161	Jubayr b. Nafîr	Khâlid b. Miʿdân
ʿAl. b. ʿUmar (*isnâds* 170–179)		
170	ʿUbaydallâh b. Miqsam	Isḥâq b. ʿAl. b. Abî Ṭalḥah
170a		Abû Ḥâzim
171	Muḥ. b. Zayd	ʿUmar b. Muḥ. b. Zayd
172	ʿAl. b. Murrah al-Kûfî	Manṣûr
173	Nâfiʿ Mawlá Ibn ʿUmar	ʿUbaydallâh
173a		Mubârak b. Ḥassân
174	Sâlim b. ʿAl.	ʿUmar b. Ḥamzah
175	al-Ḥasan	Yûnus
ʿAl. b. ʿAmr b. al-ʿÂṣ (*isnâds* 180–189)		
180	ʿAr. b. Jubayr	Bakr b. Sawâdah
181	Abû Qâbûs	ʿAmr b. Dînâr
182	Shuʿayb	ʿAmr b. Shuʿayb
183	Abû Ayyûb	Thâbit

First transmitter	Second transmitter	Third transmitter
ʿAl. b. Amr b. al-ʿÂṣ (continued)		
isnâd		
184	"rajul min ash-shâm"*	Thâbit
185	Nawf b. Faḍâlah al-Ḥamîrî	Muṭarrif b. ʿAl. b. ash-Shakhîr
186	ʿAl. b. Bâbâ	Qatâdah
187	ʿAṭâʾ b. Yasâr al-Hilâlî	Hilâl b. Abî Hilâl
ʿAl. b. Masʿûd (*isnâds* 190–199)		
190	ʿAlqamah b. Qays al-Kûfî an-Nakhaʿî	Ibrâhîm an-Nakhaʿî
191	ʿAbîdah b. Qays as-Salmânî	Ibrâhîm an-Nakhaʿî
192	ʿAwf b. Mâlik Abû al-Aḥwâṣ al-Kûfî	Ibrâhîm b. Muslim al-Hijrî al-Kûfî
193	Murrah al-Hamdânî	ʿAṭâʾ b. as-Sâʾib
ʿAl. b. Unays (*isnâds* 200–209)		
200	Jâbir b. ʿAl.	ʿAl. b. Muḥ. b. ʿAqîl
ʿUbâdah b. aṣ-Ṣâmit (*isnâds* 210–219)		
210	Anas b. Mâlik	Qatâdah
211	Abû Idrîs al-Khawlânî	ʿAṭâʾ b. Abî Rabâḥ
211a		"rajul min majlis Yaḥyá b. Abî Kathîr"
212	al-Mukhdijî	Ibn Muḥayrîz
213	ʿAl. b. aṣ-Ṣubâbahî	ʿAṭâʾ b. Yasâr al-Hilâlî
Muʿadh b. Jabal (*isnâds* 220–229)		
220	Abû Idrîs al-Khawlânî	Abû Ḥâzim Ibn Dînâr
220a		ʿAṭâʾ b. Abî Rabâḥ
220b		"rajul min majlis Yaḥyá b. Abî Kathîr"
220c		Muḥ. b. Qays

* Shâkir, *Musnad*, XI, 36–38, gives a probable identification of this man as Yaḥyá b. Mâlik al-Azadî al-Maghâzî, a tâbiʿî, or Follower.

First transmitter	Second transmitter	Third transmitter
Zayd b. Khâlid al-Juhanî (*isnâds* 230–239)		
isnâd		
230	ʿUbaydallâh b. ʿAl. b. ʿUtbah b. Masʿûd	Ṣâliḥ b. Kaysân
Sahl b. Saʿd as-Sâʿidî (*isnâds* 240–249)		
240	Abû Ḥâzim	Abû Ṣakhr
al-Mughayrah b. Shuʿbah (*isnâds* 250–259)		
250	ash-Shaʿbî	Muṭarrif b. Ṭarîf
Ṣadá Abû Umâmah al-Bâhilî, Ibn ʿAjlân (*isnâds* 260–269)		
260	al-Qâsim Abû ʿAr.	ʿAlî b. Yazîd
260a		Thâbit b. ʿAjlân
261	Ayyûb b. Sulaymân	Ibr. b. Murrah
262	ʿAl. b. Kaʿb b Mâlik al-Anṣârî	Maʿbad b. Kaʿb as-Salamî
ʿAr. b. ʿAwf (*isnâds* 270–279)		
270	Muḥ. b. Jubayr b. Mutʿim	Abû al-Ḥuwayrith
271	ʿAbdalwâḥid b. Muḥ. b. ʿAr. b. ʿAwf	ʿAmr b. Abî ʿAmr
272	Abû ad-Dardâʾ	Abû Salamah b. ʿAr.
273	Abû Raddâd al-Laythî	Abû Salamah b. ʿAr.
274	ʿAl. b. Qâriẓ	Ibr. b. ʿAl. b. Qâriẓ
275	Abû Salamah b. ʿAr.	Ibn Shihâb az-Zuhrî
ʿUmar b. al-Khaṭṭâb (*isnâds* 280–289)		
280	Muslim b. Yasâr al-Juhânî	ʿAbdalḥamîd b. ʿAr. b. Zayd
Jâbir b. ʿAl. (*isnâds* 290–299)		
290	Ṭalḥah b. Jirâsh	Mûsâ b. Ibr. al-Ḥizâmî
ʿAlî b. Abî Ṭâlib (*isnâds* 300–309)		
300	ʿAr. b. al-Ḥârith	Abû Isḥâq
301	ʿUbaydallâh b. Abî Râfiʿ	al-Ḥasan b. Muḥ. b. ʿAlî
302	Abû ʿAr. as-Sulamî	Saʿd b. ʿUbaydallâh

First transmitter	Second transmitter	Third transmitter
ʿIyâḍ b. Ḥimâr al-Mujâshʿî (*isnâd*s 310–319)		
isnâd		
310	Muṭarrif b. ʿAl. b. ash-Shakhkhîr	Qatâdah
311	Yazîd b. ʿAl. Abû al-ʿAlâʾ al-Baṣrî	Qatâdah
Maʿqil b. Yasâr al-Muzannî (*isnâd*s 320–329)		
320	ʿUbaydallâh b. Ziyâd	al-Ḥasan
ʿAbbâs b. Mirdâs as-Salamî (*isnâd*s 330–339)		
330	Kinânah b. ʿAbbâs b. Mirdâs	ʿAl. b. Kinânah b. ʿAbbâs
Abû Saʿd b. Abî Faḍâlah al-Anṣârî (*isnâd*s 340–349)		
340	Ziyâd b. Mînâʾ	[Jaʿfar]
Maḥmûd b. Labîd al-Anṣârî (*isnâd*s 350–359)		
350	ʿAmr b. Abî ʿAmr	Yazîd b. al-Hâd
350a		ʿAr. b. Abî az-Zinâd
351	ʿÂṣim b. ʿUmar b. Qatâdah	ʿAr. b. Abî az-Zinâd
Jundab b. ʿAl. (*isnâd*s 360–369)		
360	Abû ʿImrân al-Jawnî	Sulaymân [Abû Muʿtamir]
361	al-Ḥasan	Shaybân
361a		Jarîr b. Ḥâzim
ʿUqbah b. ʿÂmir (*isnâd*s 370–379)		
370	Abû ʿUshânah al-Muʿâfirî	ʿAmr b. al-Ḥârith
370a		Ibn Lahîʿah
Ṣuhayb (*isnâd*s 380–389)		
380	ʿAr. b. Abî Laylá	Thâbit al-Bunânî
Rifâʿah al-Juhânî (*isnâd*s 390–399)		
390	ʿAṭâʾ b. Yasâr	Hilâl b. Abî Maymûnah
Abû Mûsá [al-Ashʿarî?] (*isnâd*s 400–409)		
400	Abû Burdah	Burayd
401	Ḥittân b. ʿAl. ar-Raqqâshî	Yûnus b. Jubayr

First transmitter	Second transmitter	Third transmitter
Abû Qatâdah b. Ribʿî (*isnâd*s 410–419)		
isnâd		
410	Saʿîd b. al-Musayyab	Ibn Shihâb az-Zuhrî
Tamîm ad-Dârî (*isnâd*s 420–429)		
420	Zurârah b. Awfá	Dâwûd b. Abî Hind
Nuʿaym b. Himâr al-Ghaṭfânî (*isnâd*s 430–439)		
430	Kathîr b. Murrah	Abû az-Zâhirîyah
431	Makḥûl	Saʿîd b. ʿAz.

C

Index to the Divine Sayings in Part III

The Sayings in Part III are arranged in alphabetical order according to either the first or the most important line of the quoted words of God in the first text of each "family" of Sayings. The following index includes not only these lines, but also the first or main lines of subsequent texts in each "family", as well as important clauses from these same lines.

Note that the Sayings in Part III and the lines in the present index are alphabetized according to the English alphabet into which the first and main lines are all transliterated. For the purpose of keeping like Arabic words together, all short vowels of a kind precede all long vowels of the same kind (e.g., ab, am, az, âc, âl, âz, etc.). The definite article *al-*, *ar-*, etc., is ignored in the alphabetizing, as is word division (e.g., *akhrijûhu* precedes *akhrijû min*).

First or main line or clause   Saying number

Bibliography

Abbott, Nabia. *Studies in Arabic Literary Papyri.* 2 vols. to date. University of Chicago Oriental Institute Publications, vols. LXXV, LXXVI. Chicago: The University of Chicago Press, 1957–1967.

ʿAbdalbâqî, Muḥammad Fuʾâd. *al-Muʿjam al-mufahras li-alfâẓ al-Qurʾân al-karîm.* Cairo: Dâr al-Kutub, 1364/1945.

Abû al-Baqâʾ b. ʿAbdalqâdir al-Ḥanafî. *al-Kullîyât.* Bûlâq, 1281/1864.

Abû Dâwûd, Sulaymân b. al-Ashʿath as-Sijistânî. *as-Sunan.* Edited by Muḥ. Muḥyîddîn ʿAbdalḥamîd. 4 vols. Egypt, 1369/1950.

Abû al-Ḥusayn al-Baṣrî. *al-Muʿtamad fî uṣûl al-fiqh.* Edited by Muhammad Hamidullah *et al.* 2 vols. Damascus: Institut Français de Damas, 1964.

Abû Nuʿaym Aḥmad b. ʿAl. al-Iṣbahânî. *Ḥilyat al-awliyâʾ wa-ṭabaqât al-aṣfiyâʾ.* 10 vols. Cairo, 1351/1932–1357/1938.

Abû al-Yamân al-Ḥakam b. Nâfiʿ al-Baḥrânî. *Aḥâdîth Abî al-Yamân al-Ḥakam b. Nâfiʿ ʿan Shuʿayb b. Abî Ḥamzah ʿan az-Zuhrî.* Edited by Mohammad Mustafa Azmi, in *Studies in Early Ḥadîth Literature* [see Azmi entry]. Part II, pp. 137–162.

Ahlwardt, Wilhelm. *Verzeichnis der arabischen Handschriften der Königlichen Bibliothek zu Berlin.* 10 vols. Berlin, 1887–1899.

Ahrens, Karl. *Muhammed als Religionsstifter.* Abhandlungen für die Kunde des Morgenlandes, vol. XIX, no. 4. Leipzig: Deutsche Morgenländische Gesellschaft, 1935.

ʿAlî b. Sulṭân Muḥ. al-Qârî al-Harawî. *al-Aḥâdîth al-qudsîyah al-arbaʿînîyah.* Edited, together with *Mishkât al-anwâr* ... of Ibn al-ʿArabî, by Muḥ. Râghib aṭ-Ṭabbâkh. Aleppo, 1346/1927.

al-Alousî, Husâm Muhî Eldîn. *The Problem of Creation in Islamic Thought: Qurʾan, Hadith, Commentaries, and Kalam.* Photographic reprint of 1965 Cambridge University dissertation. N.p., 1968.

Anawati, G.-C., and Louis Gardet. *Mystique musulmane. Aspects et tendances, expériences et techniques.* Études musulmanes, edited by Étienne Gilson and Louis Gardet, no. 8. Paris: J. Vrin, 1961.

Andrae, Tor. *Islamische Mystiker.* Translated into German by Helmhart Kanus-Credé. Stuttgart: W. Kohlhammer Verlag, Urban Bücher, 1960.

——. *Mohammed: sein Leben und sein Glaube*. Göttingen: Vandenhoeck & Ruprecht, 1932.

——. *Die Person Muhammeds in Lehre und Glauben seiner Gemeinde*. Archives d'Études Orientales, edited by J.-A. Lundell, vol. XVI. Stockholm: P. A. Norstedt & Söner, 1918.

Arberry, Arthur J., trans. *The Doctrine of the Ṣūfīs* [see Kalâbâdhî].

——, trans. *The Koran Interpreted.* 2 vols. London: George Allen & Unwin; New York: The Macmillan Company, 1955.

al-Ashʿarî, Abû al-Ḥasan ʿAlî b. Ismâʿîl. *Maqâlât al-islâmîyîn wa-ikhtilâf al-muṣallîn* (*Die dogmatischen Lehren der Anhänger des Islam*). Edited by Hellmut Ritter. 2nd edition. Wiesbaden: Franz Steiner Verlag, 1963.

ʿAṭṭâr, Muḥ. b. Ibrâhîm Farîdaddîn. *Tadhkirat al-awliyâʾ*. Edited by Reynold A. Nicholson. 2 vols. Persian Historical Texts, vol. V. London: Luzac & Co.; Leiden: E. J. Brill, 1905–1907.

Azmi, Mohammad Mustafa [ʿAzmî, Muḥammad Muṣṭafá]. *Studies in Early Ḥadîth Literature, with a Critical Edition of Some Early Texts*. Beirut: al-Maktab al-Islâmî, 1968.

[Bell, Richard]. *Bell's Introduction to the Qurʾân*. Revised and enlarged by W. Montgomery Watt. Islamic Surveys, vol. VIII. Edinburgh: Edinburgh University Press, 1970.

——. "Muhammad's Visions", *MW*, XXIV (1934), 145–154.

——. *The Origin of Islam in its Christian Environment* (The Gunning Lectures, Edinburgh University, 1925). London: Macmillan and Co., 1926.

Bijlefeld, Willem A. "A Prophet and More than a Prophet? Some Observations on the Qurʾânic Use of the Terms 'Prophet' and 'Apostle'", *MW*, LIX (1969), 1–28.

Blachère, Régis. *Introduction au Coran*. 2nd, partially revised ed. Paris: Libraire G.-P. Maisonneuve, 1959.

Bland, N. "On the Muhammedan Science of *Taʿbîr*, or Interpretation of Dreams", *JRAS*, XVI (1856), 118–171.

Brockelmann, Carl. *Geschichte der arabischen Litteratur*. 2nd, revised edition. 2 vols. Leiden: E. J. Brill, 1943–1949.

——. *Geschichte der arabischen Litteratur: Supplement*. 3 vols. Leiden: E. J. Brill, 1937–1942.

Buhl, Frants. *Das Leben Muhammeds*. Translated from the Danish by Hans Heinrich Schaeder. Leipzig: Quelle & Meyer, 1930.

al-Bukhârî, Muḥammad b. Ismâʿîl. *al-Jâmiʿ aṣ-ṣaḥîḥ*. Edited by Ludolf Krehl and Th. W. Juynboll. 4 vols. Leiden: E. J. Brill, 1862–1908.

——. *al-Jâmiʿ aṣ-ṣaḥîh* (*Les Traditions islamiques*). Translated by O. Houdas and W. Marçais. 4 vols. Publications de l'École des Langues Orientales Vivantes, 4th series, vols. III–VI. Paris: Imprimérie Nationale, 1903–1914.

Bursalı, Mehmed Tahir. *Osmanlı müellifleri*. 3 vols. Istanbul, 1333/1913–14.

Chapira, B. "Legendes bibliques attribuées à Kaʿb al-Aḥbâr", *Révue des études juives*. LXIX (1919), 86–107; LXX (1920), 37–44.

ad-Dârimî, ʿAl. b. ʿAr. *as-Sunan*. Edited by ʿAbdallâh Ḥâshim Yamânî al-Madanî. 2 vols. Cairo, 1386/1966.

The Encyclopaedia of Islam. 4 vols. and Supplement. Edited by Th. Houtsma, *et al.* Leiden and London, 1913–1938.

The Encyclopaedia of Islam New Edition. Edited by H. A. R. Gibb, *et al.* Leiden and London, 1954– .

Eliade, Mircea. *The Sacred and the Profane: The Nature of Religion*. Translated by Willard R. Trask. New York & Evanston: Harper & Row, Harper Torchbooks, 1961.

Eliash, Joseph. "'The Šīʿite Qurʾān', a Reconsideration of Goldziher's Interpretation", *Arabica* XVI, (1969), 15–24.

Ess, Josef van. "Zwischen Ḥadīṯ und Theologie: Studien zum Entstehen antiqadaritischer Ueberlieferung". Unpublished paper delivered at Harvard Conference on *Kalâm*, Harvard University, April, 1971.

Fahd, Toufic. "Les songes et leur interprétation selon l'Islam", *Les songes et leur interprétation* (Edited by Serge Sauneron *et al.* Sources orientales, edited by Anne-Marie Esnoul *et al.*, vol. II. Paris: Éditions de Seuil, 1959), pp. 127–158.

"al-Fatâwá wa-l-aḥkâm: al-aḥâdîth al-qudsîyah", *Liwâʾ al-Islam* (Cairo), V (1370/1951), 188–189.

Frazer, James George. *The Golden Bough: A Study in Magic and Religion*. 1922. 1 vol., abridged ed. New York: The Macmillan Company, 1963.

Freeman-Grenville, G. S. P. *The Muslim and Christian Calendars; Being Tables for the Conversion of Muslim and Christian Dates from the Hijra to the Year A.D. 2000*. London, New York, Toronto: Oxford University Press, 1963.

Fück, Johann. "Beiträge zur Ueberlieferungsgeschichte von Buḫârî's Traditionssammlung", *ZDMG*, XCII (1938), 60–87.

——. "Die Originalität des arabischen Propheten", *ZDMG*, XC (1936), 509–525.

——. "Die Rolle des Traditionalismus im Islam", *ZDMG*, XCIII (1939), 1–32.

Geiger, Abraham. *Was hat Mohammed aus dem Judenthume aufgenommen?* Bonn, 1833.

al-Ghazzâlî, Abû Ḥamîd Muḥ. b. Muḥ. *Iḥyâʾ ʿulûm ad-dîn*. 5 vols. Cairo: Maṭbaʿat al-Istiqâmah, n.d.

Goldziher, Ignaz. *Abhandlungen zur arabischen Philologie*. 2 vols. Leiden: E. J. Brill, 1896.

——. "Kämpfe um die Stellung des Ḥadîṯ im Islam", *ZDMG*, LXI (1907), 860–872.

——. "Mélanges judeo-arabes: isra'iliyyat", *Révue des études juives*. XLIV (1902), 62–66.

——. *Muhammedanische Studien*. 2 vols. in 1. Halle: Max Niemeyer, 1889.

——. "Neutestamentliche Elemente in der Traditionslitteratur des Islam", *Oriens Christianus*, II (1902), 390–397.

——. *Die Richtungen der islamischen Koranauslegung*. (Olaus-Petri Lectures, University of Upsala, 1913) Veröffentlichungen der de Goeje-Stiftung, No. VI. Leiden: E. J. Brill, 1920.

——. "Ueber muhammedanische Polemik gegen Ahl al-kitâb", *ZDMG*, XXXII (1878), 341–387.

——. *Vorlesungen über den Islam*. Religionswissenschaftliche Bibliothek, edited by Wilhelm Streitberg and Richard Wünsch, vol. I. Heidelberg: Carl Winter, 1910.

——. *Die Ẓâhiriten: ihr Lehrsystem und ihre Geschichte. Beitrag zur Geschichte der muhammedanischen Theologie*. Leipzig, 1884.

Grünbaum, Max. "Beiträge zur vergleichenden Mythologie aus der Hagada", *ZDMG*, XXXI (1877), 183–359.

Grünebaum, Gustav von. "Von Muḥammads Wirkung und Originalität", *WZKM*, XLIV (1937), 29–50.

Guillaume, Alfred, trans. *The Life of Muḥammad* [see Ibn Isḥâq].

Ḥâjjî Khalîfah, Muṣṭafá b. ʿAl. Kâtib Čelebî. *Kashf aẓ-ẓunûn ʿan asâmî al-kutub wa-l-funûn* (*Keşf-el-zunun*). Edited by Şerefettin Yaltkaya and Kilisi Rifat Bilge. 2 vols. Istanbul, 1360/1941–1362/1943.

al-Ḥâkim an-Naysâbûrî, Muḥ. b. ʿAl. *al-Madkhal ilá maʿrifat al-iklîl* (*An Introduction to the Science of Tradition*). Edited with introduction, translation, and notes by James Robson. Oriental Translation Fund (Royal Asiatic Society), New Series, vol. XXXIX. London: Luzac and Co., 1953.

——. *Maʿrifat ʿulûm al-ḥadîth*. Edited by M. Ḥusayn. Beirut: al-Maktab at-Tijârî, [1966?].

——. *al-Mustadrak ʿalá aṣ-ṣahîhayn*. 4 vols. Ḥyderabad (Deccan), 1334/1915–1342/1923.

Hamidullah, Muhammad [Muḥammad Ḥamîdallâh]. *The Earliest Extant Work on the Hadith: Sahifah* [*sic*] *Hammam Ibn Munabbih*. 5th, revised edition. Translated into English by Muhammad Rahimuddin. Publications of Centre Cultural Islamique, no. 2. Paris, 1380/1961.

——. *Le Prophète de l'Islam*. 2 vols. Études musulmanes, vol. VII. Paris: J. Vrin, 1959.

Hammâm b. Munabbih. *Ṣaḥîfah*. Edited by Muḥammad Ḥamîdallâh ["Muhammad Hamidullah"] in: "Aqdam taʾlîf fî al-ḥadîth an-nabawî: ṣaḥîfat Hammâm b. Munabbih wa-makânatuha fî taʾrîkh ʿilm al-ḥadîth", *RAAD*, XXVIII (1953), 96–116, 270–281, 443–467 (also reprinted in Hamidullah, *Earliest Extant Work* [see Hamidullah]).

Hamzah, Aḥmad, *et al.* "Nadwat *Liwâʾ al-Islâm*", *Liwâʾ al-Islâm* (Cairo), VI (1371/1952), 760–764.

Hartmann, Richard. *Al-Ḳuschairīs Darstellung des Ṣūfītums*. Türkische Bibliothek, edited by Georg Jacob & Rudolf Tschudi, vol. XVIII. Berlin: Mayer & Müller, 1914.

Haywood, John A. *Arabic Lexicography: its History, and its Place in the General History of Lexicography*. 2nd edition (Photomechanical reprint). Leiden: E. J. Brill, 1965.

Horovitz, Josef. "Alter und Ursprung des Isnād", *Der Islam*, VIII (1918), 39–47.

——. "The Earliest Biographies of the Prophet and their Authors", *Islamic Culture*, I (1927), 535–559; II (1928), 22–50, 164–182, 495–526.

——. *Koranische Untersuchungen*. Studien zur Geschichte und Kultur des islamischen Orients, edited by C. H. Becker, vol. IV. Berlin & Leipzig: Walter de Gruyter & Co., 1926.

——. "Muhammeds Himmelfahrt", *Der Islam*, IX (1918), 159–183.

Horst, Heribert. "Zur Ueberlieferung im Korankommentar aṭ-Ṭabarīs", *ZDMG*, CIII (1953), 290–307.

Houdas and Marçais, trans. *Les Traditions Islamiques* [see al-Bukhârî].

al-Hujwîrî, ʿAlî b. ʿUthmân. *Kashf al-maḥjûb* (*The Kashf al-Mahjúb: the Oldest Persian Treatise on Sufism*). Translated by Reynold A. Nicholson. E. J. W. Gibb Memorial Series, vol. XVII. New ed. London: Luzac & Company, 1936 (reprinted, 1959).

al-Ḥurr al-ʿÂmilî, Muḥ. b. al-Ḥasan. *al-Jawâhir as-sanîyah fî al-aḥâdîth al-qudsîyah*. Baghdâd, 1384/1964.

Ibn ʿAbdalbarr an-Namarî, Yûsuf b. ʿAl. *Jâmiʿ bayân al-ʿilm wa-faḍlihi*. 2 vols. Cairo: Idârat aṭ-Ṭabâʿah al-Munîrîyah, n.d.

Ibn al-ʿArabî, Muḥ. b. ʿAlî Muḥyîddîn. *Mishkât al-anwâr fîmâ ruwiya ʿan Allâh subḥânahu min al-akhbâr*. Edited together with *al-Aḥâdîth al-qudsîyah* of ʿAlî al-Qârî, by Muḥ. Râghib aṭ-Ṭabbâkh. Aleppo, 1349/1927.

Ibn al-Athîr, ʿAlî b. Muḥ. ʿIzzaddîn. *Usd al-ghâbah fî maʿrifât aṣ-ṣaḥâbah*. 5 vols. Teheran, 1377/1956–57.

Ibn al-Athîr, Majdaddîn ash-Shaybânî al-Jazarî. *an-Nihâyah fî gharîb al-ḥadîth wa-l-athar*. 4 vols. Cairo, 1322/1904.

Ibn Ḥajar al-ʿAsqalânî, Aḥmad b. ʿAlî. *al-Iṣâbah fî tamyîz as-ṣaḥâbah* (*A Biographical Dictionary of Persons who Knew Muḥammad*). Edited by Muḥammad Wajîh, Aloys Sprenger, *et al.* 4 vols. Bibliotheca Indica, no. 20. Calcutta: Royal Asiatic Society of Bengal, 1856–1873.

——. *Tahdhîb at-tahdhîb*. 12 vols. Hyderabad, 1325–27/1907–09.

Ibn Ḥanbal, Aḥmad b. Muḥammad. *al-Musnad*. Edited by Muḥammad az-Zuhrî al-Ghamrâwî, with the commentary of al-Muttaqî, *Muntakhab kanz al-ʿummâl*, on the margin. 6 vols. Cairo, 1313/1895.

——. *al-Musnad*. Edited and annotated by Aḥmad Muḥammad Shâkir. vols. I– . Cairo, 1949– .

Ibn Hishâm, Abû Muḥ. ʿAbdalmalik. *at-Tîjân li-maʿrifat mulûk az-zamân fî akhbâr Qaḥṭân*. Hyderabad, 1347/1928.

Ibn Isḥâq, Muḥammad. *Sîrat rasûl Allâh*. Compiled by ʿAbdalmalik Ibn Hishâm. Edited by Ferdinand Wüstenfeld with introduction, notes and indices. 2 vols. Göttingen: Dieterische Universitäts-Buchhandlung, 1858–1860.

——. *The Life of Muḥammad: A Translation of Ibn Isḥâq's Sîrat Rasûl Allah*. Translated by Alfred Guillaume. 1955. Reprint. Lahore: Oxford University Press, Pakistan Branch, 1967.

Ibn al-Jawzî, Abû al-Faraj ʿAr. b. ʿAlî. *Kitâb al-quṣṣâṣ wa-l-mudhakkirîn*. Edited and translated by Merlin L. Schwartz. Récherches de l'Institut de Lettres Orientales de Beyrouth, ser. 1 (Pensée Arabe et Musulmane), vol. XLVII. Beirut: Dar el-Machreq Éditeurs, [1969?].

Ibn Khaldûn, ʿAr. b. Muḥ. *Muqaddimah*. Edited by M. Quatremère. 3 vols. Paris: Benjamin Duprat, 1858.

——. *The Muqaddimah: An Introduction to History*. Translated by Franz Rosenthal. 3 vols. New York: Bollingen Foundation; London: Routledge & Kegan Paul, 1958.

Ibn Mâjah, Muḥammad b. Yazîd. *as-Sunan*. Edited and annotated by Muḥammad Fu'âd ʿAbdalbâqî. 2 vols. Cairo, 1372–73/1952–53.

Ibn Manẓûr, Abû al-Faḍl Muḥ. b. Mukarram. *Lisân al-ʿarab*. 20 vols. Cairo, 1308/1890.

Ibn Saʿd, Muḥammad. *Kitâb aṭ-ṭabaqât al-kabîr* (*Biographien Muhammeds ...*). Edited by Eduard Sachau *et al.* 15 vols. Leiden: E. J. Brill, 1905–1940.

Ibn aṣ-Ṣalâḥ ʿUthmân b. ʿAr. *ʿUlûm al-ḥadîth*. Edited by Nûraddîn ʿAtar. Madînah: al-Maktabah al-ʿIlmîyah, [1386/1966].

Ibrâhîm b. Ṭahmân b. Shuʿbah al-Khurâsânî. *al-Juzʾ al-awwal wa-th-thânî min mashyakhah Ibrâhîm b. Ṭahmân*. Zâhirîyah Library, Damascus. *Majallah*

107/10, ff. 236–255 (Photocopy in the possession of M. Tahir Mallick, Orientalisches Seminar, Universität Tübingen).

Ismâ'îl Pâshâ al-Baghdâdî [Bağdatlı İsmail Paşa]. *Hadîyat al-'ârifîn, asmâ' al-mu'allifîn, âthâr al-muṣannifîn.* Edited by Kilisi Rifat Bilge and Mahmut Kemal İnal. 2 vols. Istanbul, 1370/1951–1374/1955.

——. *Iḍah al-maknûn fî adh-dhayl 'alá kashf aẓ-ẓunûn 'an asâmî al-kutub wa-l-funûn (Keşf-el-zunun zeyli).* Edited by Şerefettin Yaltkaya and Kisili Rifat Bilge. 2 vols. Istanbul, 1364/1945–1366/1947.

Izutsu, Toshihiko. *The Structure of the Ethical Terms in the Koran: A Study in Semantics.* Keio University Studies in the Humanities and Social Relations, edited by Nobuhiro Matsumoto, vol. II. Tokyo: Keio University, 1959.

Jeffery, Arthur. The Foreign Vocabulary of the Qur'ân. Gaekwad's Oriental Series, vol. LXXIV. Baroda: Oriental Institute, 1938.

——, ed. *Islam: Muhammad and His Religion.* Indianapolis & New York: Bobbs-Merrill, Library of Liberal Arts, 1958.

——, ed. *Materials for the History of the Text of the Qur'ân: The Kitâb al-Maṣâḥif of Ibn Abî Dâwûd....* de Goeje Fund, no. XI. Leiden: E. J. Brill, 1937.

——. "The Qur'ân as Scripture", *MW*, XL (1950), 41–55, 106–134, 185–206, 257–275.

Jomier, J. "La notion de prophète dans L'Islam", unpublished paper [1971?] [made available through the offices of Mr. Christian Troll, S.J., of London].

Jong, P. de, and M. J. de Goeje. *Catalogus codicum orientalium bibliothecae academiae Lugduno Batavae.* 6 vols. Leiden: Lugduni Batavorum (E. J. Brill), 1862–77.

al-Jurjânî, 'Alî b. Muḥ. *at-Ta'rîfât.* Edited and annotated by Gustav Flügel. Leipzig, 1845.

Juynboll, Gualtherus H.A. "Aḥmad Muḥammad Shâkir (1892–1958) and his Edition of Ibn Ḥanbal's Musnad", *Der Islam*, XLIX (1972), 221–247.

——. *The Authenticity of the Tradition Literature: Discussions in Modern Egypt.* Leiden: E. J. Brill, 1969.

al-Kalâbâdhî, Abû Bakr Muḥ. b. Isḥâq. *at-Ta'arruf li-madhhab ahl at-taṣawwuf.* Cairo, 1380/1960.

——. *at-Ta'arruf.* Translated by A. J. Arberry as: *The Doctrine of the Sūfīs.* Cambridge: Cambridge University Press, 1935.

al-Khatîb al-Baghdâdî, Abû Bakr Aḥmad b. 'Alî. *al-Kifâyah fî 'ilm ar-riwâyah.* Hyderabad (Deccan), 1357/1938.

al-Kisâ'î, Muḥ. b. 'Abdallâh. *Qiṣaṣ al-anbiyâ'.* Edited by Isaac Eisenberg as: *Vita Prophetarum.* 2 vols. Lugduni-Batavorum: E. J. Brill, 1922.

Knight, George A. F. "The *Shekinah* in Jewish and Christian Thinking", *Trans. Glasgow Univ. Or. Soc.*, XII (1944–46), 1–3.

Kristensen, W. Brede. *The Meaning of Religion: Lectures in the Phenomenology of Religion.* Translated by John B. Carman. The Hague: Martinus Nijhoff, 1960.

al-Kulînî [al-Kulaynî], Abû Jaʿfar Muḥ. b. Yaʿqûb. *al-Kâfî.* Edited by ʿAli Akbar al-Ghaffârî. 8 vols. Teheran, 1381/1961.

Lane, Edward William. *An Arabic–English Lexicon.* Book I, in 8 vols. [Book II never compiled] (Vols. VII, VIII, edited by Stanley Lane-Poole). London: Williams and Norgate, 1863–1893.

Leeuw, Gerardus van der. *Religion in Essence and Manifestation.* Translated by J. E. Turner. 2 vols. New York: Harper & Row, 1963.

Lidzbarski, Marcellus. *De Propheticis, quae dicuntur, Legendis arabicis.* Leipzig, 1893.

Macdonald, D. B. "The Doctrine of Revelation in Islam", *MW*, VII (1917), 112–117.

al-Madanî, Shamsaddîn Abû ʿAl. Muḥ. b. Aḥmad. *al-Itḥâfât as-sanîyah fî al-aḥâdîth al-qudsîyah.* Hyderabad, 1323/1905. 2nd edition, Hyderabad, 1358/1939 [All page references are to the second edition].

al-Makkî, Abû Ṭâlib Muḥ. b. ʿAlî. *Qût al-qulûb.* 2 vols. Egypt, 1381/1961.

Mâlik b. Anas al-Aṣbaḥî. *al-Muwaṭṭaʾ.* Edited by Muḥammad Fuʾâd ʿAbdalbâqî. 2 vols. Cairo, 1370/1951.

Margoliouth, D. S. *The Early Development of Mohammedanism.* The Hibbert Lectures, 1913. 2nd series. New York: Charles Scribner's Sons; London: Williams and Norgate, 1914.

Massignon, Louis. *Essai sur les origines du lexique technique de la mystique musulmane.* 2nd, revised edition. Études musulmanes, edited by Étienne Gilson and Louis Gardet, vol. II. Paris: J. Vrin, 1954.

——. *Recueil de textes inédits concernant l'histoire de la mystique en pays d'Islam.* Collection de textes inédits relatifs à la mystique musulmane, vol. I. Paris: Paul Geuthner, 1929.

al-Masʿûdî, ʿAlî b. al-Ḥusayn. *Murûj adh-dhahab* (*Les Prairies d'or*). Edited and translated by C. Barbier de Meynard and Pavet de Courteille. 9 vols. Collection d'ouvrages orientaux, Société Asiatique. Paris: Imprimerie Impériale, 1861–1877.

Mez, A. *Die Renaissance des Islâms.* Heidelberg: Carl Winters Universitätsbuchhandlung, 1922.

al-Muḥâsibî, Abû ʿAl. Hârith b. Asad. *ar-Riʿâyah li-ḥuqûq Allah.* Edited by Margaret Smith. E. J. W. Gibb Memorial Series, vol. XV (new series). London: Luzac & Co., 1940.

Muqaddimat kitâb al-mabânî [Author unknown]. Edited by Arthur Jeffery, with Ibn ʿAtîya's *Muqaddimah* to his *Tafsîr*, as: *Two Muqaddimahs to the Qurʾânic Sciences*. Cairo, 1375/1954.

Muslim b. al-Ḥajjâj, Abû al-Ḥusayn al-Qushayrî an-Naysâbûrî. *as-Ṣaḥîḥ*. Edited by Muḥammad Fuʾâd ʿAbdalbâqî. 4 vols. and indices. Beirut, [1374/1955–1375/1956].

Nagel, Tilman. "Die Qiṣaṣ al-Anbiyāʾ. Ein Beitrag zur arabischen Literaturgeschichte." Ph.D. Dissertation, Bonn, 1967.

Nakamura, Kojiro. *Ghazali on Prayer*. Tokyo: The University of Tokyo, The Institute of Oriental Culture, 1973.

Naʿnâʿah, Ramzî. *al-Isrâʾîlîyât wa-âthâruhâ fî kutub at-tafsîr*. Beirut and Damascus, 1390/1970.

an-Nasâ'î, Aḥmad b. Shuʿayb. *as-Sunan al-mujtabá*. With the commentary of Jalâladdîn as-Suyûṭî. 8 vols. Cairo, n.d.

Nasr, Seyyed Hossein. *Ideals and Realities of Islam*. New York and Washington: Frederick A. Praeger, 1967.

an-Nawawî, Yaḥyá b. Sharaf. *al-Arbaʿûn ḥadîthan*. Edited with commentary by ʿAbdalmajîd ash-Sharnûbî. Cairo, 1300/1883.

Nöldeke, Theodor. *Geschichte des Qorâns*. Göttingen: Verlag der Dieterichschen Buchhandlung, 1860.

——, *et al. Geschichte des Qorâns*. 2nd, revised edition. Vols. I, II, revised by Friedrich Schwally, Vol. III revised by G. Bergsträsser and O. Pretzl. Leipzig: Dieterich'sche Verlagsbuchhandlung, 1909–1926.

Nwyia, Paul. *Exégèse coranique et langage mystique. Nouvel essai sur le lexique technique des mystiques musulmans*. Recherches de l'Institut de Lettres Orientales de Beyrouth, series I: Pensée Arabe et Musulmane, vol. 49. Beirut: Dâr al-Mashriq (Imprimerie Catholique), 1970.

Okiç, M. Tayyib. *Bazı Hadis Meseleleri Üzerinde Tetkikler*. Ankara Üniversitesi İlâhiyat Fakültesi Yayınları, no. 27. Istanbul, 1959.

Otto, Rudolf. *Das Heilige: Ueber das Irrationale in der Idee des Göttlichen und sein Verhältnis zum Rationalen*. 1917. 31st Edition. Munich: Verlag C. H. Beck, 1963.

O'Shaughnessy, Thomas. *The Development of the Meaning of Spirit in the Koran*. Orientalia Christiana Analecta, no. 139. Rome: Pont. Institutum Orientalium Studiorum, 1953.

Paret, Rudi, trans. *Der Koran*. Stuttgart: W. Kohlhammer Verlag, 1962.

——. *Der Koran: Kommentar und Konkordanz*. Stuttgart: Verlag W. Kohlhammer, 1971.

——. *Mohammed und der Koran: Geschichte und Verkündigung des arabischen Propheten.* 2nd ed. Stuttgart: W. Kohlhammer Verlag, Urban Bücher, 1957.

——. "Die Lücke in der Ueberlieferung über den Urislam", *Westöstliche Abhandlungen, Festschrift für Rudolf Tschudi* (Wiesbaden, 1954), pp. 147–153.

Pautz, Otto. *Muhammeds Lehre von der Offenbarung quellenmässig Untersucht.* Leipzig: J. C. Hinrichs'sche Buchhandlung, 1898.

Pedersen, Johannes. "The Islamic Preacher: wâʿiẓ, mudhakkir, qâṣṣ", in *Ignace Goldziher Memorial Volume* (Edited by Samuel Löwinger and Joseph Samogyi. 2 vols. Budapest, 1948–1958), I, 226–251.

Pickthall, Mohammed Marmaduke, trans. *The Meaning of the Glorious Koran.* New York & Toronto: The New American Library, Mentor Books, [1953].

al-Qâsimî, Muḥ. Jamâladdîn. *Qawâʾid at-taḥdîth min funûn muṣṭalaḥ al-ḥadîth.* 2nd edition. Cairo, 1380/1961.

al-Qasṭallânî, Ibn Abî Bakr. *Irshâd as-sârî li-sharḥ saḥiḥ al-Bukhârî.* 10 vols. Cairo, 1304–5/1886–7.

al-Qushayrî, Abû al-Qâsim ʿAbdalkarîm b. Hawâzin. *ar-Risâlah fî ʿilm at-taṣawwuf* Cairo, 1379/1959.

Râghib Pâshâ [Raghıb Paşa]. *Safînat ar-Râghib wa-dafînat aṭ-ṭâlib.* 2nd ed., revised by Muḥammad aṣ-Ṣabbâgh. Bûlâq, 1282/1866.

Rahman, Fazlur. *Islam.* London: Weidenfeld & Nicolson, 1966.

Reckendorf, Hermann. *Arabische Syntax.* Heidelberg: Carl Winter's Universitätsbuchhandlung, 1921.

——. *Die syntaktischen Verhältnisse des Arabischen.* Leiden: E. J. Brill, 1898.

Rescher, O. *Sachindex zu Bokhârî nach der Ausgabe Krehl-Juynboll* (*Leiden,* 1862–1908) *und der Uebersetzung von Houdas-Marçais* (*Paris,* 1903–1914). Handwritten facsimile (lithograph). Stuttgart, 1923.

ar-Riḍâ, ʿAlî b. Mûsá b. Jaʿfar. *Ṣaḥîfat ar-Riḍâ.* Edited by Ḥusayn ʿAlî Maḥfûẓ. 2nd ed. Baghdâd, 1390-1970.

Ringgren, Helmer, *Studies in Arabian Fatalism.* Uppsala Universitets Årsskrift 1955, no. 2. Uppsala: A.-B. Lundequistska Bokhandeln; Wiesbaden: Otto Harrassowitz, 1955.

Ritter, Hellmut. *Das Meer der Seele. Mensch, Welt und Gott in den Geschichten des Farîduddîn ʿAṭṭâr.* Leiden: E. J. Brill, 1955.

Robson, James. "The Form of Muslim Tradition", *Transactions of the Glasgow University Oriental Society,* XVI (1955–56), 38–50.

——. "The Isnad in Muslim Tradition", *Transactions of the Glasgow University Oriental Society,* XV (1953–1954), 15–26.

——. "The Material of Tradition", *MW,* XLI (1951), 166–180, 257–270.

——. "Muslim Tradition: The Question of Authenticity", *Memoirs and Proceedings of the Manchester Literary and Philosophical Society*, XCIII (1951–52), 84–102.
——. "Tradition: Investigation and Classification", *MW*, XLI (1951), 98–112.
——."Tradition, the Second Foundation of Islam", *MW*, XLI (1951), 22–33.
Rudolph, Wilhelm. *Die Abhängigkeit des Qorans von Judentum und Christentum.* Stuttgart: W. Kohlhammer Verlag, 1922.
as-Sarrâj, Abû Naṣr ʿAlî aṭ-Ṭûsî. *Kitâb al-lumaʿ fî at-taṣawwuf.* Edited by Reynold Alleyne Nicholson. E. J. W. Gibb Memorial Series, vol. XXII. London: Luzac & Co.; Leiden: E. J. Brill, 1914.
Schacht, Joseph, *The Origins of Muhammadan Jurisprudence.* 1950. 4th, corrected impression. Oxford: Clarendon Press, 1967.
Schapiro, Israel. *Die haggadischen Elemente im erzählenden Teil des Korans.* Schriften der Gesellschaft zur Förderung der Wissenschaft des Judentums, I. Leipzig: Buchhandlung Gustav Fock, 1907.
Schrieke, Bertram. "Die Himmelsreise Muhammeds", *Der Islam*, VI (1915–16), 1–30.
Sezgin, Fuad. *Buḫârî'nin Kaynakları hakkında araştırmalar.* Istanbul: İbrahim Horoz Basımevi, 1956.
——. *Geschichte des arabischen Schrifttums.* Vol. I: *Qurʾānwissenschaften, Ḥadiṯ, Geschichte, Fiqh, Dogmatik, Mystik bis ca.* 430 *H.* Leiden: E. J. Brill, 1967.
ash-Shahrastânî, Abû al-Fatḥ Muḥ. *al-Milal wa-n-nihal* (*Book of Religious and Philosophical Sects*). Edited by William Cureton. 2 vols. London: Society for the Publication of Oriental Texts, 1842–1846.
Shorter Encyclopaedia of Islam. Edited by H. A. R. Gibb and J. H. Kramers. London: Luzac & Co.; Leiden: E. J. Brill, 1961.
Siddîqî, Muḥammad Zubayr. "Aṭrāf al-ḥadīth", *Studies in Islam*, VIII (1971), 17–28.
——. *Ḥadîth Literature: Its Origin, Development, Special Features and Criticism.* Calcutta: Calcutta University, 1961.
Sidersky, D. *Les origines des légendes musulmanes dans le Coran et dans les vies des prophétes.* Paris: Paul Geuthner, 1933.
Smith, Wilfred Cantwell. "A Human View of Truth", *Studies in Religion*, I (1971), 6–24.
——. *Islam in Modern History.* New York: The New American Library, Mentor Books, 1959.
——. "Law and Ijtihad in Islam", *International Islamic Colloquium Papers,* December 29, 1957–January 8, 1958. Lahore: Punjab University Press, 1960.
Speyer, Heinrich. *Die biblischen Erzählungen im Qoran.* Gräfenhainchen, private publication, [1939].

Sprenger, Aloys. "On the Origin and Progress of Writing Down Historical Facts among the Musalmans", *JASB*, XXV (1856), 303–329, 375–381.

——. "Ueber das Traditionswesen bei den Arabern", *ZDMG*, X (1856), 1–17.

Stetter, Eckart. "Topoi und Schemata im Ḥadîṯ". Ph.D. Dissertation, Tübingen, 1965.

Stieglecker, Hermann. *Die Glaubenslehren des Islam*. Paderborn, Munich, Vienna: Ferdinand Schöningh, 1962.

Ṣubḥî aṣ-Ṣâliḥ. *ʿUlûm al-ḥadîth wa-muṣṭalaḥuhu*. Damascus: Maṭbaʿat Jâmiʿat Dimashq, 1379/1959.

Suhayl b. Abî Ṣâliḥ. *Nuskhah*. Edited by Mohammad Mustafa Azmi, in *Studies in Early Ḥadîth Literature* [see Azmi entry]. Part II, pp. 13–24.

as-Suyûṭî, ʿAr. b. Abî Bakr Jalâladdîn. *al-Itqân fî ʿulûm al-Qurʾân*. Edited by "Basheerood-Deen" *et al. Bibliotheca Indica*, vol. XIII. Calcutta: Asiatic Society of Bengal, 1852–1854.

——. *al-Laʾâlî al-maṣnûʿah fî al-aḥâdîth al-mawḍûʿah*. Cairo, 1317/1899.

aṣ-Ṣaʿîdî, Muḥammad Afandî. "al-Farq bayn al-Qurʾân wa-l-aḥâdîth al-qudsîyah", *al-Manâr* (Cairo), IV (1319/1901), 497–500.

aṭ-Ṭabarî, Abû Jaʿfar Muḥ. b. Jarîr. *Jâmiʿ al-bayân fî tafsîr al-Qurʾân*. 30 vols. Cairo, 1321/1903.

at-Tahânawî, Muḥ. ʿAlî b. ʿAlî al-Fârûqî. *Kashshâf iṣṭilâḥât al-funûn* (*A Dictionary of the Technical Terms* ...). Edited by Muḥammad Wajîh *et al.* 2 vols. Bibliotheca Indica (Old Series), vols. XVII, XVIII. Calcutta: Asiatic Society of Bengal, 1862.

Taylor, W. R. "Al-Bukhārī and the Aggada", *MW*, XXXIII (1943), 191–202.

at-Tirmidhî, Muḥammad b. ʿÎsâ b. Sawrah. *aṣ-Ṣaḥîḥ*. With the commentary of Ibn al-ʿArabî al-Mâlikî. 13 vols. Cairo, 1350/1931–1353/1934.

Vaschide, N., & H. Piéron. "La rêve prophetique dans la croyance et la philosophie des Arabes", *Bulletins et Mémoires de la Société d'Anthropologie de Paris*, 5th ser., III (1902), 228–243.

al-Wâqidî, Muḥ. b. ʿUmar. *Kitâb al-Maghâzî*. Edited by Marsden Jones. 3 vols. London: Oxford University Press, 1966.

——. *Kitâb al-maghâzî* (*Muhammed in Medina*). Translated into German and abridged by Julius Wellhausen. Berlin: G. Reimer, 1882.

Watt, W. Montgomery. "The Early Development of the Muslim Attitude to the Bible", *Transactions of the Glasgow University Oriental Society*, XVI (1955–56), 50–62.

——. "Early Discussions about the Qur'ān", *MW*, XL (1950), 27–40, 96–105.

——. *Free Will and Predestination in Early Islam*. London: Luzac & Co., 1948.

——. *Islamic Revelation in the Modern World.* Edinburgh: Edinburgh University Press, 1969.

——. *Muhammad at Mecca.* Oxford: The Clarendon Press, 1953.

Weber, Max. *Wirtschaft und Gesellschaft. Grundriss der verstehenden Soziologie.* Edited by Johannes Winckelmann. Köln & Berlin: Kiepenheuer & Witsch, 1964.

Weil, G. *Biblische Legenden der Muselmänner.* Frankfurt a.M., 1845.

Wellhausen, Julius. *Muhammed in Medina* [see al-Wâqidî].

Wensinck, Arendt Jan, *et al. Concordance et indices de la tradition musulmane.* 7 vols. Leiden: E. J. Brill, 1936–1969.

——. *Handbook of Early Muhammadan Tradition.* Leiden: E. J. Brill, 1927.

——. "Muhammed und die Propheten", *Acta Orientalia,* II (1924), 168–198.

Westermann, Claus. *Basic Forms of Prophetic Speech.* Translated by Hugh Clayton White. Philadelphia: The Westminster Press, 1967.

Widengren, Geo. *The Ascension of the Apostle and the Heavenly Book.* Vol. III of *King and Saviour.* Uppsala Universitets Årsskrift 1950, no. 7. Uppsala: A.-B. Lundequistska Bokhandeln, 1950.

——. *Literary and Psychological Aspects of the Hebrew Prophets.* Uppsala Universitets Årsskrift 1948, no. 10. Uppsala: A.-B. Lundequistska Bokhandeln; Leipzig: Otto Harrassowitz, 1948.

——. *Muḥammad, the Apostle of God, and His Ascension.* Vol. V of *King and Saviour.* Uppsala Universitets Årsskrift 1955, no. 1. Uppsala: A.-B. Lundequistska Bokhandeln; Wiesbaden: Otto Harrassowitz, 1955.

——. "Oral Tradition and written Literature among the Hebrews in the Light of Arabic Evidence, with special Regard to prose Narratives", *Acta Orientalia,* XXIII (1959), 201–262.

Wielandt, Rotraud. *Offenbarung und Geschichte im Denken moderner Muslime.* Veröffentlichungen der Orientalischen Kommission, Akademie der Wissenschaften und der Literatur, vol. XXV. Wiesbaden: Franz Steiner Verlag, 1971.

Wolfensohn, Israel. "Kaʿb al-Aḥbār und seine Stellung im Ḥadīṯ und in der islamischen Legendenliteratur", Ph.D. Dissertation, Frankfurt a.M., 1933.

Wright, W., trans. and ed. *A Grammar of the Arabic Language: Translated from the German of Caspari and Edited with Numerous Additions and Corrections.* 3rd ed., revised by W. Robertson Smith and M. J. de Goeje. 2 vols. Cambridge: Cambridge University Press, 1964.

Zwemer, Samuel M. "The So-called Hadith Qudsi", *MW,* XII (1922), 263–275 [reproduced in Zwemer's *Across the World of Islam* (1929) and his *Studies in Popular Islam* (1939); German translation: "Das sogenannte Ḥadīṯ qudsī", *Der Islam,* XIII (1923), 53–65].

Index

Religion and Society

1. *Ibn Taimīya's Struggle against Popular Religion.*
   With an Annotated Translation of his
   Kitāb iqtiḍā' aṣ-ṣirāṭ al-mustaqīm mukhālafat aṣḥāb al-jaḥīm,
   by Muhammad Umar Memon
   (University of Wisconsin)
   1976, XXII + 424 pages. Clothbound
   ISBN: 90-279-7591-4

2. *Tibetan Religious Dances.*
   Tibetan Text and Annotated Translation of the 'chams yig,
   by René de Nebesky-Wojkowitz.
   With an Appendix by Walter Graf.
   Edited by Christoph von Fürer-Haimendorf
   1976, VIII + 320 pages, with illustrations. Clothbound
   ISBN: 90-279-7621-X

3. *Johann Christian Edelmann.*
   From Orthodoxy to Enlightenment
   by Walter Grossmann
   (University of Massachusetts)
   1976, XII + 210 pages. Clothbound
   ISBN: 90-279-7691-0

4. *Sharastāni on the Indian Religions,*
   by Bruce B. Lawrence
   (Duke University)
   With a Preface by Franz Rosenthal
   1976, 300 pages. Clothbound
   ISBN: 90-279-7681-3

5. *The Precarious Organisation.*
Sociological Explorations of the Church's Mission and Structure,
by Mady A. Thung
With an Foreword by C. J. Lammers
1976, XIV + 348 pages. Clothbound
ISBN: 90-279-7652-x

6. *The Many Faces of Murukaṉ.*
The History and Meaning of a South Indian God,
by Fred W. Clothey
(Boston University)
1977, Approx. 270 pages. Clothbound
ISBN: 90-279-7632-5

7. *Na-khi Religion.*
An Analytical Appraisal of the Na-khi Ritual Texts,
by Anthony Jackson
(University of Edinburgh)
1977, Approx. 380 pages, with illustrations. Clothbound
ISBN: 90-279-7642-2

8. *Divine Word and Prophetic Word in Early Islam.*
A Reconsideration of the Sources, with Special Reference to
the Divine Saying or Ḥadîth Qudsî,
by William A. Graham
(*Harvard University*)
1977, XVIII + 266 pages. Clothbound
ISBN: 90-279-7612-0

Mouton Publishers · The Hague · Paris